Texas Film and
Media Studies Series

THOMAS SCHATZ
Editor

Hollywood Exile

UNIVERSITY OF
TEXAS PRESS
Austin

OR HOW I LEARNED

TO LOVE THE BLACKLIST

A Memoir by

BERNARD GORDON

Requests for permission to reproduce material from this work should be sent to Permissions, University of Texas Press, P.O. Box 7819, Austin, TX 78713-7819.

♾ The paper used in this book meets the minimum requirements of ANSI/NISO Z39.48–1992 (R1997) (Permanence of Paper).

LIBRARY OF CONGRESS CATALOGING-IN-PUBLICATION DATA

Gordon, Bernard, 1918–
    Hollywood exile, or, How I learned to love the blacklist : a
memoir / by Bernard Gordon. — 1st ed.
        p.   cm. — (Texas film and media studies series)
    Includes index.
    ISBN 0-292-72827-1 (alk. paper)
        1. Gordon, Bernard, 1918–   .   2. Motion picture producers and
directors—United States Biography.   3. Screenwriters—United States
Biography.   4. Blacklisting of authors—United States.   I. Title.
II. Title: Hollywood exile.   III. Title: How I learned to love the
blacklist.   IV. Series.
PN1998.3.G662A3   1999
791.43'0232'092—dc21
    [B]   99-21696

To Jean,

wife and closest companion for over fifty years, who knew all the bad
times and supported us with good cheer, though her own wish
for a peaceful and settled life was never realized.

If there is a proper start for the years of Hollywood blacklisting, the date would be October 1947, when nineteen Hollywood writers and directors were subpoenaed to appear before the House Un-American Activities Committee (HUAC) in Washington, D.C. This created the sensation the committee desired, not only in the Hollywood and Los Angeles press, but throughout the nation. Hollywood!

My intent is not to write a political account of the Hollywood blacklist, which is already available in a number of excellent books. I want to tell of how I survived after I was blacklisted and of my unique experiences as a blacklisted screenwriter: how my life became exciting and rewarding, how I wound up with more screen credits (credited and uncredited) than any other blacklisted writer, and how I found myself improbably running a movie studio just outside Madrid, Spain.

Though I was not among those invited to Washington for the initial hearings in 1947, at one of the public sessions a "friendly" witness named me before the world as one of the Hollywood reds. Charles Katz, an attorney representing the unfriendly witnesses, had worked with me when I negotiated a union contract for the Screen Readers Guild. Katz protested that I was his client, that I was not present, and that I had no opportunity to defend myself from accusations or to speak for myself. He was gaveled down, and the hearings went on to other matters—and other names.

There is evidence that, early on, some powerful studio bosses like Dore Schary, Louis B. Mayer, Harry Cohn, and Sam Goldwyn were opposed to blacklisting. Many Hollywood stars joined in signing petitions and placing newspaper ads condemning the procedures of the committee. But, already shaken by the effect of the blatant anti-Semitism of Congressman John Rankin and by the clearly imputed Hollywood-Jew-Communist thrust of the entire procedure, the studio opposition folded. Big name stars, including Humphrey Bogart, Danny Kaye, Myrna Loy, and Katharine Hepburn, were intimidated into distancing themselves from any form of support for the victims, and the studios formalized their refusal to employ people who declined to cooperate with HUAC, thus starting the blacklist.

I was eventually subpoenaed by HUAC on April 14, 1952, and was scheduled to appear before the committee at a hearing in Los Angeles, but the hearings were adjourned before the committee actually called me to testify. I received a telegram notifying me of the postponement and instructing me that I was still under subpoena for a hearing at a later date. I suppose that almost fifty years later I am still on call, but I did, happily, outlive the HUAC and never did get to testify. As a result of that, my name does not appear in any of the books about the blacklist, and nowadays I can afford to find it irritating that I had the game (being blacklisted) but not the name. Still, the motion picture studios were well informed of my "unfriendly" status and barred me from employment.

These were times of great change for Hollywood, the era of the demise of the major studio system as we had known it. A host of factors led to this change. The Paramount consent decree of 1948 severed the cozy tie between the studios and the distributors and theaters, put an end to block booking, and created a situation where each new film became a crapshoot. The emergence of television also had a devastating effect. The United States survived World War II with unprecedented power and wealth, so that its vast sphere of influence became a market for Hollywood films, and, with the domination of the dollar, it became possible to produce films abroad at bargain-basement rates. Creative talents like Stanley Kubrick moved to England to produce films like *Lolita* and *2001*. Sam Spiegel produced *The African Queen, The Bridge on the River Kwai,* and *Lawrence of Arabia,* using studios in England and locations in Africa, Spain, and the Far East. John Huston worked in Mexico, Italy, and England. Spain, where I principally worked, was a favorite stamping ground, not just for bullfight films but for many others, because of the favorable rate of exchange and the welcome offered by Francisco Franco, who needed hard currency—dollars—and made his soldiers, uniforms, tanks, and guns available to filmmakers at irresistible rates. Spain also offered a landscape that nicely mimicked the American Southwest for the purpose of filming spaghetti Westerns.

With the onset of the blacklist, many outstanding creative people like Dalton Trumbo, Michael Wilson, Carl Foreman, Ring Lardner Jr., Donald Ogden Stewart, Albert Maltz, Bertolt Brecht, Waldo Salt, Guy Endore, Adrian Scott, Jules Dassin, Sidney Buchman—Academy Award winners among them—left Hollywood for Mexico, New York, and various capitals of Europe, depriving Hollywood of some of its best creative spirits. That this was indeed a blow is attested to by noting the fine films that these same writers, directors, and filmmakers produced during and after the blacklist, largely outside of Hollywood. What is generally labeled the "McCarthy era" exercised a profound effect on American filmmaking and the content of films, an effect that continued through the 1950s, 1960s, and 1970s, and reverberates even today, as Hollywood is finally assessing its role in abetting the HUAC.

For myself, I was involved in a very odd assortment of occupations inside and outside the industry. Eventually, I was fortunate to be employed in curious, exotic, sometimes downright wacky filmmaking enterprises abroad, working in a Hollywood outside Hollywood, a Hollywood *in extremis* that promoted and produced motion pictures at a time now gone. Some of the films with which I was associated as either writer, producer, or both, were *El Cid, 55 Days at Peking, The Thin Red Line, Krakatoa, East of Java,* and *Day of the Triffids.* I worked with a gallery of fascinating film personalities: motion picture stars like Charlton Heston, David Niven, Sophia Loren, Ava Gardner, James Mason, and many others; with directors like Nicholas Ray, Frank Capra, and Anthony Mann; and with a number of interesting producers and promoters, who operated scrupulously and otherwise in a golden if tarnished era.

During the worst of those years, I was fortunate to earn big Hollywood dollars in Europe when the dollar was absolute king in France, England, Italy, and Spain; to live in the finest hotels on "the company"; to become familiar with the Michelin Guide when looking for three-star restaurants; to enjoy off-time in resorts from Monaco to St. Moritz; and to work on films of greater and lesser importance as both a writer and producer. I worked with the Samuel Bronston organization, which produced some of the blockbuster films of the era, and especially with Philip Yordan, a redoubtable figure, famous for his Oscar and for his many important writing credits and infamous for the questionable provenance of many of his scripts. Filmmaking under these circumstances was a splendid adventure that I came to cherish. Later, I learned that the CIA spent some of those good American dollars checking up on my activities over there—to monitor my presumed threat to the United States.

Acknowledgments

A memoir is an exercise of memory. It has been said, with justice, that memory is an exercise of the imagination. I know from preparing this volume that various participants in the same episode will recall it differently. Self-interest prevails. So what is a writer to do? What is a reader to believe? I can only report that I have consulted daily agendas covering the years, that where appropriate I have discussed matters with other participants, that in many instances I have informed the reader that different recollections exist. I have considered it my responsibility to report the inglorious as well as the commendable, even when public icons are involved. But finally, it comes down to one's best efforts to be accurate and fair. I hope I have succeeded.

For many years, Philip Yordan was the talk of Hollywood. Regarded by some as a fraud, by others—including important stars and directors—as a genius, he amassed an improbable number of screen credits and seemed incredibly prolific. He plays a major role in this book as he did in my life. When I asked him to help with information about his past, he cooperated willingly; when I warned him that he might not approve of everything I would write, he shrugged and said, "So long as you spell my name right." Surely, he will disagree with much I have written, but I hope he emerges not as the caricatured bad-boy of Hollywood but as a man of energy, wit, talent, and productivity. If he can be criticized for some of his actions and motives, how many in Hollywood are fit to cast the first stone? I regard him as a good friend and hope that when he reads this book he will still feel that way about me.

Julian Zimet has been my closest friend for sixty-five years. How does one do justice to such a friendship? This book is about Hollywood, the blacklist, and filmmaking abroad, in all of which Julian was involved with me. But it is not about personal history. If I failed to portray Julian with all of his humanity, wit, and endless kindness, it was because I had to omit and delete much of a personal nature. I know he will understand.

Mollie Gregory is a dear friend who encouraged me to write about my life in those "interesting" times, insisting that a personal account of the blacklist and filmmaking abroad would be a unique and valued documentation of a significant era. She got me started, kept my feet to the fire, criticized, edited, supported. She also nurtured me through the travail of using a computer, spending endless hours cleaning up my computerized messes. Without Mollie, no book.

Paul Jarrico was a friend for many years both in Hollywood and in Europe. He was a spokesman for those who were blacklisted and was always unstintingly available when called for information about blacklisted people and events. He was the moving spirit at the Writers Guild for assigning proper credit to those who wrote under assumed names during the blacklist. Finally, at an industry-wide ceremony on October 27, 1997, he was handsomely recognized for his years of effort. But he died tragically in an automobile accident only one night later. His loss was shocking. An eloquent and unapologetic radical, he will be sorely missed by all who are earnest about justice.

They say that the day of great literary editors like Maxwell Perkins is long gone. Though I am no Hemingway or Thomas Wolfe, I feel blessed to have found myself in the hands of an editor like Thomas Schatz, who kindly but insistently nudged this stubborn author into chopping great swathes of favorite material and reshaping whole sections of the work. It was a constant source of amazement to me that a man so busy with his duties at the University of Texas and engaged in numerous projects of his own could find the time to offer so much detailed and constructive criticism. I will always be grateful and always consider him a special friend.

Others who helped generously are Leonard Neubauer, who read a rough first draft and liberally penciled it with thoughtful suggestions; Frances Ring, a friend since we were readers together at Paramount Pictures over fifty years ago, who uncomplainingly read several drafts with her professional eye; Fred Haines, himself a fine author, who took time to install marvelous computer software that I will never understand but that made my work much easier; and finally, my daughter Ellen Kitty, who read the work and exclaimed with delight that she had learned much about my working life that she had never before understood.

Despite all of this help, I am certain there are errors and omissions that will plague me and for which I alone am responsible.

I was born in October 1918 during the flu pandemic that took the lives of over twenty million people in America and throughout the world. It was a wonder that my mother survived the ordeal of childbirth in the New Britain, Connecticut, hospital where the hallways were stacked with coffins for the flu victims. I grew up in New York City, graduated from the public school system, and enrolled at CCNY (City College of New York), which was then, in the thirties, considered the Harvard for poor guys scholastically and a hotbed of radical activity politically.

At CCNY I became passionate about filmmaking and neglected my opportunity to get a good education because I was too concerned with films. During those years, a few friends and I organized the Film and Sprockets Society, which was one of the very first efforts to introduce serious film study at an American college. To justify my credits in the extremely permissive art department, with my closest friend and co-worker, Julian Zimet, I wrote, directed, photographed, produced, and even acted in an hour-long film. It wasn't much, but it earned us both an Honors in Arts degree from CCNY. In October 1940, a few months after graduation, I put together $60 by pawning my Graflex camera and a very old microscope, plus ten bucks from a grudging father, and set off for California and my future by paying $16 for a share-the-ride trip.

I arrived in Hollywood with $20 and teamed up with my fellow cinemaniac, Julian, who had preceded me there and had a job as a reader at Republic Studios. In a short time, Paramount hired me as a reader. I was knocked out to enter as an employee through the great fabled iron gate of that studio where so many celebrated stars had worked and so many historic films had been produced.

For seven years I enjoyed walking through that gate, working as a reader, then as an assistant story editor. Whenever I could get away from my office, I sneaked down to a sound stage to watch directors like Mitchell Leisen and Billy Wilder at work at a time when, for example, Wilder was making such films as *Double Indemnity, The Lost Weekend,* and *Sunset Boulevard.* On one memorable occasion I got onto the set of a film being directed by René Clair, the great French director who had come to work at Paramount during the war years. For his classic French films, he was one of my heroes. Though he was only directing a piece of fluff called *I Married a Witch,* starring the girl with the peekaboo bob, Veronica Lake, I was so intent on following the director's thinking that when he engaged in a spirited discussion with the cameraman for the next set-up, I crept closer and closer until we were a threesome. Finally, undecided, Clair turned to me and, in all innocence asked me what I thought. Of course, he had no idea who I was or what I was doing there. Thoroughly rattled and embarrassed, I mumbled something incoherent and fled. I missed my opportunity to contribute to a René Clair film.

The world outside the studio was looking bleak indeed. World War II was on: France had fallen; England was on its knees and fighting desperately against German air raids in the Battle of Britain; the Soviet Union, also fighting valiantly, was being butchered and bled on the eastern front by the Panzers of the *Wehrmacht.* It looked as though Hitler could not be stopped.

Finally, on a Sunday morning in December of 1941, while listening to Toscanini and the New York Philharmonic in a comfortable home in the San Fernando Valley, we heard the program interrupted by news of Pearl Harbor and realized that we were in the war, too. But war or no war, I was still comfortably at work at Paramount, reading books, stories, scripts, trying to find gems that could be turned into films for the studio's program of more than thirty films per year. I was certain that in time I would be elevated to one of those offices or bungalows where the producers and contract writers worked.

Why then, with all of that before me, would a twenty-two-year-old kid join the Communist Party? The short answer is that it seemed the right thing to do, but no one today can be expected to comprehend that. So I'll try again.

In 1942, when the decision was upon me, I had lived through the devastating depression that had started in 1929. I didn't have to be persuaded that deep and intractable problems were rooted in our economy and government. Through all of my thinking life I had seen breadlines of hungry, freezing men standing long hours waiting for a handout of coffee and a bun. I had known the "Apple Annies," shabby men and women who came into shops pleading for an opportunity to sell a piece of fruit for a couple of nickels. I had seen my father transformed from an ambitious entrepreneur into an anxious, depressed man who worried each month how to pay the rent for his little hardware shop and agonized about how to pay the doctor bills for my chronically ill mother.

I had witnessed the rise of Hitler and his virulent anti-Semitism, had watched the Republican government of Spain overwhelmed by the tanks, guns, and planes of Germany and Italy, while France, Britain, and my own country stood silently or approvingly by, had seen photos of the mass execution of Republicans in the Spanish bullrings. I was aware that Blacks were being lynched and railroaded to execution in the South, that Jews were denied jobs in almost every major American industry. I knew I had been excluded from Columbia University because of its quota system for Jews. I was aware that Japanese were "funny" people who were limited to virtual slave labor in the gardens of Beverly Hills and that Filipinos were prosecuted as criminals if they dared to marry anyone at all in California.

Like many thoughtful people at the time and like many writers I respected, from George Bernard Shaw to Upton Sinclair, I felt that capitalism was a failed and brutal system that compounded poverty, caused shiploads of oranges to be dumped at sea rather than fed to the needy, and sent marshals to evict tenants and scatter their few miserable possessions on the sidewalk. For the thinking people I knew, it appeared clear that capitalism had failed even to function as a viable system in a world plunged into economic chaos. Roosevelt's efforts to revive America from a devastating depression had certainly not succeeded until war came along. The boom-and-bust economy needed war. It was a system that feasted on the bones of colonial peoples in Africa, Asia, South America, and that had supported and encouraged the rise of fascism in Germany and Italy. One didn't have to be particularly radical to believe these things. But what was the answer? Socialism was the only answer we knew; the socialist program was accepted by masses of people in other countries and even by substantial numbers here at home. Lincoln Steffens, the respected American journalist who had visited the Soviet Union in 1919, wrote in his autobiography a sentence that thrilled many of us: "I have seen the future and it works."

What about Stalin? What we knew then, what we knew for certain, was that he was heading the most ferocious, bloody, and heroic fight against Hitler. We also knew that he had tried to involve Britain and France in an alliance to stop Hitler when Germany invaded Czechoslovakia. But despite solemn treaties of mutual support, the Western powers had declined to join Stalin's fight. Given their long and bitter enmity for the Soviet Union, going back to its very inception in 1917, we believed the hope and policy of the Western alliance was to turn Hitler east against the Soviets.

And given Hitler's oft-stated anticommunism, who could doubt that this would happen? But now, in 1942, our own government was finally doing everything possible to supply Stalin with help, sending him planes, tanks, all kinds of munitions, as well as food. He was now our ally, and without him it looked as if the Germans surely would triumph.

In the Nazi onslaught against the Soviet Union, it was believed by friend and foe alike that the survival of socialism was at stake. But it seemed that the only ones who were actively and courageously fighting for it were the Communists. Viewed from the perspective of that time, the question for me then became *not* why join the party, but how can a principled, self-respecting person refuse? It was simply a question of which side you were on.

There was one other decisive factor. Along with all the other young men, I was due to be drafted into military service. But when my draft board called, I was repeatedly rejected because of a heart murmur. While friends of mine were sweating and dying in the fight against fascism, I was left sitting pretty in Hollywood. I felt keenly guilty about this and considered it my duty to do whatever I could to join in the struggle for a better world.

Membership in the party meant being assigned to a "club," never called a "cell." Six or eight of us, all script readers, would meet once a week. The meetings were typically held in the evening after dinner in the home of one of the comrades. We had a chairman (this was before the switch to chairperson), chosen by vote from among ourselves, and an educational director, usually one of us dragooned into the job of planning educational discussions around Marxist literature and cajoling the others to buy and read the pamphlets which were endlessly available. We were also required to subscribe to the *Daily People's World*, which was the official Communist daily edited and published in San Francisco, the west-coast version of the *Daily Worker*. I well remember the postman disgustedly flinging the paper at our front door instead of politely dropping it into the slot with the rest of the mail. I, of course, found this annoying, but, as a good comrade, I was required to reflect on the unfortunate lack of class consciousness of the underpaid employee of the postal service.

There was usually some political focus for the work of the moment, such as the annual subscription drive for the *People's World*, when the club would have to accept a quota for selling new subs. Getting friends and acquaintances to subscribe to the Communist daily was a painful chore and we were seldom successful. Or there would be an election campaign, which meant door-to-door canvassing with our leaflets and literature, and which usually meant a door slammed in our faces. During the war, there was the agitation for opening a second front to draw the Germans from their total concentration on destroying the Soviet Union.

For those who are anticipating titillating accounts of clandestine activity in the party, I have only disappointment to offer. The weekly meetings were a chore. The weight of the world was heaped on us, but there was really very little we could do about it. Going to meetings was much like going to that exercise class to which you subscribed and paid your money. It was good for you. But who liked exercise?

What kind of people were we? All kinds . . . bright and not so bright, hard workers and goof-offs, motor mouths and quiet ones, intellectuals and blue collars, dedicated Marxists and people who were eternally puzzled by theories of scientific socialism and never cracked a copy of *Das Kapital.*

Joining the party was certainly not a path to success, either financial or professional. Right or wrong, people were there because they were outraged about the existing woes and evils of the world and wanted to do something to correct them. The meetings were painfully boring, but this was the price we had to pay for saving the world.

If this all sounds dull and fruitless, I'm sorry. That's the way it was during the years I was in the party. But I don't mean to be scornful about the movement or the members. We were not just unthinking sheep. We knew of the creditable and effective role of the party through the 1930s and 1940s in helping to organize the CIO and the great demonstrations in New York of the unemployed. The party also played a part in the hunger marches, the rent strikes, and the bloody fight for Negro rights. Most of all, we knew that party members and sympathizers had played a crucial role in organizing the talent unions of Hollywood for the writers, actors, and directors, as well as battling for more democratic craft unions against the International Alliance of Theatrical and Stage Employees (IATSE), which was the producers' pet union and whose leaders had been convicted of corrupt practices in collaboration with some studio heads. During the war, we worked together with most Americans to win that war against Hitler and the Japanese. But, too, we were honorable soldiers in another war for a brighter future for all.

Today most of us feel that the party made grievous mistakes in its uncritical support of the Stalinist regime, but that the movement for democratic socialism was and still is right and necessary. We who were comrades in those days still feel pride in our commitment, even though it has cost pain and isolation from many of our fellows.

The war was certainly not a hardship for us on the home front. A prosperous public (everyone had a job) needed entertainment and diversion. Theaters were full seven days a week—many of them showed features around the clock. Every film made money. The studios were fat with profits. At Paramount, under the leadership of Buddy DaSilva, our executive producer, we turned out some patriotic war films like *Wake Island*, but the emphasis was on escapist comedy, and the biggest hits were the *Road to* pictures with Bob Hope, Bing Crosby, and Dorothy Lamour, and musicals like *Holiday Inn*. Studio employees were privileged to see these films evenings in the screening room. I confess that in spite of my sober commitment to party and union, I thoroughly enjoyed the entertainment.

All through the war years I worked in the story department, first as a reader, then as an assistant story editor. I was in charge of culling Paramount's vast library of produced and unproduced stories and bringing promising stories to the attention of producers, who were always looking for new projects. I was also put in charge of the junior writers, who were apprentices learning the screenwriting trade at $50 per week.

When I had been employed as a reader at Paramount for less than a year, I was elected president of the Screen Readers Guild—largely because no one else wanted the job. Lacking clout as a bargaining unit, the readers had never won a union contract from the studios or been able to improve their pathetic pay scale. It became my project to fight for a contract.

Because my studio work was not demanding, I devoted major energies to my efforts as a trade union leader, first trying to win a contract for the readers through endless nights of negotiation with producers' labor representatives. I wrote a "Brief on Readers Wages," a thirty-page document that detailed the work of earlier readers from Lillian Hellman to Dalton Trumbo and that outlined the many contributions that readers had made to finding important story properties. This was sent to all the studios. I was surprised to receive a phone call from B.B. Kahane, chief attorney and vice-president of Columbia Pictures, who complimented me on the work. But still no cigar. When nothing else availed, I led the readers into the newly organized Conference of Studio Unions (CSU), a progressive and militant group which included the painters, screen office employees, laboratory technicians, service employees, and others.

Although by this time I had been promoted to assistant story editor, my very relaxed boss, William Dozier, permitted me to continue negotiations for a readers' contract, and I was included with the leadership of all the Conference unions during those negotiations. We met around a large table at the headquarters of the Producers Association. Herb Sorrell headed our delegation, which included the business managers of each union. The producers were led by tough, professional labor relations men; they were also represented by the chief labor relations executive of each studio. As the readers' representative, I was not exactly a wheel. Usually I watched and listened.

We finally got down to the issue of sick leave for members of the Screen Office Employees Guild (SOEG), the office employees' union. This union was headed by a very good-looking young man, Glenn Pratt, the heartthrob of many of the women in that union. I sat back and listened with growing indignation as the producers knocked down any consideration of sick leave. I waited for Pratt to argue his case. But he sat mute. When it appeared that no one would speak up for the office employees, I felt obliged to have my say.

"Listen," I piped up, "most of these women have been loyal employees of the studios for years. I think they're entitled to some consideration."

The honchos on both sides looked at me in surprise. But I knew what I wanted to say. "Many of them are mothers with children at home. They have to get up at dawn to get the kids dressed, fed, and ready for school. They probably make lunches for their lunchboxes. Then they have to get themselves ready for work, dressing nicely, watching the clock, hustling off to a bus stop for a ride to the studio . . . maybe an hour's ride."

They were still listening, so I added my punch line. "And these people are women, which means that sometimes they have a rough period. You know . . . the monthlies. And you say they can't even have a day off for sick leave, not a single day ever?"

I glanced at the bunch of men, who, despite the insignificant cost, were refusing even to consider offering these women an occasional day of sick leave. The reaction at the table from both sides was basically indifference. They wanted to get on with the main issues. Finally B.B. Kahane of Columbia Pictures, who had complimented me on my "Brief on Readers Wages," spoke up.

"Bernie, you forgot to mention that while the women are waiting at the bus stop, it starts to rain, and they've failed to bring an umbrella."

This got a great laugh and I was properly put in my place. However, while I was speaking my piece, I saw Charles Boren, the Paramount executive in charge of labor relations, scribble something on a scrap of paper that he circulated among his buddies. Afterward I learned from one of the union people that the scrap of paper he was passing around was a crude drawing of a hammer and sickle. He was labeling me.

At the time I shrugged it off. But I felt a first cold chill. Of course, it was foolish to have believed that my militant trade-union work had gone unnoticed, but to have one of my studio's executives label me a commie seemed like the start down a very slippery slope. Though being labeled was no great surprise, it certainly helped explain why I'd been ignored for any significant promotion. I knew that two of the producers I'd worked with, bringing them ideas for film stories, had suggested to the studio heads that I be considered for a producer's berth. Their suggestions were ignored.

Sorrell, too, was red-baited. Was he a party member? I never knew and had no way of knowing. Even if he had once been, this fact would not have been bruited about, even to other party members. Burly, red-faced, blue-eyed, he had started as a painter and became head of the painters union; he looked and sounded like a working man's working man. And he put the fear of God into the studios because he, apparently, could not be bought like the leaders of the IATSE, which was virtually a company union that did the bidding of the studios. The potential of an independent, aggressive union group moving into the studios was perceived as a serious threat to the producers. My conviction that Sorrell was no Communist was confirmed when, unable to achieve contracts for his people, he called for a strike, even though the war was still on and the no-strike pledge was widely respected. His call for a strike was an acute embarrassment for the Communists. We still believed that winning the war came first, but we were also tied to our conviction that workers must be supported.

Whether he was or ever had been a member of the Communist Party is altogether beside the point. What is the meaning of the question in these circumstances? Sorrell was an active and aggressive trade union organizer, attempting to improve the wages and employment conditions of workers. He was not advocating the overthrow of the government; he was not even advocating the public takeover of the film studios. (He probably would have found that notion laughable.) He was not in any sense a threat to the existing economic and political order. So red-baiting him was only the old red herring that smeared him as undesirable, played to the prejudices of conservative and reactionary workers (probably a majority), and weakened his influence on workers and on the community.

There is, interestingly, one sense in which the producers were right and in which they shared the convictions of the Communist Party. We believed that by leading the unionized workers with pork-chop issues, by helping them gain better wages and working conditions, we would establish our *bona fides* and earn the right to lead them at some appropriate time into more militant demands for an entire menu of goodies, not only better wages and working conditions, but pensions, sick leave, unemployment pay, and even a chance to have something to say about the social content of the films we worked on (at least if we were writers, directors, or hired producers). We also hoped that somewhere, way down the line, we could organize more workers, make them more political in their demands, and turn them into a class-conscious force to demand socialism.

I don't know if the producers were worried about socialism "down the line," but knowing that they could not buy off the leftist union leaders as they had bought off the IATSE, they urgently needed to cut down the effectiveness of Communists, leftists, fellow travelers who were beyond the producers' influence. They feared that if we gained power, we would be a threat to their immensely profitable and comfortable way of doing business. And they were already making plans to have things their own way. In any event, with or without the consent of the party, the strike was called, and the readers (now called story analysts) went out on the picket lines.

My own position was painful. Since I was no longer a member of that union and I held an executive job, I would know no mercy after the strike if I walked out now. I decided my only honorable course was to put it up to the readers themselves. If they wanted me to go out, I would. I discussed it with the current leadership, asked them to put it to the membership. They did, and they advised me to keep on working, just as did members of the Screen Writers Guild and others who were not directly involved in the strike.

During the strike I wandered freely about the studio as usual, and I was able to witness the ugly business of the Paramount bosses planting a studio camera and crew in a corner window where they could photograph for future identification all the people walking the picket line. This crude operation fascinated me; I associated it with the kind of behavior I'd expect in an auto- or steel-mill strike, not in a Hollywood workers' strike. It led to another discovery. The camera had been set up at a corner window on the second floor. This large room was filled with filing cabinets that held copies of all the stories and scripts the studio had accumulated over many years. Hanging out there, pretending to do my regular work browsing through the files, I accidentally found one labeled J. Edgar Hoover. A closer look verified that over the years the studio had purchased original story material from Hoover. None of this story material had ever been used, but the files showed he'd been paid for his contribution to our cultural resources, not once but a number of times. How surprising to find that Hoover was in the pay of the studios. I wondered how many times the head of the FBI collected from other studios.

I had other problems. My old nemesis, Charles Boren, came back into my life. Among the union workers on strike were the service employees, the people who did the janitorial work, vacuuming and cleaning the offices. The studios had hired replacement workers to do this work. Knowing they were regarded as scabs by many of the people still working at the studio, these men sneaked in and out of the offices as quietly as possible, even avoiding eye contact. This happened in my office, too. But I never made any comment to the cleaning man or made any effort to interfere with his work.

One day Boren complained to my boss, Bill Dozier, head of the story department, that I had thrown the cleaning man out of my office. When I denied this and demanded a face-to-face meeting, one was arranged. Next morning I waited with Boren in his office as the cleaning man was called. I was uneasy. It was the classic dilemma: how do you prove you are *not* guilty? Boren made no effort to be polite to this lowly employee when he entered, demanding abruptly: "Is this the man who told you to get out of his office?"

The man, surprised, stared at me and shook his head. "No," he said.

"What do you mean?" Boren demanded. "What did you tell me yesterday?"

The man shook his head again. "It wasn't him," he insisted, pointing at me. "It was the man across the hall from him." He was talking about a writer I knew slightly, one who didn't like crossing the picket line any more than I. But writers were not regular employees and were not in Boren's jurisdiction.

"Okay," Boren muttered, dismissing the man with a wave of his hand. He stood up and waited for me to go. Not a word of apology. I was both relieved and incensed.

I sat in the chair. "What are you going to do about this?"

"What do you mean?"

"You made an accusation about me. Now call Bill Dozier and tell him you were wrong." I pointed to the phone on the desk. "Call him. Now."

Boren shook his head. He wasn't going to do it. "Not now. I'm busy."

"When?"

"Later," he snarled, and waved at me to get out of his damned office.

Boren never did call Dozier. I didn't believe Boren was through with me.

We won the strike, contracts were signed—the readers' first ever, with a substantial wage increase from $35 to $55 per week, plus a handsome retroactive payment of about $50,000 that was divided among the members. I received none of this, but I was rewarded with a thoughtful gift, a copy of Vernon Parrington's *Main Currents in American Thought*, which was inscribed "To Bernie Gordon . . . With the sincere unanimous best wishes of the members of the Screen Story Analysts Guild, Local 1488, all of whom remember with gratitude and affection your contribution in making us . . . The Fighting 94."

Though Hollywood was happily coining money, that wasn't its only contribution to winning the war. Early on, a group of people decided to follow the lead of the New York Stage Door Canteen and open a Hollywood Canteen. It was planned to involve all of the trade unions, who would contribute their labor as needed, free of charge; the studios would contribute talent to entertain the men in uniform who were passing through on their way to the Pacific. Indirectly this involved me.

Almost as soon as I arrived in Hollywood in 1940, I began keeping company with a young woman, Jean Lewin. She was an active member of the Screen Office Employees Guild, which had succeeded in organizing the secretarial workers at many of the studios.

Five feet tall, a hundred pounds, fair skin, blue eyes, and blonde hair in the wavy style of the period, Jean had left her home in Morgantown, West Virginia, for New York when she was eighteen, just before the Depression struck in 1929. Despite her youth and inexperience, she found a niche for herself in the Village where she was taken in hand by the legendary June Mansfield of *Henry and June*, who was already involved with the writer Henry Miller. June arranged for Jean to live with her, not only because she felt a maternal affection for the innocent kid from the sticks but because it was convenient. She used Jean as a buffer between Henry Miller and her other lover, a moneyed man who paid the rent, showered June with gifts, and provided the funds June spent supporting Miller, who was supposed to be in the dark about this liaison. Occasionally Jean had to answer the door and keep one of them from entering and finding June engaged in the bedroom with the other man. It was a change from Morgantown. Jean was growing up fast.

But the mercurial June eventually took off for Europe with Henry, coolly abandoning Jean. By now, the crash of 1929 had occurred. Jobless, penniless, Jean was fed up with New York and eager for adventure. With another girl—both dressed as boys to avoid problems—they took to the road, hitchhiking to California. That trip was cold, bitter, and dangerous. Fortunately, Jean's companion packed a small revolver which she used to fight off the advances of one Samaritan who offered them a lift and then discovered he had actually picked up a couple of girls, not boys.

In California Jean knew the kind of poverty and hunger that I had witnessed only from the outside. Finding work was almost impossible, especially for someone with no training or profession. With small jobs here and there, and with some help from the Work Projects Administration (FDR's work program), Jean survived. Finally, she was able to buy a Remington portable typewriter for a dollar down and a dollar a week, taught herself to type, and started to earn a little as a freelance typist. She wound up with a secretarial job at Republic Studios, but Jean never forgot what tough times meant for the underprivileged.

Soon after the United States entered the war, an organizing meeting of the Hollywood Canteen was called. Jean was co-opted to represent SOEG. She soon found herself working with Bette Davis and Jules Stein, the potent head of MCA, a major talent agency. (After the war, Stein purchased Universal Studios and became a major force in television production and arguably the most powerful man in Hollywood.) Jean left her job at Republic and became the executive secretary of the Canteen, its only paid employee. Money was raised principally through the efforts of Stein, who had enormous clout with the studios because MCA controlled many of the stars they needed.

Jean began a career that was to continue for more than four years and was to consume her time and effort, frequently sixteen hours a day, six and seven days a week. However, their enterprise began in a homely way, with Jean and Jules Stein sitting on the floor of a dusty office, working a screwdriver to force open an old, cranky file cabinet. More demanding tasks lay ahead. For a Canteen that operated seven nights a week, talent had to be programmed, bands had to be lined up, food had to be procured and prepared, hostesses had to be signed up and scheduled as dance partners for the men in uniform. People were needed in the kitchen, behind the food bar, at the doors. Jean was the heart of the Canteen, a venture that mushroomed with each passing day.

Despite an early life that would have hardened most people, and despite her extraordinary organizing ability, Jean remained modest, low-key, and nonconfrontational—qualities that may have helped her deal with volatile movie stars like Bette Davis, potentates like Stein, and the dozens of others from all the studios who contributed to the work of the Canteen.

The musicians union was an important participant, responsible for providing the bands needed at every session. In that segregated era, there were still two separate musicians locals, a White one and a Black one. Racism was very much alive, even in the trade union movement, and, of course, in the armed forces. It was racism that raised one of the ugliest and most intractable issues at the Canteen.

All servicemen, regardless of race, color, or ethnic origin, were admitted equally to the Canteen, and each session included a time when the men could dance with the hostesses. The happy presumption was that the servicemen would have a chance to dance with a Hollywood star. There were a few occasions when Hollywood stars like Bette Davis would appear on the floor and dance with a man, but, in truth, most of the hostesses were recruited from the ranks of secretaries and other women employees at the studios, young women who were pleased to show up at assigned intervals and participate in the Canteen's entertaining and exciting events.

But what was to be done if a Black serviceman asked a White girl to dance? What was the Canteen's policy? If this seems odd or trivial today, it was a contentious issue then. For one thing, there were many women who would object strongly to dancing with a Black man. Even more important, the studios, whose participation was vital to the functioning of the Canteen, were literally terrified of a public scandal over the Black-White issue. It could be very bad for business. The Canteen had to have a policy. Was it to be segregation? A number of party members, as well as Jean herself, were active in the affairs of the Canteen and would not tolerate a policy of discrimination or segregation. But movie stars and movie moguls could not be ignored.

First, Jean and others recruited as many Black women as possible to attend as hostesses. But this stopgap measure could not ensure a peaceable resolution. The meetings of the Canteen's board of directors were the battlegrounds of this conflict. Jean, tiny and down to ninety-five pounds, pushed for total desegregation. From outside, and with the help of other trade union comrades, we did what we could to support her and the no-discrimination policy. Finally, Jean proposed a rule which the board grudgingly accepted: There would be no rule against inter-racial dancing, but no hostess would be required to accept a dance invitation from any serviceman, regardless of race. This allowed hostesses to be free to refuse invitations from anyone—too short, too tall, too hairy, too bald, too sweaty or whatever—without reference to race, and that seemed to us on the left a reasonably acceptable resolution. That worked well. With this rule in effect during a time of so much blatant racism, and considering the tens of thousands of men who attended each month, men from every state, I have often thought that the Canteen accomplished something really worthwhile toward the eventual improvement of race relations in the country.

I've always regarded Jean's attitude about race and ethnic differences as remarkable, even unique. She had grown up in a border state, West Virginia, and it was surprising that she was so free of prejudice. Most of us had to overcome deeply-rooted feelings imposed by a culture that constantly hammered at racial differences and attitudes about superiority and inferiority. We grew up, some of us, and learned that such prejudices were wrong, vicious, and we worked to overcome that conditioning. Jean simply did not have any prejudices or such feelings. People were people. Period. Color, religion, or ethnic origin had no meaning for her, except when discrimination occurred. Then, mild-mannered or not, she would become outraged and obstinate. I sometimes wished I could learn the secret from her and supply it to the rest of the world.

Despite the success of the new policy about dance partners, another problem persisted. The Navy, in its ancient wisdom, assigned a permanent MP (military policeman) to duty inside the Canteen to control rowdiness or any problem that might arise. This sailor, tall, strong, and handsome in his uniform, was named Mickey. Disregarding Canteen policy, Mickey, abhorring the sight of Blacks mixing with Whites, found it intolerable that a Black man might dance with a White woman. And this did happen, especially when some progressive White hostesses made it a point of honor to dance with Blacks. To her horror, Jean learned that Mickey had a policy all his own. He pulled such an unregenerate Black off the floor and into the men's room, where he proceeded to beat him up thoroughly. When Jean learned about this, she raised the matter with Bette Davis, who played an active role at the Canteen. The question was how to deal with Mickey. An attempt was made to talk to him; he stoutly denied his culpability and smoothly promised to see that no one else got away with such behavior.

But the beatings continued. Jean and Bette Davis decided to deal directly with the local Naval office in charge of Mickey's assignment. They made an appointment downtown with the Navy captain. Jean drove the big old station wagon as she and Bette Davis nervously went over what they wanted from the captain—Mickey must be shipped out.

They were ushered into the captain's office with the utmost courtesy. The captain seemed wowed to be in the presence of the great movie star.

"Anything I can do, Ma'am, *any* way I can help," he quickly assured them as he indicated the chairs they could take before his desk. Politely, he addressed them both, but he looked only at Miss Davis. Jean was not surprised that he ignored her, but she was struck by his distinct southern accent. Davis looked nervously at Jean as if for help to get started. Jean just smiled. The ball was clearly in Bette's court.

"It's about your shore patrolman—Mickey," Davis blurted out without preliminary. "He's been beating up some of our soldiers and sailors."

The captain was nonplused. "Why would he do that?"

"Because some of the boys are Black and they're dancing with White girls."

The captain had to digest this. It didn't seem likely he'd think Mickey's behavior reprehensible, but he had to deal with Bette Davis and a weird Hollywood crowd. He finally managed to murmur, "That's not right. Not right at all. I can't believe Mickey would do that."

Emboldened, Davis replied, "He's doing it. He's been seen doing it repeatedly."

"You talk to him about this?" the captain asked.

Davis looked at Jean who nodded. "We've talked to him," Jean said. "He denies it, of course, but some of our people have seen him in the men's room actually working over a soldier."

"Disgraceful," the captain muttered. "I'll talk to him."

Egged on by a glance from Jean, Davis said, "Maybe he could he re-assigned."

Even in the presence of Miss Davis, the captain bridled. After all, nobody dictated to the Navy.

"I'll talk to him," he repeated. "I'll surely take care of it, Miss Davis." But he didn't promise, and he never did ship Mickey out to sea where he could work out his aggression against the Japanese.

With Mickey still around, the problem persisted. Jean arranged for enough of our own people to visit the men's room frequently to limit Mickey's freedom of action. The beatings became less frequent, but Mickey and his ilk, of course, survived. Well, perfect integration was not achieved, but I like to believe that because of the gutsy efforts of people like Jean and the energetic persistence of party people, some small progress was made. Many hundreds of thousands of servicemen from all over the country were exposed, for the first time, to a memorable social situation where integration was the rule. Though largely ineffectual on major issues, the party was not entirely unproductive.

After the war ended in 1945, it took less than two years for the House

Un-American Activities Committee to get going in full gear. When I was named during the first hearings in 1947, I learned about it the next day when the Hollywood trade papers, *Variety* and the *Hollywood Reporter*, printed a very full account, and I had reason to know how publicly and thoroughly I had been nailed. This worried me, but I recall taking some pride in becoming part of the big show. When I discussed it that night with Jean, now my wife and very much pregnant, we both decided it was not important. After all, no one had yet come to grief for having been named a Communist. And look at our friends who were there in Washington, standing up so courageously, telling off the fascist-minded committee.

Though no studio executive mentioned my public red label, the blow was not long in coming. Two months after the hearings, in December 1947, Paramount terminated me. Jean and I were expecting our first child in January.

2

The October 1947 HUAC hearings in Washington had been tempestuous. When interrogating "unfriendly" witnesses, committee members were interested only in two questions: "Are you now or have you ever been a member of the Communist Party?" and "Are you now or have you ever been a member of the Screen Writers Guild?" The so-called unfriendly witnesses all tried to introduce prepared statements decrying the proceedings and setting forth their reasons for considering the questioning a violation of their constitutional right to keep their political and trade union associations to themselves. But the committee chairman, J. Parnell Thomas, invariably gaveled down any effort by a witness to speak his mind, demanding a yes or no answer to *the questions*. Finally, in each case, and on the advice of his attorney, the witness had to decline to answer on the grounds that he was relying on the First Amendment of the Constitution to protect him from such interrogation. But quite a few shouting matches ensued, with witnesses like John Howard Lawson and Lester Cole trying to have their say over the gaveling and shouting of the chairman. Eventually, ten of these witnesses were threatened with contempt of Congress citations.

In addition to the "unfriendly" witnesses, there were a number of "friendlies" who had agreed to appear and make the kind of statements (allowed by the committee) denouncing the "Communist influences" in Hollywood. Actors like Gary Cooper and Adolph Menjou spoke up. All of this resulted in nationwide headlines. Although there were some thoughtful journalistic pieces about the undemocratic and unconstitutional proceedings, the general impression conveyed to the public was exactly what the committee desired: Hollywood and Communism.

Despite some resistance from a few West Coast moguls like Louis B. Mayer, Sam Goldwyn, Dore Schary, and Darryl Zanuck, the studios, especially the East Coast businessmen who controlled them, were solely concerned with the influence of all this outcry on the business at the theaters. A number of right-wing organizations like the Legion of Decency threatened theater boycotts if any of the Hollywood Ten should be employed. And it was this pressure that prevailed. Any of the Ten who were employed at studios were fired, after which they found it impossible to obtain studio employment. Was this a "blacklist?" The studios and their spokesmen denied the existence of a blacklist; they were simply refusing to hire alleged Communists. And this logic chopping was supposed to make sense. In any event, the other writers, directors, and actors (eventually more than two hundred) were not yet on a list because they had not yet been called to testify before HUAC. But congressional pressure proceeded with contempt citations against the Ten, which meant that they were subject to imprisonment if the citations were upheld in the courts.

The initial support garnered for the witnesses among motion picture stars and in unions like the Screen Writers Guild quickly faded after the film companies issued their "statement" at a conference at the Waldorf hotel, when the studios declared they would agree not to hire any of the Ten. Still, there was a general belief that the rights of the Ten would surely be upheld by the courts and that this would put an end to the persecution and even to the power of the committee.

In addition to these political problems, there was considerable turmoil in Hollywood on another front. In 1947, Sorrell and the Conference of Studio Unions were attempting to negotiate a renewed contract, but found themselves up against a determined, united front among the studios. Evidently, with the war over, the time had come to break the CSU and return to the comfortable prewar days of friendly relationship with the IATSE. The producers flatly turned down the union demands and cleverly separated the CSU from the carpenters, the only other potent union that had the power to shut down the studios and that did not belong to the IATSE. The CSU was forced to walk out and was isolated. A prolonged and bitter strike ensued. Since it was necessary to focus their forces somewhere, the strikers concentrated their picketing and efforts at Warner Bros. in Burbank. But the Burbank police were entirely creatures of Warners, their only big industry and employer, so they stood by as the IATSE members not only drove disdainfully through the picket lines but also attacked the picketers with tire irons and chains. The strike was prolonged and bloody. People like Jean and I did what little we could to support the strikers by contributing small sums weekly to a strike fund, but, in retrospect, it is clear that Sorrell never had a chance. He had no meaningful alliances and the producers were determined at any cost to get rid of him. They did.

Big changes were occurring not just in Hollywood, but in the entire country. All of the major companies were flush with profits from war production. Our industries had won the war and were now ready to win the world. What was good for General Motors, it was said, was good for America. Henry Luce preached "The American Century." We had, for the moment, exclusive control of the atom bomb. Western Europe was completely dependent on our largesse. Our only potential enemy was the grievously wounded Soviet Union, no longer an ally but a contender for control of Eastern and, perhaps, Western Europe. And more. The Soviet Union's successful battle against the Germans had greatly increased the prestige and appeal of Communist and socialist ideas. Socialist and Communist parties were gaining alarming strength in England, France, Italy, Germany, China, and in many formerly colonial countries now freeing themselves. The specter of Communism really haunted our capitalists even as they were at the very top of the heap in world power. Measures had to be taken—and they were.

In the midst of such enormous macrohistorical developments, it may seem ludicrous to intrude something as parochial as the Hollywood blacklist. But for me, more clearly in retrospect than at the time, it seems obvious that the successful engendering of antiCommunist hysteria in the name of always-headline-worthy Hollywood was an enormously clever tactic that turned the country away from all of the liberal and progressive trends that had grown out of the Depression, the Roosevelt era, and the war. In a way, the blacklist was the lead goat that ushered the American people to McCarthyism and much else that ensued, up to and including the Vietnam War, fought so fruitlessly in the name of anticommunism.

For me, it is now encouraging and meaningful to read, fifty years later, in 1997, that people are talking of the success of the Teamsters in winning a big strike against United Parcel Service, auguring a reversal of so many years of declining power for the trade union movement. At the very least, I can testify that we saw the beginning of that decline in Burbank in 1947.

When I was terminated at Paramount in December of 1947, I had worked in the story department there for seven years and nowhere else. Though my dismissal was clearly political, that seemed to be a private matter between me and Paramount. Despite the firing of the Hollywood Ten, there was, as yet, no talk of a general blacklist, nor even of a "graylist." In retrospect, I think I can consider myself as having been prematurely blacklisted. Despite all of the events occurring in Hollywood and the world, it was necessary for me to contemplate the matter of earning a living. My old friend Julian, back from army service, was denied work at Republic (owed to all returning veterans) and also had to restart a career. He moved back into the apartment I had vacated when Jean and I were married. The two of us joined forces to become writers and chase the success that had initially drawn us to Hollywood.

A friend from the Paramount story department, Johnny Weber, also back from the war, had landed a job as an agent at the powerful William Morris Agency, and he agreed to try to get us an assignment as a writing team. From the perspective of Hollywood today, this sounds preposterous—a writing assignment for a couple of writers who had neither individually nor together acquired any writing credits worth mentioning. But back then studios still had "B" units that churned out films for less than $100,000, and these units had overheads and schedules to deliver product to the theaters. One of them might try out a couple of cheap, bottom-of-the-barrel writers whose combined salary was less than what single writers earned. Why not give it a shot?

At Columbia Pictures, we met the young assistant, Bobby Cohn, who owed his job to a relationship with the Cohns who owned and ran Columbia. Bobby was being groomed for better things, serving his "internship" under an experienced old-timer, executive producer Burt Kelly. They wanted an inexpensive cops-and-robbers melodrama. Julian and I kicked around some ideas, went back to Bobby, pitched them, and got an assignment.

Columbia's B unit was housed away from the main studio on a ramshackle lot with a dusty old office bungalow and a couple of stages. Still, seven years after our arrival in Hollywood, Julian and I relished finding work as writers at a major studio, each of us earning $200 a week. We'd come up with a story premise for a different crime film, where the principal criminal was a decent, middle-aged, middle-class man trapped in tragic circumstances. We turned out a screenplay and, with a number of rewrites, managed to stay on payroll for several months. The producer liked the final script, the executive producer liked it, and we were fired, the usual fate of screenwriters. The film was never made for reasons never disclosed to us.

What I recall most about this assignment were two criticisms of Burt Kelly, the executive producer. He was a handsome, white-haired man who seemed old to us though he probably wasn't more than fifty. But he was an old-timer in the sense that he'd held down production and executive jobs at various major studios and had come from a theatrical background. That background explained his first comment. After reading what we considered the first act, he complained, "You're still dusting off the iron apples." This referred to the old theatrical routine in which the curtain rises and the butler moves around center stage, dusting fake fruit on the table. Kelly meant: get moving, get into the story, stop stalling. His other complaint came at the end of the script: "No, no, no. They're outside cranking up the Fords," which meant: you're losing the audience, they've already left the theater, finish the picture.

Otherwise memorable was our effort to follow the party line and create a role for a Black actor, nearly all of whom found it virtually impossible to find work in Hollywood. Even a lousy bit part meant a job for at least one Black. We described a taxi driver as Black. When Bobby Cohn caught this and asked us why, we merely said that it added atmosphere and credibility. He just crossed out the word Black, explaining that it would only create trouble for distribution in the South. So, there, the truth is out: we did try to follow the party line and sneak propaganda into our films. During the war, we were proud when John Howard Lawson was able to create a heroic role for one Black actor, Rex Ingram, as a soldier in the film *Sahara*, and again when Lawson wrote *Action in the North Atlantic* with what we considered unique and meaningful roles for ordinary workingmen. The net result of all this came out during the HUAC hearings when Dalton Trumbo was denounced for sneaking the phrase "share and share alike" into his script of *Tender Comrade*. The hearings had actually produced proof of Communist propaganda in Hollywood.

Perhaps a more significant instance of red subversion occurred in the film *Crossfire*, arguably Hollywood's first effort to confront racial bigotry. The story involves the murder of a Jew—with three soldiers suspected of the crime, so that the film also examines the matter of racial prejudice in the armed forces. The film was released in 1947, shortly before the HUAC hearings in Washington at which the Hollywood Ten were cited for contempt of Congress. All of the ten were writers, except for Edward Dmytryk, director of *Crossfire*, and Adrian Scott, producer of the film. Coincidence?

Meanwhile, our daughter, Ellen, was born a month later than predicted, in February 1948. Jean was now working part-time and at half-salary for the Canteen Foundation. We had help caring for the baby. Things were looking up. We even managed a move from our tiny one-bedroom court apartment to a new and spacious two-bedroom apartment in the San Fernando Valley. Johnny Weber, still at the William Morris office, came through again with an assignment for Julian and me. We went to work at Warner Bros. at their large and splendid movie-making plant in Burbank, where the rows of great sound stages seemed to stretch to the horizon.

The producer we were assigned to had only recently been hired. Hugh King, a friendly man, grinned and confided to us that when he met with Jack Warner, the big boss asked him how he wanted to be listed at the studio. King said as a producer-writer. Warner had snarled, "Forget the writer crap. I hate writers!" Laughing, King repeated the well-known Jack Warner crack: "Writers are shmucks with Remingtons." We kicked this around with King, trying to understand Warner's attitude, concluding that writing was the one area where the studio really had no control over the product. Even directors, creative as they might (occasionally) be, were craftsmen who were assigned a script, told to go down to stage X Monday morning, and start shooting for X number of days, and they damn well had to bring the film in on schedule if they wanted to work again. Actors acted; composers composed; cameramen did their jobs, as did film editors, scenic artists, wardrobe people, carpenters, lab workers. Everyone was paid to do a job and did it. Except writers. How could you run a business when you had to hire writers, pay them thousands, and wait for pages, only to ultimately find out that you didn't like the results? So you scrapped the scripts or filed them, hired other expensive writers to rewrite them, and you still never knew what the hell you'd get back. Every studio had rooms of file cabinets stuffed with unproduced scripts, drafts of scripts, and stories whose only value was as a tax write-off.

Hugh King agreed to be hired strictly as a producer. We had a fine relationship with him and started to turn out pages that he liked. But something happened between King and Warner. Before we were halfway through the script, King was terminated. We would have been fired, too, except that the story editor liked us and managed to shift us to another project and another producer. The new producer was Anthony Veiller, a distinguished writer with a couple of Academy Award nominations (a *writer* again!), recently credited as writer of a major hit, *The Killers*, from the Hemingway short story of the same title.

Ironically, we were assigned to write a screenplay based on a novel by a man who subsequently went to jail as one of the Watergate conspirators. *Bimini Run*, by Howard Hunt, was an adventure tale of big-game fishing around the island of Bimini in the Bahamas. We loved the action and came up with plot, character, and scene ideas that delighted our producer. Our offices were over a machine shop in a building just off the main lot, but the rooms were large and well furnished, and we had other writers as companions. One was Richard Tregaskis, the war correspondent who had written a best-seller, *Guadalcanal Diary*, that Warners had bought and hired him to script. The saturnine man next door to us, Alfred Hayes, had written another best-seller, *The Girl on the Via Flaminia*. He told us that he'd written the lyrics to the old left-wing song "Joe Hill." This was hard to believe, since Hayes appeared to be in his thirties, and he sneered at all left-wing notions. How could he have written the lyrics to "Joe Hill?" But he had.

A job bonus was eating lunch every day in the Green Room, the large dining room where a table was always reserved for the writers. Accepted as equals, we lunched with some of the great men and women who wrote scripts for stars like Humphrey Bogart and Bette Davis. We joined in the jokes and games, especially the match game where for small stakes we guessed the number of matches in someone's fist as they moved around the table. We talked about the progress of the case against the Hollywood Ten, which was then still moving through the courts. Given my inevitable bias, I consider writers generally well-informed and, consequently, liberal people. At the writers' table, there was a substantial feeling of sympathy and solidarity for the writers who were being hounded in the courts. We also had a sense that the idiocy of threatening writers with jail would be exposed for what it was, and dropped. Left or right, none of us had any premonition of what was to come.

As a measure of our newly found sense of making it in Hollywood, Julian decided to date a movie star. Patricia Neal was one of the attractive, up-and-coming young stars at Warner Bros. She was also bright, well-informed, and a favorite with the writers. Julian took her to dinner. She was warm and friendly, but informed him kindly that there was no future in their relationship because she was dating Gary Cooper. That kind of competition would put a crimp in the aspirations of almost any would-be lover, even Julian.

When we completed our script, Veiller congratulated us on an exciting and original piece of work and sent it on with high hopes to Steve Trilling, the man who oversaw production for Jack Warner. There was talk of a term contract for us; we were on our way. The days dragged by without a response; we began to worry. Finally, the answer was negative. Warner had once again "been screwed" by writers who turned out a script that wouldn't be used. So far as we have ever known, this decision was not political. The studio heads just disagreed with Veiller about what made a good film for their program.

The legal proceedings against the Ten progressed from the end of

1947 until June 1950, when the Supreme Court upheld the convictions and all ten were packed off to various federal jails. The shape of the future was alarmingly clear. The Los Angeles City Council got in on the act, passing a resolution requiring all members of the Communist Party to register with the police! I don't know of anyone who complied with this demand, but it added to the chilling sense that anything could happen. More ominously, the bold, open construction of a concentration camp began in Griffith Park. With barbed wire perimeter and elevated watchtowers, this was certainly a *gulag* (a term we didn't yet know). And camps like Manzanar, which had been prepared for the Japanese during the war, were being refurbished for possible "subversives." Oddly, the press remained mum about this, but word got out. In recent years, a study of FBI files revealed the truth that a half-dozen such camps were constructed around the country in the early 1950s to imprison left-wing radicals. These pens would never be used, but who knew that at the time? We all remembered Germany and the Jews who blithely refused to believe that Hitler would move against them.

Some of our friends decided to get out of Hollywood and out of the country. Those who could headed for Europe, where they hoped to find work in a better atmosphere. Julian had friends in that group and decided to head for Europe, too. With a two-and-a-half-year-old daughter and very limited resources, Europe was not an option for Jean and me. We decided instead to head for Mexico and join up with another family there. We cashed in the $2,500 in Savings Bonds that Jean had accumulated during her years at the Canteen. This was our entire capital.

From September to the end of December, we lived in Mexico City, and I tried to find a way to do filmwork . . . or anything that would pay our way. While life below the border was interesting, even exciting, the possibility of earning money there was nil, and it was, in retrospect, a foolish notion. By December we were running out of funds and knew we would have to return to Los Angeles. The Chinese had entered the war in Korea, attacking from the north and almost decimating our forces there. Hysteria seized America.

Julian was urging me to come to Europe, where he believed he had work prospects for us. Jean and I packed up and returned to the States. Jean and Ellen settled in at her mother's home; I flew to Europe. Except for her sister, Marjorie, none of Jean's family had any idea what was going on or why we were flinging ourselves around to Mexico and then to other lands. While I was away, HUAC held major hearings in Hollywood, where the informers named everyone they could think of (and some others) as members of the party. Even older people totally out of the political circuit, like Jean's mother and stepfather, were glued to the radio or television to witness this great circus. Jean huddled in her bedroom with Ellen, shuddering at the thought of what she would have to say when my name came out.

It almost did. One of the star witnesses was Sterling Hayden, who gave only seven names at the committee's insistence. "One of them was someone named 'Bernie,'" he said, "but I never knew his last name. He was a sort of intellectual type and led the educational discussions." Alone upstairs, listening to her portable radio, Jean waited for disaster. But "Bernie" wasn't enough of a key. There were several Bernies in the local movement and speculation usually focused on the better known ones.

Years later in his autobiography, or confessional, Hayden manfully acknowledged his regret at having cooperated with the committee, admitting freely that he had done it strictly to preserve his lucrative professional career. "I was a real daddy-long-legs of a worm when it came to crawling . . . I (then) swung like a goon from role to role . . . They were all made back-to-back in an effort to cash in fast on my new status as a sanitized culture hero."

In Europe Julian and I worked for five weeks in London, researching and writing a treatment for a film about Martin Luther. Then we went to Paris and Berlin to try to put together a production deal. Other blacklisted friends were knocking around the continent in similar quests. Some of them were better connected than we. After four months of futile efforts, I concluded that our hopes were vain, that Julian's promising contacts were not going to deliver, and that I had to get back to my family. Footloose and unencumbered, Julian stayed on in Europe. It seemed ironic and sad to me that years later, in 1958, a major British biography of Martin Luther was produced, but that had nothing to do with us.

Having failed to find refuge or income in either Mexico or Europe, I returned to Hollywood and family totally broke and learned that Jean had been on the verge of selling our old 1946 Chevy just for eating money. The reunion with family, while warm and loving, was anything but cheery. Already in my thirties and with family responsibilities, I had to imagine an entirely new life and career for myself. The old fantasy of Hollywood glory could not have seemed more distant and preposterous. But as a screenwriter *manqué*, I should have guessed that life doesn't always follow a prescribed script.

3

Whichile I was away in Europe, Julius and Ethel Rosenberg were tried and convicted of spying and passing atom bomb secrets to the Soviets. The principal agent for the prosecution had been Roy Cohn, a Jew, and the judge who had been chosen to hear the case was also a Jew. Irving R. Kaufman was presumably a man who would have no choice but to pronounce the maximum sentence of execution on a couple of other Jews. Which he did. Hitler was dead, but anti-Semitism still flourished in the United States. The savage and pitiless sentence, the first one ever levied on civilians—and in a time of peace—was also evidence of the anticommunist hysteria being whipped up in the country.

Of course, these developments made those of us on the left very uneasy. We considered the Rosenbergs innocent of the charges. It seemed clear even then that the Rosenbergs were poorly equipped to understand or transmit serious scientific secrets, and could have been little more than pawns. Meanwhile, friends on the left like John Wexley wrote heavily documented volumes "proving" that the case against the Rosenbergs was fatally flawed. We believed this, and we wondered which of us would be next. This became a peculiarly personal matter for me when I learned that Julius Rosenberg had been a student at the City College of New York at the same time as I. Although, to the best of my recollection, I had never met him, how would I ever be able to prove that?

Despite the great changes that were occurring in the world of entertainment, Hollywood continued to grind out its usual fare: expensive, glitzy productions like Cecil B. DeMille's *The Greatest Show on Earth* and MGM's *Ivanhoe*, as well as films I admired, films in the best classic mode like *Five Fingers* and *High Noon*, written respectively by Michael Wilson and Carl Foreman, friends of mine soon to be blacklisted. Another film written by Wilson (with Harry Brown), *A Place in the Sun*, had won them Oscars in 1951. And a yet-to-be-blacklisted friend, Robert Rossen, was nominated for his direction of *All the King's Men*. (Rossen was later to become a turncoat and informer, but that's another story.) So, the long arm of the blacklist had not yet reached everyone.

The changes that would eventually overwhelm the studio system did not occur all at once. Muscle-bound and top-heavy enterprises, some of the studios were still run by old bosses like Jack Warner and Harry Cohn. Such men were not able to switch gears. Even though television was becoming more ubiquitous, and TV antennae sprouted on all the roofs, the studios continued to operate as though this nuisance was just a fad that would go away. They had contempt for the product on television, mostly refused to make their films available to the new medium, and even continued their programs of making "B" films as if the double-feature system in the theaters would continue forever. This last miscalculation turned out to be a lifesaver for me.

Living on meager borrowed funds, with Jean returning to the typewriter, and trying to find work with writer friends who were still hoping to sell spec stories and scripts to producers, we found an inexpensive duplex apartment in the older flatland area of Hollywood. Ellen, only three years old, had to be signed up for preschool. Everything cost money and we had very little.

Though Johnny Weber was long gone, I was still a client of the William Morris office, and I was assigned to another young agent who would presumably try to find me employment. I had little hope. Since I had not been recognizably named in any of the hearings and had not yet been subpoenaed, there was probably no issue about my employability. The stumbling bloc was my lack of credits. In an event I still regard as miraculous, a good friend who had been a reader with me at Paramount, Alfred Levitt, called to ask if I was interested in interviewing for a writing assignment at Universal. A friend of his, William Alland, another lefty, was working there as an assistant producer and needed a writer. He would be favorably inclined toward someone like myself who might have political problems, so long as the shit hadn't yet hit the fan. With misgivings, I drove out to the San Fernando Valley for my interview with Alland. Putting all the politics aside, I'd never yet written a script on my own and wondered if I could.

In late 1951, Universal was the same old movie lot that had been in existence for many years, the site of much filmmaking. It looked a bit rundown, but it was full of nostalgic memories. Most of the executive offices were in utilitarian bungalows, but, shabby or not, Universal was a going concern with a famous back lot and historic building façades, redressed for countless films, with a standing "street," long rows of sound stages, and all the accouterment of a great studio. As I drove through the guarded gate, announcing my appointment with a producer, I could sniff the air of Abbott and Costello, of *Frankenstein*, of *All Quiet on the Western Front*, and of the hundreds or thousands of features that had been ground out there since long before the days of the Depression.

Bill Alland's office was in one of the less impressive bungalows. A slight man with a sharp ferret face, Alland had eyes that seemed to dart around as though he were looking for the next promising opportunity. He was most cordial—any friend of Alfred's . . . and he didn't embarrass me with any searching inquiry about my past credits. Alfred had prepared him, and my agent had let him know my salary demands would be the Guild minimum of $200 per week. We hit it off very well. Alland told me about the project he was working on as an assistant to the big executive producer, Leonard Goldstein. The project was a historical affair, taking place mostly at sea with pirates. He gave me a short treatment and I agreed to come back in a few days with my script ideas. After another meeting I got the job and went to work at Universal for $200 a week! I had an office upstairs in the writers' building. I even had an outer office and a secretary to sharpen my pencils, supply me with yellow pads, and, occasionally, type a few pages.

That first week I worked furiously, scribbling on a yellow pad, turning pages over to the secretary to type, watching anxiously for any sign from her whether my pages were good or bad. She had worked with professional writers for years and must have some opinion. But she was professional enough to keep a straight face and a shut mouth. After that first week, with fifteen or twenty pages in my fist, I ran to Alfred Levitt for his opinion. Should I turn in these pages, consider them trash, try to rewrite? Alfred said they were fine. Greatly relieved, I turned the pages in to Bill Alland, waited uneasily. He liked them. Keep going.

But it was not to be. Somewhere up the line, perhaps from the mighty and mysterious Mr. Goldstein, word filtered down to drop the project for reasons never explained to me. But luck was with me. Bill Alland arranged for me to be transferred to another project, one for which he had created the story. He liked my work well enough to want me to write it. This new project was a story about a deaf prize-fighter who, thanks to the miracles of medicine, regains his hearing, loses it again in a brutal fight—but finds true love. The fighter was to be played by Tony Curtis, his first real drama, as he'd only been cast before in bottom-of-the-barrel, "tits and sand" epics where he dashed around the desert on a horse rescuing unsullied heroines from Arab pursuers. On the prizefight film, Mona Freeman was cast as the good woman, Jan Sterling as the bad woman, and a young, first-time director from New York, Joe Pevney, was assigned to helm the picture. Maybe this wasn't a DeMille epic, but it would do.

From the start Alland kept insisting that I meet Mr. Goldstein. While I didn't object or refuse, I had no enthusiasm. I wanted to leave well enough alone. If Mr. Goldstein was content to keep me on the payroll and voice no objections to the pages I turned in each week, why did I have to meet the man? Maybe he wouldn't like my looks. My timidity reflected my general feeling that I was at Universal only temporarily on a pass and that the good times were sure to end. In the meantime, I enjoyed the role of genuine screenwriter with a genuine office and secretary at a genuine studio, a screenwriter who ate with other writers at a genuine studio commissary.

One Saturday morning Bill Alland cornered me. He had arranged a meeting with the big man, and he dragged me over to one of the fancier bungalows. We were admitted to an outer office that was clearly more important than any I had yet seen. An older woman who looked like a super-efficient gatekeeper announced us, and Alland led the way into the inner sanctum. It was plush, with the expected large mahogany desk, fine sofas and easy chairs, plants, discreet venetian blinds that modulated the light so that Mr. Goldstein behind his desk looked important and handsome. He was in his fifties, a bit on the fleshy side, but gave every sense of having been freshly barbered and shaved. He even smelled good, some expensive scent, no doubt. Alland introduced us. I muttered my pleasure at meeting Mr. Goldstein, who immediately let it be known that he was about to leave for Palm Springs for the weekend and would have to cut this meeting short. What was I supposed to say to this? Alland jumped in with a lifesaver. "Tell him that joke about the lawnmower," he begged the boss.

"He knows the joke about the lawnmower," Goldstein replied impatiently.

"No, he doesn't," Alland insisted. "Do you?" He turned to me.

I figured we were reaching tricky ground but I could not afford to offend either Goldstein or Alland. It was an old joke, even then, but I managed to smile and say, "No," with as much enthusiasm as I could muster. "I don't know the joke."

Sighing and glancing at his watch, Goldstein told me the lawnmower joke. It's about the man who wants to borrow the lawnmower from his neighbor, imagines he'll be turned down, works himself up into a rage, and with no provocation whatever goes to the fence, calls his neighbor over, and tells him to take his lawnmower and shove it up his ass. Big laugh. After which, Goldstein offered his hand and told me to go on with the good work, and we were dismissed.

Outside, Bill Alland assured me the meeting had gone well. As we were leaving, a car pulled up bearing one of the studio's charming young actresses. The car was driven by her mother. The actress might have been too young to get her own license. Alland whispered to me that Mr. G. was having an affair with the girl and was undoubtedly about to leave for "the Springs" with her, which could explain why we had gotten such short shrift. Later, I thought Goldstein was a virile and rather attractive man and that, despite the age difference, it was possible the actress was involved because she liked him, not merely for crass casting-couch reasons. The actress, who is still around, became a very good and appealing star. In subsequent years, watching her on the screen, I remembered that moment so early in my writing career.

The writing went well; I was beginning to feel confident. I enjoyed having Tony Curtis drop in on me and urge me to keep going. He couldn't wait to get this first real script into his hands.

"How's it going?" he would ask in the distinct New York accent he hadn't begun to alter.

"Okay, Tony," I'd reply modestly. I hadn't yet learned that in Hollywood, every writer had to say, "Great!" Besides, who was I to boast?

"Call me Bernie," he said. "My name is Bernie just like yours." He grinned. "Bernie Schwartz." We were quickly pals, at least on the basis of a first name. I had no notion that he was going to become a big star. Fifteen years later I bumped into him in a Beverly Hills shop. He'd completely forgotten me and looked resentful when I greeted him as "Bernie."

However, there was a darker side to this studio experience. Most mornings when I dropped into commissary for a coffee, I bumped into the writer Borden Chase, who was usually there breakfasting with his latest wife. She happened also to be his adopted stepdaughter. He cheerfully introduced her to me, exchanged small talk, and probably grinned at my discomfiture. Jean's sister Marjorie had been Chase's personal secretary for years but had been fired when she had refused to cross a picket line with him during one of the Hollywood strikes. She knew Chase, his then-wife, and the stepdaughter, who had been three years old when Chase became her father. I had frequently seen Chase in the old days during the war when he and my sister-in-law were around together. Chase had been a militant anticommunist even when the Russians were beating the Germans back from Stalingrad; he and I had argued politics on more than one occasion, and he knew perfectly well where I stood politically. In the postwar era, Chase was one of the leaders and organizers of the Motion Picture Alliance for the Preservation of American Ideals. He had served on the original board of directors. At meetings of the Screen Writers Guild, Chase was a rabid red-baiter, along with other members of the Alliance; he was also a principal source of information to the Un-American Activities Committee about radicals and radical activities in Hollywood.

Chase proudly reminded anyone on any occasion that he'd started as a "sandhog": that is, one of the workers who labored in caissons beneath the Hudson River to build the Holland Tunnel. He had written a book about this experience, which brought him to Hollywood and a literary career.

Added to all these accomplishments, Chase was a notorious womanizer, and his affair with his twenty-four-year-old stepdaughter caused a considerable scandal. It never seemed to bother him at all. According to reports in the Los Angeles press at the time, while he and the girl were in bed, his then-wife had made a recording that eavesdropped on Chase and the girl discussing the feasibility of "doing great bodily harm" to the wife (and mother)—eliminating her from the scene. The Los Angeles police relieved Chase of his gun and gun permit. A nasty divorce ensued and Chase wound up marrying the girl.

All this went through my mind during our morning encounters in the commissary. Chase made friendly small talk. I'd try to keep up my end as I wondered when he'd drop the other shoe and either ask me about my politics or simply tell the committee to get after me.

I tried to shut out these matters and concentrate on writing pages about my hero, Tony Curtis, and his struggles to fight and/or to hear. Subpoenas were being served left and right in preparation for another big session of the committee that was scheduled to be held just down the road in Hollywood. My friend Alfred Levitt and his wife were both subpoenaed, as well as dozens of others I knew. I was not yet among the chosen, perhaps because I had come to screenwriting much later than the others and was not known to the informers as someone they'd met in their screenwriter clubs. But how long would I escape my fate?

I kept at it, turning out pages of *Flesh and Fury* that Bill Alland approved and passed on to Mr. Goldstein. Word came back that he was pleased, too. As soon as I wrote "Fade Out" on the last page, the film went into production. Instead of being terminated, as was usually the case, I was immediately assigned to another project. Bill Alland happily assured me that a term contract was being prepared for me.

A contract for me? How crazy could this get? How long before the axe would fall? I was certain that one of the informers would name me, and, if not, Borden Chase was sure to finger me. In retrospect, I find it curious that I was able to continue to function effectively as a writer under these pressures.

I was assigned to work on a Western based on a more-or-less true story of a historical character, John Wesley Hardin—a notorious killer, but a man with an honorable attitude toward his gambling debts. I had some historical material to go on; Bill Alland took credit for the original story. He was flying with excitement because this was to be his own first production, independent of Leonard Goldstein. It was going to make his career and everything must be super. Before I began to write, a young actor who had only appeared in the lowest category of "B" Westerns had been cast to star: Rock Hudson. I met Hudson at lunch in the commissary. I was impressed with this tall, handsome, well-built young man who held out his hand warmly and launched into an account of how the director of the picture he was now working on had been so helpful in guiding him as an actor.

"I had to do this scene," he explained, "where I'm walking down this flight of stairs with the camera below shooting up at me. And I don't know how I'm supposed to look, what I'm supposed to do. I mean I'm nervous wondering about all this.

"Then the director tells me, 'Rock, just make your mind a blank. Don't think of a damn thing. Just come on and walk down the stairs. That way you'll come off completely natural.'

"Well," Hudson smiled happily, "it worked. I just had to make my mind a blank. I stopped being nervous. It worked fine. It was a big help." He looked at me with his big, open, clean-cut smile.

"Great!" I managed to say—I was learning. But my heart sank. This was my star. I was trying to write a character with some complexity, a compulsive gambler with a sense of honor. Just look blank!

While I was writing the script for the film that was to become *The Lawless Breed*, shooting on my first opus, *Flesh and Fury*, had begun and was progressing rapidly. By now I was so well integrated at the studio that I even got to go on the set and watch Joe Pevney direct some of the scenes I had written. In one instance, I foolishly complained about some of the action.

"Why," I asked Joe, "do you have the actor playing the fight manager go out of the scene so forcefully and slam the door behind himself as though he's going somewhere? So far as I know, he isn't going anywhere. The point of the scene is that he has nowhere to go."

"Then why did you write it that way?" Joe asked sullenly.

Suddenly, I wondered if the mistake was mine. We picked up the director's script and studied it. I'd written nothing about the manager rushing out of the scene and slamming the door. But we didn't have time to worry about such niceties. The slam remained in the finished film and no one else ever minded.

Now, in the spring of 1951, the Hollywood hearings of the Un-American Activities Committee were on, not in Washington, but in a hearing room near Hollywood and Vine. The proceedings began, as I recall, with the testimony of Martin Berkeley, an ex–party member who proceeded to give the names of some 150 people he claimed he had known in the party. How he knew that many was a mystery; how many of them had actually been party members, I still don't know. His membership and his connections had all occurred before I'd become a writer or member of the party. I had never met Berkeley, had never even heard of him. Nevertheless, as the writers gathered around the small portable TV in the office adjoining mine, eagerly watching and listening to the show, I tried to buckle down, ignore the sounds that came through the wall, and concentrate on my Rock Hudson Western. It wasn't easy. Berkeley never named me. But other informers followed, some of whom had known me.

The friendly writers next door invited me repeatedly to join them at the TV. It was all too exciting to miss, and writing work at the studio had crashed to a standstill—all except mine. I excused myself apologetically, explaining that I was working to meet a deadline and could not afford the luxury of spending my day at the tube. Bill Alland by now knew perfectly well where I stood and was almost as anxious as I that my name not be mentioned, at least not until I'd finished the precious script that was going so well. I couldn't help hoping that by some miracle my name would never be mentioned. Was it conceivable that I would escape and go on to a successful career as a Hollywood screenwriter? Hope springs eternal. Borden Chase, "Boring Chase," as my sister-in-law called him, was waiting in the wings.

As a result of these last hearings, virtually everyone I knew on the left was blacklisted. A number of friends with more resources or better connections were able to settle in Mexico and make a life there screenwriting (but under much reduced circumstances). Among them were Dalton Trumbo, Albert Maltz, Gordon Kahn, Jean and Hugo Butler, and John Bright. Another friend, Michael Wilson, stayed in Hollywood and managed to get under-the-table work writing scripts at minimum pay for incredibly trashy films. He handled his situation with typical panache, placing the Oscar he'd won for *A Place in the Sun* on his mantel with a black velvet ribbon tied around its eyes. Distinguished writers like Samuel Ornitz moved into tiny apartments in the Valley and survived on no one knew what. The actor J. Edward Bromberg died a sudden and untimely death from a heart attack that was attributed to his summons from the committee. Another actor, Phil Loeb, a cast member for many years on the serial *The Goldbergs,* committed suicide. Others tried without much success to sell life insurance to their old comrades who had no money for such luxuries. I knew several who settled for clerking in department stores. Others continued to write original stories for films, hoping to make sales under pseudonyms. Much has been written about the political meaning of the blacklist. It is worth recalling that there were personal tragedies, too.

At Universal, *Flesh and Fury* had almost completed post-production. Christmas had arrived and all the people working at the studio who had children were invited to a huge Christmas party on one of the stages. Jeanie and I brought Ellen, who was enchanted with the show that was put on for the kids and who, along with the others, received a fine Christmas present, compliments of the studio. It was all very warm and gave us a feeling of belonging. For a few hours we were able to forget the friends who were no longer eligible for such niceties because of the blacklist. And the fact that I drove to the studio each day in a prewar model Plymouth sedan with a cracked windshield and a missing front bumper, a vehicle I had acquired from a neighbor for $125, was never commented upon by my fellow writers, some of whom sported the best in new cars.

I remember that shabby old Plymouth on the night scheduled for the sneak preview of *Flesh and Fury* at a theater on Sunset Boulevard many miles west of the studio. No one was on the lot at dinnertime that night except the producer, Mr. Goldstein, the director, Joe Pevney, Bill Alland, a couple of top studio executives, and me. We sat down at a nicely decorated table in the commissary to a good steak dinner that had been specially prepared for us. My car, parked among the others, would have been a standout, so I'd parked it out of sight in the shadows of a building. The dinner was good; wine was served; and a jolly spirit prevailed. After dinner, a big canister of Cuban cigars, Uppmanns, was passed around. I chose one and put it into the pocket of my dress-up jacket (my one and only). Bill Alland sent me a disapproving look.

Later, as I was waiting to get into the limousine with Goldstein, Alland whispered to me: "You're supposed to give the cigar to Goldstein. That's what everyone does. He likes the Uppmanns." I was offended by the idea. I'd never smoked an Uppmann, and this was the night I was going to do just that. Goldstein and I contentedly puffed away in the limousine. The air must have been foul with cigar smoke, and by today's standards insupportable to the others in the car, but Goldstein and I smoked on. The big producer gave no hint that he begrudged me my pleasure.

The marquee of the theater out on Sunset Boulevard proclaimed a sneak preview. We had been warned not to reveal the time and place of the event so that the audience would not be salted with friends who would fail to respond fairly to the questionnaires distributed to the viewers. Jeanie and a few others had wormed the truth out of me, and she winked at me in the lobby before the performance. I sat through the film, really seeing it for the first time. I squirmed at some of the scenes I had written and regarded the whole film as mediocre and silly. But the audience responded favorably. The executives were pleased.

The Hollywood Reporter, as always, tried hard to be enthusiastic and started its review, "A rousing action-filled drama of the prize ring. *Flesh and Fury* offers a novel twist that lifts it out of realm of ordinary fight pictures. This tale of a deaf-mute who battles his way to the championship is an intriguing one. . ." Other reviews were mixed, but not negative. *Cosmopolitan Magazine*, less a creature of producer's whims, even gave a special citation to Tony Curtis for his performance, and I figured I deserved some of the credit for that. In any event, that night of the full Hollywood treatment was a gratifying climax to years of effort and ambition, and regardless of the dark clouds gathering, I fully enjoyed it. So did Jeanie, who drove home with friends (while I returned in the limo with the brass).

It was dark and late on the Universal lot when I sneaked over to my Plymouth, sighed with relief when it actually started, and drove with a light heart from the valley back into Hollywood to a proud and loving reception from Jean.

4

Next day I was back at work at the studio, struggling to concentrate on the lawless, sometimes brutal actions of my hero, John Wesley Hardin, and trying to ignore the brutal HUAC hearings just a short way down the road in Hollywood. The deluge of names of alleged Communists supplied by Martin Berkeley, Richard Collins, and others continued. Then the "unfriendly" witnesses were called and gaveled down when they tried to have their say about their rights to privacy for their political beliefs. As a result, they were all forced to end with a demand for their Fifth Amendment right to remain silent. In the eyes of the industry and of the public, this amounted to a "confession" of "guilt," despite the fact that the amendment had been included in the original Bill of Rights precisely to avert false and forced confessions, as in the Star Chamber proceedings of the early English courts.

A word here about this all-important technicality. At the time of the original hearings in 1947, the Hollywood Ten were cited for contempt even though they'd claimed their First Amendment right to remain silent when it came to discussing their political beliefs and associations. Still, they had been indicted and found guilty, and ultimately, the Supreme Court upheld their convictions. They went to jail. As a result, the attorneys representing those witnesses called before the Hollywood committee had no choice but to inform them that the only basis left for refusing to answer the committee's questions was the Fifth Amendment, which gave witnesses the right to remain silent.

Why was it important to remain silent when a Fifth Amendment defense automatically labeled you a Communist in the eyes of the public and of the industry? Because if you once opened the door by admitting membership in the party, you had to continue to answer *all* the committee's questions about who you knew in the party; you were forced to become an informer. Even more important, by answering the committee's question— about party or union affiliations—you implicitly acknowledged the committee's right to ask such a question, to invade your precious political privacy, a privacy that had been won after centuries of struggle against tyrannical governments that used such interrogations to attack every kind of political dissident, every type of trade union organization, and any kind of opposition to the powers that be. In the opinion of scholars as well as radicals, no part of the Constitution is as vital to democracy as the Fifth Amendment and the right it guarantees—to remain silent.

It is a great and bitter irony that only in 1977, in a little-noticed case, did the Supreme Court reverse its earlier pusillanimous position and declare, in the words of Chief Justice Burger:

> . . . it was a matter of supreme importance, coming under the scope of the First Amendment, a protection which includes the right to speak freely or *refrain from speaking at all* . . . A system which includes the right to proselytize religious, *political and ideological causes* [emphasis added] must also guarantee the concomitant right to decline to foster such subjects. The right to speak and to refrain from speaking are complementary components of the broader concept of "individual freedom of the mind."

According to Lester Cole, one of the Ten, the attorneys arguing before the Supreme Court in 1950 used those *precise words* in defense of the Ten. They had been rejected then. Now, at last, after *twenty-five* years, persecutions, and jail terms, the Ten were vindicated and the First Amendment properly sustained. But in 1952, when I was listening to my friends testifying before the committee, they had no choice but to rely on the Fifth Amendment. Under the circumstances that then prevailed, the use of the Fifth Amendment was not a coward's way of avoiding trouble; it was a courageous way of defying a corrupt committee, a craven system of justice (reaching even to the Supreme Court), an industry eager to get rid of its most militant workers, and a public cowed and misled by politicians and media into believing that a handful of radical dissidents were a threat to our nation's existence.

Hearings or no, my work on the script of *The Lawless Breed* had to go forward. I continued to plug away, and as the script approached conclusion, I asked Bill Alland what was happening about the promised term contract. He became more and more tight-lipped, saying only "some difficulties had arisen." It wasn't difficult to guess what was happening, but I was surprised that Alland, with whom I had become friendly, was unwilling to level with me. He was evasive and did not detail the "difficulties." I had become close to him. Jean, Ellen, and I often visited with Alland and his attractive second wife. They had bought a home far out in the Valley, a virtual farm of more than an acre that even boasted a chicken coop where Bill Alland happily raised chickens for his table. Being city folk, we snooped around, fascinated at this facsimile of rural, independent life. I recall watching Alland move around among the chickens as a one-legged chicken hopped after him devotedly.

"I love that little chicken," Bill said. "He was born crippled, with only one leg, and the other chickens were ready to peck him to death and eat him. They'll do that. But I picked him up and rescued him, and I've protected him. So he follows me around like a dog. They're not dumb," he continued. "Not dumb at all."

Weeks later, I asked Bill how his pet chicken was.

"I ate it," he said.

I was appalled. "How can you eat your own pet?"

Bill chuckled. "That little chicken had a destiny. Its destiny was to be eaten by me and my family. And," Bill assured me, "I've never enjoyed a chicken dinner so much." Maybe I'm a chicken-hearted kid from the streets of the Bronx, where chickens only seem to grow on the hooks of butcher shops or in plastic refrigerator packs, but I never felt the same about Bill Alland. Maybe it should have alerted me to things to come.

When I wrote "The End" to my script of *The Lawless Breed*, Bill Alland hugged me with delight, assured me that he would go right into production, and told me I was fired. He even summoned the courage to whisper to me that word had reached the studio brass that I would be subpoenaed.

Back home, in realistic anticipation of this, Jean had gone to work in a secretarial job with a company that was preparing a big production of *Finian's Rainbow* to be made as an animated feature. The creative force behind this production was John Hubley, a good friend who had made a distinguished career in animated film with such characters as Mr. Magoo and, also, with the "Disney zoo." John, working outside the studio system, went on in spite of the blacklist to win several Academy Awards for his work. Just now he was heading up a team to produce the *Finian's Rainbow* feature, and the musical voices for the film included people like Frank Sinatra and Ella Fitzgerald. Despite the friendly atmosphere and the glamour, Jean was anything but happy. Whatever contemporary feminists may feel, Jean wanted none of this career. She had been through so much poverty and struggle in her earlier years, had endured so much downright hunger, had labored to exhaustion through the war years at the Hollywood Canteen, all she really wanted was a safe haven, a home that was reasonably secure, and an opportunity to be a full-time mother to our beloved daughter.

The work at *Finian's* meant keeping a dozen high-strung and highly paid creative people (artists, musicians, performers, promoters) happy, calm, and away from one another's throats. Jean would arrive home after a day's work exhausted, irritable, and in no condition to offer Ellen the loving attention she wanted to give her. Also, on occasions when the musical score had to be recorded at night because of the performers' other commitments, Jean would be needed on the sound stage to keep track of things. On one occasion, she came home late and told me, not at all amused, that Sinatra had been recording surrounded by a gang of his protective thugs—all very polite to be sure. But one of them had been clearly making eyes at her as she tried to keep out of his way. Another one of the gang, seeing this, had approached her and told her to ignore the asshole; he'd be taken care of if he tried to make any trouble.

Knowing there was a subpoena out for me, we decided to try to duck the process-server when he appeared. This evasion was practiced by most of my friends, though it seldom availed. The idea was that if you could avoid being served a subpoena until after the current hearings, you might actually escape appearing before the committee and, conceivably, escape being blacklisted. In no time at all, the man with the subpoena was knocking at our door. We enlisted the help of the housekeeper we now employed, mainly to take care of Ellen while Jean and I were away. But whether I was home or not, Sarah was to answer the door and say I was not home and she didn't know when I would return. We explained the situation to her. Sarah was Black and extremely loyal. She may not have understood all the implications of blacklisting, but she certainly understood harassment from the authorities, cops, courts, anyone up there, and she was eager to stand with us if we were in trouble.

The problem with four-year-old Ellen was trickier and more delicate. She loved to run to the door to open it for anyone who wanted in. We told her she was to tell a little lie and say that we were not home, explaining that "the problem" was people constantly bothering us, trying to sell us magazine subscriptions we didn't want; but we didn't want to hurt their feelings. We'd simply say I wasn't home. She was quite bright for her age, but this story seemed to go over.

Our apartment sat at street level, and by ducking behind the window blind, we could see out and watch the marshal park in front of the house, waiting patiently for me to appear, either coming home or leaving. He drove a shiny new Oldsmobile. I wondered how much he was paid and how much it cost the public to have him sit for hours, waiting for me. I confess that I also bitterly contemplated how unlikely it was that I'd ever be able to own a fine new automobile like that, but that ignorant slug had nothing better to do than loll in his new car and wait to nail me . . .

Well, I may have done the poor man an injustice. Maybe he was a talented process-server, a loving father and husband. He may have had no more use for the committee than I, except that it provided him with a decent livelihood.

When *The Lawless Breed* was completed, I was not informed of any sneak preview, but I did learn of the film's premiere at the Pantages Theater on Hollywood Boulevard. Jean and I attended as private ticket buyers (aggravating!) and were ignored by the studio brass who were present. This time, I felt that the film more than lived up to my expectations and that the director, Raoul Walsh, had done a fine job. The *Hollywood Reporter* headlined its review "'LAWLESS BREED' FINE OATER" and went on to praise it as "well-made, somewhat off-beat Western loaded with rousing action and brimming with good performances . . . Hudson does a splendid job as Hardin, playing him with absorbing conviction and sincerity." I wondered if he were still walking down that staircase keeping his mind a blank. The unusual thing about the review was that, contrary to custom, the name of the writer was omitted from the text where all the other contributors—producer, director, actors, cameraman—were individually praised. Even though I had not yet been served a subpoena, I had to assume the word was out.

Further information of interest was sneaked to me by Bill Alland. After I had left the studio, Alland said, Borden Chase had been assigned immediately to rewrite my script with the intent of eliminating my credit. But Alland proudly assured me that he had thrown out all of Chase's efforts, retained my work intact, and, consequently, the studio was required to give me sole screenplay credit. But beyond this, Alland kept his distance. No more chicken dinners at the "farm." I learned a good time later that he did have reason to be concerned, since he eventually became an informer for the committee.

While I was still at Universal, I'd been approached by an ambitious and energetic independent agent who assured me he wanted me as a client. He'd heard raves about my work and was certain he could take me far. I agreed to switch to him.

My new agent, Bernard Feins, didn't seem to know the reasons I'd been flung out of Universal. He called regularly and told me that he was working on getting me a new assignment. When he said he thought he might have a job for me at Warner Bros., I was surprised. Then I learned that a friendly story editor, who knew me from the past when I had worked there with Julian, remembered me kindly and arranged an assignment with Bryan Foy's "B" unit at the studio. The friendly story editor could not have known about the man with the subpoena who was hanging around outside my home. The studio's line to the committee was not yet completely perfected. I drove over the hill to Warner's in Burbank where I met with "Brynie" Foy, as he was affectionately called. He put me to work immediately on a "shoot-em-up crime pic." What the hell, I'd just done a prizefight picture, knowing nothing about the prize ring, and a Western, never having ridden a horse, so why not a crime pic?

I went back to the large, airy office where I'd worked before with Julian, across from the main auto gate and over the machine shop. This time, though, I was alone, and none of the old friends were in adjoining offices. I was given some small-talk about the kind of story they had in mind, and I set to work doing a treatment, a story outline of the script that would eventually be written.

About fifty, Foy was a large, hearty man, the son of a famous theatrical family, the Foys. He sounded like a man who had never gotten past grade school, maybe never even into it. Perhaps he had been raised in that proverbial trunk backstage while the Foys were doing their act up front. But he was pleasant and easy enough to work for. He didn't have much interest in story or script, leaving most of that to his assistant. He only read completed material, such as the finished treatment, when I got to that point.

His assistant was something else. Joe Breen Jr. was the son of the famous Joseph Breen who had for years been the official censor of films for the Hollywood Production Code Administration, known as "The Hays Office." Joe Jr. looked like a priest. Even without the collar, dressed in the most casual corduroys and T-shirt, hair almost shaved off, and thin wireframe glasses, he couldn't be mistaken for anything but a priest, or a priest *manqué*. He, too, was pleasant and bright, but, unlike Foy, he was interested in story and script problems and discussed my work intelligently. The thirty-page treatment I quickly wrote was approved, and I was set to do the screenplay. At home I kept ducking the process-server, but it was becoming increasingly difficult, since I was now tied to regular hours.

At Warners I was writing under the gun again, concentrating on the cops and crooks in my little story while waiting for calamity. But I was enjoying the work. At last, on this, my third script, I felt I had achieved the status of a professional writer, on my own, without a collaborator. For the first time I felt I really knew my craft, and more than that, that I could write these scripts with a special spin. I had learned a good bit about Freudian psychology and, of course, I was a small-time expert on dialectical materialism; applying these areas of expertise to the crummy characters I had to invent helped to give me the sense that I could dig deeper and add something fresh to the routine material. Evidently it worked. As the script progressed, I received enthusiastic praise from Joe Jr. and on a couple of occasions from Brynie himself, after he allegedly took pages home for the weekend and read them.

Jean and I talked it over. We decided that we couldn't keep it a secret for long that I was working at Warners. Items came out regularly in the trade papers about Brynie Foy's program. My name would crop up. I had better take the subpoena at home rather than have them come after me at the studio. So. I answered the door when the man with the new Oldsmobile knocked, accepted service, and wondered how long it would be until Warners was informed. Not long.

After only a few days I was called down to a meeting with Foy. He told me he had read the pages, which were, in effect, the first act, or first third, of the script. "They're damned good. I really like them." He smiled. "I think you're going to have a future with us." Wasting no time, he said, "I hear those SOBs served you with a subpoena." I nodded. "Don't worry about it," he went on. "We can fix it up for you one, two, three. We've got plenty of clout here at the studio." I knew better, but a tiny corner of me couldn't help hoping that he meant they had the power to quash the subpoena and let me go on as if nothing had ever happened. "All you have to do is talk to them, cooperate a little, and, one, two, three, [again] it's all over. I promise you you've got a future here. You wouldn't want to louse that up. Would you?" he asked searchingly.

I mumbled something about having to think about it. Brynie was completely understanding. I dragged myself out of there, back to my office. They left me alone for a couple of days. Surprisingly, I continued to turn out pages.

I got another call to come down to see him. Still friendly, he practically grabbed my arm and led me out of the office. "Come on. There's someone I want you to meet." He led me down the hall to the office of Blaney Matthews, head of security. Matthews was a white-haired, older man, but still bulky. He'd been some kind of cop, then took over security at the studio. He was notorious as the principal villain when the Burbank police had smashed the Conference picket lines and beat up the strikers.

He was waiting for me. He stood up behind his desk and reached over to shake my hand. "Glad to meet," he said, greeting me as one of the boys, and indicated an easy chair. "Sit down. Make yourself comfortable."

Brynie and Joe Breen Jr., who'd also accompanied us, sat down in other over-stuffed leather chairs. I was surrounded.

"Look, Gordon." Matthews got right to the point. "You know why you're here. We want you to think about your own situation, your own interests. We want a little cooperation from you, and it's all over. Understand?"

Despite the warm, hail-fellow atmosphere, I could only manage a feeble nod. I sure as hell did know why I was here.

"No coercion," Matthews continued, "no one wants to push you around. You take your time. You want to think about it?"

I managed another nod. It was clear to them I wasn't ready to cooperate.

Should I get it over with and tell them all to go fuck themselves? I hesitated. But I had my rationale. I figured that every day I could stall this nasty farce, was another day at $250 a week. God only knew when I'd make that kind of money again.

They gave me a couple of days' breather, and I continued to write. The next time I was called down to Blaney Matthew's office, we had another full-press conference with the same cast. This time they applied more pressure. Blaney picked up the phone on his desk, dialed, and got William Wheeler on the line. He held out the phone to me. "This is Bill Wheeler. You know who he is."

Did I ever. Wheeler was the committee man in town, the investigator who arranged which people got subpoenaed and which got to be "friendly" witnesses—informers.

"Go ahead," Blaney said, smiling at me. "Just talk to him. He wants to talk to you. What will it hurt?"

I shook my head, completely at a loss to know what to say.

"He's on the line. Just say hello," Matthews urged. "Why not just say hello?" Matthews simply couldn't understand.

"I'm not ready to talk to him. I have to think about it." I figured they'd about lost patience with me, but they weren't ready to give up.

"Okay. Okay. Take your time. But think about it. Just think what it means. To you, your family, your future. It's all in your hands. Just a little cooperation. What have you got to lose?" I was permitted to leave the office. I had another reprieve.

Now something new was added. Joe Breen Jr. started to drop in on me to chat. Nothing was said about the committee or the subpoena. These were just friendly visits and a chance to become better acquainted. We didn't even talk about the script. Joe first told me about some very unpleasant encounters he'd recently had with the local police during traffic altercations. As he no doubt suspected, I was very sympathetic with his criticism of the arrogant cops. Since the details were convincing, I was a bit surprised that Joe shared my anticop biases. But I was suspicious of his motives.

Next day he was back for another visit. He told me some fascinating stories about his experiences as a soldier during the war. "I was studying for the priesthood at the seminary when the war started. I wouldn't have been drafted. But I figured I had to go, get in the fight with the other guys. So, I quit the seminary and joined up."

He continued with a hint of embarrassment, "The guys in the company got my number and started calling me 'Father' and coming to me for help and advice. We got into the fighting in France, ran into plenty of Germans, and some of the fellows were killed. It was no picnic, but we sure became friends."

I was listening with real interest.

"We were a tank company moving head on toward Germany. One time," he paused to recall, "we captured a rag-tag crew of Germans. Seven of them. They were demoralized, out of touch. They just surrendered. We didn't know what to do with them because we were racing as fast as we could after the remains of their army." Now he stopped, shook his head, finding it hard to go on. "Well, the captain decided what to do. He told the frightened prisoners to lie down, side by side, then he turned to the man driving our tank and said, 'Drive over them.'

"He wanted to drive over them with the tank!" All those years later, Joe was still anguished remembering the scene. "I just couldn't hold still. I couldn't let it happen. I turned to the captain and said, 'You can't do that, sir. It's cold-blooded murder. They're prisoners. It's against the rules of war.'"

Another long pause. Joe swallowed hard before he could go on. "The captain turned on me, gave me a hard look, and said, 'Okay, Father, I'll make you a deal. Pick out one of them, any one you want. The rest have to go. But you get to save a life.'"

I reacted to this story with the appropriate sympathy and horror for the predicament Joe had been placed in. But I never got to know how Joe resolved his awful problem. Maybe I didn't have the stomach to know. He went on to tell me another harrowing, even more meaningful story.

"It was only a few days later. The war was practically over. We crossed into Germany and we were moving through some small town. I don't even remember the name. But there was no opposition. Whatever Germans were left were running away. I was walking through a small park with my closest buddy, a Jewish fellow. He stepped on a mine that blew up and just about blew away all the lower half of his body. I grabbed him, what was left of him. I hugged him close, told him it was going to be all right."

Joe turned to me and asked, "What can you say? What can you do? I just kept repeating that it would be all right. It'll be all right. I just wanted to hold him close and comfort him. And it didn't take more than a couple of minutes. He died while I was holding him. That was the worst thing that happened."

Joe went on to tell me that he was writing a script for Brynie, a war story, and he had written this scene into the script. He'd written from the heart because his agony about this had never diminished. The scene was about fictional characters in a screenplay, but when Brynie read the scene, he'd scowled. "What kind of shit is this? Are these guys faggots or what?" When Joe told me this, and told it with real feeling, I had to believe that he wasn't just there to pump me and find out if I were going to cooperate with the committee. I had to believe he felt the same way about his boss and the whole damned studio that I did.

Foolish as it seems now, I felt at that point I had to level with him. "I suppose you're wondering. But I'm not going to talk to Wheeler. I'm not going to cooperate with the committee. I'm not going to become an informer."

I've never been satisfied that I knew the whole truth about Joe Breen Jr. Was it possible that all of the heart-to-heart talk was just a ploy to sound me out? Was there any sincerity in his apparent wish to get close, to confess his own problems, to imply sympathy with my predicament? Was it just a case where his Jesuitical smarts were a lot better than my Marxist ones? Was it that his anticommunist feelings were so strong that he would go to any lengths against me?

Whatever the answer to any of this, I was called down next day to the office of the friendly story editor and told that I was fired. For the record, I asked him why I was fired. He looked at me hard and replied, as he had to, "Mr. Foy finds your work unsatisfactory." He knew that was a lie. He knew that I knew it was a lie, and he hoped I knew there was nothing he could do about it.

When I loaded up with supplies this time, I figured they would really have to last.

I got into my creaky old Plymouth and drove home. I supposed that now I was officially blacklisted. I was especially incensed because I was being penalized even though I hadn't appeared before the committee or testified under oath. Regardless of the larger significance of all this, it seemed to me the studio's action was more than normally outrageous. I did get a sympathetic lawyer to write a threatening letter to Warners, declaring the studio would be held responsible for depriving me of my right to work merely on the basis that I'd received a subpoena. They never bothered to reply.

An ironic coda to my predicament was a call from my agent, Bernie Feins, who was widely considered a firm liberal. "How could you do this to me?" he screamed. "Don't you know what this means? I could be barred from the lot!" He was furious not at the studio, or the committee, or the lousy world that caused all this, but at *me*. It was my fault. I told him to go fuck himself and hung up.

How did Jean and I feel about this? Heroic? Certainly not. We were scared. We were depressed. The future looked bleak. Once again we wondered how I would ever make a living with studio work and screenwriting closed to me. Unlike some of my friends who were distinguished screenwriters with major credits—like Dalton Trumbo, Mike Wilson, Hugo Butler, Albert Maltz, John Lawson, Ring Lardner Jr., Waldo Salt, and others—I was a new writer with few credits of no particular distinction. Producers were not going to seek me out to work on the black market at reduced rates, which was beginning to happen to others.

In recent decades it has surprised me that the blacklistees are regarded by many not only as victims but as heroes. Victims we certainly were. But heroes make hard choices, and Jean and I never felt we had a choice. We had political reasons for refusing to cooperate with the committee; we all felt they were trampling on what was best about America, the Constitutional right to speak or remain silent about beliefs; playing their game was unconscionable and unthinkable. It meant validating the committee. Becoming an informer meant dragging the names of our friends into the muck like criminals—because cooperating with the committee meant giving names. It never seemed possible to do that; it never occurred to us that was a choice. It certainly never seemed heroic.

Beyond these considerations of principle, another factor may seem small in view of what was at stake, but it was not small. We who had been party members for years had now worked and hoped and struggled for a long time alongside our fellow members; they were usually our closest friends. We were a besieged company and that drew us closer together. To turn on such friends for reasons of fear or personal gain would be an act of betrayal, not only of principle but of personal loyalty. How was that possible? It wasn't even considered. It was not a heroic decision; it was simple decency, the sort of thing I'd expect from most people. I continue to honor and love those in that band with Jean and me, those who are still alive and the many who have died, even though we sometimes altered our political convictions in the long years that followed.

5

My subpoena, dated 14 April 1952, commanded William Wheeler to summon me to

appear before the Committee on Un-American Activities or a duly authorized subcommittee thereof of the House of Representatives of the United
States of which the Hon. John S. Wood is chairman, in their chamber in the
city of Los Angeles, Calif., on September 5, 1952, Room 518, Federal Building, at the hour of 10:00 a.m., then and there to testify touching matters of
inquiry committed to said Committee . . . not to depart without leave of
said Committee.

From April until September gave me plenty of time to brood about the
upcoming hearings and to prepare for them.

The standard routine for those of us who were declining to be
"friendly" witnesses was a briefing by a panel of progressive or sympathetic attorneys. The victims gathered as a group in an office after work
hours, where we acted out the scene we'd face at the committee hearings.
The attorneys played the role of the inquisitors, and we were supposed to
learn how to respond to the questions they would put to us, paying special
attention to the danger of giving a reply that, inadvertently, would cause
us to forego the privilege of the Fifth Amendment. We met one evening
each week. As we became familiar with our roles, the attorneys got tougher
as inquisitors, baiting us, gaveling us down, behaving quite realistically—
all to prepare us for what to expect.

Since the attorneys devoted their time to this work, we had to pay
them. Most of us in the class of 1952 had little or no financial resources—
we had problems paying the rent and groceries, never mind legal fees. But
we considered it an obligation to pay the attorneys and also to make it a
political matter to raise the funds by appealing to friends to contribute to
the cause of fighting the committee. My own letter of solicitation went

out to twenty or more people, many of whom responded with contributions of anything from $5 to $50, almost invariably in cash (no one wanted to leave a paper trail). I raised $500 this way and was considered one of the more successful performers. As a matter of personal curiosity, I sent letters to several people I considered dubious prospects. One went to Bill Alland, who responded with several ten dollar bills folded into an envelope, which was left at our doorstep inside a book I'd loaned him. I respected his fear of the committee, but thought he could have managed the donation with more style.

I sent out another letter to Joe Breen Jr. I wondered if I'd hear from him. I hoped to get some kind of a response. I suppose it would have made me feel like less of a sucker to his sympathetic act. I never heard anything. Another close friend picked me up in his car and, after driving around for several blocks to make certain that we weren't followed, tried to slip me some cash but with the warning that I must never let his wife know about this. I refused to take this money. Perhaps I was unduly stiff-necked. I report this now to make the point of how fearful people in Hollywood were of the committee.

While all this was going on, I began my first job—post-blacklist. Ray Marcus was a good friend who was operating a small factory downtown in the commercial and industrial section of Los Angeles. He manufactured vinyl plastic items for household use—bowl covers, dust covers for toasters, and larger covers for patio furniture. Ray hired me for $50 a week as a salesman, needing sales to build his business and to help me deal with unemployment. Unfortunately, the marriage of true need and good intentions was less than successful. I was surely one of the world's worst salesmen. I drove around to the scattered department and notions stores in the vast Los Angeles area and tried to persuade the owners or buyers that they needed Ray's plastic merchandise.

I recall one early experience when I visited a notions store where Jean and I had often purchased an egg slicer or a packet of sewing needles. I felt I had a relationship with the proprietor and could expect a friendly reception. I bumbled in with my case full of neatly packaged items and tried to strike up a conversation with the impatient owner. He listened for less than a minute, then grabbed my case, emptied it on the counter and spread out the merchandise, snarling angrily that I was wasting his time. If I had something to sell, set it out and let him look at it. What kind of salesman was I, anyway? Humiliated, I wound up selling the man nothing. He was right, I was totally inept, I should have come in smiling, hearty, telling a few jokes or talking about the Dodgers.

None of this helped me sell plastics for Ray. I worried how long Ray's shaky enterprise could continue to support my drain of $50 per week. Jean was still working on the *Finian's Rainbow* project, and she earned somewhat more than I. Together, we managed, though the full-time help to care for Ellen reduced our income considerably. Five-year-old Ellen went to kindergarten and she also helped around the house. Relieved of the job of lying to the process-server, she had enthusiastically taken to answering the telephone. I arrived home one evening to have her report that I had a telephone call from a Mr. Charlie Schneer. The name sounded odd in her five-year-old voice and took a bit of study, but she was clear about the message. Mr. Schneer wanted me to call him about work! I knew Charles Schneer slightly; he was working as an assistant to a producer at the Columbia B unit. I called him next day.

"Hello, Charlie," (this was before I learned he preferred to be called Charles), "this is Bernie Gordon. You called?" .

"Yeah. Hi, Bernie. I saw the Rock Hudson picture you wrote for Universal. I'm working down here at Columbia with Katzman. We're looking for a Western. You have anything you'd like to show us?"

This was the crudest kind of violation of guild rules. Producers were not supposed to ask writers to write anything on spec. But by putting it this way, he wasn't asking me to write anything, just to pull something appropriate out of my trunk for him to read. I had other things to worry about beside this routine violation of the rules. I was waiting for him to mention my blacklist status, but he didn't. Could he be ignorant of this? Could the miserable Columbia B unit, so far off the beaten track in its crumbling facility down near Vermont Avenue, be out of the circuit and not even know about the blacklist? I really didn't know how to react.

"Let me think about it, see what I can dig up."

At first, I thought it was a waste of time to get involved in this situation, which would inevitably wind up as it had at Warners. I wouldn't even get to the point of being hired once the contracts and paperwork began. I also felt that even though my salesman's employ was certainly not going to last indefinitely, there was no point in giving up $50 per week for a long-shot crack at a job that might never materialize. So I sought a way of checking out the situation without burning my bridges.

I recalled that some good friends of mine who were also blacklisted, Janet and Philip Stevenson, had written a play for Broadway about Billy the Kid. Though I had never read the play, I thought this sounded promising. I proposed to the Stevensons that they prepare a short synopsis of their play, which I would submit as my original story. If an actual job materialized, I would pay them one-third of the fee for the whole scripting job. The Writers Guild minimum schedule for a script of this category was then about $2,500. The Stevensons agreed and sent me their synopsis. I ran the pages over to Schneer, who was the assistant to Sam Katzman, executive producer at Columbia's B unit. Nothing was said about the blacklist.

I kept Ray Marcus apprised of what was going on. Soon I received a call from Schneer telling me that the story had been approved. When could I begin work? Since I had no agent to represent me, and since I had no intention of asking the Katzman unit to pay more than the guild minimum, the whole matter smelled very fishy to me. I stalled before making a final commitment.

Sure enough, Schneer called. "There's some damn business going on. They're asking everyone to give a loyalty oath. Will you write something and send it in?"

Could he really be ignorant of the political situation? I played along. "Sure, Charlie, I'll send you a statement." Which I did. The statement made no mention of political matters. I merely said that I was a loyal, law-abiding American citizen with no police record. Period. I assumed this would end all discussions about hiring me. Amazingly, I was told that this was satisfactory and that I could begin work at the minimum fee. Contracts, as always at the studios, would come along eventually.

I was confronted with the same problem all over again. I assumed that once the paperwork started and the legal department at the main studio got into the act, the stuff would hit the fan. *They* could not be unaware of what was going on in town. I didn't want to give up my profession in plastics, and Ray Marcus was very understanding. But writing a script meant any number of meetings with the producers at their behest and convenience, plus the time-consuming effort to turn out pages, send them in for discussion, do rewrites, and so on. I couldn't do that and run around town as a salesman. I resolved this problem by involving another blacklisted friend, Bob Williams, who actually had considerable experience writing Westerns at Republic and Universal. My deal with Bob was that I would be the front man, taking meetings with the studio, conveying to him the sense of the meetings, and then he and I would share the writing chores. For this, we would split the two-thirds that remained of the script fee. He was delighted.

By now I was down to $800 or $900 for my remaining third of this deal. But what the hell. We'd all make a few dollars. Bob and I began to turn out pages. I continued working in the plastics industry. I met with Schneer to discuss the script. The lot where we worked was far from the main studio on Gower Street, and there was little likelihood of my meeting anyone I knew. The problem that came up was totally unexpected, and it had nothing to do with politics or the blacklist. I couldn't get Bob to write scenes that seemed right to me, that I was prepared to turn in to the producers. I wound up rewriting Bob. I couldn't understand this, since he was a more experienced writer of Westerns than I. I finally concluded that it was unrealistic to expect a writer to deliver scenes to a producer he never talked to, so I wound up writing my own scenes, rewriting his, and trying not to hurt his feelings. So far as Schneer and Katzman were concerned, the work went along splendidly. I still hadn't met Katzman, but word came to me through Schneer that the boss was content.

Using some excuse that now escapes me, I persuaded Schneer that it would be best to use some name other than my own on the contracts. I believe I concluded at the time that Schneer knew what was going on and chose to close his eyes to the politics. But we never discussed the blacklist. The name I used for the contracts had to have a social security number, so I settled on using the identity of Bob's young brother, Jack Williams, who worked at a Westwood photo shop and was more than willing to lend his name and number to the enterprise.

After the script was finished and paid for, and the film, *The Law Versus Billy the Kid*, was actually made, I discovered that using Jack Williams's social security number led to an additional complication or irritation. Since it was reported that he had earned the whole fee for the work, he had to report this to the IRS and pay the income tax. While it was theoretically possible for him to seek a rebate on this income he had never actually received, the whole process struck us as tricky and was never resolved. The result was that I finally netted some $500 or $600 on the deal. But because the blacklist had never really come up, I was the fair-haired boy at the Katzman unit. I looked forward to more assignments.

Ray Marcus thanked me for my efforts as a salesman and terminated my employment. Life seemed to be looking up—except for a long dry spell when we had trouble paying the rent. I was casting around for a means of making a living while occupied for months with preparations for the upcoming hearings: writing fundraising letters, drafting a statement to be presented to the committee (which they wouldn't let me read before my testimony), and attending the practice sessions with the attorneys.

On the day of my appearance before the committee, I drove downtown to the Federal Building alone. Jean was at work; there was no point in her accompanying me, because we never knew how many days we would wait before being called to testify. The hearing room was set up like a courtroom, with a raised platform in front where members of the committee and their "prosecutor" sat at tables to direct their questions to witnesses. About a hundred seats were arranged for witnesses and spectators. I sat with friends who were due to be called. The friendly witnesses testified first. Roy Huggins was one of the few friendly witnesses I'd actually met at party meetings. Seated close to the front, I was able to stare unblinkingly at him as he reeled off about twenty names. I knew he could see me clearly. I waited for him to name me. But he didn't. This was not considerate oversight. Huggins and I had never had any personal relationship. The omission must have been a typical example of the committee telling its witness in advance the names it wanted him to produce, which he then produced.

I was scheduled to appear in public as a "Fifth Amendment Witness." I assumed that any chance I might have to slip between the cracks and keep on working at Columbia would vanish. I was resigned to this and waited to be called. The principal unfriendly witnesses at that session were the local doctors and lawyers who had been included with the few remaining Hollywood people still in the inquisition. These were the very lawyers who had represented the Ten in the earlier hearings and court cases; they were also the same attorneys, in many instances, who had been preparing us for our testimony. The lawyers, and even the doctors, were exceptionally well equipped to deal with the committee. They refused to be gaveled down. They refused to answer questions as the committee demanded—with a simple yes or no. They knew their rights and argued vociferously, angrily, ferociously, and at length. One doctor, who had been awarded medals for valor during World War II, threw his medals on the table, returning them to the country that had once honored him and was now behaving disgracefully. Another doctor explained with great feeling that, among Jews, an informer could not be buried in the same sacred ground as other Jews. Informing on one's friends, associates, and fellows was an unforgivable sin.

As a result of the vigorous and time-consuming battle mounted by the doctors and lawyers, the committee ran out of time and never called some of the last Hollywood people, like myself, who remained to be nailed. We received telegrams notifying us that our hearings had been postponed, that we were to consider ourselves still under subpoena, and that we would be told where and when to appear. More than forty years later, I suppose I am still under subpoena. But the fact is that I was never called to testify. So far as I know, my name doesn't appear in any of the committee records except for the very earliest one in 1947, which was prior to the time when the committee really got into the act, forcing witnesses to invoke either the First or Fifth Amendments.

This left me in an irritating limbo. The fact that I never testified did not relieve me of my blacklist status—I had to work under a pseudonym, and that continued for about ten years until the blacklist was finally broken. But this did keep me in some ways from achieving the honorable status of a resistance fighter. My name does not appear in any of the major books written about the blacklist. So here I am writing my own account which will, I hope, cast some additional light on the history of myself and others who suffered through that era without the official stamp of disapproval.

I suppose I could prove my case that I was truly, one hundred percent blacklisted by seeking the testimony of someone like William Alland, my first producer at Universal. He should qualify as an expert since he eventually testified that he had once been a member of the party and then went on to name names, including his ex-wife (the mother of his daughter). His was one of the worst instances of crawling during the entire nasty era. About a year after the committee hearing discussed above, I ran into Alland in a hardware store. He attempted a weak smile. I glared back, then ignored him. He left the shop, but waited outside, across Sunset Boulevard. When I came out of the store, he was watching for me and tentatively raised a hand. I crossed the boulevard. I was curious to hear what he'd say.

His pitch was direct. "Bernie, for God's sake, I have to talk to you. You have to come to your senses and talk to the committee. Now, you're going down the drain."

"Talk? Become an informer?"

"Bernie, be sensible. That's just a word. Who would you be hurting? They already have all the names. You're the most talented writer I've ever known. And what's to become of you?"

I shook my head and delivered the only *coup de grâce* I could think of. "Talk to the committee and then live the rest of my life with friends like you and Borden Chase?" I started away.

Sly as ever, Alland had the last word. "You wanted to talk to me. You crossed the street." This was true. But what else was there to say? I went back across Sunset carrying the light bulb or extension cord I had purchased.

At home, I told Jean about meeting Alland. We agreed it was a case of misery loving company. He would enjoy having me join him in the ranks of the informers. I never learned what happened to his farm out in the San Fernando Valley or whether he rescued any more chickens for his table. I did hear that in time he'd had some success producing low-budget films. Years later, I hoped he saw my name up on the screen as the writer of more important films.

$\mathbf{T}$*he Law Versus Billy the Kid* had been filmed, but I had no way of knowing if I'd ever work again. I was out of the plastics business, but my next venture had more pizzazz. I became a private investigator.

I had become acquainted with Jack Burke, who was working as a secretary in the law offices of Margolies and McTernan. He had an intriguing history as an investigator in Washington, D.C., for the old LaFollette Commission, which during the Roosevelt era had conducted some progressive investigations. Jack now wanted to set himself up as an independent private investigator, and he invited me to join him in a partnership.

"Me? A private investigator?" I laughed. But Jack was serious.

"Look," he explained. "Forget all the Humphrey Bogart bullshit. We'd be working for regular-guy attorneys who are doing personal injury work. You know—like car accidents where people are hurt or killed and the attorneys need someone to go out, get the facts about the accident, and try to get witnesses. We'll be working for the injured parties who are trying to collect from insurance companies. What's wrong with that?"

I was listening.

"The way it works now," Jack said, "the insurance companies are the ones who have the investigators. They send men out into the field the same day as the accident, get the information and get witness statements, and are all set to beat down the demands of the injured parties. It's not the way you hear—that the insurance people get taken for big settlements. Nine times out of ten, it's the poor slob who gets hurt, who doesn't know what to do, finally gets to a lawyer weeks or months later, if ever, and winds up with nothing. You want to look at it from a social point of view, it's the little guy against the big corporations, which have all the clout, the experience, and the high-powered attorneys working for them. We'll be on the right side. Besides, a lot of the plaintiff lawyers are inexperienced and don't want to lay out money for investigation."

"Exactly what would we be doing?"

"We get to the scene, if it's an auto accident, measure the skid marks, take photos of the damaged cars, of the intersection, and the injured people, if necessary. We try to find witnesses and get statements for them to sign."

Although I felt foolish, I was able to tell myself that at least this was socially acceptable, And who knew? Perhaps one day this real-life experience would be useful in some future writing career. So I signed on.

I had one true "private eye" job involving a criminal case and an actual trial. In the course of it, while ducking hostile police in the hot, dusty precincts of Bakersfield, California, I asked myself what a screenwriter was doing there.

Leo Branton was Black and an extremely bright and promising lawyer. After the Bakersfield incident, he went on to a distinguished career—in fact, he later successfully defended Angela Davis in her dispute with the University of California and in her trial as a Communist. Leo asked me to help him decide whether he should become involved in a criminal case in which a young Black man was being tried in Bakersfield for allegedly raping a White woman. The defendant, Osceola McClinton, a twenty-five-year-old student at Bakersfield Junior College, was accused of raping Lela M. Shanley, a woman of forty, in her car on the night of May 4, 1955. Osceola, universally called "Coke," admitted there had been sexual intercourse but said that it had been consensual.

In the course of less than two days of investigation, which was all the time we had before the trial, I was tailed by the local police, denied a copy of the police report, refused a discussion with the doctor who had examined the plaintiff, and even ejected from the courtroom during the trial on the grounds that, just sitting there, I might be influencing witnesses. Still, I was able to come up with some very damaging information about the alcoholic and corrupt husband of the alleged victim. I was even able to produce, miraculously, a highly respected local white gynecologist who testified for the defense. Leo was absolutely brilliant, managing to work into the testimony all of the meager information I was able to provide.

However, my most satisfying work was done while sitting in our motel room between court sessions. Leo turned to me.

"What it gets down to," Leo said, "is that we need a convincing story I can tell the jury, a scenario of what happened in that car to convince them it wasn't rape but consensual sex."

The word "scenario" turned on a light in his head. "Get out your typewriter, Bernie," Leo said, "and write me a scene, something the jury will buy."

As I got out the light portable that I carried for taking witness statements and set it up on the wobbly telephone stand, the two local attorneys who were working with us looked at Leo, puzzled. "Bernie has another background," he explained. "He can do this." Nothing more. I was back into screenwriting.

While the three of them kicked around the legal approach to the case, I settled at my typewriter and banged out a couple of single-space pages that, I hoped, told a plausible story. Making use of what little I already knew about the couple of Shanleys, I wrote that while driving Osceola home (no dispute), Lela Shanley began to tell the sympathetic "Coke" about her miserable life with Shanley, who drank up most of their money (the money she earned as a nurse's assistant), which left them without money to pay for their one room. He abused her, humiliated her with the other roomers in the house, was unable to hold a job, and stood in the way of her seeing her two daughters by a previous marriage, who had to live in another town. By the time I got to this phase, Lela was sobbing bitterly. Coke, only demonstrating his concern, put an arm around her comfortingly. She rested her head against him gratefully, then raised her face to his, nuzzled his cheek. He bent his mouth to hers. They kissed. It was a surprise for both of them. But the kiss led to another, more passionate. Soon this troubled, needy woman was clasping him close.

Coke was aroused. She was aroused. He started to fumble with her clothes; she tore them away, gladly offered herself to him. And that's how it came about.

I handed the pages to Leo who read through them quickly, passed them to the other two. Here I was, waiting again for approval of my script! After the others finished reading, having nothing to say, Leo said, "Okay. Good. I can use this fine."

Leo used the scenario to good effect. He brilliantly impeached the testimony of the police and found the gynecologist an invaluable support. With the trial virtually over after the second day, he and I were able to return to Los Angeles, leaving the final summation to the local attorneys. We were confident of an acquittal. The next day, Leo called to tell me that Osceola had been acquitted. Osceola McClinton was immediately released from custody, and it seemed the matter was closed.

Four years later, after many changes in my own life, I decided to go back to Bakersfield to learn what more I could about the people and events I had investigated. I thought there was a story in it, even a motion picture. I drove up to Bakersfield and began my search for the answers I felt I had missed the first time around. I spent another hot day in Bakersfield driving around and talking to a number of women who were wildly amused at how I had misunderstood everything—but everything!—about the situation that had existed here those years ago. The story I finally put together was that Osceola had been a star basketball player on the local junior college team and was liked for this by people both Black and White; that he had joined a dramatic society at the school (which also admitted outsiders), which is how he had become acquainted with Lela Shanley, who also played at being an actress in the group; that he and Lela had become lovers; this was well known and had gone on for quite a while. It was hinted that the alcoholic and perverted husband had encouraged the relationship and even tried to arrange to witness the lovemaking.

To my astonished questions of why no one had come out with these facts at the time of the trial, I only got loud and knowing laughter. To this day, I have been puzzled and have only been able to speculate about what this meant, about why McClinton, a man largely accepted by the local White community, could be sure a White court in Bakersfield, California, would never railroad him to prison. I don't know if he ever understood that except for some luck on my part and a brilliant job by Leo Branton, he would probably have gone up for fifty years. In any event, it looked like the laugh was on me. Ruefully, I had to examine my pride in the work I had done as an investigator in my one real criminal case.

From 1953 to 1955 I worked with Jack Burke as an investigator, but I interrupted my efforts to measure skid marks and photograph bent fenders or damaged limbs when I was hired by Schneer and Sam Katzman to do a rewrite of *The Earth Vs. the Flying Saucers.*

I had learned by now that it was not necessary to use a "front" like John Williams, that it was simpler to use the name "Ray Marcus" and append my own social security number. This was perfectly legal and done frequently for a variety of reasons; it was not unusual for an individual to have more than one name under the same social security number. That is how I proceeded for the rest of the years of the blacklist, and, because I used my own social security number, it has been simpler in recent years to prove to the Writers Guild that the scripts I wrote under the Marcus pseudonym were, indeed, mine. Thus it has been possible for the guild to award me more proper credits as a blacklisted writer than any other guild member.

The Earth Vs. the Flying Saucers was based on an original story by Curt Siodmak. George Worthing Yates had drafted a screenplay, but the producers weren't happy with it. To tackle the rewrite, I was offered the splendid sum of $1,500, and I accepted. As it turned out, my "rewrite" involved total page-by-page changes, including adding new characters and reworking many of the science fiction ideas—basic ones, such as how the space aliens finally manage to communicate with the Earthlings, how they learn everything they need to know about us, and how they are finally beaten back (but not until they've done a good job of destroying almost all of Washington, D.C.). I was proud of my sci-fi ideas since I hadn't known I had them in me. I invented and named something the aliens called "an infinitely indexed memory bank" that was virtually an anticipation of computer memory, which came years later.

During this work, I met with the special-effects man Ray Harryhausen, who went on to become a significant figure in the field of special effects and the darling of science fiction lovers everywhere. He was a lovely, talented artist and technician. Even working on the minuscule Katzman budget, he turned out credible (and incredible) effects—space ships hovering and landing and wonderful wholesale destruction. Mainly because of his work, the film actually opened at New York's Paramount Theater and went on to become a cult classic. But I am assured by the tireless admirers of such films, who continue to run and re-run the film whenever they get together, that my story and screenplay are also appreciated.

In terms of actual screen credits for the script, the Writers Guild decided that the credits should read "Screenplay by George Worthing Yates and Raymond Marcus." I was outraged that my name should come second (these matters are important to screenwriters), and Charles Schneer expressed his astonishment to me. But producers had nothing to say about credits. Schneer suggested that I protest to the guild and demand a review. But this would have involved more direct dealing with the guild than I—as Raymond Marcus—felt safe doing.

About thirty years after this effort, I was approached by a journalist who was curious to know how, during some of the worst days of the Cold War, it had been possible to write a script or make a film portraying the Americans and the Russians working together to save the world by defeating a threat from outer space. When he discovered that the actual writer had been blacklisted, he felt he had the answer. So, there was the smoking gun that HUAC had always searched for and never found: outright proof that "we" had smuggled awful red propaganda about the United States and Russia working together into an innocuous sci-fi film that opened at the Paramount in 1955.

After withholding taxes, my $1,500 fee for *Earth Vs. the Flying Saucers* did not last long. I went back to work with my friend Jack. Jean was still working with the same people who had been developing the *Finian's Rain-*

bow project, but even after a great deal of money had been spent on art-work, music, recording, contracts, etc., the film (as so many projects) was put aside never to be resuscitated. John Hubley went on to produce animated commercials for television, and Jean went with him to become the executive secretary of a very busy and successful enterprise.

During this period I was able to get several writing jobs for television, none of which worked out very satisfactorily. First, I was approached by my old friend, Walter Doniger, the man who nervously offered me $50 when I was collecting funds to pay the blacklist attorneys. I had refused the money when he pleaded with me to keep the matter secret from his wife.

I had once helped Walter sell his spec screenplay of *Rope of Sand* to Hal Wallis, who produced it at Paramount. Walter had now connected with a promoter and was planning to produce and direct a series about Warden Duffy of San Quentin. He asked me to write some scripts for this series and explained, of course, that he would have to put his own name on the scripts. This was more than acceptable to me. I did not regard this as a comedown and was delighted with the prospect of long-term work on a series.

I wrote two scripts which turned out well. I recall that one of them was intentionally comic despite the grim background. It concerned a famous professional chef, now in prison, who ran the prison kitchen as he had once run his great restaurant, commanding respect from fellow prisoners, guards, and even the warden, who enjoyed the improved cuisine. Yet, after two episodes, Walter disappeared. I was left to understand that his partner, the man in touch with the network, had concluded it was too risky to employ me. I never heard from Walter again

I had an almost identical experience on another series when I was hired by Charles Schneer, now working for a television producer, to start writing half-hour scripts for their new series, *The Web*. The scripts were approved, and I was even invited to meet with the enthusiastic director, a man who was reputed to be a liberal who would have no objection to working with me. But shortly after that meeting, my employment with the company ended. It was typical that none of the nice guys like Doniger or Schneer, who really wanted to work with me and initiated the jobs, ever felt free to tell me that the blacklist had closed in on television as well as the motion-picture industry. The term "blacklist" was *verboten*, and anyone working in either industry was careful to avoid what was, in principle, a procedure forbidden by law.

In this same period, the problem arose for me even more blatantly. I had been approached by Bob Cohn, for whom Julian and I had written our first script, *The Millen Case*. Cohn was now working for his relatives at Columbia Pictures, but in the studio's newly created and successful division, Screen Gems, which was producing a number of television series. He was eager to employ me but explained that he would have to get the consent of his older brother, Ralph Cohn, who was in charge of Screen Gems. This looked promising to me since I had known Ralph Cohn in the past and knew him as an outspoken liberal. He would only be asked to close his eyes to the fact that I would be working under a pseudonym. I was surprised, angry, and bitterly disappointed when word came down that I was not to be employed under any circumstances. Any illusions I had about decent people at the studios cooperating to help us evaporated completely.

The conditions controlling the blacklist in television were not precisely the same as at the film studios. Because in those days so much television programming was produced by smaller independent venture operators and was not concentrated in the hands of a few major studios, it was easier to slip in, find producers who wanted good work done cheaply. Such people felt less vulnerable to the proliferating pressure groups that, with publications like *Red Channels*, made it their business to expose any blacklisted writers who might be working, or, for that matter, to expose anyone they considered left-wing, whether Communist or not. With writers working at home and having no contact with studios, it was easier to conceal identities by using people who for reasons of principle, friendship, or money were willing to act as fronts for the real writers. Increasingly, this did occur. My friends Alfred and Helen Levitt worked quite steadily under the aegis of their good friend Jerry Davis, who took credit as both writer and producer of many shows. This was true even more so in New York, where the media were more scattered than in our company town. Writers like Abe Polonsky, Walter Bernstein, Ring Lardner Jr., and Ian Hunter, and others eventually began to work quite regularly. Interestingly, too, after a time a very progressive woman with access to funds, Hannah Weinstein, started a serious studio operation in London where she produced the successful *Robin Hood* series exclusively using blacklisted writers, many of them the same writers who had been working in New York.

There was also a negative side to this. The *Red Channels* fanatics were constantly on the search for blacklistees who might be working, and they had great leverage because of the threat to pressure advertisers to withdraw their sponsorship of any program tainted by the commies. Advertising was where the bucks were for the TV stations and networks, who were even more fearful of such reprisals than the studios were of a theater boycott. Personally, I know of no instance when a station or a network had the courage to stand up to this threat and agree to hire or use a blacklisted writer, actor, or director. So the under-the-table work continued.

I had another friend who had no connection with the studios or networks. Joe Steinberg had made some money in real estate investment. He was still young, financially comfortable, not rich. He had attended the Yale drama school in its heyday and had developed a love for drama and the arts. In his thirties, he was eager to get into filmmaking and play a creative role. An extremely warm and forthcoming man, and completely sympathetic to the left, it was natural for him to cultivate film people who were blacklisted. His very good friend (and mine) was Irving Lerner, a man who knew everything about filmmaking, a brilliant film editor who knew music and all the convolutions of laboratory work and photography. He had also directed several low-budget but well-regarded films. He too was blacklisted. Joe and Irving decided there might be an opportunity in the young television medium for a fresh approach to a series of films about sports.

After we met, I gave the matter some thought and suggested that an original series of films or episodes could be developed by focusing on the personal stories of people involved in a sport, whether a team sport or sporting activity. I recalled that in 1936 during a course on filmmaking at the Museum of Modern Art, the distinguished British documentary filmmaker Paul Rotha had run a clip that indelibly impressed me. The shot was of an elderly woman seated in the corner of a room speaking excitedly about her experience in chasing down and hitting a rat with a broom! The camera never moved, not even to go in for a close-up; there was absolutely nothing filmic in the usual sense, but that bit of film conveyed a feel of total reality stronger than anything I'd ever seen. Almost twenty years later, I still remembered that film clip, and it suggested to me a different approach to a series of sports films, with the emphasis on the personality, lifestyle, and history of the players speaking informally, directly, and candidly right to the camera.

Joe and Irving liked the approach. For my first assignment I flew up to Ennis, Montana, the heart of the best trout fishing country in the Rockies. I studied the streams, the hatcheries, the historic Lewis and Clark territory, and the local people who lived by and for the hunting and trout fishing. Ennis was only a few miles from the gateway to Yellowstone Park, which was not yet open for the season but was opened for me. My time

there was invigorating—a wonderful change from accident investigations. I wrote a script that Irving shot, using the locals as actors, and millions of trout in great breeding tanks for splendid photography.

Though the film was regarded as successful, Joe found that he needed
more than one such film to promote a series. My next assignment was to
script an "inside-the-game" account of a minor league baseball team in
Visalia, California. Here, more than in the fishing film, I was able to use
my idea of interviewing the players and their wives during the progress of
a ball game. I told a variety of personal stories about kids coming up as
rookies and old timers who had once played in the World Series but were
now reduced to playing for peanuts the game they loved and couldn't quit.
The result was touching and real. We were very high on it, and when serious interest developed for a major series with sponsors like Colgate, we
were certain we were on our way and I would, at last, beat the blacklist.

The negotiations dragged on and another offer fortuitously came
along through my old boss at Columbia, Sam Katzman, who had a new
team working to make his B pictures. A new man, who used the professional name James Gordon for reasons that had nothing to do with the
blacklist, was the story editor and the principal writer for the unit, but he
couldn't keep up with the job of turning out scripts. He had known my
work from the earlier films with Katzman and called me to come up with
some ideas for cheap horror films.

It took about five minutes for me to suggest something about underwater zombies. Brilliant. I had the job. I decided then that things were
looking up enough on several fronts, so I gave up my career as a detective
and my Bogart persona. Now I was a blacklisted writer who couldn't use
the name Gordon, working for a writer who wasn't blacklisted who wasn't
really named Gordon. The other Gordon was a low-key man who knew
just how to get along with Katzman, and I tried to learn from him. My
first script on this stint was made as *The Zombies of Mora Tau*. I was asked
to come up with second one. Overnight I managed another brainstorm
that became *The Man Who Turned to Stone*. After that, a third script, based
on a newspaper item, became a nonhorror thriller about a prisoner who
escapes from San Quentin by airplane.

Though I do not count these credits among my prouder achievements,
the $3,000 or $4,000 for each screenplay went a long way toward easing
our financial situation. And the "real" Ray Marcus began to take pride in
the number of films bearing his name. I well recall the night I took Jeanie
and Ellen to Hollywood Boulevard to look at the marquee of the Egyp-
tian Theater that boasted both of my horror films on the same bill. With,

I confess, a certain degree of pride, I put down my money at the box office for three seats. And the thought occurred to me that millions of others all around the world would be doing this. Cheesy or not, these were my own.

It's true that there was a raucous laugh from the audience at one of the ridiculous moments in *Zombies* that was supposed to be horrific, but I felt that it was not my fault. The scene I had written called for the underwater zombies to get out of their caskets en masse and start about their destructive ways. The director, Edward Cahn, had dutifully laid the caskets around the walls of the "underwater" chamber, then signaled for the bit players to emerge from the caskets and get on their feet as the camera rolled. They did as instructed, or tried to. But since they were all lying down cramped into the caskets to start with, they struggled clumsily to climb out and get onto their feet. It was a laugh riot. These clumsy oafs were the invincible zombies? When I first saw the footage at the studio, I complained to the director: "Couldn't you see what they looked like? Why didn't you do it over? Stand the caskets up and let them get out from a standing position?"

Eddie Cahn looked at me wearily. "I've got six days to shoot this damned ninety-minute film. Do you think I have time for retakes?"

In any event, none of this troubled Sam Katzman. He felt warm enough toward me to offer me a free Christmas gift for my wife—a bottle of Chanel No. 5 . . . counterfeit. He got the bottles by the gross and offered to sell me as many as I needed at his own cost of two bucks apiece.

Quite a few months had passed before Joe Steinberg got the final word from the network and Colgate. They liked the show very much and had considered it carefully but had finally concluded that there was really no place on television for a purely sports subject. It meant automatically losing one-half the potential audience, the women! The wisdom of this thinking has often come back to haunt us in the years since 1956, when the World Series, the Super Bowl, Monday Night Football, the Olympics, and a thousand other sports shows seem to dominate the airways. Lose half the audience? Tell it to ESPN.

In 1950 North Korea invaded South Korea. Forget the long history of brutal Japanese colonial oppression of a proud people; forget the aggressive role being played by our own country in creating and supporting a vicious and corrupt government in the south: Communism was on the march and had to be stopped, even with the blood of our own men, who were shipped over there with the conviction that our great military superiority would quickly put an end to red aggression and chutzpa. But it didn't work out that way, especially when we approached the Chinese border and found ourselves confronted for the first time ever by a potent Red Army.

I am not discussing here questions of right or wrong, only the effect this had on the temper of the times. Now our men were fighting and dying in Korea. There was fear that we might be engaged in a full-scale war against the Chinese. There was mounting and legitimate concern about atomic destruction, concern that had people building backyard "shelters" against the awful day and had schoolchildren practicing to dive under their desks at the sound of sirens posted in every neighborhood. Hollywood contributed to the concern about the end of an atom-devastated world with films like *On the Beach*. The FBI was everywhere, tailing us, keeping watch, because subversives might do . . . what? And we feared that we might at any moment be interned in the camps that had been prepared. Politicians like Richard Nixon and Joe McCarthy made the most of it, building careers out of the anticommunist hysteria.

Loyalty oaths became standard equipment in schools and universities throughout the country. Even great institutions like the University of California established a loyalty oath and dismissed instructors and professors who refused to sign it. Harvard University denied a tenured position to someone suspected of "disloyalty." This was no longer just a Hollywood blacklist; it was a countrywide witch-hunt.

More was involved than congressional bluster. Along the way, John

Foster Dulles ran the State Department, and his brother, Allan Dulles, ran the CIA. The CIA carried out U.S. anticommunist activities in the most brutal ways throughout the world. In Iran, the elected president, Mossadegh, was ousted and imprisoned so that the United States' man, the infamous Shah, could be brought back. Americans arranged the assassination of Lumumba in the Congo, of Arbenz in Guatemala, of Allende of Chile. We arranged and supported murderous military dictatorships in Argentina and Brazil. We supported the massacre of some million inhabitants of Indonesia, and even supported Pol Pot, the incredible butcher of Cambodia. Need I mention Vietnam? There is scarcely any corner of the world where, in the name of anticommunism, the United States did not intervene and literally contribute to the slaughter of millions. Though some of this occurred even after the Hollywood blacklist had finally faded away in the mid 1960s, there can be little doubt when it all began.

I find it interesting to contemplate the fact that even as I write this, in October 1997, there are two 50th anniversaries being celebrated. One is the birth of the CIA in October 1947; the other marks the date of the initial HUAC hearing in Washington on October 27, 1947. In present-day Hollywood, a major event was organized to memorialize the start of the blacklist; our four major cultural unions, the Writers, Actors, and Directors Guilds, and AFTRA (American Federation of Television and Radio Artists), financed and participated in this event, where they acknowledged their regrettable role in supporting the blacklist. I suggested that President Clinton, who had just joined ex-President Bush in extolling the CIA, be invited to join us at the event at the Academy of Motion Picture Arts and Sciences to help us "celebrate" another 50th anniversary.

In his fine book, *Red Scare: Memories of the American Inquisition*, Griffin Fariello records how it felt to live under McCarthyism. As quoted in the San Francisco *Chronicle*,

State and federal investigators grilled suspected citizens on their reading habits, voting patterns and church attendance. Support for racial equality became evidence of subversive leanings. Heretical literature was banned from public and school libraries; some communities even held book burnings. Federal agents were known to threaten the uncooperative with internment in the newly established camps, with the removal of their children, with the deportation of aging relatives.

As reported in the *Chronicle*, the atmosphere in San Francisco especially became one of paranoia and enforced collaboration. "I'd been working as a waitress in a bakery and restaurant on Van Ness Avenue," recalls Loretta Stavrus, a former labor organizer. "I'd been under surveillance for weeks."

At her home the FBI agents "broke through the door" without a warrant. "The children were hanging onto me, I was telling them 'Don't be afraid, look at these cowardly men. Five, six of them coming here, breaking into our house . . .'"

The *Chronicle* goes on to say that via this book (*Red Scare*) "readers today may understand how political expedience led to what is termed here 'right-wing hysteria' and make sure it doesn't happen again."

An especially odious instance of this kind of hysteria occurred closer to home at a meeting of the Screen Writers Guild in Hollywood. A good friend of mine, Edward Huebsch, was ducking a subpoena from HUAC but decided to attend the guild meeting because a discussion of the guild and the blacklist was scheduled. Outside the meeting hall, Eddie spotted the federal marshal who had been trying to serve him. Eddie ducked into the hall and saw that the marshal was trying to follow him into the closed meeting. Eddie immediately asked the chair to have the marshal barred, because only members of the guild were permitted. One of the right-wing members raised a point of order and moved that the marshal be given temporary membership in the guild and permitted to enter the hall. This was promptly seconded; the chair called for a vote. A few of our blacklisted friends tried to speak against this outrageous motion, among them John Howard Lawson and Lester Cole, both of whom had been original organizers of the guild and past presidents. They were hooted down. The membership voted in favor of the motion. The marshal walked over and served Eddie the subpoena. Does this mean that a majority of the guild members favored the blacklist? I don't believe so. It means that fear of the consequences was so pervasive for anyone who was seen to oppose the extreme right wing that no one dared to take such a stand openly.

It was fairly early in this period that I experienced, at least emotionally, what I consider the nadir of my political ordeals. In 1953, having been tried, convicted, and sentenced to death, Ethel and Julius Rosenberg had exhausted all of their legal appeals. A date had been set for their execution. Appeals for clemency were sent to President Eisenhower from all over the world, from heads of state of western powers, even from the Pope. Ike didn't budge. Without rehashing the question of guilt or innocence, it is worth noting, as a reminder of the political atmosphere of the time, that the Rosenbergs were the only civilians in the history of the nation ever sentenced to die for espionage; that their alleged acts had occurred during peacetime and involved another nation with which we were not at war; and that the charge had been "conspiracy to commit espionage," which made it possible to convict both husband and wife without the necessity to prove that each was involved.

The Supreme Court was in recess for the summer. A last-minute appeal to Justice William O. Douglas resulted in a stay of execution. It was standard procedure for a single designated justice to rule on a case until the full court could consider it. In this instance, good, old, warm, friendly Ike took an unprecedented action. For the first time ever, he called all the scattered justices of the Supreme Court back into session. They considered the matter summarily, overruled Douglas, and adjourned to go back to their vacations. The execution date was immediately rescheduled. There was no possible recourse except a last-minute decision by Eisenhower for clemency, something that was clearly not going to happen. The press and the media played up all the hideous details: the husband and wife's final encounter, their last meeting with their devastated attorney, their last meeting with their two young children, and the delicious detail that Ethel was the stronger character of the two and had been chosen to go to the execution chamber first.

On the evening of the execution, we were asked by the party leaders to convene outside the Federal Building in downtown Los Angeles to form a picket line in a last, desperate hope that public reaction would influence Eisenhower to act. Jean and I were among the picketers. Our sad group of a few dozen faithful circled outside the main entrance with whatever courage and determination we could muster, while hecklers gleefully assailed us with epithets about "Jew blood going to fry." One of the group leaders asked me to join a few others who were going up to the federal attorney's office where we could send a last, desperate telegram to the president.

A half-dozen of us from the picket line took an elevator up to the office of the federal attorney. Although it was now almost nine o'clock at night in Los Angeles, thus approaching the midnight hour of execution in New York, the offices were still open. We were received politely and when we explained our mission, we were offered a room with a conference table and even some paper and pencils to prepare the wording of the telegram. We all appended our names to the message. Then we handed it to a secretary, who assured us that it would be sent promptly to Washington.

We were back on the picket line in a few moments when we learned that the execution had proceeded. Our hecklers raised the level of their venom and their glee until we disbanded and adjourned to a nearby meeting hall where we sat—miserable, but, at least, together—and listened to a few speakers who tried to make sense of all this and say some comforting words.

To appreciate the true magnitude of this atrocity, it is useful to know a few facts that have only recently been revealed and published. In 1997, Daniel Patrick Moynihan, senior senator from New York, wrote a report on government secrecy (Government Printing Office, 1997; published as *Secrecy: The American Experience*, Yale University Press, 1998). Through the Freedom of Information Act, Moynihan obtained previously classified documents that showed that

[T]wo scientists at Los Alamos, Klaus Fuchs and Theodore Hall, did convey valuable atomic information to the Soviets; but neither had any connection to the Communist Party. . . .

Moynihan makes it clear that when the FBI put Julius and Ethel Rosenberg on trial for atomic espionage in March 1951, it had already learned, in May 1950, that real atomic secrets had been given to the Soviets by Theodore Hall. . . . Hall was never charged with espionage and eventually moved to Britain, where he lived a long and happy life, while the United States executed the Rosenbergs for stealing "the secret of the a-bomb."

The decoded Soviet cables show that Ethel was not a Soviet spy and that, while Julius had passed nonatomic information to the Soviets, the trial case against them was largely fabricated. . . .

Moynihan calls the execution of the Rosenbergs "a harsh injustice . . ."

Why didn't the FBI go after Hall? . . . Did the government execute the Rosenbergs and let Hall go because it didn't want to admit it had prosecuted the wrong people as atom spies? (John Wiener, *The Nation*, December 21, 1998)

After the Rosenbergs' execution, the political atmosphere in Hollywood became even more poisonous. The studios that were run by Jews had to make it endlessly clear that there were Jews in America who were not atomic spies, that, in this instance quite literally, they were holier than the Pope. Any thought of an easing of the Hollywood blacklist now seemed hopelessly remote. What had once seemed a temporary political aberration, a moment in a changing world (and we believed that things did change), now seemed like a trap from which we would never escape.

The party? During the early days of the blacklist, we had hung together. A cold wind was blowing and we needed each other for warmth, companionship, and mutual support. When Stalin died in 1953, rumors of the appalling nature of the dictatorship in the Soviet Union began to leak out. In early 1956, Khrushchev spoke publicly about Stalin's atrocities. This was quite different from Henry Luce of *Time* magazine or the Chandlers of the *Los Angeles Times* unfurling their anticommunist propaganda. This news could not be ignored. But by 1957, as the scope of Stalin's abominations became clear, many of our people had scattered to Mexico, New York, Europe; few of our members remained in the section, and functioning was desultory.

In the party, we felt betrayed. A lifetime of dedication and sacrifice to help make a better world had put us on the side of an inconceivable butcher. We still felt that humane socialism was necessary to correct the brutality and inequity of our own system, but the party had lashed itself too tightly to the fate of the U.S.S.R. Unannounced, informally, most of us simply stopped attending meetings. We just faded away from the party.

Whether we were in the party or out made no difference to the establishment, to the media, or, indeed, to the public. Communists, ex-Communists, fellow travelers, leftists of different stripes were all demonized. Remember, there was the atom bomb. And if we were all to be atomized, it would be no one but the Russians and their sympathizers who would do it to us. I think it is possible to put an exact date to the start of this hysteria. It was in Fulton, Missouri, in 1946, that Winston Churchill uttered one of the most memorable and effective phrases of our time or any time. He spoke of the "Iron Curtain," that presumably would impenetrably separate us forever from the demons on the eastern side. Then the term "Cold War" came along and reinforced the conviction that we were hopelessly separated into a world of good guys and bad guys who were determined to destroy each other. In this atmosphere, despite some small personal victories, the blacklist flourished with more intensity than ever.

8

Though I was having a good run of work through the mid 1950s, it wasn't possible to relax and assume this would continue. I had no agent or any organized way of getting jobs; whatever came along was from the few contacts I had in the industry. Would that continue with the blacklist in force? Jean kept working with the company producing animated commercials. She had a responsible position and a good relationship with her employers, but she was not reconciled to being away from Ellen all day, every day.

Charles Schneer, the man who had asked me to write the scripts for *Billy the Kid* and *The Earth Vs. the Flying Saucers,* had family connections and was now back at Columbia Pictures. He had a much improved position and was headquartered at the main studio building on Gower Street, where he was producing films that were still labeled 'B' but that had budgets much more generous than Katzman's $100,000 epics. My first assignment with Schneer redux was *Hellcats of the Navy,* and for me it had special piquancy. First, I was to do a rewrite of a script by David Lang, an especially malodorous informer who had notoriously given the committee names of people he had never met. I knew this because he named my best friend, Julian Zimet, whom he had no way of knowing. It was a pleasure to come in and try to write him out of a credit—or at least out of a sole credit. That Schneer had first hired an informer did not sit well with me, and I complained about this, but Schneer seemed untroubled by political principles.

Second, Ronnie and Nancy (Davis) Reagan had been cast in this film. (It would turn out to be the only film in which they appeared together.) This was long before Reagan's state or national political triumphs, but at the time everyone in Hollywood knew he had played a major role in creating and enforcing the blacklist. Although a minor star, best known as host of the General Electric Theater on television, he was working local politics and became president of the Screen Actors Guild. This, of course, was when the SAG and all the local unions were at their most reactionary. Still, it was not yet known that Reagan, while president of SAG, supplied names of guild activists and political suspects to the FBI.

Based on a nonfiction book by some naval officers, *Hellcats* was about the use of sonar for submarines fighting the war in the Pacific. In the final, breathless action sequence that I wrote, the sub captain, played by Reagan, had to perform a solo dive down into the treacherous waters of the Sea of Japan to free some cables fouling the propeller and thus rescue the sub and crew from an approaching storm of Japanese depth charges. For years after this, friends chided me that I had let Ronnie come up from the depths of the sea and survive for bigger and meaner projects. But of course, I had no way of knowing at the time the full measure of Reagan's treachery, or, indeed, of the role he would eventually play as governor of California and president of the country.

Hellcats also gave me the opportunity to write a speech for Admiral Nimitz, who consented to appear in an introduction to the film. I wondered how he would feel knowing that a Commie had written the words he spoke. And later, when Reagan inhabited the White House, clips of the film were repeatedly played on television. There was our president mouthing some of the better lines I'd written for him, speaking the tender words I'd created for him to say to the love interest who, it turned out, became the first lady. I fantasized about contacting Reagan, informing him that I was the uncredited, blacklisted writer who had written one of his better roles and, consequently, believed I was entitled to an invitation to one of the White House dinners. Why not, since he denied there had ever been a blacklist? But I let him off the hook and dropped it.

Another good break sent my old chum, James Gordon, from Katzman to the Edward Small Production company, where he hired me to do a script for the film *Chicago Confidential.* Most of this work was crammed into 1956 and 1957, when things were looking so much better that we moved from our dingy duplex to a still-modest but larger, pleasant house in the same neighborhood. At last we had a place that seemed like a home. It was a charming white clapboard affair in Dutch farmhouse style, with red-brick and white-picket fencing. There was a front yard with grass and a couple of birch trees and a backyard with room for Ellen's toys and a brick barbecue. We loved it and even bought some new furniture to dress it up. Meanwhile, Julian had been living in Mexico, where he'd written a widely-praised novel that had been published by Simon and Schuster—*The Young Lovers. The Book-of-the-Month Club News* said, "This concentration upon sexual experience . . . may astound some readers; but the beauty, confusion and urgency of young passion are wonderfully captured." The *New York Herald Tribune* spoke of "Vivid realism . . . warmth, humor, and tenderness." We were proud of Julian, but there had been problems. Even among New York publishers, the blacklist issue was raised, and Julian had to adopt a pen name for his book. He became Julian Halevy, a name he used for more than ten years when he worked as a screenwriter. But well before publication, another problem arose when Julian sent me the manuscript from Mexico for a critique. The package had been stopped at customs at the Los Angeles airport, and when I went to collect it, the custom's agent said he wouldn't permit the book into the country.

"Why not?"

"Because I looked at it, and there's a fucking match on every page," he snarled.

I knew this wasn't true, but true or not I was astounded and incensed that they were exercising such censorship. I told him that there were hundreds of books on racks in every drugstore with much more open sex. He didn't disagree but said that he had no control over what was published inside the country, only what could be allowed to enter. I battled with the customs headquarters in downtown Los Angeles and threatened to sue. I called Julian in Mexico and urged him to make a public issue of this. It could make the book a best-seller and put him in a class with James Joyce. But Julian had no stomach for this kind of fight, so his manuscript was thrown into the furnace in Los Angeles. Naturally, he had another copy, which he carried into Los Angeles himself.

The publication of the book and the subsequent tortured negotiations for a film version with the Samuel Goldwyn Jr. company (more blacklist problems) eased Julian's financial squeeze, but he still had to find a way to make a living. Having decided to move up to California from Mexico, he was sleeping on the daybed in the office of our Dutch farmhouse. I was working on another script for Schneer, *The Case against Brooklyn.* Although I was well into the script, it was unseemly for me to go on working for pay while Julian sat around twiddling his thumbs and wondering how to make a buck. I offered to let him collaborate with me on the script and share the fee. Clearly, though, I could not go to Schneer and tell him that his blacklisted writer (me) was collaborating with another blacklisted writer, so the arrangement was strictly *entre nous.* The script turned out fine, and for once I was awarded a solo screenplay credit (this time not deserved), but still as "Ray Marcus." A further miracle was that I managed to squeeze an extra $500 from Schneer for the work—money Julian was happy to share with me. When the blacklist was gone, I reported to the Writers Guild and the Academy that Julian had collaborated with me, and, recently, the guild has awarded him an appropriate credit.

The Case against Brooklyn was exceptionally well received. One of the trade papers said that despite its limited budget, it looked more like an 'A' than a 'B' film. Julian and I, while waiting for another assignment, decided to write a script on spec with the hope, always high among screenwriters, of hitting the jackpot. The summer weather was warm, and it seemed just as easy to talk over story ideas while lolling on the beach at Santa Monica. Julian was a great swimmer; he'd plunge into the sea and swim far out, out of sight, to consort with the fish and any other denizens there beyond the breakers. Even when we were boys in Rockaway Beach, New York, Julian drove his mother crazy with this behavior. After all these years and countless safe returns to shore, I took his antics calmly and relaxed in my own cowardly way on the warm sands of the California coast.

Julian had countless fascinating stories to tell of his years in Mexico, any one of which seemed material for a film. But when he spoke of his times in Acapulco and of his encounters with the expatriate beach boys who survived there on cheap Mexican food and drink and, occasionally, on exploiting the better heeled expatriate women, a bell rang in my head. *The Beach Boys* would make a great film title; the subject matter ideal for an action-adventure film set in a fresh background. Julian agreed, even though he'd been too close to the material to see it, and we set to work.

Although the blacklist continued unabated in 1957, we believed and hoped that a spec script submitted to the market with our established phony names would slip through. It was a great pleasure to be working for once on our own material, which reflected our personal views of people and the world, rather than writing about zombies for Katzman or cops and crooks for Charlie Schneer. We luxuriated in the experience, took our time, and did our best to get it right.

In December of 1957, Julian and I felt ready to submit *The Beach Boys* for sale. Because of his experience in selling *The Young Lovers* to Samuel Goldwyn Jr., Julian had a valuable agency connection. The people there had a good notion that the Julian Halevy on the book cover actually represented a blacklisted writer (whatever his real name), but like most of the wheeler-dealers in Hollywood, they preferred not to know the entire truth. Julian took the script to the agency with both his name (Halevy) and mine (Marcus) on the title page. Their reaction was enthusiastic, although there were concerns about submitting it with our names, even the pseudonyms. Mary Baker, a partner in the agency who was handling the project, proposed that the Halevy name remain on the script but the Marcus name be dropped . . . just one author—the one who had written a well-received novel.

When Julian brought this proposal back to me, I'm afraid I erupted. Under no circumstances would I agree to remove my name, and I attacked him for even considering it. Julian assured me that he agreed and was only conveying Mary Baker's thoughts about the best way to market what seemed like a valuable property. Market it or not, I insisted that my name remain. And so it did. Since the Christmas and New Year's holidays were almost upon us, when traditionally little business was transacted in town, Mary Baker decided to wait until January to test the waters. But she was most encouraging about our prospects for making a substantial sale. That Christmas, in addition to the bells, whistles, and glass baubles, a great deal of hope hung on the tree.

For once, optimism and high hopes were justified. Soon after submissions in January, offers started to come in. Kirk Douglas personally offered $35,000 to acquire the script. MGM upped the bid to $61,000. We were amused at that extra $1,000, but assumed it was there to beat out anyone who might offer $60,000. Finally, Mary Baker decided we should settle for $75,000 from Columbia Pictures and its guaranteed employment for ten weeks at $1,000 per week each: a grand total of $95,000 minimum! It was February and we were expected to report to work at the main studio on Gower Street.

This was the same place where I'd worked for Charles Schneer, who, when he heard of the deal, complained to our producer, Roger Edens, that now he would never be able to afford to hire me again. Edens had just moved to Columbia from MGM, where he had worked as associate producer to Arthur Freed on many major musicals like *The Band Wagon, Deep in my Heart*, and, most recently, *Funny Face*, with Audrey Hepburn and Fred Astaire. He was a delightful man and wildly excited at having acquired *The Beach Boys* for his first production at Columbia. In fact, it would be his first important feature film as a full producer on his own. He greeted us enthusiastically and promised that he would make *The Beach Boys* the most beautiful production we'd ever seen. As far as we could tell, he knew nothing about our being blacklisted. We had no way of knowing if he would care.

At the studio we were given fine adjoining offices with a secretary and plenty of supplies. We were expected to report to work more or less regularly, but were nervous about entering the place. Every time we got into an elevator, we wondered whom we would confront who would know exactly who we were. But the contracts were duly signed. I recall vividly that morning when, with my accountant, an old friend, I opened a new bank account with a check for $33,750—half of $75,000 minus the ten percent agent's fee. I knew I wasn't the richest man around—I just felt that way. Jean immediately quit her job and went to work doing what she really cared about: taking charge of Ellen and fixing up the house.

At the studio Julian and I conferenced with Roger Edens, who had notions for script changes that we found quite reasonable. We were able to agree about everything. After these meetings, Julian and I went back to our offices and knocked out revised pages, which were sent up to Edens, who, curiously, sat at his own typewriter and retyped the new pages. When we expressed surprise at this, he explained that by typing the pages himself he incorporated them *into* himself—as though he had actually written the pages—and this way felt part of the creative process.

After a couple of weeks of this happy time (and collecting $1,000 per week in paychecks), a totally unpredictable disaster occurred. The studio head and absolute boss, Harry Cohn, dropped dead. Cohn had approved the script purchase, the hiring of Edens, and the whole project. Once gone, new people with their own ideas were in charge of the studio. But first, a huge memorial service was scheduled on one of the stages, and all employees were "invited" to attend. Julian and I did not feel like tried-and-true Columbia employees, nor, despite enjoying his money, did we have any feelings of affection for Cohn, who was a notoriously brutish studio head. Also, we were still gun-shy about meeting people there. We decided to skip the occasion. Edens was surprised but shrugged off our understandable indifference to the Cohn obsequies. Our fears for the future were well justified.

This time our problem was not political—it was pure Hollywood. Though it was not clear exactly who was running the studio, our new bosses had their own ideas about what to do with *The Beach Boys*. They wanted it recast to star Kim Novak! She was a lovely lady and a Columbia contract star but she wasn't a beach boy. We'd written a story for a couple of male leads like Burt Lancaster and Kirk Douglas. Moreover, Novak, attractive as she was, didn't have shapely legs and refused to be photographed in a bathing suit. All we had to do now was rewrite the script to fit these new specs: *Beach Boys* for a girl who wouldn't go to the beach! Edens was little help. He was new at the studio, new as a producer, and insecure. He didn't join us in fighting this insanity. The meetings with the top brass did not go well. I'm afraid that I was my usual obstinate self in dealing with authority and didn't earn any Brownie points. Still, they couldn't take back the money they'd paid nor abrogate the ten-week employment deal. We still felt the picture could work out, that we had a good shot at a great film that would win the Academy Award and set us up as major screenwriters for now and forever.

Meanwhile, the agency had arranged a publication deal for the novelization of the script, which would be published simultaneously with the release of what was expected to be a major motion picture. Financially this was no big deal, not the kind of thing one encounters today. The total advance was less than $10,000, but it was certainly welcome; we were not so long into our new affluence as to spurn such a sum, and the prospect of seeing our story between covers was exciting.

In May 1958, we finished our stint at the studio. Julian and I decided to go down to Acapulco where we would write the book. Since I had never been there, it seemed fitting we should spend a couple of months writing and enjoying the ambience of the fabled resort. Jean and Ellen would join us as soon as Ellen's school was out for the summer. As far as we knew, the script was in order and approved. Even so, we were apprehensive. It was not studio practice to inform writers if changes were needed; they would just hire other writers. Besides, the next step was assigning a director, who would undoubtedly have his own ideas for alterations and improvements.

Julian flew ahead to Mexico City to see the friends he had made during his five years there. I followed in my Buick, because I enjoyed the drive and because we would need a car to roam the many scattered beaches around the area. On a fine afternoon I left Jean and Ellen and the Dutch farmhouse on Curson Avenue and headed for the Mexican border at Nogales. I was stopped at customs. I had no idea what they might make of the Sears Roebuck junk I had packed into the trunk for Mexican friends of Julian, and I didn't want delays or complications, so I offered the customs man ten pesos to hurry me through without opening the trunk. He accepted the money graciously but informed me that I would also have to fork over ten pesos to his *compañero*. I handed over the second banknote and drove off, feeling smug at my competence at handling such a matter, even though there was no conceivable way that anything in my car might be considered contraband.

I was driving along cheerfully when I was passed by another American car full of young women. They were in the lead when we suddenly came to a roadblock. There, deep in the interior, the Mexicans had put up another customs checkpoint. I watched as the girls' car was summarily waved through. I was stopped. The customs man asked me to open my trunk. I complained that I'd already been through customs at Nogales. The officer nodded agreeably. Realizing the routine would have to be repeated, I gave him ten pesos; he accepted graciously, then told me I'd also have to give ten pesos to his fellow officer. I did. Then, I asked in the best Spanish I could muster how it happened that the car before me, the one with the girls, had been waved through but that I had been stopped. The customs man smiled and replied in acceptable English, "Well, señor, what do girls know about business?" It was all so friendly and, indeed, businesslike that I felt I had really crossed into another world. I drove on contentedly.

In Acapulco Julian had rented an apartment for us in a building perched on one of the steep hills near the center of town. It was plain, even barren, but perfectly adequate for a couple of young bachelors. I remember most keenly climbing almost a hundred stony steps to get up to it. When carrying a five-gallon jug of drinking water, the trek just about did in this "bachelor." To begin the novel version of our script, Julian and I set up an office with the typewriter I had lugged from L.A. Mostly, in the first week or two, Julian showed me around the town . . . the morning beach, the afternoon beach, the wonderful little island just a stone's throw off the morning beach, which could only be reached by swimming (Julian) or taking a heavily laden open ferry that packed in about twenty people.

I kept hearing accounts from some of the expatriate residents of what a wonderland this place had been ten and more years earlier, before the tourists discovered it, and how Robert Louis Stevenson had put in here by ship long before that. But to me, Acapulco was wonderland. The tropical warmth and humidity made it a matter of indifference whether you showered or not because you were always wet—but comfortably so. We could reach up and pick mangos and cashews off the trees in the garden. We found coconuts and almost every imaginable fruit in the marketplace for pennies (or pesos, which were worth even less). Fresh fish was cheap in the restaurants, and tequila and orange juice cost little more than water. Perhaps because of the tropical climate, I had no sense of the kind of poverty we'd seen in Mexico City, where hungry people huddled on cold sidewalks waiting for price-controlled *masa* and *tortillas* to be doled out. In Acapulco it was easy for me to understand how our "beach boys" came to live here happily on practically no income.

We also spent time looking around for a good place to rent for Jean and Ellen's arrival. Before that event, however, our idyll came to an abrupt end. Roger Edens telephoned that he and the director and the cameraman were arriving to reconnoiter the locations for the picture. The director was Charles Vidor, a substantial name in the business; he'd directed many hits, including *Cover Girl* and *Gilda* with Rita Hayworth. To our delight, the cameraman was James Wong Howe, a top artist and someone I knew personally.

We picked them up at the small airport just a short ride out of town and drove them to the hotel in my convertible with the top down. Naturally, they were booked into the best hotel, the one with the terrace restaurant that overlooked the cliff from which the local divers plunged down to the shallow sea below, always in time to catch an incoming wave to give them enough depth of water to survive. This was one of the scenes in our script.

Before dinner and a discussion of the picture, we settled them into their suites and began to get acquainted. I took an immediate dislike to Vidor, who was boastful, arrogant, and crude. He lost no time telling us which beautiful movie stars he had laid, but he really wasn't choosy. While we were listening to his account of how he had snared Rita Hayworth away from Harry Cohn, he was looking at the young woman who was doing some housekeeping in the suite.

Vidor turned to Julian, our Mexican expert. "You think she understands English?"

Puzzled, Julian shook his head. "No."

"How about asking her if she'd come back later when we can be alone? You know," he smirked. "Ask her how much she'd charge."

Julian was no innocent, or a stranger to sexual liaisons, but this request was so brazen and such an ethnic slur—Vidor obviously felt that any poor Mexican woman could be bought for a few pesos—that Julian was momentarily speechless. Finally Julian just said, "No, I'm sure the woman would not be interested."

Afterwards I chided Julian. "If you really had our interests at heart, really wanted us to go on and do more work on the script and protect our credit," I said, "you should have arranged for Vidor to get laid." I added that Julian could have suggested that he stay in the room with the two of them so that he could use his excellent Spanish to convey Vidor's wishes to the woman. "You know, do this . . . do that . . . go up, go down . . ." Julian was not amused.

That evening we all had dinner at the hotel's terrace restaurant to watch the divers perform. Jimmy Howe, the cameraman, said there was no way he could light up that entire cliff to photograph the action, not with every brute (5000-watt arc lamp) in Mexico. Of course, it could be shot "day-for-night," using a blue filter to simulate a night effect while shooting in the daytime. But that was a shoddy technique, used for cheap Westerns and action pix; it never looked convincing and was not appropriate for a major film like ours. In any case, Howe would never accept it. I believed the necessary effect could be achieved by using powerful spots to follow the divers down from the top of the cliff into the wave, but I didn't dare argue with Jimmy Howe.

The next day we toured the area, showing the producer, director, and cameraman the various locations for the scenes in the script. Jimmy Howe observed everything quietly, said nothing; as an old hand, he may have considered it unsuitable for him to make any comments that might reflect on the project. Edens was cautiously enthusiastic about some of the colorful, occasionally splendid, locations and settings. But Julian and I felt he was nervous about his relationship with Vidor, who probably had enough clout at the studio to make trouble for him as producer. Vidor looked at the steep, green-clad hills, dotted with handsome villas, that rose dramatically from the road or dropped breathtakingly to the sea below, and he nodded agreeably but seemed lost in other thoughts. Julian and I kept up a pitch about the scenic potential.

It turned out that Vidor had something else on his mind . . . the same old thing. Finally he asked Julian, "Isn't there a nightclub or some place in this town where we can find some good-looking girls?" A whorehouse? A bordello? Julian was on the spot again. Though he had an active and varied love life, it had never occurred to him to make it a commercial transaction. He promised Vidor that he would see if something could be arranged for the evening.

After dinner, with Julian directing me, I drove the four of us (Jimmy Howe stayed out of this) to an unfamiliar back section of town. We stopped at a ramshackle wooden structure that was virtually open to the elements. It didn't look promising, and it was a place Julian had never before visited. We entered a large, undecorated, dimly lit room full of dozens of bare, wooden tables occupied exclusively by men. Waiters came around and took our orders for drinks. The wine and liquor were the worst I had ever tasted. Music was provided by a mariachi combo. Poorly dressed women shunted back and forth, escorting clients through a curtained doorway that led back to the rooms or cribs beyond. Drab and dreary, this was not what Vidor had in mind; it was not reminiscent of Ciro's on the Sunset Strip. He complained bitterly about being taken to such a dump. Julian and I felt guilty; we had committed a gaffe. We got out of there promptly, dropped them at the hotel, agreeing to meet there the next day to discuss the script.

That meeting was nearly a disaster. There was virtually no substantive discussion of the script, because Vidor just wanted to get back to Hollywood. He told us he wanted us to return with him and get started on revisions at the studio.

I was on a spot. I didn't want to blow it with Vidor, but Jean and Ellen were due here in a week. I shook my head. "I'm sorry," I said, "but I can't leave now."

"Why not?" Vidor was surprised and sharp.

"My wife and daughter are coming down next week. I have to find a house for them, get things ready, help them get settled."

"You can find someone else down here to help them," Vidor insisted.

"Look. They don't speak Spanish. They're complete strangers here. I can't just let them drop in and shift for themselves."

"We want you back at the studio. We have to get going," he said, ignoring my problem.

Julian stayed out of this. So did Roger Edens. This was supposed to be one of the best times of my life, yet here was this arrogant son-of-a-bitch free to walk all over me. I couldn't restrain my anger.

"Look, Mr. Vidor," I said, "I've already made enough money this year to hold me. If you tell me I have to come back right now, the answer is 'no.'"

As soon as I said it, good as it felt, I thought I'd blown it.

Looking back with some perspective, I was stupid to be so confrontational. There was too much at stake for us. I should not have risked our chance to stay with the project and protect our script and credits.

But Vidor backed down. "When can you make it?"

"In two weeks."

"Okay," he said. "We'll send you two tickets."

Edens, Howe, and Vidor took the next plane out. I was greatly relieved that I hadn't ruined everything by shooting off my mouth. I apologized to Julian and, together, we speculated that perhaps the bully responded to someone who didn't yield to his bullying. Was Vidor the stereotypical "ugly American" with his disdain and contempt for local people and places? I don't think so. For one thing, he was *Mitteleuropa*, and his style suggested this more than anything American. I suspected that he was just as arrogant and insensitive at home, a man who enjoyed his wealth and the considerable power that came with his position as a big-time film director.

Soon after their departure we drove to the airport again to pick up

Jean and Ellen. Jean was very unhappy to learn that I wouldn't be staying on. Apart from missing me, she dreaded the prospect of coping with all the housing and family problems of a strange town and strange language. We solved some of these problems. We found a fine house for the family. And one of Julian's American lady friends was delighted to move in and expertly help with all the local problems. Back in Hollywood, we reported to work at the studio, conferencing chiefly with Vidor, who was serious about twisting the script into a vehicle for Kim Novak. We tried. We wrote and rewrote, but it never came out right. After another ten weeks of this, on pay, we were released with vague promises and no real understanding of what would now happen to the project. Jean and Ellen got back home after their four-week stint in Acapulco. Julian and I continued to work on the novel version.

9

Suddenly, momentously, we found we could get our passports!

Back in 1953, around the time I had been blacklisted, I had been denied a passport. Well, not exactly denied, but after making the usual application, I received a letter from the State Department requesting answers to questions about my political affiliation. Outraged, as usual, I replied that they had no business inquiring into my politics and threatened to sue them if they didn't come across. For some reason, the State Department was indifferent to my threat, which had as much effect on them as my similar letter to Warner Bros. had had on the studio. They even ignored my demand that they return my four- or five-dollar application fee. I suspect that somewhere in their files they kept all of this correspondence in the hope of using it against me one day if the opportunity ever arose.

Through those mean years, our inability to get passports, even though there had been little money or few opportunities to use one, had had an oppressive effect. We felt forcibly detained, if not imprisoned. The author and artist Rockwell Kent had taken the matter to the Supreme Court, which finally ruled that the State Department had no right to refuse passports to United States citizens on political grounds. All of my blacklisted friends stampeded to the nearest State Department office and to the closest one-hour photo shop to get their passports. We all chortled at the story of what happened to Ring Lardner Jr. when, like all of us, he rushed to get his passport photos made. "When can I come back for them?" he asked.

The man said he would have a print the next day. Ring said he needed it right away. The man said sadly the only way to get that was to put a coin in the photomat machine that made pictures without a negative. But he warned Ring, "You'll end up looking like a Communist."

So far as I know, neither the State Department nor the nation has suffered any ill effects from returning to us our basic right to travel abroad.

With precious passports in hand and with money to burn, we all agreed a trip to Europe was in order. With no family to hold him here, Julian had pretty much decided to go abroad to live; he got passage on a freighter and took a leisurely thirty-day voyage to Italy. Jean and I elected to make a year of it over there and immediately started to plan a glorious trip. The granting of the passports was strictly a narrow legal ruling of the Supreme Court and had nothing to do with the blacklist in Hollywood or elsewhere in the country. We still had no notion of what the future might hold for us as writers, but the money earned from *The Beach Boys* was very substantial for the day, and even a year in Europe for the entire family would not put a great dent in it. Further, I felt that with a credit like *The Beach Boys*, there should be more work and more lucrative work somewhere, somehow ahead.

We flew to New York to board the Italian liner *Cristoforo Colombo* for an ocean voyage that would end in Cannes on the French Riviera. At the pier, while we waited for our tickets and passports to be examined, I felt a distinct uneasiness. I couldn't quite believe my passport was real. Would there be a last-minute hitch? Was the FBI hanging around in the celebratory crowd of travelers and well-wishers? Near the boarding ramp, officials of the Italian line sat in a small shack to examine our documents before permitting us to board. When it was my turn, I handed over our tickets and passport as requested. The officer in charge studied them and nodded. "Okay," he said, starting to collect the passport from the counter between us.

I reached in and grabbed the passports. "My State Department said that I was not to surrender my passport to anyone anywhere." Defiantly, I looked at him as I pocketed the precious booklets. He stared at me as if I were crazy. "You've examined our passports. You know they're in order. I see no reason why you have to keep them." He conferred with another man in the shack. The line behind me was at a standstill. It seemed the very departure of the great vessel was stopped. Finally, while I waited anxiously to learn whether we were sailing to Europe, the two men decided the most important move was to get the ship to depart on time. They waved me off with a perplexed but contemptuous Italian gesture and told me to get aboard.

The trip was a blast. I still cherish the memory as the best trip I've ever had. We drank. We danced. And God, did we eat. Ellen discovered scallopini of veal marsala and scallopini of veal *al limón*. She ordered one or the other every night, to the delight of the wonderful Italian waiter. She also discovered Baked Alaska. Ellen was a most beautiful child of ten and became the pet of the entire class of passengers as well as the handsome officers, who thrilled her with their attention. This was, I believe, the very height of an era when unimaginably great ships carried most travelers across the sea—before jet planes came along and spoiled it all. I felt as if the Waldorf Astoria or another great hotel had been set adrift just for our convenience and pleasure. We were being rewarded, only too well, for having lived through poisonous times.

We disembarked at Cannes, where we enjoyed the Riviera for a couple of days. On our first day there, I was walking the Croisette, the beachfront road, when I noticed a film crew working near the water's edge—the stereotyped scene of the director yelling through a megaphone. Of course, I was much too much the successful Hollywood screenwriter to stand and gawk, much less go down and brownnose the French crew like any other film-struck oaf. I walked on, a decision I seriously came to regret some months later in Paris while visiting with my old friend, John Berry, a blacklisted director I had known well at Paramount. I learned it was he on the beach that day, directing a French film. What a joyous reunion that would have been for the two of us.

We established Ellen in a school in the beautiful ski country above Lausanne, Switzerland, and, to temper the separation, we rented an apartment in a chalet near the school, where we spent six weeks surrounded by snow. I joined a beginners' ski class and worked, not very successfully, at becoming a skier. We enjoyed being snowbound in the perfect Swiss village of Chesière, and, despite the pleasures of Geneva and Zurich, of Vienna, Salzburg, Paris, Rome, Madrid, and London, I recall those weeks in Switzerland with special affection.

We picked up a Mercedes in Stuttgart, which may seem madly extravagant, but clearly indicates what the dollar meant in those days—for me, the entire American economy, and for the film industry. The new Mercedes, not even the smallest one, cost a trifle more than $2,000. With this car, we toured much of Europe for almost a year, visiting Julian in Rome, driving to Vienna for the show at the Spanish Riding School (for Ellen), calling on friends in Paris like John Berry and the writer Michael Wilson, who was establishing himself successfully as an expatriate screenwriter, working for Sam Spiegel, out of London. We visited our good friends, Norma and Ben Barzman, who had only recently relocated from

Paris to London. In their case, Ben had been free to travel because, Canadian born, he had a Canadian passport, but Norma had been without a passport and confined to France for seven years, from 1951 to 1958. Ben was an energetic and prolific screenwriter who turned out almost two dozen scripts in English and French (both credited and uncredited) including *The Blue Max, Justine, El Cid, He Who Must Die* (directed by blacklisted Jules Dassin), *Christ in Concrete* (directed by blacklisted Edward Dmytryk), and *Fall of the Roman Empire*. The Barzmans were part of a growing circle of Hollywood expatriates in London working in film and television, like Carl Foreman, Joseph Losey, Ian Hunter, Ring Lardner Jr., Abraham Polonsky, Arnold Manoff, Walter Bernstein, Bernard Vorhaus, Donald Ogden Stewart, and the actor Sam Wanamaker. Many of the writers were working on the *Robin Hood* television series produced by Hannah Weinstein.

Even in good old England not everything was roses. When, with family and car, we took the channel ferry from Calais to Dover, the British immigration authorities pulled me out of line and grilled me about my reasons for entering England. When I imprudently answered the question of my usual employment as "screenwriter," they conferred ominously among themselves and finally admitted me, but with the proviso stamped in my passport that my stay would be limited to thirty days. This proviso was to dog me every time I entered England for the next five years. I had to assume that the British were not entirely pleased with the influx of American film personnel who might be taking employment away from the locals. I could only compare this with the freedom with which Hungarians, Germans, French, Swedes, Danes, Brits, and all others were permitted to work in Hollywood (just so long as they weren't Communists).

Apart from the blacklist contingent, London was enjoying its finest hour as a center of world-class motion picture production. American stars and directors were valued there, but many fine British actors and directors emerged to play important roles on the international film scene. American financing and distribution were still essential, and the domestic American market was certainly the largest and most lucrative, providing more than half of worldwide box office returns. But the Hollywood studio system had broken down. The old moguls (tyrants?) were gone; men like Darryl Zanuck now lived in Paris and produced films out of London with locations just about anywhere. United Artists became an important player in financing and distributing films. As we've observed before, television, the Paramount consent decree, the extremely potent American dollar, the increasing importance of foreign box office, all contributed to a new era when Hollywood was no longer the only significant center for film production.

In 1958, with our European idyll over, we returned home to old problems and new solutions.

Back in Hollywood, what was I to do? My collaborator, Julian, had remained behind in Europe and was starting a lifelong residence in Rome, so any prospect was shot of the team getting work on the basis of *The Beach Boys*. In any event, our magnum opus didn't seem to be going anywhere. All I could learn from the studio was that a succession of women writers had been hired to turn this around for Kim Novak. So I was again a blacklisted writer with no significant credits. Even if I had been willing to return to the drudgery of working for Charlie Schneer, he had departed for England with Ray Harryhausen to launch a company that year after year would turn out a succession of low-budget special-effects films about "Aladdin." Using Columbia Pictures financing and distribution, taking advantage of the strong dollar and also of the British Eady Plan, which provided significant tax incentives for local production, Schneer prospered. This, of course, was part of the increasingly important "runaway production" that characterized the coming years.

Back in Hollywood I felt altogether out of that circuit, but an old friend came to my rescue with an assignment that paid little but kept me off the streets. Joe Steinberg still had the filmmaking bug. Even though the sports series for television hadn't taken wing, he wanted to try making a feature film. He had purchased the rights to a novel about the fighting in the Philippines in World War II, *Fortress in the Rice*, by Benjamin Appel. The subject matter interested Joe for several reasons, but mainly because his brother was a wealthy and well-connected American entrepreneur in the Philippines. Brother Harry would put up all the below-the-line financing for a shoot there. He could also arrange for whatever permits and prerequisites were necessary. Joe had little up-front money to pay for a script. But I was eager to get to work and I liked the material. I agreed to write a script for $5,000 cash, the rest to be paid out of gross (not net) proceeds from the sale and/or distribution of the film.

About 600 pages long, the novel covered many characters, situations, and issues related to the Japanese occupation of the Philippines during the war. My job was to mine the book for a dramatic story with a few central characters and to find a beginning, middle, and end that would fit neatly into a script's 120 pages. Here was a chance to write a film script that would have something to say about American attitudes toward the native people in those days, as the novel related the contribution, usually ignored, of the Filipinos in the struggle against the Japanese.

Joe was extremely pleased as the scenes came out of my typewriter. He felt confident that he'd be able to cast the film and bring it into production. Even then, I knew more than Joe about the vagaries of film production; I hoped that the promise would go from Joe's lips to God's ears. Irving Lerner, my good friend, was slated to be the director. Short, plump, and with large eyeglasses, Irving did not look or sound like anyone's idea of a film director. In fact, despite his extensive experience in filmmaking, Irving was a born and born-again innocent. But he had some industry contacts, and when the script was finished he was able to get it around for casting and for possible financing of the American above-the-line costs.

All of this would take time. Meanwhile, Irving had an impressive assignment directing the film version of *Studs Lonigan* from the trilogy by James T. Farrell. This was one of several films that Philip Yordan had contracted to produce for United Artists. Yordan, whom I had yet to meet, was already a legend in Hollywood. With about fifty screenplays to his credit (an improbable number, as one reviewer acidly remarked), Yordan was reputed to have a "script factory." Further, whether for convenience or otherwise, he was known to hire blacklisted personnel. Irving was one blacklisted filmmaker who had worked with Yordan on and off for years. I also knew that Yordan had employed the blacklisted writers Ben Maddow and Arnaud d'Usseau. I had pressed Irving in the past to try to get me together with Yordan. But, thus far, that hadn't worked.

Irving explained to me that Yordan had no patience for the actual filmmaking process. The notion of spending time on a set while dozens of people languidly moved lights around, set camera angles, laid tracks for the dolly, rehearsed actors, waited for the director to decide which character should stand with his back to the camera, which with his face, then turning around and doing it all in reverse—all this was absolute hell, a total waste of valuable time that could be profitably used to promote the next film. Characteristically, he had taken off for Spain to work with Samuel Bronston on a major film being produced in Madrid, leaving the making of *Studs Lonigan* to Irving and a production manager. Arnaud d'Usseau had been hired to do the script from the endless pages of Farrell's book, an unenviable task. Arnaud, a playwright, had written, with James Gow, two successful Broadway plays: *Tomorrow the World* and *Deep are the Roots*. He had also written, with Dorothy Parker, the Broadway production *Ladies of the Corridor*. It interested me that Arnaud was now in Spain working with Yordan.

By early 1960, the *Studs Lonigan* film had been shot and edited, but it didn't work. Irving asked me to look at it and come up with suggestions. After he ran it for me in a projection room, I had to agree that the continuity was confusing and the character motivation of the protagonist was unclear. Though there were some excellent individual scenes, and Irving had gotten good performances from the actors, he was nervous because Yordan was flying in from Madrid for a quick look at the film. He wanted to know what I thought could be done to help. As sometimes happens with independent productions, the budget had been spent and the cast was gone; therefore, additional shooting was impossible. The only thing that could be done was to write a narration to cover the character motivation and fill in the holes; then, by re-editing the film to match the new continuity, it might be acceptable. Irving asked me to come up with some ideas for the narration and meet with Yordan, who was due to arrive in a few days.

This was early 1960. We met on a Saturday morning at a projection room in Beverly Hills. I sat in the semidarkness with the production manager, film editor, and a few others of the post-production crew. Irving came in with Phil Yordan, but in the dim light I could scarcely see what the man looked like. He muttered a perfunctory hello, gave a handshake, and turned to Irving: "Let's get started." He was clearly a man in a hurry and a man in authority.

We sat in silence through the running of the film. I was nervous for Irving. The flaws in the film seemed magnified in the threatening presence of the boss. When the running was over, the lights came up, and we waited for Yordan's verdict. He wasted no time complaining about what was wrong or assessing blame. He turned to me.

"What do you think? What can you do?"

I shrugged and said the obvious. "There are problems with the continuity. And I don't think the motivation of the Studs character is clear or consistent."

Yordan nodded impatiently. He didn't need me to tell him what was wrong. He wanted to know what I proposed to do about it. "So what do we do?"

"You've lost the cast. You can't do any reshooting. The only thing I can think of is to write a narration to go over the film, tell us more about the character, and pull it all together."

"You have any ideas?"

I thought this was *chutzpa*. I hadn't been hired or paid, but he wanted answers. Still, I admired his directness. If he were to hire me and pay me to cure the problem, he first wanted to have some idea of my approach. As he well knew, if I wanted the job, I would have been thinking about what I might write.

While I was mulling this over, he tried again. "Give me a single line."

What I had in mind was a little more than a line. It would be the first bit of narration, something that would express the inner confusion of the protagonist and his wish for direction, a line that would set him out on some self-discovery to provide empathy and understanding of the character.

"It's right at the beginning, the New Year's Eve scene when his girl walks out on him. It could go like this in the character's own voice: 'It's the year 1920. Never can be 1919 again . . . not in a hundred million years. So what? What you gonna do in 1920? Where are you going? The world ain't a year older—just one day—one more day that's good for nothing.'"

Yordan instantly grasped the value of the approach. He said, "Okay. Go ahead. You're hired."

As we walked out of the projection room to the parking lot, nothing had been said about an employment agreement or pay. Yordan left it to me to ask about the deal. "You know," I said lightly, "I'll want to be paid."

"How long will you have to work on this?"

"In addition to writing the narration, I'll have to work with Verna [the film editor] to see how the narration will fit into the film, and we'll want to change some continuity. I figure it will be about four weeks' work."

He offered no argument. "How much do you want?"

"I get $1,000 a week."

"Forget it."

"But I'll give you a flat deal. $2,500."

"I don't have the money."

I knew this was nonsense because there had to be money for the re-edit and then recording the narration. On top of this, he had to pay for titles, lab work, dubbing, and all the considerable expenses of post-production. But who was I to argue with the big man? Instead, I smiled. "I'll lend you the money."

Yordan suffered from severe cataracts in both eyes. His vision was poor, and when he read a script (or anything) he held it within inches of the heavy, dark-framed glasses he wore, rapidly scanning page after page. His hair was thin and brushed unfashionably back; his face always seemed exceptionally smooth-shaven. Despite the heavy glasses, his eyes were large, dark brown, liquid, and, because of the visual impairment, he looked at you with what seemed exceptional intensity.

When I said I'd lend him the money to pay me for the work, he turned his stare on me, a hint of a smile on his lips. He knew that I was making a little joke; and maybe he knew that I knew he'd respect a writer with money in the bank more than one who was broke. "Okay," he said, "I'll pay you." Then he added, characteristically, a big carrot: "You want to come to Spain and work for me?"

Did I ever. I made no attempt to conceal my interest. "Yes, sure."

"All right," Yordan said, "finish this job. I'll be ready to send for you in six weeks." He got into his car and was driven away.

Six weeks and back to Europe . . . and working! Was that possible? In the years to come, I was to learn that Yordan never used an indefinite future when making promises. It was always "January 1" or "six weeks" or whatever. But always specific. This, of course, was very effective. It made the promise seem more real. Did he do this deliberately as a tactic? I never knew. But one time many years later when he had been pitching a deal at me and went on and on about the benefits that would accrue, I asked him, "Phil, when you say all that crap, do you really believe it?"

He thought seriously about this for a moment, then replied with winning candor, "When I say it, I believe it."

But I am getting ahead of my story . . . years ahead. Back in 1960, I watched Yordan as he was driven away from the projection room's parking lot, then turned to Irving, who had witnessed all of this. He had worked with Yordan for years.

"Is he serious?" I asked.

Irving shrugged. He wasn't sure. "He could be."

Back home I related all this to Jean. I couldn't tell if she was pleased or dismayed at the prospect of my going to Europe to work or possibly of us all going back to Europe. After all, we'd been back for less than a year. She only said, "If you're going over there, you'd better get yourself a decent suit." I took her advice and put enough trust, or hope, in Yordan's promise to go out and buy myself a handsome, serious, black gabardine suit. It was my offering to the gods. With this investment I tried to guarantee that his (and their) promises could not be violated. In an unexpected way, that's how it turned out.

First there was work on the film. I wrote a narration, then worked in the cutting room with Verna Fields. This was her first job as a film editor. Before this she had been a sound editor. Verna went on to become one of the most successful and powerful women in Hollywood. Years later, she took charge of the reshooting of *Jaws* at Universal, worked closely with Steven Spielberg on all of his films, became a vice-president at the studio and a significant force at the heart of much of their production. Back in 1960, working together, we wrapped up *Studs Lonigan* and hoped for the best.

10

After seven or eight weeks, I decided my wardrobe investment wasn't paying off and that Yordan's promise had been empty. Trying to come up with another project, I read an article about the Tour de France, the great annual bicycle race, a major sporting event that encompasses virtually every western—and some eastern—countries in Europe. The article described it as a kind of traveling circus where the cyclists were followed each day by great caravans of automobiles, vans, trucks, and entertainers who provided a festival atmosphere each night at the selected stopover town. It seemed like a great opportunity for a drama or comedy that could exploit the wonderfully varied countryside as well as the frequently exciting and dangerous action of the race.

Alex Singer was a close friend by virtue of his marriage to Julian's sister, Judy. Ambitious, he wanted to be a serious feature-film director like his friend Stanley Kubrick, and he had recently directed an interesting and highly praised low-budget independent film, *Cold Wind in August*. He felt he was on his way to the big time, though he had not yet cracked the ranks of major studio directors. I tried out my Tour de France idea on Alex, and he liked it. His partner, the financier of his earlier film, agreed, and we worked out a deal. They would buy me a round-trip ticket to Paris, pay for my expenses there, and make it possible for me to research the project and actually witness the big race. Then I would write a treatment and/or a script on terms that were mutually agreeable. It was now August and the race was scheduled for October.

I arrived in Paris on an early, fragrant, summer morning. The bus ride from Orly up the tree-lined Boulevard St. Germain as the cafes and fruit stands were opening for the day was reward enough for the long trip. After settling at the lovely but still inexpensive Hotel Regina on the Place du Pyramide, within sight of the Louvre, I called my old friends, the

Michael Wilsons. Around the time he had been blacklisted, Wilson had won the Academy Award for his script of *A Place in the Sun*, which was based on Theodore Dreiser's *American Tragedy*. Then, the Wilson family had left the United States for France, where, because of his well-deserved reputation as a top screenwriter, he had won important assignments. One was for the script of *The Bridge on the River Kwai*, which he had written with another blacklistee, Carl Foreman, who had settled in London. When Academy Awards came around this time, the script for the film won the Oscar, but Wilson and Foreman were ignored and the little gold man went to Pierre Boulle, the French author of the original novel, even though Boulle didn't speak, much less write, a word of English.

When I telephoned Mike, he explained that he and his family were living some distance out in the country. He drove in to pick me up, arriving in a splendid new Thunderbird, testimony to his financial well-being at the moment. The car seemed twice as large as anything else on the road in France. On the drive out, after admiring the car, I explained my mission in Paris and said I could use some help getting in touch with the right people about the Tour de France. Mike thought he knew someone who could help.

After dinner I was groggy from my trip and the time change. Mike wanted me to read his script of *Lawrence of Arabia*, which he had just finished writing for David Lean and producer Sam Spiegel. He had not even turned it in to them yet. It was hard to stay awake to read the exciting script, but it was worth the effort. Later, when Mike refused to spend a year in Saudi Arabia with Lean to scout locations and do some rewriting, Lean hired the British writer Robert Bolt to make the changes. This time, when the script was nominated for an Oscar, it was awarded to Bolt. Mike's name was never even mentioned as one of the writers, even though the Screenwriters Guild of Great Britain eventually did an arbitration and awarded co-credit to Mike.

The Wilsons had leased a lovely estate that had once belonged to the French actor Gérard Philipe, who had died tragically only the year before. The uniquely attractive modern home sat on a sizable property that bordered the River Oise. The approach from the road curved along a lane of trees, past a tennis court, a swimming pool, and greenhouses, where the full-time gardener raised wonderful French goodies like white asparagus. I was impressed and delighted to see that one blacklisted writer had made it big, even though he'd had to emigrate to France. The next morning Mike drove me to Paris, saying he would make some calls and get back to me about the Tour de France project.

He was as good as his word, and within a day he called me at the hotel and said I must come out again and meet his good friend Simone Signoret, who knew everyone who was anyone in France. Another old friend, Jack Berry, would pick me up and drive me out. Jack came around the next morning in a beat-up old Peugeot. Unlike Mike, Jack was having a difficult time. It was one thing for writers to work wherever they might be, but quite another for a director. In France he had to compete with the local talent to direct French films, and that was extremely difficult. But Jack was a cheerful, energetic, and talented man who did whatever was necessary to get by and support his family. At the moment, in between very occasional and low-paying directing jobs for both French and Italian producers, he was dubbing films from French to English.

Signoret was now a bit older than I recalled her from *Diabolique*, a bit more plump, quite self-assured, and still very lovely. When I explained what I needed, the handsome actress shook her head disapprovingly. Signoret thought it was a lousy idea. "Who in the whole world gives a damn about the Tour de France? It's just a dumb bicycle race for ignorant idiots."

Mike was not a man who suffered criticism or opposition lightly. "We didn't ask you for your ideas about the film," he said. "We asked you to help put Bernie in touch with the Tour people."

She shrugged, subsided. "I know the publisher of *L'Equipe*. That's the sports journal that sponsors the Tour. They have the exclusive rights to reporting it."

Signoret's name was magic. The following day I had a luncheon appointment with the man at *L'Equipe* who was central to this project. He spoke some English, and I found him enthusiastic about the notion of a real international film about the Tour. He ran a 16mm print of a French film that had been made about the Tour, gave me an armful of books and journals with more than I needed to know, and even arranged for me to hire a young lady who was bilingual and could help me get through the printed material and anything else I might need. It seemed I was all set. He also told me that early in October a preliminary local race would be run between Paris and the city of Tours, about a hundred miles away. I could accompany him in an open car right along with the cyclists to get a good feel for the routine. With the help of my translator, I worked my way through the literature that had been provided. My translator, who was also a typist, ground out a volume of material about the history of the race, the major personalities and stars, the stories of accidents, injuries, victories, defeats, *tout*—everything I might need to know to go back home and work up a script.

One Sunday, just about finished with the work, I was invited out to the Jack Berry home in Boulogne, on the western outskirts of Paris. This was a modest house with a small garden. I received a warm welcome from a number of friends from Hollywood who had gathered to meet me and enjoy the California-style barbecue. At the time, in addition to the Wilsons, blacklisted friends living in Paris included Paul and Sylvia Jarrico, Lee and Tammy Gold, Jules Dassin and his family, and the Berrys. For most, work was not readily come by. Paul, endlessly energetic and enterprising, roamed the continent and got work in France, England, Germany, and even in Yugoslavia, where he wrote the script of *Five Branded Women* with Mike. Jules Dassin, of course, had directed and cowritten the big international hit *Rififi* and was getting ready to move on to other work in Greece and elsewhere with the successes *Never on Sunday* and *Topkapi*.

In the midst of boisterous eating and drinking, Jack answered the telephone, came out of the house and said the call was for me! I couldn't have been more astonished. Who could possibly know I was at the Berry's for Sunday lunch in Paris? Irving Lerner was calling from Madrid where he was working with Yordan. They were having problems with a script based on a book, *The Day of the Triffids*, which Yordan was planning to produce. Could I come down to Madrid for a few weeks and do a rewrite? I explained I was already committed to the people who had paid my way to France. But I did have to kill a few weeks until the first race I planned to witness. Maybe I could squeeze in a writing job in Madrid. Irving said he'd been authorized to offer me $5,000 for a four-week stint, plus all expenses in Spain.

My people in Hollywood had no problem with the change—it saved them my expenses in Paris for the weeks I would have waited around for the races. I picked up the plane ticket at Orly and flew to Madrid. I was met at the airport by Irving, and by Phil Yordan, who was just flying out and only had time to shake my hand. "You did a good job on *Studs Lonigan*," he said. "I'm off for a week or so. While I'm away, they'll put you up in my suite at the Hilton." And he was gone to catch his plane.

At the Hilton, in Yordan's suite, I was introduced to the producer and the director who would be making the film. Steve Sekely, the director, was Hungarian. Though he did have some history of work in Hollywood, I was unfamiliar with it. The producer, Lou Brandt, was another one of the left-wingers who worked with Yordan. They handed me the script, asked me to read it, then discuss it with them. It was still early in the day after the hour's flight from Paris, so I quickly read the script I was supposed to "polish." I was dismayed. It was an illiterate mish-mash, and I suspected there must be truth to all the stories I'd heard about Yordan running a "script factory," hiring starving writers, paying them a few hundred dollars to turn out pages, hiding the writer under a rug, and proceeding from there. The script bore no name, not even Yordan's.

Irving and I walked down the wide, grassy center-divide of the main drag that ran past the hotel. (The boulevard was then called "The Generalissimo.") The evening was balmy, and the kiosks on the divide were busy selling excellent espresso coffee for the equivalent of about a dime a cup, and pretty fair wine and brandy for not much more. I regretted telling Irving that the assignment was impossible; I would have to pass. I would return to Paris at once. I didn't see even the possibility of a screen story in the material; certainly this script couldn't be polished or rewritten. It needed a totally new approach to the material, and I had no idea what that might be. Irving prevailed on me to read the novel from which all this had sprung.

Late that night, after I'd read the lengthy and admirably written novel by British author John Wyndham, I felt the book did not lend itself to filming. It was discursive, not dramatic; I saw why no one had yet tried to film the story, even though it was highly regarded, especially in England. I was discouraged. But, as with *Fortress in the Rice*, I couldn't resist the challenge. And, after all, I was not free of the blacklist; the chance to earn a decent sum for a few week's work certainly appealed. Most of all, I wanted to succeed with Yordan and become one of the group who seemed to be employed regularly here in Spain. All night I twisted and turned, trying to get a handle on the material. Finally, I decided on an approach. The next day, I told my ideas to Sekely and Lou Brandt. They accepted. It was settled. I started to write.

Yordan wasn't in Madrid to make *Triffids*. He was there for Bronston and *King of Kings*, directed by Nicholas Ray. Yordan apparently had rewritten that script, then taken charge of the casting; more important, he had come up with the idea of using the title of the original DeMille classic, which, it turned out, was not registered and protected. That film was now completed. Yordan operated on more than one track. While busy with Bronston affairs, he also worked on his own independent productions— like *Triffids*. With the great old title attached to it, everyone working on *King of Kings* in Madrid was certain it would be a hundred-million-dollar blockbuster that would put Bronston on the map and make everyone rich. Yordan had made all this happen. He was king of the hill.

Samuel Bronston was a short, rather soft-looking man with a round face, friendly blue eyes, thinning gray hair. Born in Russia, speaking with a trace of an accent, he was one of the many Europeans who had come to Hollywood and found a place in the film industry. He had become an executive at Columbia Pictures and was associated either as executive or producer with a number of respected films, including *Martin Eden, City without Men, Jack London, A Walk in the Sun.* Ambitious to do more important high-budget films, he went to work with astonishing success as a promoter. He succeeded in persuading some top American industrial executives to back him in an initial project that had considerable patriotic appeal: *John Paul Jones.* In the hope of producing this expensive seagoing epic with controllable costs, Bronston moved to Spain and had a couple of period ships knocked together by skilled Spanish workers. The ships then were berthed in the harbor at Alicante. Unfortunately, it appears that all of Bronston's attention had been focused on the production problems, not on the script. Despite assembling an impressive cast (good promoting again), the film was a total loss; it probably never earned back the first dollar of its cost. But Bronston had established himself in Spain. Further, he had established a close relationship with Pierre DuPont, head of the international chemical company. DuPont, for reasons that have always puzzled everyone, signed blank completion bonds that permitted Bronston to borrow money, almost without limit, for production.

Evidently, Bronston was not out to fleece DuPont. He found other ways of financing or helping to finance his films. Spain was an ideal site. Bronston became an international broker in complex deals sometimes involving three and four different countries, all of which were short of hard currency. He would arrange the barter of whatever products Spain could produce—trucks, locomotives, ships—in exchange for whatever Spain needed—grain or oil. For example, Spanish trucks might be exported to Yugoslavia, which would pay for them with pork, which would go to Russia for oil. Finally, the oil would come to Spain. Then, as gasoline, it would be retailed for local pesetas, which, ultimately, would pay for the original trucks.

Bronston, the organizer of all this bartering, would be rewarded with Spanish pesetas that he could use for below-the-line film production. The net result of this round robin was that each country got what it needed (trucks, pork, oil) via barter and did not have to come up with hard currency (dollars) it didn't have. And Bronston got all the Spanish currency he needed for local production expenditures. He only had to come up with dollars for above-the-line costs: cast, director, writers, composer, film, outside lab work, etc.

This set-up had really gotten rolling with *King of Kings*, and, with Yordan's help, now seemed to be moving into high gear. Yordan had managed to obtain an original story about *El Cid*, which, when I arrived in Spain, was scheduled as the next Bronston production. Director Anthony Mann, who had worked with Yordan in Hollywood on *Men in War* and *God's Little Acre*, was working down the hall from me at the Hilton, trying to make sense of the *El Cid* script. By now Bronston had even acquired a small studio on the outskirts of Madrid with a couple of sound stages, offices, a bit of a back lot, and standing sets from *King of Kings*. From what I could tell, Yordan was the indispensable man here. His deal with Bronston was to provide scripts for each project and to be paid $400,000 for each film produced from one of his scripts. For this reason, I soon learned, it was entirely in Yordan's interest to provide original ideas and scripts rather than to buy important books or other existing properties. I don't believe this worked to Bronston's advantage, but, in all fairness, Yordan provided much more than scripts. He had a great deal of Hollywood know-how and had contacts with agents and film stars, all of which he used. He also helped Bronston to establish a large, international approach to film financing, making deals in advance for territories in countries around the globe, deals which could be discounted at the bank and provide funds up-front for production. This became an essential part of Bronston's operation, and, indeed, it became standard for filmmakers everywhere. For Hollywood, this became the basis for much "runaway" film production.

11

Though I had no way of knowing this at the time, Philip Yordan was destined to become a major player in my life and my work history for many years to come. Over the years I became more and more interested in him as a person and in his life story. I am confident no one will dispute me when I label Phil Yordan one of the most colorful characters ever on the Hollywood scene. But many people debated everything else about him. Critical or admiring, everyone talked about him. The following account of Yordan's early pre-Hollywood life was offered to me recently by Yordan himself. Though over time I had heard some different and more colorful details of his early years, those stories are not still clear in my mind after the passage of much time, and the people who offered them, correctly or not, are no longer here, so I cannot check and verify them. If, like all of us, Yordan may be self-serving in his memories, I do believe that the essential facts are correct.

Yordan grew up in Chicago in the bitter days of the Depression. He speaks respectfully of a mother who was a forceful character with her own ideas of how to raise a family. As he tells it, poor or not, she never bought anything except top-quality food for her family of two sons and two daughters; he swears she never served food that was a day old. Even now, when it comes to food, he remains under his mother's spell. The father, evidently, made much less of an impression. He traveled a great deal, selling land throughout the Southwest, practically living aboard railroad trains. From an early age, Phil assumed many responsibilities and exhibited entrepreneurial skills. At thirteen he was managing a considerable business from the basement of the house. He had learned he could buy supplies for beauty shops in barrel lots, repackage them, then sell them to the shops at a considerable profit: bobby pins, nail-polish remover, cold cream, hair pins, something called "karaya" that, when mixed with water, formed a gelatinous goo useful for hair setting. Eventually he turned this into a mail-order business that netted the family of four up to $500 a week.

Being busy with this family activity all through his school years meant that when he decided to study for the law, he went to night school at a place called Kent College. By then he was prosperous enough to buy a little car, but he couldn't be bothered driving and parking, so he hired a local boy for a dollar a day to be his driver, take him to class, wait for him, then drive him home. This boy was called "the moron" by the other kids because he wore thick eyeglasses, haunted the local library, and read all the time, particularly when waiting in the car for Phil to finish his classes. Phil credits him with getting him interested in reading, though the authors he recommended didn't suit young Yordan. He didn't take to Dreiser and Faulkner. He preferred detective stories. But Yordan got into the habit of reading and began thinking of doing some writing.

He passed the bar exam in 1936 and went to work for an attorney who specialized in bankruptcy law—an excellent business at the time. Phil ran down to the local courts and registry offices, filing bankruptcy papers, but soon he decided that the law didn't suit him. Then a case came up that caught his interest. One of the businesses that went bankrupt was a large tire distributor, and it became clear to the attorney that the partners were concealing a huge amount of assets. Although highly improper and potentially a cause for criminal proceedings, this was not unusual. The two partners in this complicated case were fighting each other, each threatening to put the other in jail, and both were at risk. Uneasy about dirtying his hands, the attorney turned much of the routine to his neophyte lawyer, Yordan.

As early evidence of his enterprising spirit, Phil took it on himself to start advising the partners. First, sitting at a park bench to assure privacy, he persuaded one partner that the only sensible course was to cooperate with his enemy (the other partner), or they would both wind up in prison. The man agreed but said it was impossible to talk sense to his ex-partner. Phil decided to give that a shot, and arranged to have the other man pick him up in his car where, again, they could talk privately. The man was impressed with Phil's logic and sincerity. He pulled open the glove compartment and displayed a loaded revolver. He explained that, if he had determined that Phil was a phony, acting for the partner, he would certainly have shot him.

Phil was not shot. The two partners, grateful for Phil's help and aware that he did not really want to practice law, asked him what he wanted to do. He said he wanted to write. What would that cost? Phil said he'd need $50 a week to support himself. Each partner agreed to send him $25 every week. But, to be quite honest about this, there was yet another spin on the story. As their attorney, Phil agreed to accept service of a subpoena for them, then disappear. This was an enormous help, as it would keep them from having to appear in court. Phil accepted a *pourboire* of $35,000 in large bills; he stuffed them into a lead pipe, hid it in the family Victrola, then decamped for Hollywood, where no one knew his address or could catch up with him. Before leaving Chicago, he confided to one of his sisters the whereabouts of the loot and told her that the money was to be used for the family.

In Hollywood in the thirties, the $50 a week that he received from the two ex-partners in Chicago was more than enough to support him comfortably—a decent hotel room at the Mark Twain on Wilcox, meals out, and a typewriter. He started to write short stories. He sent at least a dozen to magazines. All were rejected. Frustrated, he wrote the editor of *Esquire* and asked for help. If they didn't like his story, why not tell him what was wrong so he could improve? The editor replied that Phil's prose was stilted but that he had a good ear for dialogue and suggested that he try his hand at writing plays instead of stories. Phil had never seen or read a play, but he took the advice, went downtown and looked at a few plays at the Biltmore Theater. He didn't dig them. At the library, he found contemporary plays, recent Broadway hits; they were sophisticated, unappealing, not his style. Finally he discovered Eugene O'Neill—the O'Neill who wrote about common people in *The Hairy Ape*. He read on. With *Anna Christie*, Phil hit the jackpot. He sat down and wrote his play, *Anna Lucasta*, about Polish people in Chicago, hard times, loss of innocence—things he knew first-hand. Did he borrow from O'Neill? Perhaps for the atmosphere and for the first name of the two principal characters; the two "Anna" plays have that much in common. But the plots are different. According to an old friend from those long-ago days, Yordan's first play was, as might be expected, inchoate and undisciplined and ran almost 400 pages. But it must have had something compelling.

Knowing no one in town, Yordan consulted the yellow pages of the telephone directory to find an agent. By luck he found someone who actually read the script, liked it, and sent it to Antoinette Perry and Brock Pemberton in New York. They optioned it (no money up front) and sent for Yordan to come to New York. In those days a train ride was rough for someone sitting up all the way. But in New York he found himself in the midst of the theatrical scene. Perry and Pemberton wanted to do the play with Joan Crawford. When that fell through, they lost interest and dropped it. Now, however, he had some contacts and was urged to write another play that, when he finished it, was put on at the New School for Social Research by Erwin Piscator, one of the talented refugees from Germany. Unfortunately, the day before the premiere the leading man dropped dead and the understudy was a *lox*. The uptown critics trashed the play, so that was that.

Yordan had, however, made significant contacts and won the admiration of people like Ferenc Molnar, who soon helped him get started with the important foreign colony in Hollywood. Back on the West Coast he began working with William Dieterle, one of the important refugee directors, who paid him $50 a week as a general assistant or gofer. Yordan found himself in impressive company at dinner parties for Thomas Mann and Lion Feuchtwanger, though, he admits, he had no idea what they were talking about, since he understood no German. The $50 a week was useful, because by now the payments from the Chicago boys had stopped. Around the time Dieterle went bust after a number of unsuccessful ventures, Pearl Harbor occurred, and all draft-age men would be going into the Army.

Never one to wait for disaster, Yordan decided to prepare himself for service more palatable than slogging through the mud with a rifle. He took a course at a school near Hollywood and Vine that taught ground navigation and meteorology to Air Force trainees. He was completing the course when his Chicago draft board summoned him to appear for induction. Once in the Army, he listed his expertise as a trainer for Air Force personnel and was promptly shipped from Chicago back to Los Angeles, where he was instructed to report for duty at an airfield in Bakersfield, a hundred miles north of Los Angeles.

The airfield was nothing but a dusty track with barracks for the trainees—not an airplane in sight. The owner and benefactor of this operation was an anti-Semite who instantly decided that Yordan would not fit in. The trainees were all young men who had been selected because their slight build and weight let them fit into the cockpits of the pursuit planes of the time, and they were almost all from Texas and other Southern precincts.

The owner had a heart-to-heart with Yordan, explaining that these Southern boys just didn't like Jews and it would be better if Yordan went back to Los Angeles where he could do whatever he liked for the rest of the war. Yordan readily consented to this arrangement, swallowing his annoyance that the man in Bakersfield continued to collect for Yordan's services for the duration of the conflict and never offered to share a single buck with him.

With the war on, Yordan soon made a connection writing for the

King Brothers. Even at the low end of Hollywood film production, the King Brothers stood out as low. They cranked out exploitation films for $25,000 that were distributed by Monogram. Yordan had found a home. He accumulated more than half a dozen credits in a couple of years. The distributor, Monogram, loved them. Yordan was so productive and successful with the King Brothers that he persuaded them to give him a contract for one-third of their profits on each film. This did not amount to a fortune, but it was better than the minimum pay he had been receiving.

Yordan learned fast. You didn't write scenes where you would have to go outside with a crew. That was expensive. Stay indoors, and stay in one set, if possible. There was no point in spending an extra nickel on production because the audience wouldn't care and the distributor wouldn't ever pay back that nickel. Like the training about food that he'd received from his mother, the production principles he absorbed with the Kings stayed with him, as I was to discover years later. Ultimately Yordan became more ambitious and persuaded his bosses to spend a bit more money on the production of *Dillinger*. For about $100,000, and with a better cast than in previous films, they turned out a hit that opened at the New York Paramount. The film eventually grossed over $4 million. Yordan's end would have been more substantial had he been able to refuse a cash offer of $75,000 for his share, a sum that was then considerable.

During this period he learned that someone had written a story about his play *Anna Lucasta* in *Variety*. That was news to Yordan, who found a copy of the sheet and read that his play had been produced by a Negro company in Harlem and had received rave reviews from the mainstream critics. He vaguely recalled receiving a postcard long ago asking for permission to produce the play and offering a $1 royalty, something he'd never bothered to answer. But the play was a hit in New York, even with an amateur cast from the American Negro theater. Inquiries started to pour in; one of them concerned interest in a Broadway production. Yordan hauled himself back to New York—on the train again.

One backer offered to raise the $11,000 needed to start a Broadway production—for the usual fifty percent for financing. Yordan readily consented. After the usual aggravations, the money was actually produced, but no respectable theater on Broadway would consent to housing the play. They didn't want a Negro audience that would "stink up" the theater forever for Whites!

The man who had directed the production and who had been, evidently, responsible for all the creative aspects, was an old-line director— Harry Wagstaff Gribble. Long out of the circuit, he had devoted himself to the Negro theater. There are conflicting stories about Wagstaff's contribution. One friend of Yordan's from those days said that not only did Gribble convert the play from Polish to Negro, but that he cut the four hundred pages down to size and contributed greatly to the success of the work. Yordan vigorously denies all this. He remembers Gribble as an irritating perfectionist who spent hours trying to get an amateur actress to say a single word to his satisfaction. This was altogether unrealistic, considering the funds and time available once a theater had been leased. The theater was a horrible dump on 49th Street; the play had to open on schedule. According to Yordan, they finally premiered the play without ever rehearsing the third act. It was August. There was no air conditioning; the heat was unbearable. Traffic noise from the street penetrated the flimsy theater walls, but the show went on. When it ended, there was a minute of stunned silence, then raucous applause. The play was a hit. The audience poured out of the theater sweatbox onto the sweltering streets of New York and stood around until one o'clock in the morning talking about the play.

Yordan and a few others repaired to the apartment of Canada Lee, the only professional actor in the cast, and waited for the newspapers and reviews. Even hard-bitten critics were enthusiastic. Yordan recalls that it was during this week that his film *Dillinger* opened at the Paramount. Two giant billboards on Broadway featured his name. The play went on to tour the country, in both large cities and small towns. Many years later, when we were all living and working in Paris, Yordan recalls meeting Sidney Poitier in the company of Paul Newman. Yordan knew Newman, who introduced him to the other actor. Poitier shook Yordan's hand and said, "You kept me eating for a year and a half with your play."

Back in 1944 it was time for another train ride to the West Coast to resume film work. Now that Phil Yordan was a somebody, the agent Irving "Swifty" Lazar approached him and asked if he wouldn't like assignments at the major studios. Yordan's real film career had begun. From 1944 until 1960 Yordan had a unique whirlwind career in Hollywood, principally as a writer, but also as a producer. He is credited officially with fifty to sixty screenplays and productions, an output that seems inordinate. For that reason, as well as others, he is widely said to have run a script factory. Of course, the same was said about the literary output of Zola and Dumas. Personally, I know of instances when Yordan put his own name on scripts that were written by blacklisted screenwriters (including my own), but there was real justification for that.

In the course of his nonstop career, Yordan got one break that every Hollywood writer dreams about. In 1949 he wrote and was credited with the script for a film at Twentieth-Century Fox, *The House of Strangers*, based on a novel by Jerome Weidman. Five years later, in 1954, the same producer decided to make a Western using the basic personal relations of *House of Strangers* for the new film, but the film was scripted by another writer. When the Academy awarded an Oscar for the story of *Broken Lance*, the statuette went to Phil Yordan as the writer of the earlier script. An Academy Award is potent medicine in Hollywood. Yordan made the most of it.

Stories about him abounded. It is widely believed that he took assignments at two, three, and even more studios at the same time on different scripts and collected a salary on all of them. Eventually, of course, he had to turn in scripts, and he did. Did he write them himself? That depends on whom you believe. But word got around among studio heads and producers, and matters became more difficult for him. The following story was related to me recently by the man who was Yordan's agent at the time. He does not count himself as a friend of Yordan's and may indeed be prejudiced. But, for what it's worth, and it does sound plausible to me, I offer it.

Unable to obtain work for Yordan at any of the other studios, the agent went to the head of Columbia and asked for an assignment. They were looking for a writer-producer for a couple of films. Yordan had been writer-producer on one of their major productions, *The Harder They Fall*, Humphrey Bogart's final film. When the agent proposed that they hire Yordan again, the head of the studio, Sam Briskin, chuckled and shook his head. Everyone knew what went on with Yordan and his scripts. Under no circumstances would they hire him. The agent had a proposition. He told Briskin that he would guarantee Yordan's presence on the lot and make certain that Yordan himself wrote the scripts, and if he, the agent, learned that Yordan was up to his usual tricks, he would personally come and report this to Briskin. Since the agent worked for the prestigious MCA agency, which valued its studio relationships, this was not an empty promise. He said he would make this arrangement clear to Yordan up front. This appealed to Briskin, who okayed the deal for two pictures. Good as his word, the agent explained it to Yordan, who accepted the terms without complaint. Contracts were drawn up; Yordan started to work.

After a couple of weeks, though, Yordan (according to this account) was up to his old tricks, only reporting in to the studio each Friday in time to pick up his check. When the agent learned about this, he went right to

Briskin and reported, as promised. Briskin looked at the man and said, "I'm very glad you came and told me this, because we already know it and we were about to fling Yordan."

The agent reported to Yordan. The upshot was a meeting in Briskin's office—the agent, Yordan, and Yordan's attorney, the redoubtable Herb Silverberg. As soon as he could get a word in, the tough attorney protested that all the accusations against Yordan were hearsay, unreliable, and untrue. Under no circumstances would he permit the studio to cancel the contract. In fact, he would sue them if they tried. Briskin laughed at this and assured the attorney the studio would sue if Yordan didn't repay every dime he had already collected. They argued back and forth. The agent turned to Yordan, who hadn't said a word, and demanded, "Phil, what about it? Tell us the truth."

Yordan shrugged. "I've got my attorney here to talk for me." End of session. Later, the studio did sue and collected $25,000 from Yordan, despite the attorney's bluster.

Can this story be dismissed as false, or a figment of the agent's imagination? I hardly think so. If there's a bottom line to the Yordan story, I don't pretend to know it. During the twenty years we worked together in Paris, Madrid, and elsewhere, we developed a close professional and personal relationship. I sweated with him through more than a dozen film projects; I thought I knew what he could do and what he couldn't do. From early on, Yordan was a fascinating, contradictory, enigmatic character and someone I would spend two decades trying to figure out. The man who, in his glory years, worked on many top Hollywood films, worked for some of the toughest producers, most demanding directors, and most exigent stars, and won their respect and affection, cannot be dismissed as a fraud. But it's also true that the stories about his "script factory" cannot be dismissed as fabrications.

After the dispute at Columbia, Yordan was unable to get an assignment in Hollywood. His agent came up with something different: Samuel Bronston was operating in Spain. He had already produced one expensive flop, *John Paul Jones,* and was in the middle of another film about the life of Christ. Nicholas Ray was directing, but they didn't have a usable script. Ray had worked with Yordan on *Johnny Guitar* and other films; he had a great deal of respect for Yordan and confidence in him. He wanted Yordan to come to Madrid and work on the script. Bronston offered to pay Yordan's salary and guaranteed $25,000 after the first month's work. Yordan refused. Everyone knew Bronston was broke and would never pay.

After pointing out that Yordan didn't have many options, the agent suggested he accept a first-class round-trip air ticket to Madrid, stay at the Hilton, work for four weeks, and then not turn in any pages unless the promised fee was forthcoming. If it wasn't, he could keep the pages and use the return-trip ticket home. What did he have to lose?

Yordan agreed.

12

In 1960, when I began working in Madrid on *Triffids*, my deal was with Yordan's personal company, Security Pictures, Inc., which did pay my salary and deposited the money in my bank in Los Angeles. My work with Yordan at the time was totally separate from any Bronston operation. It appeared to me and everyone else there that the hotel expenses for people like myself and the Sekelys, who were also working for Yordan, were nonetheless assumed by Bronston, who was not a man to niggle over a $100,000 here or there, especially since these costs were paid for in Spanish pesetas of which there seemed to be an unending supply. Today Yordan assures me that the expenses for people working on Security Pictures projects were, in fact, paid for by Security Pictures. However that may be, secretaries, typewriters, office supplies, and peseta cash expense money were all paid through Bronston. It is possible, no doubt, that proper bookkeeping could have assigned such expenses back to Security.

In any event, by the time I reported for work in Madrid on *Triffids*, the film *King of Kings* was already in the can and ready for distribution. Hopes were high for a blockbuster success that would put Bronston in business forever, and no one seemed inclined to worry about matters like the $50,000 bill it was rumored had been run up at the Hilton. Of course, none of this concerned me. My expenses in Madrid were paid by someone, and my only concern was to turn out pages for a new version of Yordan's project, *Triffids*. During the first week I managed to get through the 30 pages of script—the quota I'd set myself if I was to turn out 120 pages in four weeks. I still had no notion how I would end the story, but I had to leave that problem for later.

The Day of the Triffids tells of a series of events that first blinds almost everyone on earth and later begins populating the earth with deadly three-legged plants ("triffids") that roam about freely, attacking the helpless, sightless humans who remain alive. The story concerns the few people who, for logical reasons, have escaped being blinded and who must contend with the proliferating and unstoppable plants. Well, it doesn't sound like much. But it's science fiction. For me, the problem of the book was that the story meanders through many episodes and never comes to a meaningful end. The good guys among the survivors simply hole up in a defensive place and devote their energy to fighting off the plants and hoping for the best. This doesn't provide the happy or hopeful ending Hollywood demanded.

Writing a screenplay from an existing novel can be at once easier and more difficult than working on an original story. It's easier because the books may contain good character and situation material to be mined instead of invented. It is more difficult because the natural continuity of the novel may have to be abandoned, great stretches of story omitted, characters lost, and a new pattern imposed on the story. On a more meaningful level, of course, a good novel is a creation of *words*, not of visual images; so a film, no matter how good, however faithful to the novel, can never capture the special magic of the author's words. But such elevated concerns were not my problem for my four-week assignment on *Triffids*. There were other practical complicating factors. Yordan had plans to use foreign characters from France and Spain, unlike the strictly British principals of the book. This meant moving the story out of England and across France and Spain, where, for reasons of budget, it would make sense to shoot some of the film. Good reasons had to be invented for all this. My biggest problem, though, was a moral one. How could I give some meaning to the story? Would this be merely a meaningless succession of actions and adventures, or could I make some point about life, society, humanity? It may sound pretentious to attempt to supply such meaning to just another sci-fi picture, but science fiction does have a long and honorable history of commenting on our world and where our planet may be headed. I felt Wyndam's book was too good in terms of its characters and its writing to be dismissed as humanly meaningless, but I couldn't dig any meaning out of the book.

Fortunately I chanced on a story in a newspaper or *Time* magazine about William Faulkner's speech to the Nobel Committee when he received the prize for literature. I paraphrase this poorly, but in essence he said that mankind will have a way of triumphing over all odds, that at the end, when the sun has grown cold and its last rays are touching the peak of our highest mountain, even then, a human being will be there representing all mankind, representing the triumph of mankind. I clipped this piece, pinned it to the wall I faced as I wrote, and typed away at the script. It gave me the clue I needed about how to end the story.

I turned the first batch in to the director, Steve Sekely, a man of about sixty with an assertive wife who always seemed to be present. Though they more or less approved of my work, Sekely, like so many directors, wanted to pick away at the details, but I didn't have time for that if I was to complete a draft in the time I had. I made this clear to Sekely and, in effect, declined to discuss anything with him and the producer unless major story problems arose.

On my first Sunday, after about a week on the job, I felt I needed a few hours' break. Irving suggested we rent a car and drive out to a rural town about fifty miles from Madrid to visit an old chapel he'd heard about and have an al fresco lunch. Even the best available rental cars were old-model Fiats, manufactured in Spain under license. These were called SEATs (pronounced say-at). It was an adventure to climb into this hoary antique and take off, but fun. On the highway, about an hour north of Madrid, a couple of *Guardia Civil* hailed us peremptorily by waving their rifles in our direction, signaling us to stop. Given our political history, Irving and I were instantly nervous. What could these rural cops possibly know about our radical background or our thoughts about Franco? If that wasn't it, why were we being stopped?

Even with my primitive Spanish, I quickly understood. They were friendly and were merely asking us for a ride to their barracks less than a mile up the road. They climbed into the rear of the car, settled their rifles, and expressed their gratitude for our help. In a few minutes we reached their destination, were thanked again with true Spanish courtesy after they got out of the car. Then Irving and I were on our way, laughing at ourselves and our knee-jerk reaction to fascist authority. Our concern was not quite as ludicrous as it then seemed. Early on, I heard that the local police were keeping their eye on Irving, obviously for political reasons. And if on him, why not on me? Much later I personally came to know that the CIA actively followed Americans (*some* Americans) in Spain, occasionally annoying the Spanish authorities, who considered this interference in their domestic affairs.

A few days later I learned that Yordan was returning to Madrid. I moved out of his suite and into one of my own, not much different, and then I bumped into him in the hallway. He told me he had read my first thirty pages and liked them. "Keep going."

Life there was deluxe—Hollywood in Madrid. After only a few days on the job, a man came around from the studio and handed me a bundle of Spanish pesetas worth $200—my weekly expense allowance. I really didn't need them for anything more than the Paris *Herald Tribune*. The fine dining room was at our disposal for three excellent meals a day, or as many more as we might like—all we did was write in the tip and sign the check. It was summertime, and they served meals in a great central garden courtyard with a good musical combo. Even the harpist was pretty.

Though I was feverishly turning out pages, I kept hearing bits about life in Madrid. These fascinated me. One of the stories was about a uniquely Spanish bordello, a fine roof-garden with music, dancing, good food, and some of the loveliest women in the world. The Marques de Riscal, on the street of that name, was renowned as a place where women of good breeding could be met. Patrons could politely ask the woman of their choice to have a drink. She might agree or decline. If the drinks went well, she might agree to dance with you. So, drinking, dancing, even eating, you might pass an evening together, get acquainted, decide whether you enjoyed each other's company. Then, at the end of such a pleasant evening, you could ask her to spend the night at your place or hers. She might say yes. She might say no. Furthermore, it was said some of these young women would have along with them their duenna to keep a sharp eye on the proceedings. Could this be for real? I was determined not to leave Madrid without checking this out. But I couldn't find a soul in the whole damned company who had been there or was interested in going.

Finally, on a Saturday night, I took my courage in hand, got into a taxi, and asked for the Marques de Riscal. Except for the very minor foray in Acapulco with Charles Vidor, I had never been in a bordello of any kind in any country, and, apart from the unbelievable stories I'd heard, I had no idea what to expect or how I was supposed to comport myself. The taxi let me out in front of what looked like just another apartment house. In the lobby I found an elevator to the roof-garden. The elevator seemed to be hammered together from pieces of an old aluminum airplane fuselage, but the aged uniformed operator appeared to trust it as it rose shakily up six or seven stories.

I emerged with several other clients and found myself in a crowded anteroom that also served as a stand-up bar. On this Saturday night the place was crowded and jumping. The music boomed from the large adjoining room that was full of tables where people ate and drank. The dance floor was jammed and the band kept a good beat. I walked to the main room's entrance and saw dozens of attractive, well-dressed young women interacting with the equally well-dressed crowd of Spanish men. True, the fake palms were dusty, but the Marques de Riscal seemed much as advertised. I stood in the entrance, relieved to see that there wasn't an empty table in sight, not even a single seat. Waiters raced around the room, but no one bothered about me. I was not going to have to test my courage or my Spanish any further. I could leave in good conscience and not label myself a coward. After taking in the colorful scene for a few minutes, I relaxed, turned back to the elevator. As I waited for it to arrive, a handsome middle-aged man with thick white hair joined me.

"How do you like this place?" he asked in perfect English. He was American and had recognized that I was too.

I smiled. "My first time here. I wasn't even able to find a seat."

My new friend was shocked. He couldn't permit this to happen to a fellow American. "Come with me." He grabbed my arm and virtually pulled me into the big room to a table already crowded with half a dozen men. "My friend is here for the first time. He couldn't find a seat." A chair was immediately found for me, and I was a member of the party. They were different nationalities, but all understood English.

One of the men insisted on ordering me a whiskey. In those days when you ordered Scotch whiskey in Spain it came in a tall "gin and tonic" tumbler half-full of whiskey. They didn't seem to distinguish between wine and distilled spirits. My host, who had ordered the drink for me, was about fifty, dark-haired, less than five feet tall, and voluble. He came from Romania, bore some kind of title, was married to a titled Spanish lady, and he absolutely loved the Riscal. He glanced admiringly at the various young women who were seated, or dancing, or circulating.

"I come here every week," he confided, "and I've been in love with every one of those girls." I wondered about his titled wife. But what did I know about titled wives? "When you see one you like—anyone," he said, "I'll get you together with her. No problem."

I was overwhelmed by the hospitality, but extremely apprehensive. I had not come here with the idea of leaving with a woman. How would I get out of it? I took another gulp of the huge Scotch, offered to return the favor and buy drinks, but they would have none of it. I was their guest. Seeing that I was undecided, my Romanian friend began describing the fine points of various girls, all of whom he had known. Then he had an inspiration. He pointed out a couple of pretty women across the room. "You see those two over there? They're sisters. I know the older one very well. The younger one is here for the first time," he said, gleefully, "and you're here for the first time. Why don't I get the two of you together?" He seemed delighted with this prospect.

I am not proud to confess that I finally made some lame excuse and skulked out of there alone. I probably did irreparable damage to the reputation of American manhood. But, though I didn't see or recognize any duennas, I did find that the Riscal deserved its splendid reputation.

Though trained as a radical to frown on the exploitation of women who were forced to sell their bodies in order to survive, I failed to respond as my comrades would have approved. I found the Riscal a fun pace where even the well-dressed, available women seemed to be enjoying themselves. Maybe it was all an act. Or perhaps it was an ancient practice in this traditional land where, even in the smallest town, according to Cervantes in *Don Quixote*, the local pub or inn was also a gathering place for the men, who openly socialized with the one or more ladies who would take them upstairs for a go. The men included the mayor and the police and any other men of greater or lesser importance who came to eat, drink, and be merry. There was nothing clandestine, nothing illegal or shameful. It seemed to be the natural and native form of entertainment before people had television to watch. Could the pleasant atmosphere of the Riscal derive from such a tradition? Whatever the answer, I was enjoying living in a different culture.

Now, in 1960, only two years after my first visit, when the country had seemed cold and gray, much was changing. Eisenhower had made a deal with Franco to establish major air force and naval bases on Spanish territory. Just outside of Madrid one of the greatest American air bases in Europe was sited at Torrejón. The thousands of servicemen who worked there needed living space, schools for their children, restaurants, and recreation. A new section of Madrid had risen, with modern apartment houses for the airmen who chose to live off-base with and without their families. The area was dubbed "Korea" by the Spanish, who were, of course, aware of our military action in that country. The main street of "Korea" was named "Dr. Fleming," after the man who had discovered penicillin, which the Spanish regarded as one of the great scientific discoveries of all times, because toreadors gored by the horns of a bull were not so likely to die of infection. Penicillin cured them.

Bronston was not the only American producer who had discovered the advantages of filmmaking in Spain. *Alexander the Great*, directed by Robert Rossen, with Richard Burton, Fredric March, and many more stars, was produced in 1956. This picture may have set the tone for the big historical epics that could be turned out so economically in Spain. There followed a veritable flood of greater and lesser films like *Patton*, *The Hunting Party*, *Son of a Gunfighter*, *Doctor Zhivago*, *The Hill* with Sean Connery, *Travels with My Aunt* with Maggie Smith—many with major

American and British stars, and all financed by American companies like United Artists, MGM, and others. All of this certainly constituted "runaway production" and signaled the very end of the era when the major Hollywood studios were the site of all the important filmmaking.

Then the Italians landed, too. After the international success of *A Fistful of Dollars*, Sergio Leone bought a stretch of land down in Almeria province where the landscape nicely matched the American Southwest. He built a permanent set that he used for spaghetti Westerns with Clint Eastwood or that he rented to other producers, mostly Americans, for their Westerns. It's interesting that it was frequently cheaper for Americans to come over to Spain with cast and much of their crew than to work in their own backyard at home.

In addition, American films completely dominated the screens in Madrid. Down on the Gran Via, which was the Broadway of the city, all the film palaces featured American films. The only concession to the Spanish was that the films could not be exhibited in English with Spanish subtitles. This was strictly prohibited, so they were all dubbed. This, of course, did give some business and income to the local sound studios for dubbing, but that was trivial.

Along with the filmmaking (and the dollars that brought in) and the film exhibiting (and the dollars that took out), the Americanization of this old culture had really begun. Coca-Cola and Marlboro billboards dominated the landscape. American music was even more ubiquitous. American food was slower in coming. There were only two small Mexican restaurants in Madrid, patronized almost exclusively by our servicemen. Spaniards hated Mexican food. Though there was only one Chinese restaurant in Madrid in 1960, ten years later there were dozens. Was this, too, a form of Americanization? I thought so.

As I continued to work on *Triffids*, I turned in pages each week and Yordan generally approved of them. He gave me only one serious criticism about a scene where the heavy confronts the hero with a gun. I had to get out of the scene with the hero on top or the film would be over prematurely. I'd written that they tussled, that the hero got control of the gun, turned it against the villain, and survived to fight another day. Yordan said, "You can't get out of such a situation by having the hero just knock the gun out of the other man's hand. You have to come up with an idea, something clever that the hero does to turn the situation around, or you'll lose the audience." I don't recall now what clever idea I finally came up with, but I have always remembered that good advice. I've sneered at many action films since, when the writer, not having the advantage of Yordan's counsel, settled for merely knocking the gun away.

As I was finishing the assignment, Yordan grew impatient—not with me, for he was pleased with the script—he needed more writing help and wanted to use me or at least pick my brains. He even got me together with Tony Mann, the director who was struggling with *El Cid*. But that didn't work out. I thought Mann's story suggestions were unworkable and we didn't get along. With less than a week to go before I had to return to Paris, I was introduced to a new associate.

Sheldon Reynolds had had a successful career in France producing a detective series for American television, *Foreign Intrigue*, which followed the adventures of an American private eye who always wore the same trench coat as he wandered from city to city around the continent, chasing down bad guys. Apart from any virtues the scripts may have had, the package was wildly successful because it permitted the exploitation of what were then still-exotic European locations for the American public, and all at bargain-basement prices, using strong American dollars to pay for everything in Europe. The series, started in 1954, had run its course by 1960, and Reynolds wanted to do something more substantial—direct a feature film. He had persuaded someone close to Yordan that the project should be a film about the pirate Captain Kidd. Apparently, the deal was a go if Yordan would agree to produce.

Shelley Reynolds arrived in Madrid gung-ho to get started, but he didn't have a story, much less a script. Yordan didn't consider him equipped to write a feature film script. When I turned in my final pages of *Triffids*, Yordan asked me to spend a day with Shelley to see if we could come up with a story about the pirate. The *Triffids* script was barely on the shelf when I was into *Captain Kidd*.

Shelley and I hit it off instantly. He was slender, handsome, amiable, sophisticated, and more than ready to embrace me as the experienced writer who would make his whole project go. We kicked story ideas around for a couple of days until Shelley insisted that we had it licked and wanted to run over and tell the story to Yordan. I said I thought we were still far from having a suitable story for a script and declined to tell it to the boss. Shelley went anyway. Not long afterwards, I got a message that Yordan wanted to see me at breakfast in a small private dining room.

"You should have known better than try to sell me that garbage," Yordan said. "I thought you were smarter than that." He was referring to the story that Shelley had rushed in to sell him.

I could only tell him the truth. "I agree with you. I told Shelley and refused to go with him." Though this was true, I thought it sounded like a cop out. "But I shouldn't have let Shelley go. I should have stopped him. It's my fault."

Later that day Irving told me that Yordan had been impressed with my honesty and sense of responsibility. That evening we were all sitting in the great, circular, marble hotel lobby where waiters carried drinks from the bar out to the ample sofas and easy chairs. This was my last evening in Madrid. Tomorrow I was flying back to Paris.

Yordan turned to me. "You want to stay here and work with me?"

I tried to sound casual and matter-of-fact. "Sure."

Yordan got right to the point. "What do you want?"

I told him I'd have to return to Paris, settle up with the Tour de France people who were expecting me, square it with the people who had originally sent me to Paris, and that I'd have to have a deal for enough time to make it worthwhile to bring my family over.

He nodded thoughtfully. "Okay," he said.

I was hardly prepared for this. "Okay?"

He nodded.

"Write it out," I finally managed.

He glanced around the lobby. "Write it out where?"

I offered him the back of one of the bar bills lying on the table. "Write it on this."

"I don't have a pen."

I produced a pen and handed it to him.

"Real writers don't walk around with pens in their pocket," he sniffed. "When are you leaving?"

"Tomorrow morning. Ten o'clock flight."

"I'll see you in the morning."

Next morning I woke up early and anxious. I packed and ordered room service. I didn't dare to leave my room. Less than an hour to go. No word. Irving came in. He was planning to go with me to the airport, and he was eager to know if I'd heard from Yordan. We waited. The time to leave was coming closer every minute. Finally, when I had about given up, Yordan called. "Come on down here."

When I entered his room, there were no preliminaries. "You sure you know what you want?"

I was prepared. I told him I would have to have a six-month contract that would pay me $1,250 a week (the same as I'd been earning for my four weeks on *Triffids*), and I wanted another $250 per week for expenses for living abroad with my family; I needed two round-trip tickets for my wife and daughter; he would have to agree to reimburse all the expenses I had incurred on my original trip to Paris, to be paid to the people who had sent me there. This amounted to a couple of thousand dollars. Finally, it had to be written into the agreement between us that it was contingent on my being released from my Tour de France commitment. He didn't haggle. He'd had time to think this over and was prepared to deal.

"Sit down," he said, indicating his desk with the special typewriter which, because of his impaired vision, typed very large characters. "Type it out."

I sat and hesitantly began to peck away. He became impatient, pushed me away, sat at the machine and typed a paragraph that effectively included all the terms and conditions agreed upon. Still, it was only a single paragraph on a flimsy sheet of paper. Was it real? Was it enforceable? I had no idea.

"I'll get in touch as soon as I work things out in Paris."

He nodded. Before I could dash out to make my plane, he loaded me down with a full-size guitar in a case and a sealed envelope to be delivered in Paris to his ex-wife, who was staying with their son at an apartment he kept at the Prince de Galle hotel. I raced off without even a handshake. Eventually I learned that Yordan was unhappy when he made deals that involved spending money—his own money. But I was off and flying in more ways than one.

I had to get another opinion from someone about whether the scrap of paper I had from Yordan was meaningful—and binding. As soon as I got back to Paris and the Hotel Regina, I called my good old friend, Paul Jarrico. Like other blacklisted friends, Paul and his wife, Sylvia, were living in Paris. Their apartment on the Rue de Rivoli was close to my hotel. During some of the meanest days of the blacklist, Paul had been the producer of the film *Salt of the Earth*, a project conceived by a group of blacklisted men and women who decided to continue their filmmaking careers independently of Hollywood by producing a film created entirely by blacklisted artists. *Salt of the Earth* was a story of a mining strike in the Southwest and of the development of union consciousness and feminist consciousness by the men and women who participated in it. Roy Brewer of the IATSE forbade any of his union members to work on the film; laboratories refused to process film or rent out editing rooms, sound studios, equipment. The Mexican actress, the lead, was deported while the film was in progress. The filmmakers were attacked in Congress. Vigilante action was initiated at the location sites, and shots were fired at the car of one of the lead actors.

Despite this, when the film was previewed in New York, both the *New York Times* and *Time* magazine gave it excellent notices. But the studios joined to threaten distributors that they would withhold future product if the distributor handled the film. Personally, I recall having to see the film on Hollywood Boulevard in a theater that had been rented (four-walled) by the production company. So bitter was the attack that when the producers appealed to progressive individuals for "loans" to help complete the film, even good left-wing people were fearful of attaching their names to such loans. One friend asked my permission to use my name as a front for the loan. Freedom of expression? Freedom to dissent? In the Land of the Free? Not always.

From his new base in Paris, Paul, always resourceful, was racing around Europe scaring up writing jobs wherever possible. I met Paul for coffee, showed him the "contract," and asked his opinion. Paul had a good deal more experience than I with studio contracts and film business in general after his experience with *Salt of the Earth*. He studied the one-paragraph agreement and opined that it was clear enough and a deal was a deal, even without all the usual boilerplate.

When I got back to my hotel room, I telephoned Alex Singer in New York and explained the situation. I told him I would see that he and his partner were reimbursed for every dollar they'd spent on this trip for me, that I would send them all of my typed research and give them full right and title to my idea of a film on the Tour de France. Alex and his partner agreed to release me from any further obligation.

I called Jean and brought her up to date on what was happening. But I urged her to sit tight until I returned to Madrid, made sure that there were no last-minute hitches, and had actually obtained the tickets for her and Ellen. Yordan had said that we would all be moving to Paris, where we'd be working. All that had to be planned and dates set before I could tell Jean what to expect.

I called my contact at *L'Equipe* to announce that I was back in town and to find out if the race to Tours was still on as scheduled. Even though I had no plan to go through with the project, I thought it might be useful to have the experience and, perhaps, get back to it later. The race was scheduled for Sunday, two days off; we arranged to meet at the journal's office early that morning.

This left me with one more chore: deliver the guitar for Yordan's son and the envelope to his ex-wife at the Prince de Galles. The ex-wife was the actress Marilyn Nash, who had been Chaplin's love interest in *Monsieur Verdoux*. I was curious to meet her. I found that she was still a great beauty, rattling around in Yordan's spacious suite, alone except for the son, Danny, who was then off with friends. Marilyn had been touring Europe with her present husband, a doctor from some small town in central California, but he had gone back home to his practice and Marilyn was due to follow soon. Since I had time on my hands before the Sunday race, I asked her if she'd like to have dinner with me, and she accepted. I can still remember the succulent *blanquette de veau* and the great *tarte Tatin* (a kind of open apple pie which doesn't even come close to describing that marvel of French pastry). Most of all, I recall the effect of this gorgeous, tall woman sweeping in on my arm, wearing a mink coat that looked much too expensive to have come from an ophthalmologist in a small California town. After dinner we made our way to Harry's American Bar and found ourselves downstairs in a room that was full of revelers, most of them Americans, lustily singing the lyrics to the show tunes banged out on a piano. I guess it was corny, but with good food and enough wine and cognac, the mood was so relaxed that even I began singing, though I could never carry a tune. When the place closed down, we left reluctantly.

The taxi took us back to her hotel. I asked the driver to wait while I walked her to the elevator. Dubiously, he looked after me and the lady and the great mink coat. I suppose he'd seen us sitting close together in the back of the cab. When I came back and got into the car, he asked me incredulously if I really was not going in with the woman. I smiled and shook my head. My French wasn't very good, but I could certainly follow him when he muttered sympathetically, "*Quel dommage.*" I asked him to take me to the Regina. He hesitated, as if certain something else was called for. Then he asked me if I'd like him to drive me to an *hôtel privé*. I'd never heard that expression before but I knew what he meant. I declined.

Sunday, October 1, was sunny but chilly. I found myself in a convertible Peugeot with the top down, sharing the ride with several officials of the race. Cyclists, working in teams, sped along the highway to Tours. The trip to Tours took several hours. By the time we arrived, I was windblown and worn out from trying to follow the explanations in French. I suppose the cyclists were tired too. I wasn't prepared for the rain when it arrived and became separated from my friends in the town of Tours, but I found the railroad station and took a warm train back to Paris, glad not to have to return in the Peugeot.

Back in Madrid, while we were waiting for Shelley to return from Rome, Yordan threw another task at me. The Bronston organization had decided to get Sophia Loren to play the lead in *El Cid*. She had read the script and complained that she had no love scenes to play, and had turned down the assignment. They were in a hurry to insert some love scenes into the script to woo her back. I returned to my typewriter. The love scenes I wrote for Sophia Loren and Charlton Heston were forwarded to Rome and did the trick. Sophia agreed to do the picture. Though my contribution was important, I never asked for credit on the film because the twenty-odd pages I wrote were not sufficient by Guild standards to entitle me to a screen credit.

I called Jean. Yordan had informed me that we would be moving to Paris by the end of October. He was buying an apartment there. Shelley would be there, and I was to tell my wife to meet me there. He promised to arrange for his accountant in Los Angeles to send the two first-class round-trip tickets, Los Angeles, Paris, Los Angeles, to Jean. I was finally satisfied that the deal was real. I suggested to Jean that she arrange for a friend to live in our home as caretaker while we were in Europe. For how long? I had no idea. At least six months. I urged her to take $1,000 and buy herself a new wardrobe and, of course, get Ellen's school records so that she could be enrolled in a school in Paris. (In those days, $1,000 was a lot of money to me and could actually buy some nice clothing.) Jean was pleased that I would be earning good money for at least twenty-six weeks, but I don't think she was thrilled about the need to pack up and head for Europe again, and she was worried about how upsetting this would be for Ellen.

While I was working on *El Cid*, I kept hearing about a woman living in a penthouse suite at the hotel who was becoming increasingly annoyed that I hadn't bothered to pay a call on her. Her name was Clem, and she'd been Yordan's personal secretary for some fifteen years, following him around from studio to studio, typing up his scripts.

I didn't understand why I should be involved with her or why she should care, but the whispers became insistent, and I was urged by people like Irving Lerner and Lou Brandt, also long-time associates of Yordan, to go up and pay my respects. I finally called the woman, saying I'd like to come up and get acquainted.

My visit coincided with an afternoon salon that Clem evidently hosted fairly regularly. In the large penthouse living room, six or seven middle-aged women, both Spanish and expatriate, were sipping sherry and nibbling cookies. Clem was a small, shriveled woman in her fifties who could only walk with the help of a couple of canes. She evidently had suffered from childhood polio. Since she, and Yordan, had been in Madrid for many months, the room was filled with personal decorative items and seemed more like a living room than a hotel room—except for the large IBM typewriter that dominated the decor.

I introduced myself, accepted some sherry, and tried to join in the conversation. After a short, uncomfortable time, I tried to make my escape with the usual phrases about "back to work, you know," but Clem virtually ordered me to stay. She wanted some time with me alone. When the others were gone, she graciously offered, since I was a man alone in Madrid, to fix me up with one of the women or some other woman. I smiled politely and swallowed. Then she got to the point. She waved at the typewriter and told me flat out that *she* wrote all of Yordan's scripts. She clearly said "wrote," not typed. I figured she was just a crazy old lady. Whether there was any truth in this, it seemed to me that she was sizing me up, because, from what she'd heard, I was now the one who was doing Yordan's writing. Later, when I discussed this with some of Yordan's old associates, they were careful to mind what they said, but what came out was something like this: Yordan was good at coming up with ideas, scenes, the material of drama, and, of course, dialogue. But he was impatient about writing the "long, dull" paragraphs of description that went with the action. Maybe he depended on Clem to "English" the scripts, as the saying used to go in Hollywood.

I don't have any idea whether Clem wrote anything, but I do know that when I was finally leaving, she hit me up for some money. She told me that Yordan wouldn't let her have any Spanish money, that she was stuck up here in a hotel room and couldn't afford to get out, didn't even have pesetas for a taxi. Could I lend her a few thousand pesetas? Feeling creepy, I emptied my pocket of about $20 worth of pesetas and made my escape.

This led to one of the very few times Yordan attacked me. Shortly after my visit to Clem, he and I were alone in a hotel elevator. Angrily, he demanded if it was true that I had given Clem some pesetas. Startled at his tone, I said that yes I had. He barked at me, "Don't ever do that again." He went on to explain that his arrangement with her was that his accountant deposited her entire salary in dollars in her California bank, from which she wrote checks to support a useless adult son who lived in San Francisco; further, like everyone else here, she got a decent peseta allowance, and I had no business getting involved. My promise to him was heartfelt. I had no wish to be further involved with Clem.

Next thing I heard, Clem was gone. I have no idea what arrangements, if any, Yordan may have made for her termination, but I always felt slightly guilty that my appearance on the scene may have precipitated her departure.

Yordan was now ready for his move. Shelley Reynolds and the *Captain Kidd* project were also moved to Paris along with me and a number of other Yordan personnel. Yordan would be making his headquarters in the French capital.

13

At last everything was settled. Jean had the tickets. She and Ellen were to arrive in Paris via TWA on October 29. It would be exactly two years since my birthday in Stuttgart when we had picked up the Mercedes. Hoping to make Ellen's arrival more festive, I went to downtown Madrid and found a handsome Spanish leather saddle that would be her very own when she started to ride horses in France, as she surely would. Of course I was very happy with all of this. It seemed that at least so far as I personally was concerned, the blacklist was over.

When I arrived in Paris, the customs men at the airport were curious about the large, unwieldy box I carried. I showed the saddle to them and explained that it was for *ma fille*. They acted amused, as if I'd said it was for my lady friend. Maybe they misunderstood my French. In any event, daughter or girlfriend, they were happy to oblige and waved me through. Back at the Hotel Regina, I got two adjoining rooms with a connecting door and carefully settled the saddle across the brass railing at the foot of what would be Ellen's bed. The following day I reached Orly in plenty of time but found myself waiting hour after hour for the plane to arrive. I could find out nothing about the reason for the delay. When Jean and Ellen finally dragged in, I learned what they'd been through.

The flight, due to set down at Montreal on the way from Los Angeles, lost its brakes and was diverted to New York, which had the longest runways. The passengers were alerted, and the New York runway was prepared with fire engines, foam machines, and all the emergency paraphernalia for a crash landing. Passengers were instructed how to settle themselves and prepare for the worst. Jean had evidently been wonderful with twelve-year-old Ellen. Without arousing any panic, she had instructed Ellen to be sure, if there were a crash, to head directly for the escape chute and get out of the plane without waiting for Jean or worrying about her. But there was no crash. The plane had skidded safely to a stop, but they were delayed further when they had to switch to another plane before heading for Paris.

It was a letdown that Ellen did not pay much attention to her saddle when she first saw it, but she had been too excited by all the events. When she went to bed that night, she pulled the saddle under the covers and slept with it close. Fortunately, I had a few days to help get things started for the family in Paris, because Shelley was in Rome and Yordan hadn't yet come in from Madrid. Shelley had arranged for me to use his Alfa Romeo convertible while he was gone, so I was able to drive Jean and Ellen around in style. It was now early November 1960. Many of the expatriates gathered one evening in the living room of the Jarricos' apartment on the Rue de Rivoli, just a few steps away from our hotel. We were there to listen to the radio and the reports of the American election. Of course, we were all bitterly opposed to Nixon and were delighted when he lost to Kennedy by a squeak. Or was the election rigged in Chicago? We knew nothing then about that and wouldn't have cared. Nixon was the enemy. Kennedy was young, handsome, forward-looking, we believed, and made good speeches about "what you can do for your country." Maybe Camelot was about to happen. Though, to be sure, we had our reservations when Kennedy chose Lyndon Johnson as his vice president for purely political and tactical reasons.

It turned out that we were only half-right about Johnson, who, when he got his chance, turned out to be one of our better presidents on domestic matters, and might have turned out good altogether if he hadn't been trapped in the Vietnam War, to which Kennedy had first committed our fighting men. Much closer to us at the time was a sense that, with Eisenhower gone and Joe McCarthy finished after the Senate hearings, the political atmosphere in the country was improving. Whatever else, and regardless of his father's nasty history, Kennedy was scarcely a rabid right winger. Could there be light at the end of the tunnel? A time when the blacklist would be behind us?

W hen I got back to work on the *Captain Kidd* script, it was up to Jean to find us a place to live and arrange for Ellen's school. We decided to enroll her at the English School of Paris, because the Wilsons' daughters, who were just about Ellen's age, were both pupils there, and we figured that it would be best for Ellen to start school with some friends of her own. But classes had already begun for the year, and the school was quite a distance outside of Paris. Jean managed to get around, get Ellen settled in the school, then try to find us a house or apartment. She had no French, and the burden was considerable. I was working under my new contract, and although everyone was kind and helpful, I still had to spend my days at work with Shelley.

Jean finally settled for a crazy house in the suburb of Vaucresson, about twenty minutes outside of Paris and ten minutes from Versailles. This had the advantage of being close to Ellen's school. The house was on a substantial piece of land with mulberry trees, a decaying tennis court, and even a gatehouse lived in by an old Russian retainer who watched after the property and stoked the furnace. The house had been put together over a long period of time from old bits of houses acquired here and there—a door or two, a window, a stairway that went up at an odd angle. The windows didn't fit quite tightly, so the interior was protected from the wind with billowing sheets of plastic. The kitchen was downstairs; for no known reason, another one was upstairs. The bedrooms were anything but square. Though it did suggest an elf's dwelling from a Grimms' fairy tale, it hung together with undeniable charm. It certainly gave us the feeling that we were not living in Los Angeles or the Bronx.

Jean went into Versailles and registered with employment agencies for household help. This was a vexing chore and seemed to be getting nowhere. But one day, quite independently of the agencies, a woman appeared, told us that she'd heard we needed a *bonne*, and that she had decided she would be it. We didn't seem to have any choice in the matter. Marat was about fifty, built on a five-by-five chassis. She came from Brittany, had firm opinions about everything, and certainly knew how to run a household. She was also a splendid cook. But Marat did not take well to criticism or instruction. When we had our first big party on Thanksgiving for all of our American friends, Marat was in the kitchen preparing a feast. After an hour passed beyond the scheduled dinnertime, Jean finally got up the courage to go into the kitchen to inquire. Marat coolly explained that it was still early and indicated the kitchen clock, which had stopped. Jean told Marat the right time. Enraged, Marat seized the clock and flung it down onto the tiled kitchen floor, shattering it. Jean, hampered by the language problem, didn't know how to cope. Neither did I, but I suggested Jean give Marat her own wristwatch as a peace offering. Dinner was finally served. Late but good.

Apart from these homely developments, I had to write. I had arranged a fine workroom upstairs in one of the bedrooms. A table, typewriter, and a working fireplace. But I frequently drove into town and worked on *Captain Kidd* with Shelley in his hotel suite.

Yordan finally bought an apartment of considerable splendor in Paris. Once belonging to the Guggenheim family, it had also been a home-away-from-home for the German naval command during the war. In 1960 an apartment of this stature could be bought for $150,000; today, it would be worth millions (of dollars). Right at the edge of the Bois de Boulogne, at the foot of Avenue Victor Hugo, it was on two levels; the entry hall looked down a grand staircase into an enormous two-story living room. Upstairs, the master suite was accompanied by an incredible bathroom that featured gold plumbing fixtures and a green Italian-tiled tub. Below these chambers, and around them, swarmed a warren of smaller rooms and hallways that Yordan eventually used for staff offices for writers and associates of all kinds. Fortunately, I was spared this indignity and was favored with a fine office at an *hôtel particulier* near the Champs Elysées. Once a fine private mansion, it was now transformed into the office building of a French film distribution company with which Yordan began to work.

At this time political affairs were heating up in France. De Gaulle had definitely committed to leaving Algeria. The French army were adamant opponents of this and threatened to rebel against their old general. There was a serious alarm that the army, based in Algeria, with its guns, tanks, and planes, would stage a coup by flying into Paris and taking over the government. Early one morning, Marat woke us with news from the radio that de Gaulle had called on the citizens of Paris to collect arms—which would be distributed among them—and to prepare to resist an invasion. We listened to the radio ourselves and could only understand a few of his words when he called on the *citoyens de Paris*. "*Aidez moi! Aidez moi!*" The other citizens were urged to stay home, stay off the streets. I didn't think I was called on to collect a rifle, so decided to stay home. When I called Yordan and told him why I wouldn't be coming into Paris that morning, he could only grumble that any excuse served to keep people away from work. In truth, I can't recall in all the years I was to spend with him ever hearing him express any interest in anything political or, indeed, in anything other than the project or projects currently engaging him.

The invasion didn't occur. The scare was over temporarily, though for several more years the diehards in France engaged in terrorist tactics, planting *plastique* bombs aimed at left-wing Frenchman who favored severing the colonial connection with Algeria. A number of my left-wing French friends were targets for these bombs. But for us it was work as usual, turning out pages on *Captain Kidd*.

Yordan and Shelley were pleased with the way the script was going. In fact, it was going so well that Shelley, in early December, persuaded Yordan to let us both drive up to St. Moritz where Shelley had an apartment. Shelley wanted to ski and he promised that we would work as hard as ever up there to turn out pages. We took off in his Alfa Romeo. Jean and Ellen were decently settled in Vaucresson, where Marat had things under control. Ellen had connected with the local riding stable, and Jean had many friends from our Hollywood colony. I felt guilty at leaving them but was able to live with it.

Shelley and I had scarcely unloaded our bags in his St. Moritz apartment when he insisted we go over to the Palace Hotel to pay our respects to Cappy, whom I had never met. Cappy was Phil Yordan's second ex-wife and another beauty. She had only recently divorced Phil and had quickly married a Mr. Badrutt, who was the principal owner of the Palace Hotel. It's no exaggeration to say that this was the premiere resort hotel of Switzerland. Everyone from the Shah of Iran to the Opel motor heir stayed at the Palace when in St. Moritz. It boasted that the concierge staff was so well trained that any guest who ever stayed there might come back years later and the staff would know all of the guest's preferences—room, food, service, and what have you. I never got a chance to check out this charming legend. But I did finally get to meet Cappy, another legend.

One story about her sounds apocryphal but isn't. A friend of mine was present when Cappy was asked, at a Hollywood party, "If there were one thing you wanted more than anything else in the world, one thing, what would that be?" Without hesitation, Cappy (then Mrs. Yordan) replied, as if it were a single word, "fursandjewels." Now Cappy was queen of one of the great hotels of the world. She had plenty of furs, quite a few jewels, and she presided over the Palace as though it were her private palace and the guests were all her *invités*. Yordan had never quite reconciled to the divorce, and I learned that many of his absences, from Madrid and Paris, early on, had been in vain pursuit of Cappy, who had finally turned him away and married Badrutt, heir to one of the great properties and traditions of Switzerland.

Cappy greeted Shelley and me regally, asked after Phil, then sent us on our way because she was about to go skiing in her very latest and most beautiful ski outfit. Shelley and I actually turned out some script pages. Shelley was a night owl who sat up half the night, banging out pages that he would proudly show me in the morning. Whatever his other talents, he wasn't much of a writer, and I usually had to explain why we couldn't use his pages as I set about rewriting them. Shelley was an avid skier and was out on the slopes much of the day anyway while I stayed in and wrote.

I did find time to enjoy some skiing. Determined to make me a good skier, Shelley introduced me to his ski professional, who gave private lessons for a reasonable hourly fee. Soon I was up on the slopes, trying the man's patience with my clumsy efforts. But I did feel I was making progress. The ski slopes were crowded with brightly clad, skillful skiers in a perpetual holiday atmosphere. These were mostly people who didn't have to wait for holidays or a vacation to get away. Even with a professional *skimeister*, the few days at St. Moritz were not sufficient to turn me into a confident athlete on the snow, but we had to get back to Paris. Subsequently, there were other trips to St. Moritz and Jean, too, got to enjoy the Palace Hotel.

As an unreconstructed red, I was troubled by the Swiss. At that time I knew nothing about the Swiss banks grabbing and holding the money and property of German Jews. But I did know that they had been only too ready to turn fleeing Jews back to Hitler rather than admit them into their own squeaky-clean country. Besides, from top to bottom they all seemed so determined to be the perfect hosts for the free-spending visitors. It wasn't natural. And I had heard that, despite appearances, the working class was poorly paid and lived in less elegant quarters than the Palace Hotel. I knew that they used unpasteurized milk and that their toilets, like the German toilets, were constructed so that whatever was deposited in them was protected from the flush of water so that it could be scooped up and used for night soil. Even so, feeling guilty as hell, I had to admit that I enjoyed feeling rich, feeling like one of the top dogs. Well, not the "top"—after all, the Shah and the Opel heir were still in nearby rooms.

By now Yordan was commuting back and forth from Paris to Madrid and sometimes to London or Rome. *El Cid* was shooting in Madrid, and though Tony Mann seemed to be in control, Yordan was involved with many problems of casting and distribution. On one trip back from Madrid, he brought Merlyn and installed her at Boulevard Suchet. Merlyn was nineteen or twenty, with a great body and no education. She was from somewhere in the American Deep South, claimed her father was the captain of a shrimp boat, but more likely he was another sailor or dockworker. She had originally come to Madrid as the girlfriend of a company attorney, then returned with him to New York, where, though a young man, he died. Merlyn decided she liked the looks of things in Madrid and arranged to get back. Irving, always the gofer, was delegated to meet her plane. He told me that the first thing she said at the airport was, "Who's the most important man here?" So far as Irving was concerned, Yordan was the most important man, and that's what he told her. Yordan, recently divorced, was at loose ends. In no time at all, the two had paired up.

Merlyn was tall, extremely buxom, and very pretty. In order to be somewhat discreet, Yordan put her up downtown at the Madrid Palace Hotel instead of with the rest of us at the Hilton. When I delivered script pages for Yordan to their Palace suite, Merlyn confided to me that Phil was a great and considerate lover; she gave me astonishing details. A pretty and complaisant girl to sleep with was one thing, but it surprised me that Yordan would get this involved with a girl who was so young, who had clearly been around the block in more ways than one, and who was so ignorant that she didn't know who Charlie Chaplin was. *That* really threw me.

Installed in my fine offices on Rue Dumont d'Urville, I had other things to think about, and I had to finish *Captain Kidd*. When pages were sent to Yordan, he almost invariably approved. In retrospect, I think he was so busy with other projects he didn't pay much attention to our script. I finally finished a draft, turned it in, and waited with the usual writer's anxiety for reaction from the boss.

Meanwhile, back in America, Joe Steinberg was trying to arrange a distribution pickup or some kind of deal on the Philippine script I'd written. He sent me a copy, which I showed to Phil, who sat down then and there, held the script within inches of his face, quickly turned the pages, then looked up, and said he thought it was quite good. I was very annoyed at what I felt was a cavalier treatment. "You can't possibly read it that fast and know what's there," I complained.

He shook his head. "I read it and I know what's there."

"Then what do you think of the character of Maria?" I asked. There was no such character, and I wanted to trap him in a lie.

"There's no Maria in this script," he snapped.

I had to conclude that he had read and digested the script. What I wanted from him was help getting the film made—I hoped he'd want to take over—but he wasn't interested. However, he did want to know what my deal had been with Steinberg. When I told him that I'd been paid only $5,000 but had five percent of the producer's gross, he exploded angrily. It was altogether unreasonable, he insisted, to get a piece of the producer's gross. Even movie stars never got that. He was genuinely incensed that I had made a deal so unfavorable to a producer. I was amused and comforted by the thought that I had made a good deal for myself. I also gave the script to Shelley to read. He was very enthusiastic and began to think in terms of getting involved in a production.

Captain Kidd was put aside while Yordan sought opinions from half a dozen other hangers-on who inhabited his cellar warren. Meanwhile, he wanted me to get involved in another project. He had gotten into the habit of asking me along on his lengthy walks, which led, very pleasantly, along the edge of the Bois de Boulogne, down past the Auteuil racetrack, and back up Boulevard Suchet to his place. On these walks, we talked mostly about his obsession: what picture to make next. Because his deal with Bronston called for him to be paid $400,000 for each film he initiated, he had to come up with the story (or project) and the script.

On our walks he explained that television had changed the film business; now we needed "must see" pictures, films that could get an audience out of their living rooms and into the movie theaters—big, important, promotable films, not just another story. He was thinking of films like *Kwai, Ben-Hur, Lawrence of Arabia*. We batted ideas around. I came up with a suggestion that didn't seem "must see," but I had a notion that might make an unusual film. The idea was to do a circus picture—not the standard story of the girl trapeze artist and the lion tamer—but one that would have a free form—the great circus moving all around the world wherever a colorful site could lend itself to a unique and daring stunt. I was thinking of the aerialist Blondin walking a tightrope over Niagara Falls. We could use film to convey great and unforgettable images to an audience.

Sold.

Nick Ray had a deal for a second picture with Bronston and was pressing Yordan to come up with a project. He liked the circus idea, and I was set to work developing a treatment. When Nick came to Paris I became involved with him in story conferences. Nick was a tall, well-built man of about fifty with thick iron-gray hair and a curiously hesitant manner of speech. A friend of his said, "If you telephone Nick Ray and no one answers, that's Nick." He had been a hippie product during the pre-hippie days in the forties, a serious abuser of alcohol, and even of drugs before drugs were fashionable. But he was talented and liked by almost everyone. He had scored big with *Rebel without a Cause*, and, though Yordan had received no credit for that film, they had apparently worked together on it. Yordan had also been credited with the script for *Johnny Guitar*, another of Nick's successes. Despite his physical bulk and unquestioned accomplishments, Nick was an insecure man who needed to lean on someone like Yordan. By now I was deep into a treatment for the circus story and I delivered pages for Nick to read. He liked them and he and I hit it off well. I had the impression that Yordan wanted me to cement a relationship with Nick to relieve some of the demands Yordan felt he carried. I spent long hours at the hotel and enjoyed fine dinners with Nick.

Things were going so well that Yordan began talking to me of altering our deal so that I would become his "story editor," in charge of developing all scripts. He offered a further promise—that at least one picture a year would be mine to produce in participation with him as a half-owner of the film. That sounded grand to me, of course, and it motivated me to work harder.

Back from the States, Arnaud d'Usseau was put to work on a script project that, like many others of Yordan's, was based on a story or script he'd owned for a long time. I also found a couple of American writers who were living in Paris and eager for work at the short pay Yordan offered. Without any official change of title, I did become a sort of story editor who was consulted on all scripts.

I continued to work on the circus story and kept an eye on the other projects in progress. Yordan commuted back and forth to Madrid. Shelley continued to try to raise the money to produce *Captain Kidd*, though Yordan seemed to have lost interest in it. Joe Steinberg kept me informed of his efforts to finance our Philippine film, with Paramount Pictures in Hollywood getting hot and then cold. I heard less and less about the grand prospects for *King of Kings*, which received rotten notices in the press and seemed destined to become a flop. But it was onward and upward for Bronston and Yordan. *El Cid* was being shot, and other projects were needed.

My initial six-month contract with Yordan was due to expire on April 10, 1961. I kept reminding him of this and asking for a new deal. As usual, he put me off for weeks. Other matters always seemed more pressing, including word from Shelley that he had concluded a deal with Cinemiracle to produce *Captain Kidd*. Finally, on April 1, Yordan signed a new deal with me that guaranteed another year of employment at $1,500 a week and stipulated that I would produce one film a year as a full partner. These films I was to produce were not the Bronston films, but like *Triffids* and other scripts we were working on, they were Yordan's personal projects, financed by him with money from Hollywood studios and distributors. By now I was beginning to understand something about Yordan's "promises," like his initial promise to send for me from Los Angeles "in six weeks." He is a man who means what he says when he says it. But who can help it if circumstances change? At the time I liked the sound of becoming a producer but didn't take it too seriously, just so long as he didn't try to use that to bargain away my salary. Almost invariably, the way he liked to work with writers and anyone else was to offer them "expense money" for now and a promise of participation in profits—eventually. Except for myself, everyone else in Paris working for him at the time was stuck with such a deal. So I was skeptical. However, in some curious ways, it did eventually work out that I would become a producer for him.

Just before signing me up for another year, Yordan returned from Madrid, saying the deal for the circus picture had been set with Bronston. Everything was going so well that Yordan set off for Nice to discuss deals with some people at the Cannes festival. He arranged for me to leave Paris a day or two later and meet him in Rome. I had told my old friend and collaborator, my almost-brother, Julian, everything I was doing in Madrid and Paris. In Rome he met my plane and took me to the Grand Hotel where Yordan was staying and where he'd reserved a room for me. I would have preferred staying with Julian, who had an apartment in an old palazzo in Rome's *centro historico* district, but I was there on business and was expected to be with Yordan. However, Julian and Yordan met and hit it off nicely, which was one of my hopes.

The next day, Yordan and I met with Nick Ray, who had a lovely home in a nearby suburb. We lunched with Tony Mann and Michael Waszynski, Bronston's line producer. I took advantage of the extravagant meal at the top restaurant in Rome to order something I had never before tasted: wild boar. I found it tough and salty. I couldn't eat it and had to send it back. The brass from Madrid were in for a wrap party for *El Cid*. Some of the film had been shot in Rome, just a token to qualify for the Italian nationality that conferred considerable financial advantages. That afternoon, at a stage at the studio, Julian and I enjoyed the wine and hors d'oeuvres, staying close to Yordan, who was never at his best in a crowd and did not want to be left standing idly while everyone gathered around the stars, Heston and Sophia Loren. Heston had been sweet-talked into attending with a gift of a tax-free Jaguar.

In the hours we had alone together in Rome, Yordan and I walked the sunny, pleasant streets, and he unburdened himself to me about his problem. Should he marry Merlyn? Or should he make an effort to get back together with Cappy, who might be willing? I was not about to advise him. But I tried to be helpful, urging him to think long and hard, consult his true feelings, and not act on impulse. Maybe I was trying to convey that either choice might be a mistake.

On the way back from Rome we stopped at Nice to take in the Cannes Film Festival. Somehow, we were able to get rooms at the Carlton Hotel, the unofficial headquarters for all the wheeling and dealing. Yordan was busy using his many contacts from Hollywood, London, Rome, Madrid. He didn't like me to be idle when on payroll, so I was supposed to be thinking up a project suitable for Merlyn. Cast her as a star? Sure. Can she act? Sure. I let it go without inquiring whether she'd ever even tried to act. But I did worry whether my first film as a producer with Yordan would be one starring Merlyn.

Evenings we went to the casino. When I entered, they asked me if I had a membership. I said I'd gotten some kind of card there several years before (when Jean and Ellen and I had landed there after our voyage on the *Cristoforo Colombo*). They pulled out their card file, and there I was. Yordan and Shelley were impressed by the world traveler and gambler status I now seemed to enjoy.

14

Throughout that first year in Paris, my first year with Yordan, the French factions opposed to De Gaulle continued to set off *plastique* bombs all around the city, battling to preserve the French presence in Algeria. We, the expatriate film community, were acquainted with some of the left-wing people who were actually targeted and wounded by these bombs.

Despite the major political turmoil around us, I continued to work away at the script for the circus film, but it wasn't all hard work. Jean and I, and sometimes Ellen, took in the Louvre, the Musée de l'Homme, Versailles, Fontainbleu, and spent many Sundays with friends who had a place in the country. We also visited frequently with Michael and Zelma Wilson, had dinners with them and the Jarricos in Paris. Some nights we took in the Folies Bergères, the Blue Note Café, and the Crazy Horse Saloon.

Yordan took Merlyn on his regular trips to Madrid. After one of these he told me they had been married. There was no public announcement and nothing much had been said to anyone. Jean and I wondered how to respond. We knew that a party to celebrate the occasion would give Yordan a fit. But we had to do something, and finally decided on a wedding gift.

What do you get the boss who has everything and really doesn't seem to be delighted with his new status as a thrice-married man? An inexpensive, token gift wasn't right, but neither was anything showy or extravagant. We finally decided to just go for it and to hell with the consequences. At the fine Jensen silver and jewelry shop, we selected a lovely Jensen-designed sterling silver coffee service—pot, sugar, creamer, and tray. Not large, but good. The whole set cost some $600, which wasn't peanuts at that time.

When we presented the nicely boxed gift to the bride and groom, Yordan was polite but even more subdued than I expected. Merlyn was delighted with the silver toy.

The reason for Yordan's restrained reception became clear a month

or two later when he told me that he hadn't really tied the knot, only announced this to shut Merlyn up. And now he had decided to ship her home
to the States and put an end to the farce. He also admitted to me that Cappy
was coming to town and he was still uncertain about where he stood with
her. He wanted Merlyn out of the apartment until he could complete arrangements for her final exit. Would Jean and I let her stay with us in Vaucresson until it was time for her to leave?

Yordan had frequently dined with us and treated our place as a home
away from home. He liked Jean and she liked him. He seemed to admire
the stable relationship we had. We had been married almost fifteen years,
and he found Jean a solid citizen—dignified, independent, warm, but not
gushing toward him. He liked her cooking. Whenever it was necessary,
he'd send his car and chauffeur to pick her up to get her to the doctor or
bring her back from the airport or railroad station when, as was demanded
every three months, she and Ellen had to leave France, then re-enter to
keep their tourist status. My own situation was kept clear because of my
frequent trips in and out of France with Yordan.

Yordan's car and chauffeur delivered Merlyn and all her baggage to
our place. We couldn't help noting that prominent among the goodies she
was taking back with her to some little Louisiana fishing port was the Jensen silver service we had gifted her for her "wedding." We had prepared
a bedroom for her and explained the situation to Marat, just so our *bonne*
would not throw a fit at the appearance of a guest.

Jean, for all her goodwill, became impatient when Merlyn demanded
that Marat iron her clothes, even her undies. Jean told her that we did not
have upstairs and downstairs maids, that Marat was too busy with her other
chores, and that Merlyn could just get to the ironing board herself. Things
got dicey when Yordan arrived the night before Merlyn was due to fly
home. He said he was taking her out to dinner. My premonition was right.
They didn't come back. All bets were off, and Merlyn resumed her place
at Boulevard Suchet.

I worked on several projects while waiting for the completed circus
script to be studied in Madrid, after which it would either be approved or
I would be asked to make changes. Yordan was busy trying to get financing for *Triffids*. *King of Kings* seemed to have been forgotten, despite Bronston's effort to get the Vatican to endorse it. My Philippine film was finally
shooting in and around Manila with Irving Lerner directing. Joe Steinberg
had assembled a good cast: Van Heflin, Rita Moreno, and James Mac-
Arthur. Having failed to get a distribution deal or pick-up, they had de-

cided to go on spec with full financing by Joe's brother, Harry Stonehill, who was truly a big-time operator in those latitudes.

After a winter in Vaucresson, Jean and I decided to move into Paris. We found a splendid apartment in the sixteenth *arrondissement* just a few blocks' walk from my office and also close to Yordan's apartment on Boulevard Suchet. The apartment belonged to Count and Mme. de Bearn, who were evidently having marital problems. It was completely furnished with the very best pieces, including good antiques, Wedgwood china, and cupboards full of the best crystal. One of the possessions that particularly impressed me was a large chest of sterling silver flatware, so heavy that it could scarcely be lifted, which contained two dozen place settings that seemed too precious to use. The paintings on the walls were of museum quality, and there was a unique, original crayon portrait of Napoleon casually placed on an end table. It had been a gift from Napoleon to an ancestor who had been a lady-in-waiting for Napoleon and Josephine. A large, heavy, sterling silver box for cigarettes sat on the coffee table.

We worried about losing items like this and protested to Mme. de Bearn that they shouldn't be left with tenants. "But that's why you're paying so much rent," she replied. How much? It came to slightly less than $500 per month. Those were the days!

During that first year, on one of my frequent trips back and forth between Paris and Madrid with Yordan, he blew up at all of the niggling about the *Triffids* script, especially from the director, Sekely. Yordan was busy concentrating on making the deals to finance and distribute the Bronston product and was too preoccupied to pay much attention to *Triffids*. He finally decided to call a halt to what he considered the unproductive stalling of his director and producer. Yordan was occupying an enormous one-of-a-kind suite that featured a very large circular central living room with a pair of bedrooms on either side. He busied himself setting a long table in the middle of the living area with three chairs on one side and a single facing chair. He placed a *Triffids* script at each place. Next he put on a snap-brim felt hat I'd never seen him wear before, and, with a severe frown on his face, he managed to look very much like a 1930s Chicago gangster.

When all this was arranged, he said, "Don't you worry about what you're going to see. Just do what I tell you." He called for Lou Brandt and Steve Sekely and while we waited, asked me to be seated in the middle of the three chairs.

When they arrived, he didn't bother with a polite greeting, just instructed them in a commanding tone. "You," to Sekely, "sit there on Bernie's right, and you," to Brandt, "sit down on his other side." They sat as ordered and Yordan took the seat across the table facing us all.

"Now, Bernie is going to turn through the pages of the new scenes he's written so you can see them. These are absolutely the last changes that are going to be made. So the two of you turn through the pages with him and read them. And that will be that."

"Go ahead," he ordered me. I proceeded to do my part. The other two were clearly too intimidated to open their mouths. Even I, knowing I was part of an act, felt a chilling apprehension. Just to make certain there was no misunderstanding, Yordan emphasized, "I don't want any questions or comments. Just read the new scenes." When I was through with my part and closed the script, he said to the others, "That's all. You can go." Without a word, they slouched out.

When the door closed, Yordan pulled off the dated hat and shrugged but didn't smile. "Sometimes you have to do these things."

"You certainly had me convinced," I said sincerely enough.

"The two of them: sitting on their asses, living it up around here and piddling with the script." He shook his head. "What do they know about scripts?"

"I never knew you were an actor."

Now he permitted himself an easier look. "I had a little experience at the Pasadena Playhouse way back."

As it turned out, Yordan's display of authority accomplished little because he fired Brandt and hired another producer, one who knew exactly how to take orders—Bernie Glasser—who had worked with him on some television projects in Hollywood. Yordan rounded up a couple of stars, Howard Keel and Nicole Maurey, who though not exactly shining lights in the firmament, were good enough to carry the picture for the $800,000 budget that Yordan raised by selling the U.S. rights to Allied Artists for $400,000 and the rest of the world to Rank of London for $400,000. One of the sweeteners in the deal for Rank was that the film would be produced as a British quota film, entitling it to the considerable financial benefits of the Eady Plan, which Britain used to encourage local production.

As a result of this "nationalization" of the film, we had to spend most of the budget in England and hire much of the above- the-line talent from England, which determined the casting. A Britisher, George Pitcher, was paid and named as producer, although, to the best of my knowledge, he had nothing to do with making the film. Glasser, who did produce it, never got credit.

My script had assumed production in Spain. I now tortured it into a shape that permitted filming in England. That did not help the final result. Filming began at the Pinewood Studios at the edge of London, and, on one of my periodic trips, I went out to the studio and watched some of my work being filmed.

Some months later Yordan returned from a trip to London to tell me he was in trouble with *Triffids*. The completed film had been screened for Allied Artists and for Rank; they had rejected it. Actually, Yordan didn't have any legal obligation to please them, since they had no approval clauses in their deal, but he didn't want to blow his relationships with these important film people. There were always possible deals in the future. Steve Broidy, head of Allied Artists, was an old friend of Yordan's. He had recommended Yordan bring to London a fine Hollywood film editor who would go through the footage and see how much could be salvaged.

Though Yordan blamed the producer and the director for the problems, I believed the real trouble came from Yordan's unwillingness or inability to spend the money required to shoot the major action sequences that had been planned for Spain. He had been constrained by the need to spend most of the money in England in order to benefit from the Eady Plan. Whatever the reasons, Yordan followed Broidy's advice, sent to Hollywood for Lester Sansom, a real pro, and nervously waited in a Soho delicatessen while Sansom ran the film through a moviola, marked the bad sections with a grease pencil, then timed what was left—the good sections. Yordan was called back to the cutting room. The bad news: there were only fifty-seven minutes of good film. Contractually, Yordan needed a ninety-minute feature-length film. Someone had to find or add close to thirty minutes.

Apart from the cost of doing this, the other problem was that the cast—principals and all other actors—were long gone. They could not be brought back without spending a fortune. It would be cheaper to scrap the whole film. Back with me in Madrid, Yordan had already figured out in principle what had to be done. We would write and film another complete story that was related to the basic plot but independent of it, a story with different characters, therefore, different and cheaper actors. What kind of story? I was stumped. The whole idea overwhelmed me. Not Yordan. A few days later he came to me with his solution. We would do a story of two people isolated in a lighthouse, just two characters who had somehow escaped the destruction of most of the rest of the world, and we would interleave their story with the one that was already shot. I liked it.

I had to find two characters, put them in a lighthouse, figure out why they hadn't gone blind like everyone else, make them interesting enough to watch for thirty minutes, and figure out how their affairs would intersect those of the original story. Relieved of my other chores, I set to work, and soon I had twenty-five pages I liked. I gave them to Yordan. He read them and rejected them.

"Why?" I demanded angrily. "That's a good story."

"It's too good," he retorted. "Your characters are too sophisticated, have psychological problems. They don't fit in with the others in the rest of the picture." I thought he was dead wrong, but shrugged and walked away from it.

Yordan had a British writer available. After all, the original novel was a British classic; the location of our lighthouse would be somewhere on the British coast and would have British characters and actors. Yordan would get Jon Manchip-White to write the new lighthouse sequence. A day later Jon came to my room with some script pages in hand. "I didn't think Yordan could write," he said.

"What are you getting at?"

"I just read a sequence he wrote and it's really damned good." He handed me some script pages.

I glanced at them and laughed. Of course, they were the pages of my lighthouse sequence. "Did he tell you he'd written them?"

Jon nodded. I explained that they were my pages and that I had just received the most sincere compliment from one writer to another. Then I marched in to see Yordan and waved my pages at him.

He shrugged. "What's the difference who wrote them?"

Maybe that's the way he really felt. Maybe he never told Jon he'd written them. Maybe Jon just assumed he had. In any event, those were the pages that were shot, and many people have told me, since the film has become a cult favorite, that they like the lighthouse story best.

Getting the lighthouse story into work meant starting up a full production in London. Yordan had to pull it together there and find the money to pay for the new shoot. He somehow managed all this, then announced that he was sending me to London to take charge of filming the lighthouse sequence.

Characteristically, he didn't bother to tell the *Triffids* producer, Bernie Glasser, who was in London, that I would be arriving to take over. On some unconscious level, Yordan worked on the principle that the more people he had doing the same job (writers, directors, producers, lawyers, accountants), the more likely someone would come up with a good result. It was up to me to handle Glasser in London.

I started out by renting a large two-bedroom suite in the modern wing of the Grosvenor House Hotel. I needed two bedrooms because Jean and Ellen would be coming from Los Angeles to join me in London on their way back to Paris. The very large and impressive sitting room was necessary because I would be using it as my office for casting and for interviewing directors and actors. Glasser may have been impressed with the suite, which should have announced my real authority, but he was understandably balky about cooperating with me. I needed him. He knew his way around the London film scene. I knew nothing, no one. I faced a dilemma when he as much as told me to drop dead. I knew that he wouldn't want to totally tear up his relationship with Yordan, but I had been sent to London to solve problems, not to call Madrid and toss the problem back to Yordan.

I invited Glasser to dinner, had a heart-to-heart with him, reasoning that it would be bad for both of us if I had to call Madrid and complain to Yordan. He understood. We got along fine after that and went to work considering suitable directors and performers. Maude Spector, the leading casting director in London, was not much help. She couldn't help turning up her nose at this job of finding two inexpensive actors and a very inexpensive director who wouldn't even get a credit on what she considered a minor film. She didn't know that this was my entry into a higher state of filmmaking, and she became very impatient with me when I was choosy and insisted on interviewing a number of people. Once again, the threat I didn't have to voice was that Yordan and Bronston were behind me.

Jean and Ellen arrived from California. We had a happy reunion in the suite, which was a great upgrade from the rooms we had occupied in the same hotel several years before. Jean and I had a week together (except for actors, actresses, and directors) and were able to enjoy my elevated status while recalling the days of selling plastic and chasing scofflaw drivers.

I was fortunate to find Freddie Francis, who was one of Britain's leading lighting (first) cameramen. His ambition was to become a director. He had already directed a couple of low-budget films. He read the script of the lighthouse story we were preparing to shoot, liked it, and agreed to work for a modest fee, with the understanding that he would receive director credit only for the lighthouse portion, not for the full film. He was an absolutely delightful man who cooperated in every way and was able to steer us to some actors he knew. With his help, we found Janette Scott, who had a reputation for being the best screamer around. We ran a couple of her films, and it was true. Also, she was attractive, a good actress, and agreeable. We found Kieron Moore who was a good-looking, virile actor who had made several British horror films.

With these two lined up, we rented a stage at Shepperton Studios on the outskirts of London and planned the interior of the lighthouse set. I was dubious about it, however, because the downstairs floor area, virtually the only place for playing out the personal scenes, seemed too small to permit the camera angles needed, especially when the massed triffids started breaking down the walls to get at our humans, but Freddie Francis assured me that it would be fine. Since he was one of the world's best cameramen, I subsided. He turned out to be perfectly right.

Other matters did not go as well. I'd heard that working with British film crews could be vexing, that they insisted on the strictest rules for defining the function of each union category. If an electrician picked up a wrench that only a grip could touch, work stopped, a grievance hearing was held, untold time lost. Time is a lot of money on a film set. As an old left-wing union man, I tended to discount these stories as antiunion grousing by producers. What I had heard turned out not only to be true, but true in spades. We were an American company shooting in Britain, and we could feel palpable resentment against us. I well understood the feeling among British filmmakers who were forced to struggle to keep their own industry alive while the theaters were full of American imports. Naively, I'd thought that since we were over here employing the British, they'd see we were the good guys working here instead of in Hollywood. Not so. Americans were the enemy.

The special effects were hard to achieve. To carry out my concept that seawater destroyed the triffids, we had to find a system where spraying the monsters with seawater, as from a fire hose, caused them to go up in smoke or steam and dissolve harmlessly. The special-effects people were maddeningly lackadaisical in their approach. Try one trick one day. Wait until the next day to try another. The triffids were men dressed up in costumes that made them look like bark-covered plants with moveable limbs. The object was to cover the exterior of these mobile, treelike brutes with some substance that would react appropriately when in contact with water or whatever was sprayed at them.

We all tried to come up with suggestions. I recalled from elementary chemistry that phosphorous reacted this way to water. Whether this idea was helpful or not, I don't know. I doubt it. What I remember most keenly was that one day, in the midst of this costly struggle to find a workable system, the chief special-effects man was inexplicably absent and all work ground to a halt. After frantic efforts to find him, we learned that he had decided to report to the Motor Vehicle Bureau to renew his driver's license, so hadn't bothered to report to work or even to inform us that he wasn't coming. This seemed an act of sheer hostility, and my impulse was to fire him on the spot. It was frustrating that I couldn't even consider that. There was no one around to replace him, and satisfying my fury only would have cost us dearly. Finally an excellent effect was achieved, and we were able to shoot the sequence to everyone's satisfaction.

After this, we worked in editing rooms rented in Soho, in the heart of London. Putting the new footage together and intercutting it with the old was in the competent hands of Les Sansom. But this was all unofficial. We had to keep the British film editor on to satisfy the demands of the Eady Plan. Additional work consisted of sending a crew out to the furthest reaches of Lands End for an exterior shot of a real lighthouse to establish an authentic feel for our own interior construction. Much as I enjoyed the post-production work, Yordan felt that it was now in capable hands. He wanted me back in Paris for more writing chores.

On November 28, 1962, Yordan called me from London to say he had just run *Triffids* and thought it was terrific. Two weeks later he called to tell me that Rank had accepted *Triffids* with enthusiasm, and it was a foregone conclusion that Allied Artists would also accept it. When I approached Yordan for writer credit on the film, he said he had to deny me because the original deals with Allied and Rank called for him to be the screenwriter. Thirty years later, Universal Pictures in Hollywood was considering a remake of *Day of the Triffids;* they requested clarification of the writing credit on the existing film. At that time I got Yordan to sign a letter to Universal acknowledging that I was the sole and proper author of the script and originally had been denied credit only because of the political circumstances that existed at the time of the production.

At the Hollywood Canteen, L to R: John Garfield, Carroll Hollister (a distinguished pianist and Canteen volunteer), Bette Davis, and my wife, Jean. PHOTO BY JACK ALBIN.

Hollywood Canteen, group photo in Canteen office: Jules Stein, then head of MCA, with his wife, Doris (left of Stein), Bette Davis, and my wife, Jean, far right.

Jean dear,

Your letter finally reached me with it's news of your resignation. It is indeed a sad day for us- more than for you. I am sorry to hear of your health- let me tell you this business of children and work is not apt to make us the soundest of human beings physically.

I, also, would refuse to go on with the Presidency in the event they to become active again. I have no enthusiasm left for any such projects. What I had I gave once- and could never get me, myself and I to that pitch again. I am tired of duties and responsibilities after twenty years of it- want as much freedom as I can find-am in a position now to find some- and mean to make the most of it.

Where are you or will you be in the east. I am still at Prouts Neck in maine- box 44- write me if you are any where in this vicinity. I don't know how much longer I will be here maybe weeks- who can tell.

This past six months practically finished me- the quiet and the pine woods and the rain and lots of sleep have me on the mend at this point- what an experience. !!!!

My memories of our association are warm and affectionate ones also Jean. Without you we would have had a grim time. You are one of the brightest girls I have ever known. My love to you and write me.

Bette

A letter from Bette Davis to Jean regarding her resignation from the Canteen.

Flesh and Fury (1952): Tony Curtis's first real dramatic role.
© 1952, UNIVERSAL PICTURES COMPANY.

The Lawless Breed (1953): Rock Hudson on his way to stardom.
© 1953, UNIVERSAL-INTERNATIONAL.

The Law Versus Billy the Kid (1954): They paid almost as much to get Billy as I got, net, for writing my first script as a blacklistee.

Crime Wave (1954): Sterling Hayden, who couldn't or wouldn't come up with my full name when testifying before HUAC, ironically became the lead in the film I was writing when I was blacklisted at Warner Bros. COURTESY OF PHOTOFEST.

Earth Vs. the Flying Saucers (1956): Ray Harryhausen's fine special effects helped this very low-budget sci-fi film become a cult classic. COURTESY OF PHOTOFEST.

Hellcats of the Navy (1957): Ronnie and Nancy in one of the love scenes I wrote for them. Reagan never knew it was a blacklisted writer who put the words in his mouth.
© 1957
COLUMBIA PICTURES CORPORATION.

PARTY SHOTS:
In early 1958 Julian Zimet and I sold our script, *The Beach Boys*, to Columbia Pictures. Almost simultaneously, another blacklisted pair, Nedrick Young and Harold Smith, sold their script, *The Defiant Ones*, which won an Academy script award (1958). To celebrate both sales, I held a dinner party at my home for a group of blacklistees: Dalton Trumbo (left) with Young;

Cleo Trumbo at the piano;

Julian Zimet to the right of me;

and Irving Lerner, who later introduced me to Philip Yordan.

Day of the Triffids (1962): The little girl, having slept through it all, is the only one on the train who is still sighted. The others, helpless and blind, grab on to her to lead them . . . anywhere.

55 Days at Peking (1963): The exterior set of the six-million-dollar production, a very big budget for the time. © 1963, ALLIED ARTISTS PICTURES CORPORATION.

55 Days at Peking: Nicholas Ray was totally miscast as director of a large action-adventure film. He was, however, comfortable and effective with actors, as here where he confers with Flora Robson, who played the Dowager Empress.

55 Days at Peking: I pose proudly beside my name on poster on Les Champs Elysees, Paris. My first post-blacklist public recognition.

Cry of Battle (1963):
Rita Moreno attracted great
attention from Manila
political big-wigs when she
did a nude bathing scene.
Here, she holds a local child
in her lap during a pause in
the filming.

After their real wedding at
the town hall (*mairie*) of the
16th *arrondissement* in Paris,
Yordan and Merlyn exit, with
me, the official best man,
bringing up the rear, right
behind the bride. The other
two are local witnesses who
happened to be available.

The Thin Red Line (1964): Philip Yordan's wife, Merlyn, gets her love scene with Keir Dullea in the middle of the battle for Guadalcanal.
© 1964, ALLIED ARTISTS PICTURES CORPORATION.

10, quai d'Orléans
Paris IV°
April 22, 1964

Mr. Andrew Marton
Avenida del Dr. Arce, 11
Madrid

Dear Andrew Marton,

I have now seen THE THIN RED LINE twice, and I wanted to write you about how marvelous I thought were the combat scenes in the film.

The scene where Doll kills the first Jap is of course magnificent. And the scenes in the swamp are most beautifully done. But for myself, possibly because I am so personally involved with that particular part of the story, I think the beginning of the attack on the Bowling Alley, where Tella is gutshot and Welsh goes out to him with the morphine is one of the finest, most moving combat scenes ever filmed.

I just thought you might like to know how pleased I was with the power of this particular aspect of the film.

Sincerely,

James Jones

JJ:klw

The Thin Red Line: Letter from author James Jones to director Andrew Marton praising the film adaptation of his novel.

Circus World (1964), L to R: Philip Yordan; George Weltner, Paramount executive vice president; Samuel Bronston; Frank Capra; and Martin Rackin, Paramount production head, at the happy meeting where Capra signed an agreement to direct *Circus World* and a second feature. But none of this worked out after Capra was fired from *Circus World*.

Circus World: Rita Hayworth was personally and professionally at about the end of her rope but was trying to hang on. Here she sits with my daughter, Ellen, in the big circus tent. PHOTOGRAPH BY THE SWARBRICKS OF LONDON.

Circus World: The sinking circus ship is how I started my first circus script. And here it is, many drafts later, upended in Barcelona harbor. © 1964, BRONSTON MIDWAY PRODUCTIONS AND PARAMOUNT PICTURES CORPORATION.

Battle of the Bulge (1965): Robert Shaw and director, Ken Annakin with a couple of very real tanks thanks to Francisco Franco and the Spanish army.
COURTESY OF THE ACADEMY OF MOTION PICTURE ARTS AND SCIENCES.

Custer of the West (1968): Custer (Robert Shaw) faces a well-earned end at the
Little Bighorn.

Western street at the studio outside Madrid, Spain: Originally built for *A Town Called
Hell (Bastard)*, the street was redressed for *Captain Apache*, *Bad Man's River*, *Pancho
Villa*, and *Horror Express*.

Krakatoa (1969): Detail from one of the posters that insisted that Krakatoa was *east* of Java.

Bad Man's River (1972): James Mason, Gina Lollobrigida, and Lee Van Cleef in the final scene of the film. Lollobrigida had threatened not to come for this last day's work if she weren't paid in full *immediately*. I couldn't arrange that, but she came to work anyway. © 1973, SCOTIA INTERNATIONAL.

Horror Express (1972): Christopher Lee and Peter Cushing looking for scientific clues to the identity of the monster. © 1973, SCOTIA INTERNATIONAL.

Horror Express: The director, Eugenio Martín (right), with me at the period railroad station in Madrid, discussing how to get the most production value from the authentic steam locomotive and the antique train. PHOTO BY SIMON LÓPEZ.

Pancho Villa (1972): Telly Savalas, center, upstaging Clint Walker and Anne Francis.

Surfacing (1981): Claude Jutra, who couldn't swim, sits petrified as the camera boat approaches the rapids. Tragically, he drowned a few years later in the St. Lawrence River. PHOTO BY EDIE YOLLES.

15

Yordan had to come up with a new project for Bronston and for Nick Ray, who had been signed to do another picture. In Paris Yordan and I kicked around many ideas, including *The Fall of the Roman Empire*, which he liked. I insisted that I couldn't see any way of doing a story, a script, or a film on the subject. I made long lists of possible subjects and titles for other films, brought them over to Boulevard Suchet, went through them, had them rejected. One of these ideas dealt with the Boxer Rebellion in Peking in 1900. When I was in the Paramount story department back in the forties, I had read a play that struck me as unusual, pictorial, and filmic, but stuck in Paris, submitting ideas to Yordan, I couldn't recall the title of the play or the author.

Yordan never sparked to my suggestion. However, he came back from a trip to London with a "good idea"—to work up a script from a title, *55 Days at Peking*.

"That's my idea," I protested. "The Boxer Rebellion. I can show you." I was ready to go back to my office and find the foolscap sheet with my many suggestions, including the "Boxer Rebellion."

"No," he replied. "That had nothing to do with it. I was cruising the book shops in London . . . You know how I do . . . Merlyn was with me. She opened a book and saw a chapter heading, 'Fifty-five Days at Peking,' and showed it to me. That clicked. It's a good title. Boxer Rebellion doesn't mean anything."

So Merlyn got the credit. What he told me was probably true; certainly he believed it. I would have liked to receive credit for the idea, but that wasn't as important as working on another script and staying on the payroll.

Peking was a tough assignment. We had no story, no plot ideas, no characters, and only the sketchiest notion of what the Boxer Rebellion had even been about. Yordan brought back from London a few books with historical accounts, but even these were murky and confused. The Boxer Rebellion was a puzzle even to the people who had been involved. It was a Chinese form of protest against foreigners, but the role of different factions of Chinese was extremely mixed and contradictory. Isolated in Paris, I had little help in running down the truth, but I started trying to work up a story, knocking out ideas and outlines of possible stories, giving them to Yordan. He liked some of them, not others. I went back to try again.

By December 1961 Yordan and I put together something he considered presentable. He met Charlton Heston in the Hilton Hotel in Madrid, told him the story, and urged him to sign on. Heston balked. According to what I heard later, Yordan used every means of persuasion on Heston, and when that didn't work, he threatened to throw himself out the window of the hotel room unless Heston yielded. Finally, for whatever reason, including a unique deal for a percentage of the producer's share, Heston agreed to do the picture without script approval. Heston had, of course, starred in the previous Bronston epic, *El Cid*, and he was at the height of his popularity and box-office appeal since the success of the recent release of *Ben-Hur*. More than ever, we were into the star system, when signing a "bankable" star meant that the money could be raised to make a film, and distribution and release deals could be made on little more than the name of the star.

In the last days of December 1961, Yordan returned triumphant with Heston's agreement in his pocket. Now all we had to do was write a script. Nick Ray was assigned to be the director. The pressure on me was intense. Yordan was signing cast. Nick Ray was working with the art direction, designing sets, including the great wall of the Forbidden City, the residence of the Dowager Empress and the seat of power of the ruling dynasty. This wall and the accompanying Forbidden City sets, built on a backlot outside Madrid at a cost of over $900,000, were unusually expensive for the day.

That winter, and into the spring, I worked night and day trying to come up with story ideas and suggestions for scenes that the stars and producers would accept and that the distributors would find exciting enough so the film could be sold in advance. It was just a matter of some words on paper—right? Yordan tried to work closely with me on this one. A great deal was at stake. He was good at coming up with an idea for a spectacular scene or situation; he had a good feel for what would sell the picture, but I had to go back to my office and try to sweat these ideas into a plot and into personal stories. I was pressured constantly by the first-draft deadline, February 1, when Nick was arriving in Madrid. Then I was told to ignore that and aim for March 1—or, at least, aim to have a first act by then. This continued into the spring of 1962. As usual, time was of the essence. The Bronston studio in Madrid had to be kept operating with a new picture, a new budget, and financing in place to pay the overhead and the substantial salaries of many people, including Yordan.

I was having trouble. I began getting colds and the flu and constantly ran a low-grade fever. Seeing that he was in danger of losing my services, Yordan came up with the kind of answer he knew best—to motivate me to carry on. He volunteered to pay me a bonus of $50,000 if I completed the script of *55 Days at Peking, and* if the film were made. That prospect cheered me, and I continued to work through my fever.

Busy as Yordan was with this problem—and a half-dozen other stories he wanted written by some of the poorly paid slaves he kept in his basement rooms—Yordan had time for other matters of greater and lesser importance. One spring day, he asked me to come over to Boulevard Suchet. When I arrived, I was bundled into the car with Yordan and Merlyn. We were going to the office of the *mairie* of the sixteenth *arrondissement*, where he and Merlyn were to be married. I was the official witness. We arrived at a building that was the city hall for the district. The local *maire*, or mayor, conducted the civil ceremony—in French, of course. Yordan signed the great ledger. Merlyn signed. And I signed. I presume I am now embalmed forever in the records of the city of Paris.

Yordan wanted to return home immediately, but I insisted that my role was not complete unless I could at least take them somewhere to celebrate with a bottle of champagne. Merlyn was pleased with this minimal acknowledgment of her new status. We did knock off a bottle at the bar of the George V. Whether Yordan was pleased, I never knew. I suspected he was more eager to get me back to work on the script.

Money or not, promises or not, I had to keep working on the script. Production on *Peking* was scheduled for early summer. I had to go down to Madrid and work on the script with Nick Ray. I think Yordan was hoping and praying that, working together, Nick and I would solve the script problems and leave him free for all his other machinations. The Madrid trip turned out to be more than the usual one-week stint at the Hilton. I worked on the script with Nick and found him most agreeable and supportive. We became personal friends, and I realized that he, too, had a radical background. One night at dinner in his home with him and his wife, Betty, I told them the story about my private-eye experience in Bakersfield. They seemed enchanted. Nick insisted there was a film in the story. Compared to the elephantine historical subject we were tackling, it was much more the kind of personal and ironic story with which he was comfortable.

Nick was trying hard to battle a long alcohol dependency, but his approach struck me as weird and unproductive. He didn't allow himself any wine or liquor but kept a liter bottle of an Italian *digestif,* Fernet Branca, at hand. Almost every bar had this drink in stock, ready for patrons who'd eaten too much and were suffering from acid indigestion. Ergo, *digestif.* I tried it myself. It worked much better than Alka Seltzer, but it was a vile-tasting concoction made from something like fermented artichoke hearts; sipping it was only slightly less unpleasant than suffering from heartburn. It was actually a strong alcoholic drink. From the taste, I suspected it was about a hundred proof. Keeping to his vow and his promise to stay off the sauce, Nick sat all evening, sipping his *digestif,* consuming almost the entire liter bottle. Toward the end of the shoot on *Peking,* Nick became seriously ill. I blamed that corrosive drink.

After Nick and I had worked for about four weeks and turned out quite a few pages, Yordan showed up, read the pages, and threw them all out. I was disheartened. I don't believe Nick ever regained his confidence in me. He needed someone like Yordan to tell him what to do. From this point on he went along with all Yordan's opinions. In other ways, so did I. I believed I was dealing with one of the most experienced scenarists in Hollywood, and the owner of a coveted Oscar. Who was I to argue?

None of that was any help in the spring of 1962. I had to go back to square one and write the kind of clumsy, impersonal, fat historical opus that Yordan felt the international distributors, who catered to the lowest common denominator, wanted. *Peking* was not being made to please the critics but to satisfy the judgment of businessmen who owned theaters and theater circuits in England, France, Spain, Portugal, Italy, Germany, India, Japan, and all of South America, where audiences were unsophisticated, enjoyed spectacle and simple characterization, and where fine points would be lost in translating and dubbing.

I probably never understood that and never got over a wish to please myself and my peers.

With the start date for production looming, Yordan suggested I get some help by hiring Arnaud d'Usseau to write some of the scenes, particularly those for Ava Gardner, who was approached to play the female lead. He proposed that, since he had promised me a $50,000 bonus if I completed the script and the film went into production, I pay Arnaud from that theoretical bonus. I was happy to give my consent. Arnaud was a friend, he was struggling to stay on the payroll, and he was stuck with one hopeless assignment after another. I didn't know how much Yordan was paying Arnaud, but I assumed it wasn't much. I confess I was surprised and annoyed when Arnaud held out for $2,500 a week when we offered him the assignment. I had the feeling that this was Yordan's way of making up to Arnaud for not having paid him properly until now, when in a sense his salary would be out of my pocket. But I still regarded the $50,000 bonus as a chimera, and, should it ever become a reality, I was willing to share it.

Arnaud was a good writer. He was meticulous. And he was slow. His last serious writing had been the Broadway plays he wrote with James Gow and Dorothy Parker, and I had no notion how long he spent on those polished efforts. For whatever reason, he simply couldn't find his way into our script. I wondered if, unconsciously, he found it demeaning to be "assisting" me. Perhaps it was simply the great difficulty of moving into the middle of a script someone else was already writing. I never found out. After four weeks of work on his part, there was nothing we could use. When Yordan suggested that we continue, I refused. The effort had cost me a theoretical $10,000, and I had no reason to believe that it would be productive.

Shortly after this, Julian came through Paris on his way to visit family in New York. He stayed with us and read my pages. I asked him if he would like to spend a week or two on my payroll and try his hand at a few scenes. He was happy to agree; I paid him the same rate of $1,000 a week that, not that long ago, he and I had been earning on *The Beach Boys*. Julian worked with me and eventually wrote one scene about the Dowager Empress that I liked very much and that got into the film. But these various efforts to get help did not relieve the burden on me.

Now with Ava Gardner as our female lead, we learned that David Niven, in the role of British ambassador to Peking, would be the supporting actor to Heston. Samuel Bronston had run into Niven in the lobby of the Grand Hotel in Rome and offered him the role. He also offered to pay Niven the handsome fee (for that day) of $300,000. It was an offer Niven couldn't refuse—even though he hadn't read a script, which didn't yet exist, and knew little about the story. This came back to haunt me later.

In Madrid, preparations for production were in high gear, a fact that appalled me. How could they be spending all this money and be certain that I would ever come through with an acceptable screenplay? Would they kill me if I didn't? I suppose this was all a tribute to Yordan's stature and persuasiveness. When I went to the studio in Madrid and looked at the models for the sets with Nick Ray, I complained that the way the compound, the Forbidden City and the great wall, were laid out, there was no space for the battle scenes I envisioned. Nick assured me it would be just fine. It didn't turn out that way. Nick had never directed a major production like this and was just as frightened as I.

In May I had dinner with Bronston and Heston. I had just presented them with the draft of my 140-page script. To my great relief, Heston okayed it. I knew I still had a lot of work to do, but I was taking it one day at a time. Someone came up with the idea that they find a real British writer to write dialogue for the British ambassador to be played by Niven. Bronston had a man on payroll in London who sent us a truly distinguished writer-director. Robert Hamer had made numerous films, including some outstanding ones like *Kind Hearts and Coronets*. We were warned that Hamer was now a serious alcoholic and would have to be closely watched if we hoped to keep him sober. Renilde, who had been my secretary over the years and had become a good personal friend, was assigned to pick him up at the airport and get him directly to the hotel. She did.

As my loyal ally, the first thing she did was bring him to visit me. He was a lovely man. I especially appreciated him because he said, in all candor, that he had shuddered when first offered a job to work on the film. He imagined that a Hollywood treatment of the Chinese revolt against Westerners would be dreadful—reactionary!—but when he read the script, he was pleased and relieved. He complimented me for doing a creditable job and for giving the Chinese dignity and a legitimate case. I expect he had in mind the speech I had written for the Dowager Empress, who complains to the assembled ambassadors that the Western powers have long been treating China as a cow to be milked, and now they are planning to slaughter the cow so they can eat the meat.

Needless to say, I took him to my heart. But it didn't help. Nothing helped. Renilde quickly became fond of the man, and she did her best to save him from himself, but no matter how much she watched, he was like the alcoholic of *The Lost Weekend*. He would escape and find his way to a source of liquor or beer. She described his room, where she had to step carefully to avoid falling over beer and whiskey bottles. He was too drunk to write. They finally conveyed him back to the airport and loaded him on a plane to London. Not a single word of true British dialogue for the ambassador had been written. Sometimes I thought the movie was jinxed. No one could help write this script.

For me, the height of that really wild year was July 2, 1962, when production actually started. The first scene to be shot was a night scene inside the Forbidden City, shooting toward the great Temple of Heaven, a round building that had actually been constructed full-scale and half-round. I was chauffeured out to the set at Las Matas and greeted by Nick, who took me with him in the basket of the crane that lifted us both high above the action. Jack Hildyard, the distinguished British director of photography, had gathered every 5,000-watt brute in Spain and some from France to light this huge exterior night scene. When the lights went on, it was impressive, seeing the great set illuminated for the first time.

Unfortunately, the entire first night's work had to be done over at great expense, because, even with all that light available, we didn't have enough to make the round Temple of Heaven look round. In the dailies it looked like a flat, two-dimensional fake. This kind of miscalculation plagued the production. For example, the beautifully carved interior walls of the temple, where important scenes with the Dowager Empress occurred, were painted a flat black. This was an accurate depiction of the actual temple, but the blackness of the walls made it impossible to light them to show the expensive carving detail. Despite all the efforts of the camera crew, the background beauty of the temple walls was lost.

Beyond this, no sensible control of cost was ever maintained. One day at the studio, Leon Chooluck, the production manager, came to me, tearing out his hair because the workmen in the furniture shop were applying real twenty-four-carat gold leaf to the legs of chairs that would be used in a minor way in a scene. "I asked Colosanti and Moore [the art directors, who had a close personal relationship as well as being co-workers] why they couldn't settle for gilt paint that didn't cost anything and could be applied in minutes." He shook his head. "They ignored me."

"Did you go to Bronston?"

Leon nodded sadly. "Bronston said he wants everything to be real, only the best."

When on one of our almost daily walks though the streets of Madrid, I reported this to Yordan. He shrugged. "Bronston can piss away money in lots of ways. He owes about $20,000 to some loan sharks in Rome. Instead of paying them off, he's paying them 10 percent per month. *Per month.*"

"Why doesn't he just pay them off?"

"He always needs the cash for something else."

I never saw Bronston look angry or worried, and I supposed that, like Yordan, he was able to sleep well no matter how much trouble he was in. I, who had never bought anything, even an automobile, on credit, marveled at the capacity of some men to live, and even thrive, on a daily diet of financial disaster. At that time I didn't know that any disaster was impending—it just seemed that way from where I sat. I did know that with the Castellana Hilton half-full of Bronston dependents, he had run up an enormous debt that was rising every day. I saw profligate spending of money on all kinds of nonsense, not only gilded chairs. People came and went from Hollywood and London to be consulted, at Bronston's expense, on foolish, doomed schemes for original ways to photograph the action sequences (*pace* Nick Ray). Expensive talent was hired and then dismissed and paid off on a whim. Personal expenses were unrestrained and had to come out of the budget.

One day, two fine blue limousines showed up in the parking area of the lot. One was a Rolls Royce for producer Michael Waszynski; the other was identical, except it had the Bentley radiator grill. Bronston told Waszynski, "I'm giving you the Rolls as a gift, and I'm getting the Bentley for myself. Just, please, see that no one else on the lot should have a Bentley."

Waszynski, also known as Prince Michael Waszynski, was from Poland and allegedly was a legitimate Polish prince. In his expatriate years, he'd worked as film production manager in Rome, where he met Bronston. The two men were close. Whether this had anything to do with the story of Bronston's marriage, I don't know. But it was well known that Bronston had fallen in love with Dorothea when she was married to a successful film distributor in Rome, a man from North Africa named Hajaj. When it was agreed that Dorothea would divorce Hajaj to marry Bronston, it included an amicable agreement, on lucrative terms, that Hajaj would become the sole distributor of Bronston product in Italy. Waszynski, who knew Hajaj and every film person in Rome, may have been in the middle of all this as the man who arranged for the divorce in exchange for the valuable distribution deal. Whether this was true or not, the prince cultivated princely tastes. He bought and furnished a home in a Madrid suburb, a home smaller than a palace but no less expensively furnished. I can personally attest that dinner was served on a table set with solid sterling platters under the finest china, and that we ate with what appeared to be real gold flatware.

Where did all this money come from? After the great heyday in Spain, it was claimed, even in lawsuits, that Bronston stole huge sums of money from film budgets and stashed it in Switzerland. I never believed this to be true. There was never any evidence of that. The way I read the man, it simply wouldn't occur to him that such finagling might be necessary. Caution was not his bag. He was the king. He had a prince working for him, and they would always be on top of the heap.

On Yordan's initiative, another British writer was sent down from London. Jon Manchip-White was a beefy Welshman in his thirties. He had written a number of respectable historical books and several novels.

It was hoped that he could write some dialog for the Niven character, the British ambassador, but that didn't work out. Yordan kept him on in hope of getting a story about the French Revolution. This was another notion I had sniffed at. As with the Roman Empire project, which now occupied Ben Barzman and Basilio Franchini, who had written *El Cid*, I suggested that if Yordan were interested in the French Revolution, he should go to a good novel like *A Tale of Two Cities*, which could certainly be remade, or something by Dumas, who had tackled that era. That approach didn't suit Yordan. Jon Manchip-White was put in my charge—I was to help and advise him about filmwriting.

I found Jon interesting. He was the first Oxford graduate I had met, a genuine scholar—though not necessarily of the French Revolution. He was proud, even arrogant, about his Welsh heritage—he tended to look down on mere Englishmen. An avid collector, he was no sooner in Madrid than he found his way down to the Rastro, the great local flea market, where he started to collect some of the wonderful antique ivory fans that Spanish ladies traditionally used to fan away at their flushed faces when Spanish gentlemen looked at them suggestively. He also collected used and slightly tattered *trajes de luz*, the heavily embroidered and decorated "suits of light," which Spanish bullfighters wore and ultimately discarded when their glory days were past.

Despite the almost daily demands on me to rewrite scenes during the shooting of *Peking*, I was still rewriting the circus script. I also worked with several other writers who were engaged on various minor script projects. I was continuing to run a low-grade temperature. One day the hotel doctor who came to check me out suggested that I needed some time off. I told him to tell that to Yordan. He did. As a result, it was agreed that I could take a week off and go where I pleased. When Yordan asked me what I would do, I said I'd just like to go to a beach somewhere and relax in the sun. He nodded as though he understood, but then asked, perfectly serious, "Okay, but what will you do the second day?"

I cherish many of his one-liners. He and I were returning one night from the usual Madrid dinner that typically got under way about ten o'clock. It was close to midnight when we hit the hotel lobby on our way back. Yordan detoured with me to the little notions shop off the lobby, a place that sold various sundries from Life Savers to aspirin; it also had a rack with magazines and daily newspapers. I watched, astonished, as Yordan grabbed all the astrology magazines. There must have been five or six of them. As we walked toward the elevators, I asked incredulously, "You don't really believe in that stuff?"

He paused before getting into the elevator, then delivered his zinger: "Do you know a better way to foretell the future?"

Another line of his was delivered the day I told him about the pleasures of a transatlantic voyage on a great ocean liner. He listened carefully, seemed to be picturing the luxuries I described, then shook his head. "Six days in the middle of the ocean. Do they have a telephone?"

A whole week off! Jean and Ellen were summering in California, so there was no way I could profitably use this week of rest by traveling there and back. I decided to treat myself to the most luxurious and expensive week I could think of. I made reservations at one of the fine hotels in Monaco, where I would have beaches, pools, access to all the beauties of the Côte d'Azur, and where I would have no problem about what to do the second day. I even arranged to fly into Cannes first-class and reserved a rental car at the airport.

The Hermitage Hotel was only the second best in Monte Carlo, after the Hotel de Paris, but it seemed perfect to me, right down to the dusty palms that drooped in the pale sunlight that filtered into the lobby. The rooms and decor were strictly turn-of-the-century, spacious, a bit worn, but clean and somehow honest. The hotel made no effort to be up-to-date. Its heavy Victorian furniture seemed to say, "We remember and honor the old days when princes and moguls came to stay with us, when the rich were rich and the poor knew their place." What was an old Commie like me doing here—and enjoying it? Well, why not? I wasn't taking it away from anyone else and I found it very relaxing. I was beginning to believe that the blacklist was really behind me.

When I got back to the Hermitage after dinner my second night in Monaco, there was a call waiting from Yordan. Late as it was, I reached him in Madrid. "I'm not asking you to come back, but I have to tell you Niven read the script and refuses to report for work unless it's rewritten."

"I'll come back tomorrow," was all I could say.

At Barajas Airport in Madrid, a studio limousine was waiting for me. These 1950s Cadillacs were enormous seven-passenger boats that resembled ocean liners among the small Spanish SEATs. They were unavailable except to foreign tourists and businessmen and were used by the studio for movie stars and VIPs. Yanked back from Monaco, I evidently qualified.

"Niven's being completely unreasonable!" Yordan said to me at the hotel. "I offered to release him from the contract but he refused. He wants the money, but he wants a script he can approve, even though he signed without reading a page and without demanding script approval."

The film had already been in production for four weeks, with most of the actors and actresses well into their roles. "How am I supposed to change the script now?" I wanted to know.

Yordan had already thought about this, and he had a simple answer. He knew actors. "You'll just write a *Hamlet* scene for him, and he'll shut up." I knew immediately what he meant. The British ambassador, as I had written him, was the official who pressed most vigorously for an uncompromising stand. He wanted all the foreign nationals and their ambassadors to remain in the compound even though they'd been advised by the Empress to leave for their own safety. The Boxers were raising hell all around the country, and their principal targets were foreigners; they were sure to attack the Peking compound. How would the foreigners, cut off from the outside, defend themselves against vastly superior forces? Many of the other nationals wanted to leave, but the ambassador (Niven) insisted they stay because departure meant abdicating their extra-territorial status, perhaps for good.

Yordan was advising me to write a breast-beating scene for Niven in which he could torment himself: Did he have the right to place innocent people in such jeopardy? How would he feel if there were casualties, or deaths? Was he truly acting out of principle or was he using these people as pawns for his own political purposes? And so on. What actor can refuse to play Hamlet?

I wrote four or five pages with the ambassador, Niven, pouring his heart out to his wife. They were sent to Niven. He came to work. I complained to Yordan that it was unprincipled for an actor to torpedo a production after he'd agreed to work without imposing conditions. Yordan looked at me wearily. "Stars have few principles, Bernie."

During production, problems multiplied in Madrid. Ava Gardner was an alcoholic, and getting her to play her scenes was driving Nick Ray crazy. But we all enjoyed the story of Ava and Paul Lukas, who was playing the role of the doctor in charge of the hospital in the foreign compound. Lukas was an Austrian actor with a pronounced German accent whom I had seen on the stage playing the heart-rending role of the father in Lillian Hellman's play, *Watch on the Rhine*. I had great respect for him as an actor, but my admiration was tempered by a sense that he was German through-and-through. Ava Gardner also seemed to regard him as an exceptional actor. One day she approached him on the set with a modest request that was heard by all: "Mr. Lukas," she murmured, "I have great respect for your acting and I'd certainly appreciate any tips you could offer me about my acting."

Lukas glared at her. He seemed to glare a great deal. Then he nodded agreeably and said, "Yes, Miss Gardner, I think there is something that would help a lot. If you could manage not to start drinking before noon every day." This did not improve Miss Gardner's attitude on the set. The troubles she would make were only beginning.

We had other troublemakers. On one occasion, Heston decided that he, too, had a right to be difficult. In a lather, Yordan burst in to my room at the Hilton to say that shooting had stopped on the set because Heston would not perform. He wanted a good scene, something more than just running around with a gun shouting orders at his Marines. But running around in uniform was exactly what Heston did best. As a character actor, he had, in my estimation, less animation than Ulysses S. Grant cast in bronze on a horse. Even as Moses he wore a kind of uniform. Yordan, of course, had an answer. "Give him a scene with that kid. That always works."

In our story, one of Heston's Marines was the father of a delightful young half-Chinese girl of about ten. Her mother was dead. We could kill off the father, leave the child completely orphaned and up for grabs in a country where she would never be accepted. Give Heston the job of telling the bad news to the child and somehow dealing with it.

"Write something. But hurry. The holdup is costing a fortune." Yordan had to go back to the set but said he'd return in an hour to see how I was doing. An *hour?* I didn't have time to think. I just put myself on automatic pilot, sat at the typewriter, and started to knock out a treacly scene of the little orphan girl and the deeply touched Marine major who had the painful job of consoling her. Evidently, I was right at home in this gear. I had a draft of three or four pages that I hadn't even read myself when Yordan came flying back. He grabbed the pages and read them through in his usual half-minute.

"Okay," he said and started to leave with them.

"You can't take them!" I protested. "I haven't even read them myself."

"I won't show them to anyone," he promised. "Just use them to talk from."

But he did show them to Heston, who loved them. And the show went on.

Nick Ray was running out of steam and becoming more irritable on the set; eventually, he froze up and was unable to decide where to put the

camera to start a simple scene. Yordan was sent for. He found Nick helplessly looking at a scene in the hospital where the doctor, Paul Lukas, was
supposed to examine Gardner, who'd been wounded in the fighting. Pru-
dently, Yordan acted as though he had to give this matter serious consideration, then turned to Nick with a tentative suggestion. "Maybe you could
have the doctor hold a watch in one hand and take the patient's pulse with
the other. Then start with the camera in close on the watch, pull back, and
go on with the scene." After Yordan's profound suggestion, Nick gave this
his usual protracted and thoughtful consideration. "Good idea," he eventually agreed. The shooting resumed.

This was a prelude to what occurred a few days later when we at the
hotel were informed in hushed tones that Nick had been rushed to the
British American Hospital with a heart attack. We were all concerned.
Whatever his weaknesses and idiosyncrasies, however much he may have
worn out his welcome on the film, he was never overbearing or mean. He
was a talent, even if he'd been miscast for this type of motion picture. We
were also worried about what would happen now, with the shooting more
than three-quarters finished but with considerable work left to do.

A decision was made to put the rest of the film into the hands of the
second-unit director, Andrew "Bondi" Marton, who had a great deal of experience as second-unit director on major productions like *Ben Hur*. I sat
with Marton and Yordan as we ran about forty minutes of rough cut of the
picture; we discussed the best way to move forward. We decided to let
Bondi get started on a major set-piece, a ballroom sequence that involved
a dramatic confrontation with drawn swords between our major, Heston,
and the principal Chinese heavy. The sequence was a challenge. The director needed to coordinate the many expensively costumed men and
women dancers on a brilliantly decorated and lit set, the music, and the
eventual personal confrontation. Principally, it was the kind of action that
would make a second-unit director feel comfortable. Marton did fine.
Everyone was relieved and the lead actors made no serious objection to
continuing with him. When Nick Ray was out of the hospital and resting
at home, no one was sure whether he had had a heart attack or not, but
neither he nor anyone else was suggesting that he return to finish the film.

At Heston's insistence, the director Guy Green was brought down
from London to help create and direct a single emotional scene for the
unrequited love between Heston and Ava Gardner. When Green arrived
with his wife, it fell to me to make him comfortable in town and with the
production. I took them to the Riscal, a surefire warmer-upper, but it back-
fired, because, to my amusement and Green's embarrassment, his wife de-

cided to challenge her husband: she thought he was looking too appreciatively at the local female talent. She insisted that since he so obviously wanted to, he should be a man, get up and dance with one of the girls. He had her permission to go ahead and do whatever appealed to him. This did not fly. Tails between our hind legs, we slipped out of the Riscal.

Since he had only one scene to direct, Green wanted it to be great to justify the expense of bringing him here. I felt he was pressing for an effect unrelated to anything else in the film. I tried to write another scene, but couldn't satisfy him or Heston. They had to settle for what I could deliver. Even larger problems loomed. The brass had generally agreed we needed some impressive action sequences to top off the film. I was stumped. What could the poorly-equipped rabble—the Boxers—bring to bear against the soldiers of a dozen Western nations? And what could the soldiers, isolated from outside support, their munitions gone, do against the Boxers to create a big splashy ending?

Yordan applied himself to these problems and came up with answers I thought ridiculous—but no one cared what I thought. Just write. First, there was the kind of action sequence that suited the talents of Heston. A great sewer was imagined, one that a troop of men could actually march through. It led, according to this scenario, under the great wall that separated the foreign compound from the Forbidden City, where, deep in the interior, an arsenal was stacked with barrels of dynamite. Heston, accompanied by Niven—the British ambassador!—was to lead the way through the sewer into the Forbidden City, breech the defenses of the arsenal, light a long fuse that would blow up the whole damned place with familiar breathtaking suspense—but not until our heroes got back into the safety of the sewer. Protesting all the way, I wrote this garbage while they built a huge, splendid sewer on what was now the largest sound stage in Europe. They filmed the sequence. I don't recall that any critics complained.

Even worse, we needed a tremendous final battle, though neither side had anything to battle with. Yordan put his fertile brain to work. We had an impregnable wall and forces on both sides with no armaments. He must have dug out of his memory scenes from old films where medieval castles were attacked from the outside by forces that built high wooden towers for assault. "Assault with what?" I wanted to know. "Well, everyone knows the Chinese invented fireworks. Let them use fireworks! That will photograph great! The fireworks set the compound on fire! Write it."

Bondi Marton did a good job of shooting this mess. It looked great. Who cared if it was foolish? It was movie making in the grand old tradition.

By these means we arrived near the end of the epic, but Ava Gardner decided she'd had a bellyful of the film and simply disappeared. She was missing for her final big death scene. This time they came running to me for an answer. It was simple. "What was the last shot of her?" I asked.

"She's been seriously wounded in the big final action; she's lying in the hospital bed." The doctor (her friend Paul Lukas), was looking down at her sorrowfully.

"Forget the big death scene with Heston," I said. Did we have any choice? "Just put someone else in the bed and have the doctor pull a sheet over the head. Then fade out." (Occasionally someone complains that Gardner disappears abruptly from the film, but very few care.)

In the final sequence, with all the fresh troops who come to the rescue on parade, Heston looked splendid in his new uniform. He was mounted on a fine horse for his exit. Tears in her eyes, the appealing little orphan girl was watching him go. Heston rode up to her, boosted her onto the horse behind him, and they rode off together to rousing patriotic music of the massed military bands.

During the post-production, I complained to the film editor, Bob Lawrence, that I hadn't seen one shot of the expensive wall, nothing that revealed its true dimension. Bob gave me a withering look, pulled from a bin a short length of film, three or four feet long, and ran it through the moviola "You mean something like this?" he demanded.

"Yes," I said doubtfully. It wasn't much of a shot and there wasn't enough to be useful.

"What you see is what we have. It's a bit of test film they made in pre-production. They never gave me another foot of the wall." I walked down the hall wondering if I'd been right when I complained to Nick Ray that the original set design wouldn't permit the kind of shots I had in mind. When I finally saw a rough cut of *Peking* in a room packed with a group of exhibitors from many different countries, the exhibitors seemed happy with the film. It was a big show. I was miserable. To me, it seemed to be a clumsy, old fashioned historical spectacle with a crude story and paper-thin characters.

But I was supposed to keep busy on *The Thin Red Line*. I'd been working on and off for more than a year, between other chores, to turn James Jones' 500-page, discursive war novel into an acceptable screenplay. I was also busy with Arnaud d'Usseau, who was trying to cope with *Gretta*, one of the collection of Erskine Cauldwell novels Yordan had acquired for filming. Jon Manchip-White was alternately struggling with *The Hand*, a horror picture idea, while *Crack in the World* and *The French Revolution* languished; Dan Aubrey was trying to make sense out of *The Tribe that*

Lost Its Head. All of these were projects for Yordan's personal film production. A couple of other projects that Yordan was trying to work up for another Bronston film added to the clutter of this time: *Khartoum* and *The Paris World's Fair*, a period piece set at the turn of the century. I was constantly being consulted on every one of these.

When Yordan heard my complaints about *Peking*, he sent me to see Waszynski and Bob Lawrence to discuss possible changes and improvements. They were not receptive. Waszynski wanted to believe they had a big winner—he was making plans to take the film to New York to show it to the people at the Radio City Music Hall for its premiere. I told him he was way off-base, and he resented me. Nonetheless, we agreed I should write a narration for the opening of the film. I did. Just another chore that kept me hopping. The post-production was almost complete, and the film's titles had to be decided on. I told Yordan that I wanted script credit. Joe Steinberg had already agreed to give me proper credit on *Cry of Battle*, the Philippine film, my first post-blacklist credit. I cornered Yordan in his suite one day. "Look, Phil, I've told you that I want credit on *Peking*. I've already gotten credit on Joe Steinberg's film and there's no reason I shouldn't get it on this."

He came up with a familiar answer: "I made a deal with Allied for a picture written by me. It's a big money deal. They're not so crazy about the picture anyway. I don't want to rock the boat."

"They won't ask for their money back if my name is on as writer."

He gave this some thought. "It's okay with me if your name goes on along with mine. But you'll have to get Bronston to agree."

"You mean I should talk to Bronston about it?"

"No. Go see Paul Lazarus. He's in charge of selling. If it's okay with him, it'll be okay with Bronston."

Lazarus was a new vice president who'd been brought in for his distribution savvy. He had previously been in charge of National Screen Service, the company that for years had enjoyed a virtual monopoly in the States creating and distributing to theaters posters, photos, lobby art, and trailers. I had met Lazarus but didn't really know him when I went to see him in his office down the hall from Bronston's. "You may or may not know that I've been blacklisted and haven't been getting credits on the films I write," I began. He was a pleasant man who listened with care to my demand for credit. He didn't seem at all surprised.

"I think the time for that is past," I went on. "Phil says it's okay with him if my name goes up with his on *Peking*. I guess it's up to you."

He seemed agreeable, but uncertain. How much authority did he really have? I didn't know. I used the uncomfortable silence to say, "You know, Trumbo's gotten credit on *Spartacus* and *Exodus*. If it's safe enough for them, it should be safe enough for *Peking*.

"Okay," he finally said. "But I'll need a signed loyalty statement from you."

That again!

"I'm willing to write a statement that I'm a loyal law-abiding American citizen. That's all." I really felt that he was genuinely sympathetic; maybe he secretly deplored the blacklist. But he was new to the job and thinking about his own position.

He decided. "That will be all right."

I did it. I got on the screen, a really big screen this time. My name came after Yordan's, of course. Maybe not the whole cheese, but I felt I'd won a victory for myself and for all blacklistees. It was not until 1997, when the Writers Guild was making an earnest effort to assign proper credit to all the blacklisted writers, that I called Yordan and asked him to sign a statement acknowledging that I was entitled to sole credit as screenwriter on *Peking*. He hemmed and hawed and finally declined.

"Why?" I demanded.

"Well, I'm in the middle of working on a public stock issue, and the prospectus states that I was a writer on *Peking*. My credits are an important part of the sales pitch. I can't change the prospectus now."

Although I did receive credit for nine films that I had written under pseudonyms or otherwise without receiving credit at the time, I still haven't received proper solo credit for *Peking*.

Shortly after my talk with Lazarus, I was instructed to report to the studio to have my official portrait taken for the elaborate and magnificent color brochure that was being prepared to sell the film. Since I smoked a pipe in those days, I decided that, like any true writer, I should have my photo taken with a pipe in my hand. At least I have been thus immortalized and appear for all posterity with such celebrities as Heston, Niven, Ava Gardner, Bronston, and, of course, Phil Yordan.

Peking didn't get an opening at the Radio City Music Hall, though in general the reception of the film was much better than I had expected. As the years go by, more and more people tell me how much they like the film. I am, of course, happy to be corrected in my judgment.

S ome months after the completion of the film, there was a grand premiere in Paris. Jean and I dressed in our best formal attire and hired a car

and driver to take us to the theater and pick us up afterwards. The studio
brass were out in force, as well as Heston and other important cast members. Watching the film was, for me, painful as usual, though I enjoyed seeing my name on the screen. After the filming, we went down to the splendid restaurant, Lasserre, for a gala champagne supper. Jean and I sat with
the Yordans, nestled between the Bronston and Heston tables. Everyone
was high on wine and great food and, most especially, on the sense that
the film was smashing. In fact, *Peking* became a big hit in Paris and ran at
an important first-run theater on the Champs Elysées for many months.
I was right there up front, not under the table anymore. I was treated as
part of the team by the Bronstons and the stars, even Heston, with whom
I'd never become close. Talk about finally arriving in "Hollywood!" Late
as it was after the supper, Merlyn insisted we all go to New Jimmy's, the
"in" club on the left bank. With half the cast we rolled over there, drank,
and danced for hours.

The film went into worldwide release and received generally favorable
notices. *Daily Variety* said,

Samuel Bronston has a very large production of uncommon visual excitement . . . The original screenplay by Philip Yordan and Bernard Gordon
adheres to the historical basics in its description of the violent rebellion of
the "Boxers" against the major powers of the period . . . And, indeed, while
these nations have in their Peking outpost gallant fighting men who,
although only a few hundred in number, withstand the merciless 55-day
siege, the aforementioned historic facts must stir some sympathy for the
outlaw rebels. For it is the latter who are encroached upon by diplomats and
soldiers from foreign lands in circumstances that somewhat parallels latter-
day struggles for independence at various global points.

The London *Daily Mail* weighed in with,

Old Imperial China, Charlton Heston at his most rugged, Ava Gardner at
her loveliest, David Niven at his smoothest and battle scenes resembling a
fireworks display gone mad . . . what more could an epic ask? . . . The script
(by Philip Yordan and Bernard Gordon) shows a sophistication rare in the
epic game.

In the *Los Angeles Times*, the full-page notice by Philip Scheuer was headlined: "*Peking*—Bronston's Great Leap Forward?" The actual review
starts, "If this keeps on, we'll obviously have to call him the new Cecil B.

DeMille . . . The only difference is that Bronston doesn't actually do the writing or (as DeMille did) the actual directing, himself. These he leaves to his aides—the screenplays to the incredibly and improbably prolific Philip Yordan . . ." At the very end of the notice, he manages to work in that "Bernard Gordon collaborated with Yordan on the screenplay."

The London *Times* remarked,

It is all so smooth and neat that one feels it hardly deserves to work, but, alas for principles, it does in fact work very well . . . The script could tell us more about the hows and whys . . . perhaps it is not altogether unintended that we are left feeling vaguely that the Chinese have the right of it . . . Mr. Niven plays with his habitual easy authority, helped by some unusually accurate English English in the writing (the work, perhaps, of Mr. Robert Hamer, who gets credit for "additional dialogue"[!]) . . .

To be sure, not all the notices were so kind. *Daily Variety* of May 8, 1963, had this to say:

The Yordan-Gordon script, as directed by Ray, succeeds fairly well in incorporating a personal story within the framework of the vast depiction of primitive fiery warfare, with Charlton Heston, Ava Gardner and David Niven it plays interestingly. But somehow lacks appropriate power. The characterizations don't have the intensity of the struggle . . .

The *New York Times*, predictably, was most harsh (May 30, 1963).

Rudyard Kipling was wrong. The Easts and Wests do meet, constantly and explosively in *55 Days at Peking*. As a fictional version of the final gasps of the dying Manchu Dynasty in and around the Forbidden City in 1900, it is no more historic than a Gene Autry epic.

The fact of the matter is that the principals and the multitudinous extras involved have no more depth than Occidental and Oriental figures on a Chinese tapestry and their actions—at least the reasons behind the actions of the principals—are rarely explored fully. Without authentic historic background, a viewer gets a foggy picture, if any, of the real causes of the Boxer Rebellion. With a variety of intertwined personal stories that are also superficial and vague in treatment, the characters of the principals remain largely one dimensional.

Enough!

Whether a film entertainment deserves to be savaged because it is not a true and comprehensive study of the Boxer Rebellion, I will leave to the reader, who may also want to reflect on how well *Gone with the Wind* "presents an authentic historic background" of our Civil War. In recent years, having seen the film again on television and listened to many people who find the film one of their favorites, I wonder if I should mellow and revise my original cruel judgment. While searching for some dated notices about the film, I learned that there is a club in Beverly Hills which meets annually for the sole purpose of running this film via video on a large screen for the enjoyment of the members. When I asked why I had not been invited to these celebrations, I was assured that now that I have been discovered I certainly will be asked to attend. If and when I do, I will be careful not to mention the subject of the *New York Times* review. In retrospect, I am wondering whether, despite my superior attitude, they should not have played the film at the Radio City Music Hall. The film did only moderate business in the States but did exceedingly well in foreign markets, where, of course, less sophisticated audiences enjoyed the fireworks.

16

Work on the circus film started very early in my career with Yordan and continued on and off for years. The project intersected virtually all the others with which I was eventually involved.

Despite the fact that I had initiated the circus project, had suggested the basic story of a search for the greatest acts anywhere in the world, and had worked with Nick Ray to deliver a completed script that was accepted by Ray and Yordan, matters beyond the control of any of us resulted in a series of reincarnations that, while interesting, eventually left me out of the picture—a film ultimately released in 1964 under the title of *Circus World*. According to Yordan, Bronston and his close associates in Madrid, especially his wife Dorothea, decided that *Circus* was not up to the elevated standards Bronston now set for himself. *El Cid* was in distribution and, though not a smash hit, it was regarded as a *succès d'estime*, enough to make Bronston want to deal in major historical subjects. Yordan assured me this change was not a criticism of the script I had written. No one had even bothered to read the script. It was a sudden change of direction for the Bronston enterprise.

Much later, even while *55 Days at Peking* was actually in production and there were almost daily demands on me to rewrite those scenes, I was also rewriting the *Circus* script. Yordan had not entirely abandoned it and wanted me to work up a more conventional personal story. It seemed to me at this point that most of my time was spent working away at unrewarding and frustrating assignments that seemed to go nowhere. For instance, the *Circus* script needed work in an effort to please someone. I didn't know exactly who. A half-dozen other projects were always in some stage of progress, where I was supposed to help other writers or take a crack at them myself.

Shortly after I had started on *Circus* again, word came down that Bronston had signed Frank Capra to direct it. The account I heard from Yordan, and I had no reason to doubt it, was that Bronston, once again in

Rome, had run into the eminent old director. Bronston, drunk at the time, approached Capra with a deal. Capra, of course, the beloved director of such all-time hits as *It Happened One Night, Mr. Smith Goes to Washington, Mr. Deeds Goes to Town, It's a Wonderful Life*, was apparently past his prime and not getting many offers to direct. He accepted Bronston's offer and the handsome remuneration without asking to read the script. Ah. Niven again? It was evident that Bronston wanted, above all, to establish his respectability as a great and memorable filmmaker. Using the right stars helped, and using a director like Capra would be a real feather in his cap.

I didn't know whether I would have anything more to do with the script, though, of course, I was impressed with the name Capra and thought it would be gratifying to work with him. By now, Yordan had assembled his entire script factory in Madrid. Besides myself, the Hilton now housed Jon, Arnaud, Dan Aubrey, Lou Brandt, Sidney Harmon. Frank Capra was installed down the hall to work on his version of the *Circus* story. We were all fascinated to have Capra working so near us. It was like having Renoir, Degas, or Gauguin dabbling with paint and canvas in the next room.

Everyone wondered what exactly he was doing, while I worked on a revised version of the circus script.

"What's Capra doing in there?" I asked Yordan.

"He says he's writing his own version of the script," he snapped.

"I didn't know he was a writer."

"You talk to him, he says he wrote every picture he ever made. All by himself! I wonder why they ever bothered to pay Robert Riskin."

"Have you seen what he's writing?"

"He won't let anyone see his pages. I have lunch with him every day. I'm telling him he can have any writer he wants, any writer in the world. But no. He says its going fine. We'll all be happy."

Yordan was sweating. He had a start date, John Wayne had been signed to do the lead, and Rita Hayworth and Claudia Cardinale were already on board.

The production deal had been manufactured in the usual insane way: Paramount Pictures had a commitment to pay Wayne $500,000 to do a picture but didn't have a vehicle for him. They were on the hook and might have to pay Wayne without using him. Yordan came along (for Bronston) and offered to take over and assume the Paramount commitment to Wayne. To sweeten and to guarantee the deal, Bronston agreed to pay Wayne $750,000 for the work, which greatly improved Wayne's attitude. Like everyone else, Wayne considered Capra a big plus. In return for this favor and for taking the $500,000 debit off its books, Paramount agreed to a pick-up for $2.5 million for distribution in the Western hemisphere. Bronston took their commitment to the bank to help finance the film. Everyone was happy. All they needed was a script.

After seven weeks of diligent work, Capra finally turned in his script. When Yordan marched into my office and handed it to me, he had obviously read it, but he didn't say one word and gave not a single hint of how he felt about it. I was eager to see what the great man had wrought. Was Yordan being so close-mouthed because he wanted me to see for myself what really good writing was like? Naturally, I put everything else aside and settled down to read.

I couldn't believe my eyes. It was an unimaginable jumble of fantasy ideas cavorting all over the place without continuity, characters, or story premise. I couldn't believe a professional filmmaker had produced it. But how could I be so arrogant as to dismiss a man like Capra? I took another look at the material, wondering if a creative and imaginative approach to filmmaking lurking inside those pages had eluded my conventional and limited mind. Try as I might, I couldn't make sense of this.

I went to Yordan, handed him the pages, and just shook my head. He nodded, knowing what that meant. I managed to say, "I don't understand it."

The studio brass agreed. Yordan still had to salvage something from this mess. He sent the script to Wayne in California, hoping Wayne would agree that, though the script was nutty, he would come to Madrid and try to work something out with Capra for a new version. Yordan knew Wayne was not difficult about scripts. Give him almost anything that could be shot, pay him, and start rolling the cameras—that's the way he worked. But word from Wayne was that Capra must have gone senile. No dice. Yordan pleaded with Wayne to come to Madrid and talk it over with Capra. Wayne refused. He wouldn't face the grand old man and tell him the truth.

It looked like the whole project was down the tubes, but Yordan decided to try one more ploy. He persuaded Bronston to agree to pay to ship Wayne's beloved yacht across half the world to Portugal, where he would meet with the actor and try to save the deal. Wayne was delighted with the offer. Done. Yordan went to Lisbon, where, for two days aboard the yacht in the harbor, they ate, drank, and talked. Finally, Wayne agreed that if Bronston hired a solid director like Henry Hathaway to replace Capra,

Wayne would agree to go forward with no further script approval. Hathaway, about seventy, had dozens of films to his credit, some of them mediocre Westerns, but some very good ones like *The House on 92nd Street*, *Kiss of Death*, *Call Northside 777*, *Desert Fox*. Yordan accepted this deal contingent on Hathaway's availability. When Yordan came back to Madrid, he told me he'd "nailed down Wayne."

Hathaway was ready to come. But there was still one unpleasant job to do. Bronston told Yordan to fire Capra. Yordan resisted, but finally he had to agree. Capra was devastated. He insisted that the people who had read the script hadn't read it properly, didn't see what he had in mind. But it was over. Yordan told him that he'd be paid the remaining $200,000 on his contract to direct, but Capra rejected that. He'd settle for the $50,000 advance he'd already received—plus one additional request: his wife had purchased some furniture in Madrid, and if Yordan arranged to have that furniture crated and shipped to California, Capra would appreciate it.

Yordan agreed with alacrity, and it was done.

While I had no personal contact with Capra, Ellen, age fourteen, had a very nice encounter. While Capra was wrapping things up in Madrid, he was curious to see something of the city where he'd been immured in a hotel room. As a consolation prize for Ellen, who once again had left school and friends in Paris and moved to Madrid with Jean, we had promised to buy her a horse. Our friend Lou Brandt, who was working for Yordan again, but now on Bronston projects, had arranged for Ellen to see a horse at the stable in the big central park of Madrid, the Casa de Campo. Knowing that Capra was at loose ends, Lou suggested that Capra use the time to drive Ellen to the stable and to see the great park, which was one of the features of the city.

Ellen, wearing her pretty velvet-covered riding helmet, met Capra in the lobby of the Hilton, introduced herself, and got into the limo with the director. "You like to ride?" Capra asked her.

"Yes," was all Ellen could manage to get out.

"Have you been riding for a long time?"

"Ever since I was a baby," she replied. "My father used to take me to the pony ride on Beverly Boulevard in Los Angeles."

"I like horses too," he said.

"Do you ride?" she asked.

Capra considered this, then he replied rather wistfully, "Not for a long, long time."

At the stable in the park a man was waiting to show a horse to Ellen. Capra got out of the limo to watch. Ellen mounted the horse and rode around in the ring outside the stable. After a few turns, she came back, dismounted, and handed the reins to the man.

"You like him?" the man managed to say in English.

"I'll let you know," Ellen replied. She and Capra got into the limo and started back to the hotel.

Capra was curious. "You like the horse?"

Ellen shook her head.

"Why not?"

"I don't know," Ellen replied. "Just didn't feel right."

Capra approved. "Good girl," he said. "*Trust* your feelings."

Capra had been a headache, but he was pleasant and gentlemanly. Hathaway proved to be an entirely different kind of trouble. He was a curmudgeon—an arrogant, mulish man who also insisted on writing his own script. The situation as before? Yordan tried to give help, give me, give *anyone*. Hathaway would have none of it. In order to suit Wayne, Yordan imported a writer and close friend of his, James Edward Grant, to help on the script if and when Hathaway could ever be persuaded to let a writer in on the project. With Wayne, Grant had been one of the aggressive members of the Motion Picture Alliance for the Preservation of American Ideals, the get-the-reds squad in Hollywood, which had worked hand-in-glove with the House Un-American Activities Committee to finger all the radicals. I suddenly had a sense of the blacklist reaching all the way to Madrid to touch me again.

Though Grant was a serious alcoholic, in Madrid he was on the wagon, and he had been for some time. He knew who and what I was, but he seemed to want to be friendly. We had a few exchanges that barely skirted the political situation in Hollywood and in Spain.

"How do you like it here in Spain?" he wanted to know.

I wouldn't bite. "I like it fine."

"Franco?" he asked provocatively.

"None of my business."

"Right," he answered as one pal might to another. "None of our business."

I tried to avoid him.

Though Hathaway ignored Grant too, Grant was kept around on salary as a pal of Wayne's, another "ordinary expense" of making films in the

Bronston organization. Yordan made another try. He brought in Ben Hecht, the venerable old boy whose Academy nominations went back to 1927, the first year of those awards. For $1,000 a day, he sat quietly in his hotel room at the Hilton and pecked away at scenes. At that price, no one wanted to interrupt him, but I had to meet this revered screenwriter, and I managed to get in once. He looked like a short, shabby, used-up man as he sat at the typewriter, but he smiled cordially and offered his hand. I felt I was touching Mark Twain or Charles Dickens, or, at least, Hemingway. Hecht didn't last more than a week; Hathaway would have none of him either.

For reasons only hinted at, another writer besides James Edward Grant took up residence in a special penthouse suite at the Hilton. Clark Reynolds, we were given to understand, was a close friend of Stephen Boyd, who had been signed as the lead in *The Fall of the Roman Empire*. That film was scheduled to be shot directly after *Circus World*. His arrival meant we now had two writers in addition to myself working on the *Circus* script, even though Hathaway ignored all of us.

Shortly after Reynolds' installation, Yordan approached me. "I have to go to the States, may be gone a couple of weeks, so I would like you to work with Reynolds and see if he can come up with anything we can use on the circus picture."

"Look, Phil, I took the trouble to be friendly with the man, went up to his fancy suite, had a drink with him. But he acts very superior—like a man who's in a different league from the rest of us bums in Madrid."

Yordan was impatient with my irritability or sensitivity. Such considerations never mattered in his universe. "I just want you to read the pages he turns out and talk to him about them. Try to be helpful."

"You mean you're going to tell him to turn his work in to me?"

Yordan hesitated at this. He hadn't quite thought it through, but then he had to nod in assent.

"Have you told him this?"

"I will," he reluctantly agreed.

"I want to be there, all of us together, when you tell him," I insisted. "That's the only way I'll know if I can ask to see his work."

"Okay. Okay," Yordan said.

I wondered if he would do it and waited. At the very last moment before he was due to take off, I had a call to come down to his suite and found Clark Reynolds already there. Yordan beat around the bush, talking in general about the *Circus* script, never getting to the point of why we were there. I was fascinated and irritated at Yordan's unaccustomed delicacy in dealing with another writer. I attributed it to the fact that Reynolds was here at the insistence of Stephen Boyd, the star of *The Fall of the Roman Empire*. Why did Boyd have anything to say about a writer on a totally different film? There was considerable speculation, but I thought I knew Yordan well enough to know that he had great respect for the trouble a star could make and he was not going to antagonize Reynolds. I guess I was in a mood to twist the knife.

"You wanted to talk to us about how to work together while you're gone?" I thought that was putting it delicately enough.

"Right." Yordan nodded, but he didn't continue.

"You want Clark to turn his pages in to me and discuss them?"

"That would be a good idea," Yordan muttered as though the thought had just occurred to him.

"Then it's agreed," I said, turning to Reynolds, "that you'll send me your pages after you complete each scene?"

Reynolds shrugged, a grudging consent. The meeting was over. As I recall, Reynolds did send me one scene, which I thought was all wrong. But it was all beside the point because neither his work nor anything I was then writing for the circus picture was even considered by Hathaway.

The Reynolds matter made me aware there were now two writers on the payroll who were probably earning more than I. The time had come to deal with this. I went to Yordan and said, "I'm due for a new contract."

"All right," he said.

"There's something else. I want a raise to $2,000 a week." I was still earning the same $1,500 from some time back.

"Why the raise?"

"Because I'm the one who's writing practically everything being shot here." I ticked off titles: *Triffids*, *Peking*, *The Thin Red Line* (which was almost ready to go), *Crack in the World* (which looked like it would go). "Even *El Cid*, thanks to the scenes I wrote for Sophia Loren — even *Circus World*, Capra or no. Hathaway or no. I'm the one who did the backbreaking work on it."

Yordan dismissed this argument. "That's only because you get the plum assignments."

"If I get the plum assignments, it's because you think I can get the work done. And I think I do get the work done." I went on to explain that

Jean had found an acceptable apartment for us, but we would have to sign a year's lease. I was unwilling to make that commitment unless I had another contract for a year.

"All right. All right. Go on and sign the lease. I'll give you what you want." But he held off signing anything.

Shooting was about to start for *Circus World* in the Barcelona harbor, where they would film the major production sequence of a shipwreck that set all of the circus animals (and performers) afloat. This, I believed at the time, was all that remained of my original script. Yordan had persuaded Hathaway that it wouldn't hurt to have a writer down there with the crew. My friend Julian had earlier been brought aboard to work as one of Yordan's writers in Madrid. Julian had been chosen to go. He was delighted to be put up at the Ritz Hotel along with Hathaway, Wayne, Rita Hayworth, Claudia Cardinale, and other above-the-line figures. He was on the set every day and even wrote some scenes when Hathaway, too busy as a director, needed a writer for lines of dialogue.

Mostly though, Julian sat around and watched time go by very slowly—an inevitable fate on a movie set. One day he was watching Wayne play a game of chess with one of his buddies. Wayne looked over at Julian and grinned. "Surprised?" he asked. "You didn't think I could read without moving my lips?" Actually, Julian found that Wayne was bright enough. He had made so many films by then, had actually directed *The Alamo* himself, that he knew exactly what was going on or should be going on during a shoot. Wayne was also bright enough to try to enhance his role, and he talked Julian into rewriting a scene.

When Hathaway saw the result of this, he called Julian over and gave him hell. Hathaway was a ferocious old boy. "Nobody tells you what to write," he snarled. "Not Wayne. Not anyone. You write if and when I tell you to, and only then. Understood?" Wayne was amused, refused to take umbrage at Hathaway, and shrugged off Julian's discomfiture. In the evenings after work, Wayne and Julian would walk around Barcelona. One night they ran into a crowd of sailors from an American naval vessel in port. The sailors were all Blacks. When they recognized Wayne, they surrounded him, shook his hand, and hooted with astonishment and pleasure to see this favorite actor strolling the streets of Barcelona. Wayne carried it all off graciously, but when they had gotten free of the sailors, Wayne, the great all-American, shook his head and muttered to Julian, "Niggers. I can't stand them."

The shooting of *Circus World* moved to Madrid and continued in an enormous tent that had been erected in a field on the outskirts of the city.

Much of the cast was gone, but Rita Hayworth was still in residence at the Hilton while final shooting with her on *Circus World* was in progress. By now she was a hopeless alcoholic, worse than Ava Gardner. Ava would drink, get high, and act irresponsibly, but she usually showed up to do her work—until she decided to decamp entirely. Hayworth got falling-down drunk and was unable to function; a constant watch was mounted, but it wasn't always effective.

One night, about three o'clock in the morning, Yordan received a frantic call from the Hilton management. He had to come down to the lobby immediately. He threw on some clothes, went below, and faced a chaotic scene. This is the story as it was finally disclosed: Earlier that night, about midnight, Hayworth decided to go out for some entertainment. She called for her car and chauffeur and was driven to one of the lively *cantinas* where drinking, dancing, music were in full swing. Hayworth came from a Spanish family of entertainers and originally had herself been a dancer. All of this fitted nicely with her mood that night. When the place was to shutter at two A.M., Rita decided the night was still young. She invited all the entertainers, about ten in number, to come with her to the Hilton and continue the music and dancing in the great, circular, downstairs lobby of the hotel. The employees on duty dared not interfere, and no great harm came of this until, about three-thirty, Hayworth decided she was tired and would abandon the troop and go up to bed. The Spanish entertainers demanded to be paid for their time and efforts. Rita had no money, not a peseta on her, and tried to get away. She was forcibly detained.

The frightened night porter called a manager, who appeared and then called Yordan. Fortunately, Yordan always knew how to put his hands on some ready cash. He paid off the entertainers and saw to it that Hayworth got safely to her room. I was saddened that the lovely woman, the perfect beauty who had enchanted so many for so long was now an alcoholic. I reflected that through all the years of glamour and adulation she must have been a victim of so many sexual predators.

With the Christmas holidays almost here, Hayworth's two daughters came to visit. One, Rebecca Welles, the daughter of Orson Welles, was virtually a young lady. The other, Yasmin, was the daughter of Aly Khan, who had been killed in an automobile crash in Paris in the Bois de Boulogne. Yasmin spent most of the year at an exclusive girls' school in New England. Rebecca was old enough to disapprove of her mother's drinking, fought with her about it, and took off after only a few days in Madrid. Yasmin remained but needed activity and companionship. She was exactly Ellen's age and equally avid about horses. The two teamed up, riding together in the park when Ellen arranged for a horse for Yasmin. One of the local newspapers featured a huge, full-page photo of them riding, Ellen on Ayuco and Yasmin on the horse Ellen had borrowed for her. Naturally, the interest was in Yasmin, the daughter of Hayworth and Aly Khan, so the angle of the shot made it appear that Yasmin was virtually riding alone with Ellen almost disappearing in the background. Ellen didn't hold this against Yasmin, and the girl moved in with us and slept in Ellen's room during her stay in Madrid.

Christmas Eve. The Gordons had the only real home, while most of the company lived in hotel rooms or small apartments. We threw a big Christmas party for everyone. My favorite Italian restaurant outdid itself sending up great silvery chafing dishes with splendid food served by a crew of waiters. A friend banged out popular tunes on an old piano in the second living room. It was a boisterous and very successful party. Even Rita Hayworth showed up a bit late to spend part of the evening with her daughter. Santa Claus had little packages for everyone, and we celebrated Christmas in a way that was strange to Spain, where gift-giving was usually reserved for the coming of the Three Kings on January 6. The hardship days were not so far behind us. We could appreciate without taking for granted the good fortune we were now enjoying. To paraphrase the words of another film person: "I've been on the blacklist and I've been off the blacklist and off is better."

When *Circus World* was released, the notices were predictable. The trade press and the local Los Angeles papers praised what they could about the film. The Los Angeles *Citizen News*, despite some reservations, said, "Actions, thrills, laughs and heart pervade the movie. It provides a grand show for the whole family and is directed in the grand Hollywood traditions (even though filmed entirely in Barcelona, Toledo, Vienna, Paris, and Hamburg) by Henry Hathaway."

BoxOffice chimed in with: "Bronston captures the 'feel' of the circus magnificently by using actual backgrounds of European shows . . ."

The national periodicals were more critical. *Newsweek* carped that "John Wayne lately looks more and more like a waxworks dummy of himself." *Time* magazine said, "To sit through the film is something like holding an elephant on your lap for two hours and 15 minutes . . ." but admitted that "gaps in the story line are filled by some delightful European circus acts and other diversions."

All reviews credit the screenplay to Ben Hecht and Julian Halevy and James Grant, and credit the original story to Philip Yordan and Nicholas Ray. I was never involved in any of the studio screenings of the film, nor was I in Spain when it was finally released there. It was long-gone from distribution when I finally got back to the States, so, to this day, I have never seen the film. I always assumed that my original and much revised work had long disappeared. I note at this late date from reading the reviews that my original concepts—1) starting the film with a great shipwreck that loses the acts and animals, and 2) forcing the hero to move all around Europe pulling together all of the best and most spectacular acts—remain at the heart of the story. I believe that I should be entitled to some credit on the film but chalk it up to the times—and hangover—of the blacklist. It's a bit late to concern myself with that.

17

In early 1962, when Yordan was ready to start another film for his own company, Security Pictures, he pulled one of his bargain books off the shelf and handed it to me. *The Thin Red Line*, by James Jones, was a 500-page volume that imagined in realistic and painstaking detail the battle for Guadalcanal, one of the major infantry engagements between the Americans and the Japanese in the Pacific. Despite the great success of a film from an earlier Jones novel, *From Here to Eternity*, Hollywood had passed on this one. Though the book had considerable merit as a work of imagination and as an exhaustive study of men in battle, it had no love story—not a single woman nor any of the typical tough-guy characters people expect in a Hollywood war film. On the surface, it was all about shooting, battling, firestorms, killing. As with the Philippine story, I was tossed into the middle of the war in the Pacific.

At least there was an action framework. The soldiers landed on the island, fought their way through. As usual with Yordan, he had been unwilling to lay out cash for a property that he might or might not ever get to produce, so he made a trick deal with James Jones: no cash down, but payment in the form of all the income from certain territories if and when the film was made and released. In this case, Jones received the money paid for European sales, which turned out to be a mutually beneficial arrangement. I set to work, trying to construct a character conflict between a death-loving sergeant and a life-loving private, a concept I was able to carve out of the book.

As a result of many interruptions, it was more than a year before I turned in a final draft of *The Thin Red Line*. By then my family and I had all moved to Madrid and had signed a lease for an apartment, the kind called *senorial*, whatever that meant. It was vast and beautifully furnished, not quite as high-style as the apartment in Paris, but the Spanish equivalent.

Having completed the script for *The Thin Red Line*, I was assigned to a new project, *Nightrunners of Bengal*, from the novel by John Masters. The director, Richard Fleischer, came in to help prepare a script, or at least a treatment. Fleischer, slight of build, low-key, and very pleasant, was born into the industry. His father, Max Fleischer, had created Betty Boop and other timeless animated shorts, which, next to Disney, were the most successful animated films of their times. But Dick had not just popped into films from on high. He had studied at Brown University, then at Yale, had a Master of Fine Arts degree, had directed some legitimate theater, had become a prolific film director—*Twenty Thousand Leagues under the Sea*, *Compulsion*, and at least twenty other major motion pictures. Recently, though not blacklisted himself, he had been living in Rome and had become friendly with a number of other Hollywood expatriates, including my friend Julian.

When Fleischer was installed at the Hilton, Yordan was eager for quick action on *Nightrunners*. He had me sit with Fleischer and work out a story from the book. Day after day I was closeted with him, talking story. I found it a delight. He was sensitive, knowledgeable, responsive to good ideas. We seemed to be making progress, although the complex action of the book and the interweaving of themes and characters demanded thought, a lot of cutting and restructuring. Fleischer understood what was required, and he and I were really in sync.

I felt things were going so well that I cornered Yordan and asked him for the new written contract he had already agreed upon. He gave in relatively easily and added, "You really hit it off with Fleischer." We finished the preliminary work on *Nightrunners* with an unwieldy mass of notes and called a halt because Fleischer had to go back to Rome, then to Hollywood, and would be gone for several weeks. Just before he left he said he was looking forward to getting back and working with me. Because of my new contract and a great relationship with Fleischer, a director I liked and respected, I felt better about work than ever before. My script on *The Thin Red Line* was about to start shooting. And for egg in my beer, I had persuaded Yordan to send for Julian, make him one of the writing staff.

Julian had just arrived to join the crowd at the Hilton when I told Yordan I would take a couple of weeks off without pay to take a much-needed vacation with the family. I would be back in Madrid in time to hook up with Fleischer again. Jean and Ellen and I flew to Lisbon, where we rented a VW bug and drove down half the length of Portugal to Praia da Rocha on the southern coast. We joined friends from Paris. Vasco Costa was from a prominent Portuguese family, and being "connected" as we were made for a wonderful vacation on a fine beach just around the corner from the open Atlantic. We ate ourselves silly with splendid picnic lunches prepared and delivered by one of the local restaurants and drank the very good local wines.

Never for a moment did I have to wonder what to do the "second day," though I occasionally thought of Yordan and wondered what made a man like that tick. Why the compulsion to be eternally busy? Why the sense that it was sinful to be occupied in anything that wasn't "productive?" How did a man like this make love—was it a chore, an obligation, a necessary function to be performed and gotten through? Was he thinking of the next deal, even then? But I was still under his spell, under the illusion that he was the eminent Oscar-winning screenwriter who knew all the answers, who could do no wrong. It would be a long while before I could conclude, with my half-baked Freudian concepts, that he was bedeviled by insecurities and continually had to run hard just not to lose ground.

After Praia da Rocha, Jean and I drove up to Lisbon and were welcomed there by Vasco's brother, an altogether different type. Ruy was some kind of international financier and promoter, who seized upon my presence in Portugal for a really important project. Together, he and I would do for Portugal what Bronston had done for Spain, create a great and profitable motion picture industry! I could not persuade Ruy that I had no interest in becoming another Bronston nor did I believe I had the promotional skills.

Ruy had a plan. He confided that he had access to a special man, a man of mystery, the *éminence grise* behind Antonio Salazar, the Portuguese dictator, and I could explain everything to him. Ruy warned me that, while the existence of Mr. Lester was an open secret, one did not speak openly about him in Portugal.

To my surprise the day actually arrived when Ruy showed up and told me we were going to meet Mr. Lester. We drove to the lobby of a modest hotel and waited until a man entered and Ruy rose to greet him. Mr. Lester was about sixty, dressed in black, with a flat-brimmed Segoviana hat. His eyes were colorless; his hair, also colorless, fell straight down over his ears; his skin was dead white. An albino. His flat, unrelieved black dress from head to toe accentuated his unforgettable appearance. I never did learn whether this was indeed the man who ran Portugal for Salazar, but he had a quiet air of complete authority.

Ruy introduced me as one of Bronston's major associates and writers. Lester nodded, polite and reserved. Ruy prompted me to explain the Bronston operation and how it could be accomplished again here in Portugal. I tried. I explained the fundamentals of financing that involved using soft local currency for the below-the-line costs of production, all the local labor, costumes, construction for sets, locations, etc., and hard currency costs only for the cast, director, producer, film stock, and foreign labs where necessary. Lester listened without interruption.

I explained that after producing a film thus with controlled dollar costs, the film would be released around the world and bring into the country hard money. Though I truly had no interest in pursuing this, I did feel a responsibility to sound professional and knowing. At the time it struck me as possible that I was talking to the most powerful man I might ever meet. When I concluded, Mr. Lester asked a few questions about how much money would be involved altogether in both hard and soft currency. I tried to explain about the exigencies of budgets depending on scripts. The man seemed to understand what I was saying but gave no indication of whether he was interested. I began to think that Ruy needed Yordan here to do a proper selling job. Finally Mr. Lester rose, shook my hand, and left.

Ruy assured me it had gone very well. I had no idea and could only hope that this was the end of it. If anything more should be heard from Mr. Lester, I was determined to turn it all over to Yordan and Bronston. This was not my cup of tea. No problem. We never heard from Mr. Lester again.

On my return to Madrid, unpleasant surprises awaited.

After my brief absence, I was shocked to learn that with shooting about to begin on *The Thin Red Line*, Yordan had decided to make severe cuts in the script. As I was reminded time and again while working with Yordan, his only real consideration was cost: when a deal was made with a distributor for a pick-up for a fixed number of dollars, Yordan was obligated to deliver ninety minutes of film with the subject, title, and cast agreed on. Beyond that, chances were nil that he would ever see another buck from the distributor, *regardless* of how the contract might read about net profit-sharing. Any effort to make a "better" film was childish nonsense. If he stayed within the budget, he had a built-in producer's profit or fee; if he could bring the film in under budget, that was additional money in his pocket; if he went over the budget, he was throwing away his own money. When disputes arose among us about the need to rewrite and improve the script in terms that cost money, his repeated phrase was: "It won't earn another cent."

This approach to filmmaking, which he had learned the hard way with people like the King brothers, applied to his own productions, not to Bronston, a man he regarded as an egomaniac more interested in his stature as a great filmmaker and heir to the Cecil B. DeMille mantle than in any vulgar pursuit of profit.

An example of the kind of problem that often confronted me: In *The Thin Red Line* I described the initial action of the film after the soldiers came ashore on Guadalcanal. They were weary and frightened, having withstood the shelling of their ship in the harbor, and they were trooping raggedly toward combat positions in the interior. To give some visual reality to their condition, and to help convey their misery, I had them slogging, falling, stumbling through a muddy patch of pathway. Yordan would have none of this. Impatiently, he explained to this neophyte that by writing these few words, the script told the production manager he'd have to prepare more than one set of uniforms for the actors. After they got filthy with mud, they'd have to have clean uniforms for subsequent scenes. What if the scene had to be shot more than once? How much time would be lost waiting for the laundry to return? How much extra would all that cost? Had I thought about that? Mud was out!

I protested that we were shooting a war film, that the reality of combat under the brutal conditions of the South Pacific was a crucial part of the whole and, particularly, for developing the character conflict around which I had devised the entire story. I appealed to the director, expecting support from him. But Andrew "Bondi" Marton would never side with me against Yordan. Marton, a successful second-unit director on major films, and, recently, the man who had filled in for Nick Ray on *Peking*, was eager to become a director in his own right. He was thrilled to have a film like *The Thin Red Line*, and Yordan had seduced him into believing that this was the beginning of a major career change. He refused to back me up on this or any other subsequent dispute. The mud was out.

Somehow, the most painful aspect of this contretemps was the irony that Julian, newly arrived in Madrid, had been assigned the task of making a number of cuts in the script and went ahead as ordered by the boss without consulting me or giving me a chance to be heard. Julian's seemed like the worst betrayal—my lifelong buddy, the man I had worked hard to get here, had just gone along with Yordan. So what if I hadn't been around to talk to? I was in no mood to be fair. At that moment I refused to grant that poor Julian was helpless in a new situation and had simply followed orders like any sensible man. I carped at him about what he'd done to me and what a lousy job he had made with those cuts. Well, no one is perfect, and after sweating out a difficult script for what felt like years, a writer might be excused for an unreasonable defense of his own work. I suppose I still owe Julian an apology.

Much more devastating for me was what happened on *Nightrunners of Bengal*. As Yordan told it, despite the love-feast between me and Dick Fleischer, Fleischer had gone to Hollywood and tried to hire someone else for the job, a big-name writer he had worked with successfully in the past. When that writer was not available, he had gone back to Rome and arranged to hire still another writer who was due to arrive in Madrid at any moment. As it developed, Yordan was not personally involved in any of this. He hadn't hired Fleischer or the writer who was on his way to Spain. This turned out to be strictly a Bronston initiative. But I was out of *Nightrunners*. I never saw or heard from Fleischer again. What remained with me was a painful sense that I had placed foolish trust in a relative stranger and my sense of failure with regard to the work.

Guy Endore was the new writer on *Nightrunners*. He was a successful author of several novels, including *King of Paris*, a well-regarded book based on the lives of Dumas, father and son, which had been chosen as a selection by the Book-of-the-Month Club. I knew him from Hollywood, where he had also worked extensively as a screenwriter before he was blacklisted. He and I had become friendly on Sunday mornings in Los Angeles, when we would both be at the pony-ride park where our young daughters took repeated rides while Guy and I sat on a bench deciding the fate of the world. On his very first night in Madrid he came to dinner with us.

Guy was a slender, wispy man who gave the impression he might float away. His curly, ginger hair and delicate, transparent skin seemed perfect for his gentle, fey personality. He was one of the kindest and most sensitive men I've ever known, and I couldn't hold it against him that he had been hired in my place.

For the next few months, Guy, as well as many others, was a regular at our dinner table. Jean and I were the ones with the proper home, the help, and whatever else was needed to host a home-cooked meal for assorted guests. Guy invariably brought us a large can of mangos. This became a standing joke, and the maids started to call him Señor Mango. Eventually I got to read some of the scenes he was writing, and I thought they were very good.

I have on my shelves a copy of Guy's novel, *King of Paris*, with the inscription: "To Jean and Bernie and Ellen (and the horse—God help me if I forget that beautiful white horse). With love, Guy." The long-ago pony rides were not the only horse connection between us, for, shortly after moving to Madrid, we had been able to buy Ellen a dazzling white horse of the distinct Spanish Arabian breed, sturdier of build than pure Arabians, but with the delicate, tapered head of the true Arab. Named

Ayuco, which we were told meant something like "King of the White Mountain," he was her pride and joy—and ours. Stabled in the main Madrid park, Ellen rode almost every day. She became a very good dressage rider and won many ribbons in the regular competitions held for the horsy set. Guy and all of our other friends frequently accompanied us to the park (when we could steal away from Yordan on a Sunday) to watch Ellen ride or compete, and everyone brought a lump of sugar or a carrot stick for Ayuco.

Buying a fine horse and stabling it was not a great expense in Madrid in those days. In fact the cost of living was so modest that on my substantial earnings, we were able to afford all kinds of luxuries that would have been unthinkable at home. We had two live-in maids and a full-time chauffeur and hired car for Jean. I was content to drive myself in the little Renault to the studio, though I was astonished when Renilde informed me that the Spanish workers at the studio resented the fact that I drove such a stinky car, which was parked there beside Waszynski's Rolls and Bronston's Bentley. They knew I must be making big money—enormous money, by their standards—and were critical of some kind of reverse snobbery, as they saw it. I never quite figured that out and I could not explain to the Spanish that, after the blacklist days, I was not inclined to be profligate with my money.

I regretted it when Guy's project, *Nightrunners*, like so many others, came to nothing. Projects germinated, budded; most withered. Few bloomed. That was not unusual. In fact, it was standard. That's why Jack Warner hated writers. That's why I had spent considerable time in the story department at Paramount, cataloguing and indexing the many hundreds of stories and scripts in their unproduced inventory. Bad as some of the films may have seemed, the stories and scripts for them did not come out of cookie cutters. It took a lot of people saying "yes" to a heavy investment before a script could be turned into a film: producers, directors, actors, executives, advertising people, distributors, and, frequently, the spouse of any one of these. A single "no" usually canceled a project. No one wanted to take the rap for an expensive failure.

A̲t this time, though the blacklist was fading, it was still in effect for most. In Madrid we had five blacklisted writers working for Yordan, and glad of the employment—Arnaud d'Usseau, Endore, Julian, Ben Barzman, and myself.

Late that fall of 1963, activity at the studio was tumultuous and disorganized. The Bronston organization was preparing to shoot its most expensive production yet—*Fall of the Roman Empire*. Yordan was using the Bronston sound stages to produce *The Thin Red Line*. The shooting of *Circus World* continued in an enormous tent that had been erected in a field on the outskirts of Madrid. Guy Endore was quietly plugging away at *Night-runners*, and I was now writing a treatment of Aldous Huxley's science-fiction classic, *Brave New World*.

Another project, *Crack in the World*, was taking shape. Bernie Glasser had flown down from London to take charge. This project had begun many months before when our Welsh friend, Jon Manchip-White, had come to me and said he was in trouble. He still hadn't come up with anything useful on the French Revolution. Nor had I been any help on that turkey. Yordan told him he would be terminated unless he could come up with an idea for a film. He had tried a title on Yordan: *Crack in the World*. Yordan liked it, but asked him to suggest some idea of a story to go with the title. Jon didn't have a clue. He asked me if I could help. Fortunately, I had just read an account in *Time* about an effort to penetrate the earth's crust in the Gulf of Mexico. The project had been named MOHOLE and was an effort to drill down through the mantle, reach the super-hot interior core of the planet, and thus develop an inexhaustible source of energy. I thought this would be a good start for a science-fiction yarn, and, obviously, to go along with the title, *Crack in the World*, the drilling would have to result in a disastrous fracture that threatened to destroy the planet. The details would have to be worked out later. On and off, working with Glasser and Jon, I had been developing the story for *Crack in the World*. After quite a bit of this, Glasser had said to me that he believed I was entitled at least to story credit for this film. Independently, Jon came to me one day and suggested that I share story credit with him. I nodded to both offers. In the end, when the film was completed, no one seemed to remember my contribution. The film went out without any credit for me. I let it go.

In any event, I was busy working on a treatment of *Brave New World* and, of course, considered that a much more important project. In addition, Yordan wanted to insert a scene into *The Thin Red Line* for his wife, Merlyn. This was to be something sexy and provocative to suit her appearance, and it would presumably elevate the war action of the film to a more absorbing and exploitable category.

But what the hell was Merlyn doing on Guadalcanal in the middle of the American invasion against the Japanese? That was easy, according to the ever-fertile imagination of Yordan. It would be done as a sex fantasy of the principal soldier, played by Keir Dullea, when he took time off from battle! If that didn't work, it could be a recollection of another time in his life with a wife or a girlfriend before he was drafted. My protests that this was preposterous were, of course, ignored. Had Yordan promised Merlyn? That was standard operating procedure for him. He had cast a former wife, Cappy, in a film in the old Hollywood days; he would now do the same with Merlyn. I can jump ahead to assure that he would do the same with his next wife. The women, I think, grew bored and discontented. Yordan was always so completely wrapped up in his work that, even though they loved him, they tended to drift away.

I was being well paid to write, not to quarrel with my orders, so I really tried. Version after version was read, considered, tossed. Eventually, at considerable cost, a scene was shot and actually cut into the film. All through the shooting of *The Thin Red Line*, Yordan and I had quarreled bitterly about the very ending. To end the story on a satisfying note, and to resolve the conflict between the sergeant (Jack Warden) and the soldier (Keir Dullea), I had the sergeant mortally wounded in the final battle and the soldier comforting the dying man, for by then the two antagonists had developed a grudging respect and affection for each other. True to his character, the sergeant scoffs at the imminent prospect of his death—it's what he always expected, and he is a man who joined the army, opted out of real life, and has been waiting for this moment. This is the root reason he has always felt contempt for men like our hero, who feared death, who believed living was all. Scornfully, the dying sergeant says, as the soldier is trying to comfort him, "What's the difference?" followed by the big question, "What do you want, anyway?"

How does one answer the question, "What do you want from life?" Dullea stands up, looks at the brilliant sky clear of battle smoke, an affirmation of the possible beauty of the world and of life. He drinks it all in and says, "I want everything." Fade Out.

Many people who read my version of the scene found it moving and congratulated me on it. Yordan insisted it was wrong. It was back to the old "they're cranking up the Fords" philosophy. No dialog. In the end, what we saw was Dullea fixing the sergeant's dogtag between his teeth. No dialog. Fade Out.

The Los Angeles *Herald Examiner* even included a photo of Merlyn as part of their review, but they noted, "Merlyn Yordan, the only woman in the movie, has a brief and meaningless scene with Keir Dullea." *Daily Variety:* "Merlyn Yordan participates in flashback sequence that is rather artificial and irrelevant and could be deleted." Most of the notices were raves (which surprised me), though they had nothing good to say about poor Merlyn's film debut.

The *Citizen-News* of Hollywood said: "Bernard Gordon's script is taut and exciting . . . the movie is one of the most exciting war films to come along in some time."

Daily Variety started its notice with: "Aficionados of action-packed war films will savor the crackling combat-centered approach . . . an explosive melodramatization of the Yank assault on Guadalcanal. . ." Philip Scheuer of the *Los Angeles Times* allowed that "its makers have done a terrific job of condensing, telescoping and pinpointing James Jones' bestseller . . ." And concludes: "Old fashioned warfare? Of course. But it still has the power to stun and shock."

Yordan always insisted that he paid no attention to film reviews, that they made no difference at the box office. I never quite understood or believed this and assumed it was only a sour-grapes reaction to bad notices. I was not above taking some satisfaction in praise, even though I knew that reviewers were frequently far off the mark and generally scratching the backs of the producers and theater owners who paid for the advertising.

Though I quarreled bitterly with Bondi Marton on *The Thin Red Line* and found him a dull and blustering man, I must report, in the interest of truth, a letter that Marton received from James Jones, dated April 22, 1964, in which Jones praises the action in general and goes on to say, "I think the attack on the Bowling Alley where Tella is gut-shot and Welsh goes out to him with the morphine is one of the finest, most moving combat scenes ever filmed . . . I just thought you might like to know how pleased I was with the power of this particular aspect of the film . . ."

Well, James Jones was a real gentleman and even found kind words for me, the writer, when I later met him in Paris.

I don't believe it had anything to do with my failure to write a successful scene for Merlyn, but it came as no surprise to most of us that she was packed into one of the Cadillac limousines with as many personal possessions as she could carry and shipped out for good. I witnessed a tiny slice of the very last scene. She was already in the car pulling away from the Hilton driveway when I arrived and caught a glimpse of the velvet-covered riding helmet perched on the shelf behind the back seat. Merlyn had decided some months before to do as Ellen had been doing and ride horses. She had, of course, acquired all the most expensive accouterments, including a fabulous French saddle from Hermes of Paris. I don't recall that she got up on a horse more than once or twice.

Though no one spoke of witnessing or of hearing about the final event that tore up the marriage, everyone assumed the worst. Yordan, who was in the habit of taking long walks with me in Madrid as he had in Paris, did speak one day of the financial arrangement he'd reached to take care of Merlyn and the son who had been born to them. It seemed quite generous to me.

O n October 11, 1963, *Cry of Battle*, my film about the war in the Philippines, opened at the Victoria Theater on Broadway for a two-week engagement and received a good notice in the *New York Times*. The film did well in release, but as Yordan had predicted, Joe Steinberg never realized another cent above his $100,000 guarantee. This put Joe out of the motion picture production business. Ironically, through an accidental circumstance, *Cry of Battle* achieved a notorious immortality. In Dallas, Texas, on the fateful day Kennedy was assassinated, Lee Harvey Oswald was apprehended by the police in a movie theater that was running the film. Many years later when Oliver Stone was producing his film about the assassination, his production manager reached me and asked for a print of *Cry of Battle* so that Stone's film might accurately play back the original circumstance. I was able to supply the print and a fraction of a minute of *Cry of Battle* became part of Stone's *JFK*.

Now, with *Cry of Battle* and *The Thin Red Line* both in release with my name on the screen as solo script writer, were my blacklist days over?

18

Ｉt was well into 1964 when I picked up Yordan at the Madrid airport on his return from still another trip to New York. He was full of talk about a new production setup involving Cinerama and possibly MGM, where I would be in charge of production, and, best of all, I would have a credit card on the company and could charge everything to business expenses. This sounded fine, but what really got my attention was when he virtually whispered while we were still alone in the car, "Don't breathe a word of it around here, but it looks like Bronston is through. Kaput."

I continued to drive in silence, waiting for more. "He's already blown $10 million on *The Roman Empire*. It's nowhere near finished, and he's out of dough."

I knew that Bronston was also in New York and wondered what he had been doing. "Sam is in New York, trying to raise money, but there's no chance. He's got no more credit because he gave up the DuPont production guarantees. You know about them?"

I nodded. I knew the blank completion guarantees that DuPont had signed were the basis of Bronston's credit. "What happened?"

Yordan went on: "DuPont asked Sam to give them all back to him, all the blank completion guarantees he was sitting on. I told Sam that if he did this, he'd be out of business. But Sam felt deeply indebted to DuPont and insisted on doing the honorable thing and returning them. Now he has no way to raise the money to finish *Empire* . . . or anything else. It means closing up shop. Bankruptcy."

Though it looked as if the entire enterprise would come crashing down, Yordan decided to try one more angle. He consulted a financial wizard he knew, who suggested a possible solution. Paramount was already on the hook for $2.5 million, which they had advanced for the Western hemisphere rights to *The Fall of the Roman Empire*. If the film was never completed because of Bronston's bankruptcy, Paramount was out the $2.5 million. At the time that was serious money for the studio, which didn't have great capitalization. But if Yordan could go to DuPont and persuade him to sign a deficiency guarantee for the picture for $5 million, that could be used to get $5 million more from Paramount, and the studio could depend on DuPont's deficiency guarantee (in case the film did not earn back that money).

For his part, DuPont, who was already deep in the soup, would not be placing an actual debt on his own books, because a deficiency guarantee was only contingent and not an actual accounting expense. This would give DuPont the opportunity to see the film completed with Paramount's $5 million and to have a good chance of getting out clean with the distribution of the finished film.

Even Yordan had a hard time following this. He finally grasped the idea that DuPont would put up a five-million-dollar deficiency guarantee (only a paper transaction that wouldn't show up on his books), that Paramount would advance the actual $5 million to finish the picture, relying on DuPont's guarantee if the film did not earn back the money in the Western hemisphere. Paramount would be in for $7.5 million instead of $2.5 million. But they'd still be at risk for only the lesser amount, because of DuPont's deficiency guarantee if the film didn't earn back the whole $7.5 million. With the film completed, the studio would at least have a chance to get back its entire investment instead of a sure loss of $2.5 mil. Since it seemed painless to both parties, Yordan decided to try.

He made an appointment to meet with Pierre DuPont and his attorney at the company headquarters in Maryland. Once there, he explained the plan to DuPont while they were waiting for the attorney to appear. The attorney came in wearing a shabby shirt without a tie or jacket; his ill-fitting trousers were held up by suspenders. Yordan said that though he may have been a good attorney, the man looked like a real yokel. The attorney listened to Yordan, then retired to another room with DuPont, the heir to the great fortune and the CEO of one of the wealthiest companies in the world. While they were out, Yordan waited with a DuPont brother-in-law, who told Yordan how he had warned DuPont never to get involved with Jews. Yordan kept quiet and didn't bother to inform the man that Bronston had voluntarily let DuPont off the hook. DuPont and the lawyer returned. They liked the deal and would agree to it. They drew up the necessary letter of agreement to show to Paramount.

In New York, while waiting to see the head of Paramount, Barney Balaban, Yordan was able to take care of another chore. He had promised to do a favor for his old friend and sidekick, Sidney Harmon. Sidney, a man of about sixty, had been associated with Yordan for many years. They had met in the 1930s when Sidney became the youngest producer of a Pulitzer Prize–winning play on Broadway, *Men in White*. It was Sidney who'd read Yordan's play *Anna Lucasta*, and, as Sidney told me the story, it was he who offered the play to the director Harry Wagstaff Gribble, who produced it in Harlem. Yordan does not seem to remember any of these circumstances. Sidney was one of Yordan's regular hangers-on, sometimes getting producer's credit on minor films, always reading scripts, and always involved in casting because of his many friends and contacts in the film community.

Sidney had been married to a wealthy woman for many years, but she was now seeking a divorce, offering him a financial settlement. Because of his profound respect for Yordan's negotiating skills, Sidney asked Yordan, who would be passing through New York, to deal with the wife's prestigious law firm and make as favorable a financial deal as possible. Yordan agreed, appeared at the attorney's impressive offices as arranged. He was shown into the conference room, where not one but a half-dozen attorneys sat around the big table waiting for him.

He stopped in the doorway. "There were all these cold, blue-eyed *goyim* waiting for me." He knew what they were thinking and, characteristically, came up with the right one-liner: "As you gentlemen know, I am a snake-oil salesman from Hollywood." Blue eyes or not, they broke into laughter and invited him to sit down. Yordan did negotiate a favorable deal for Sidney, which he was pleased to bring back to Madrid.

In New York Yordan got in to see Barney Balaban, head of Paramount since the late 1930s, but by 1964 getting old and senile. He made it a practice to lock up all the postage stamps at the Paramount headquarters in a safe in his office. (This was before the days of postage machines.) If anyone at Paramount wanted to mail a letter, he or she had to sign a requisition and get the stamp or stamps from Balaban and his safe. That's how Balaban controlled costs at Paramount. It was evening in New York when Yordan got in to see the old man, and time was running out in Madrid. He tried to explain this rather complex deal. Balaban thought it looked okay, but he didn't move without the company's chief attorney, who also happened to be President Lyndon Johnson's personal lawyer. When they tried to reach him, they were told he was at the White House with Johnson. Finally they got through. The attorney agreed to fly up to New York and meet with Balaban and Yordan that very evening. The two men killed time in Balaban's office with small talk. I expect Yordan kept eyeing Balaban's safe and wondering how to get at least one stamp out of it.

When the attorney showed about nine o'clock that night, he listened to the proposal, quickly understood the value of it for the studio, and agreed. All he cared about was the report that DuPont personally had an asset valuation of $470 million. Clearly, with the deficiency guarantee from him, it was risk-free. What neither the attorney nor Yordan understood (and didn't bother to check), and what the DuPonts had sneakily known all along, was that DuPont's money was tied up in a trust, and he only had use of the proceeds, not the principle. Yordan left New York with Paramount's five-million-dollar check made out to Bronston.

He flew directly to Rome, where the company was managing to get in some final hours of shooting with money from the Italian nationality funds. Yordan taxied to the stage at Cinecitta, got in to see Bronston and Waszynski, and handed Bronston the check. Seeing that, Waszynski, the Prince, took Yordan's hand, bowed low and declared that they should erect a statue of Yordan. Bronston came through with a more meaningful reward. He tapped the new funds for a gift of $200,000 to Yordan. And that's how *The Fall of the Roman Empire* did not bring down the Bronston empire—yet.

Ultimately, this deal resulted in a messy series of lawsuits between Paramount and Pierre DuPont, who must have been one of the world's greatest (and richest) idiots. He had, after all, for whatever reasons of ego or fantasies of filmic fame, signed numerous completion guarantees for Bronston in *blank*, which had permitted Bronston to borrow unlimited sums backed by these completion guarantees. Because of the inflated and uncontrolled budgets of the films, they had mostly failed to earn back their costs. DuPont lost millions. He was forced to resign from the management of the DuPont company. Bronston was eventually sued by everyone, with inflated claims of over $30 million against him, though I was told he actually owed only $16 or $17 million.

All of this came months, even years, later. Meanwhile, *The Fall of the Roman Empire* went on to completion in Madrid. I was still under contract to Yordan, who frantically pursued his own agenda while waiting for the Bronston house of cards to collapse.

K eenly aware of Bronston's vulnerability, Yordan had embarked on another independent project: *Battle of the Bulge*. The genesis of the film is a matter of dispute. A young, would-be screenwriter, John Melson, had been hanging around because he was a friend of John Wayne and James Edward Grant. To my knowledge, it was Melson who suggested the *Bulge* idea to Yordan, who agreed to put him to work developing a screenplay on a minimal salary. Yordan, however, recalls it differently. He was in New York, meeting with George Weltner, the man in charge of production at Paramount, and told him he had a film project to propose. He got another appointment for the following day. Yordan had absolutely nothing in mind and now had to come up with something to talk about. He had been cruising the bookshops along Fifth Avenue, as was his custom, reading the spines of the jackets on the shelves. He recalled having spotted one title or idea that appealed to him but couldn't now recall what it was nor where he had seen it. It was getting late, but he frantically retraced his steps until he finally chanced upon the same book jacket and decided that this was the project he would propose to Weltner—*The Battle of the Bulge*.

Yordan was now busier than ever with his own promotions, involving Cinerama and others. He was flying back and forth from Madrid to New York. Since I was busy with my own projects, Yordan asked Sidney Harmon to work on the script with Melson. The chemistry was bad; when Harmon stepped on Melson's toes once too often, Melson came to me in a fury. "I'm quitting." I was sorry about this because, whatever his inexperience and limitations, I liked some of the scenes and characters he was developing. I also felt responsible for keeping the Yordan operation going. I persuaded Melson to stay on and work with me. I promised to keep Harmon out of his hair. That's how we proceeded.

Back in Madrid again from another trip to Hollywood, Yordan surprised Julian and me by arranging to run the recently completed *Fall of the Roman Empire* just for us in the studio screening room. From what we had heard of the film, we didn't regard this with unmitigated delight, but we sat through the entire, endless length of it, alone in the theater, in silence. We emerged, glanced at each other, and we still had nothing to say. Yordan found us and asked us to drive him back to the Hilton. Tense silence. He was waiting for an opinion, but we didn't know how to respond. Finally, intensely angry, he burst out: "So, you guys didn't like it! You're so smart. You know everything! Well, let me tell you, this film has been seen by some of the biggest critics in New York—" he named a couple—"and *they* think it's really great. Really great!"

Weakly I replied that I hoped that was true and I was glad, but Yordan flounced out of the car at the hotel, still provoked. I've often thought about that surprising encounter—it was unlike Yordan. But he had a lot at stake, a whole future with Bronston; he probably needed and wanted some reassurance that the film was all right. Unfortunately, we were right. The film was a dog—an expensive dog—and it ended Bronston and the golden days in Spain. But the studio was still functioning. The offices were there and no one was asking us to leave. Rumors proliferated. People who had never talked to me before came around with tidbits of gossip, looking for others. Knowing I was close to Yordan, they sought me out for signs of the future. I only knew what they knew.

Renilde was still working for me. She was concerned about the prospect of losing her job, a possibility which preoccupied all the Spanish employees still left at the studio. She told me that a nasty kind of anti-Semitism had emerged, the Spaniards complaining that the Jews (all Americans, of course) had been pulling down enormous salaries that had bankrupted the company, and now the Spaniards would be jobless! I suppose I should not have been surprised, but I couldn't help thinking that if Jews and Americans were responsible for anything here, it was the good employment at greater than local salaries that had gone on for years.

In May 1964, though I was still working at an office at the studio, I felt I was the only person there, apart from the guards and the inevitable hallway attendant who answered the needs of whoever worked in an office. Did you want cigarettes, matches, coffee, cognac, lunch? The ever obliging Mañuel was there to help. Six years later, when I was back in Madrid and the furnishings of the bankrupt studio were being auctioned off, Mañuel was still at his little desk outside the office I had once occupied and was delighted, after all this time, to see me again.

Everyone else on Bronston's payroll who could be legally terminated (not easy in the corporate state of Spain) was gone. Everyone on Yordan's payroll was gone too. Except me. I was prepared for Yordan's announcement that the good times were over. My contract had only a few weeks left to run—to the first of July. I was prepared to agree, if he asked, to let him off the hook. Instead, Yordan phoned me from Hollywood, saying he was negotiating a production deal at Warner Bros. He wanted me to rewrite the script for *Battle of the Bulge* from page one.

If not at Paramount, I had expected Yordan to go forward with Cinerama, with whom he had now been flirting for years, but William Forman of Cinerama had turned down *Bulge* as his first production. Yordan hooked up with an old associate, Milton Sperling, who had originally been a screenwriter. He had married the daughter of Harry Warner and had moved over to Warners as a producer, where Yordan worked for him. Sperling had achieved unfortunate notoriety when a Hollywood wit claimed that Sperling had single-handedly set back the son-in-law business many years. When I later came to know Sperling personally, I appreciated the wisdom and aptness of the comment.

On the first of June 1964, I started rewriting *Bulge*. By the fourth, my agenda tells me I'd reached page twelve and was writing the Van Bogen scene and planning the mock-up scene. June 5, "write mock-up scene," and so forth . . . I mention these details because of a subsequent disagreement about credit for the script.

About the middle of June, Yordan finally returned to Madrid. He took a small suite at the Hilton, with a tiny kitchenette, and proceeded to make his own breakfast of coffee and a sweet roll and his own lunch of peanut butter sandwiches. He also shifted his smoking habit from Cuban Monte Cristo cigars at a dollar each to nickel cigars with plastic tips. He claimed that the new smokes were very good. I didn't know what to make of this poor-mouth act. I didn't think he was broke; I assumed the switch was the difference between living at the Hilton, charging it all to Bronston, and paying out his own cash to live there. Maybe it was the kind of irrational insecurity a man feels when, even having socked away more than a couple of million dollars, he's not sure when he will close another deal.

In the ten days remaining on my contract with him, Yordan wanted to squeeze as many pages out of me as possible. I was more than ready to oblige. For me, thanks to Yordan, the trough was not empty. For once Yordan worked beside me in the suite, one of us writing on a desk in the bedroom, the other on a desk in the living room, and Renilde typing away madly between. It was a rare experience for me to work with Yordan as a writer. I found it interesting, even entertaining, that Yordan would turn out a scene and hand it to me for my consideration. Much as I wanted to move forward with the script, I had to shake my head and reject his work. It was certainly a refreshing switch. I do recall, however, that in a single instance, he handed me a scene I liked. I approved it and kept it in the script. I intend no judgment here of Yordan's ability as a writer. I report as scrupulously as possible a personal experience with him at a time when he must have been in turmoil, preoccupied with other urgent matters. He was a man without a wife, without a home (his place in Beverly Hills was on lease), and without a paying project, possibly for the first time in many years.

With time running out, we worked nonstop through the final weekend of June. We reached page ninety. Yordan was satisfied that he had what he needed for Warners. I drove him and the script pages to the airport, where he took off for the States. He said he would be back in three weeks, but I wondered when I would see him again.

At the time of the present writing, I am trying to set straight the record of my proper credits at the Writers Guild, and I have discussed the history of writing *Battle of the Bulge* with Yordan. He recalls absolutely none of the above episode of our working together at the Hilton, or, in fact, of my ever writing a single word of the script. Nor does he recall that after the film was completed and it was time to assign credit, he came to me in Madrid and explained that because of the deal with Warners it was important for writing credit to go to Sperling and himself (as well as to John Melson, who had written the original draft and couldn't readily be excluded). He asked me if I would be good enough to forego a request for credit or any arbitration by the Writers Guild. I didn't think it was important, just another Yordan picture. Perhaps I felt I owed him one, so I agreed.

Now, in July 1964, for the first time since arriving in Europe in 1960, I was altogether free of any employment obligations. Despite his promises, I doubted that Yordan would come back with a job now that Bronston was gone. We had money in the bank, and it was time for Jean and Ellen and I to enjoy some of Europe. First there was a jaunt up to Biarritz and a side trip one morning to watch the running of the bulls at Pamplona. Then Ellen was happy to be shipped off for a summer vacation with her friends in Portugal. Jean and I did Egypt: the Pyramids, the Valley of the Kings, Luxor. Then Athens and a ferry ride for a wonderful week on the island of Crete, with the endless wonders of Knossos and the Aegean Palace of Minos.

One of the most memorable experiences of a lifetime was our visit to the River Styx. We were only dimly acquainted with the Greek myth telling how Cronos, then the big god, consorted with Rhea, his sister, to produce offspring, which he then proceeded to swallow in order to avert his own predicted destruction by one of his progeny. By the time Rhea gave birth to Zeus, she was fed up with the loss of her children and managed to conceal the infant in a cave on Crete. For Zeus, she substituted a stone, which Cronos swallowed. When Zeus grew big enough, he did, in fact, destroy Cronos and became the big cheese himself. Our guidebook told us that the very cave where all this occurred was in the interior of the island. We could visit it and touch base with this ancient myth. Not really believing this, we nonetheless couldn't resist making a try. We had to drive our rented Fiat through the heart of the virtually uninhabited island until we reached a town halfway up in the hills.

The journey was a bit scary. We had no way to communicate with the locals even if we encountered one. We could only hope that the rented Fiat would hold up. We were never sure that we had taken the right turn or had gone too far, but we eventually reached a small village in the hills, where, following directions, we pulled into a cafe and indicated that we were looking for a guide to the cave. Clearly we were not the first foreigners to stumble into the place, for, even without a word of Greek, we were understood, and a young man was produced who could speak some French. With our guide seated beside me, giving directions, we began driving up the mountain. The paved road gave way to an unpaved path. I worried about this and how we would ever get turned around to get back down. After another mile we reached a point where we could drive no farther. We got out and started to walk up the steep, rocky path.

Jean and I were out of breath when the guide pointed to the dark opening in the hillside—we had arrived. All we could see at the entrance was a steep, muddy slide down into darkness. The guide seemed to want us to slip down into this unknown. I was uneasy. Jean was frightened. I suggested she stay behind while I followed the guide into the cave, but she didn't want to miss the experience and agreed to let the guide hold onto her while they made the descent, which, actually, turned out to be only a matter of eight or ten feet. I had to let them go first, then I followed. We found ourselves on a ledge covered with hundreds of small votive figures, vaguely human forms of clay or stone. How long these figures had been gathering there, I don't know, but I couldn't believe they went back to antiquity.

The guide prepared small, boat-shaped floats of newsprint, expertly fixed a wax taper upright in the center of each, and set them one by one on the surface of the dark stream flowing below us. The floats with the lighted tapers drifted with the current, lighting the cavern. This was the River Styx, heading into the depths of the mountain or, presumably, Hades. Fortunately, the guide did not suggest we cross the river, which would obviously have been fatal. It was all impressive and curious, especially the votive figures, which strongly suggested that even in recent times people were paying their respect to the ancient gods. After a few minutes the floats themselves flared up as the flame reached the paper. All light went out, except for the daylight filtering from the entrance above. The guide took hold of Jean again and clambered up and out.

Was it possible that we had visited the actual spot that, in antiquity, had been considered the cradle of Zeus? The *Encyclopedia Britannica* supports that thesis, mentioning that the original cave is said to be located in the interior of the island of Crete. Of the River Styx, the *Britannica* says the location is uncertain. I prefer to accept the opinion of the Cretans whose civilization, after all, predated the Greeks, and even predated the *Encyclopedia Britannica*.

Unfortunately I had no clay with which to prepare a votive figure that might insure that the blacklist was truly past for all of us and that along with my friends I would now be able to go back to work freely as a screenwriter.

19

I was now an unemployed American screenwriter in Spain. What to do to continue my film career and earn a living? Yordan, busy with *Battle of the Bulge* and other promotional schemes, was unlikely to be offering acceptable employment now that the Bronston bags of money were gone. A return to Hollywood and an effort to kick-start a career was not appealing. Finding work in Spain or elsewhere in Europe was difficult and unremunerative at best. Julian and I put our heads together and discussed plans for the future, the work we might do separately or jointly, how we hoped to earn money. We decided to write an original screenplay, a spec script, based on a news story I had seen in *Time* magazine some weeks earlier about the death of the German general and statesman, Paul von Lettow-Vorbeck, who had had a unique and fascinating career during World War I. At the time of that war's outbreak, he'd been a colonel in charge of a ragtag collection of troops, mostly Blacks who had long been pressed into service by the German military in German East Africa. Annoyed at being excluded from the real action in Europe, he had decided against all logic to do his duty to the Fatherland by conducting his own war on the British in Africa.

The latter had considerable troops in adjoining Kenya and in South Africa; they also controlled the seas, so they could send in more troops and matériel at will. Because they could block any assistance to the Germans, it was inconceivable that this colonel could wage a meaningful war, but that is what he did for more than four years, running the British ragged, causing them hundreds of thousands of casualties, even after they poured in major reinforcements from India—troops that otherwise would have fought in Europe. The war he conducted had a kind of military honor appropriate to his Prussian background. When he captured British officers, since he had no place to imprison them, he offered them their freedom if they promised, as officers and gentlemen, that they would never rejoin their troops and fight against him again.

This theater of operations was so isolated that even the few exotic German attempts to send supplies (as by airship across Africa) failed. Even after the Armistice ending the war had been signed in Europe, the German colonel was still on the attack. The British had to persuade him that the war was really over before he agreed to quit. All of this was fascinating, but, in addition, when Lettow-Vorbeck, now a general, went back to Germany after the war, he entered parliament there and in the early 1930s became a principled opponent of the upstart Hitler. The Allies knew this history well. Toward the end of World War II, they tried to enlist him in an assassination plot against Hitler.

The story seemed irresistible film material: two great action characters in conflict, a big action spectacle, and a wonderfully ironic story with many unexpected turns. To give contemporary meaning to this "ancient" history, we thought it would be intriguing to relate how the protracted warfare—using native Blacks as soldiers (on both sides) and training them as fighters and as leaders—would hasten the day when the Blacks would be able to fight for their own freedom and independence.

In early November of 1964, Julian and I drove up from Madrid to Paris on our way to London to do some research and prowl the bookshops for the books and maps that would help us fill in the sketchy information we had. In Paris we ran into some friends who were about to go to James Jones's home on the Ile de Cité for a social evening. I was apprehensive about how I would be received by the famous author of the novel I had butchered. I prepared defensive explanations about the difference between writing a novel and writing a screenplay, but Jones greeted me warmly, said he was satisfied with the film and led me to a small guest bathroom that was shiny new and papered with what looked like tiger skin. He proudly explained that the $25,000 he had received from Yordan had paid for the new bathroom. After that he returned to hosting the bar, downing a drink for every one he enthusiastically served to the many guests.

In London we only needed to set foot in that literary treasure-house, Foyle's bookshop, where, among new books and old, we found an armful of references, plus maps of Africa. We also visited with numerous friends from the old Hollywood days.

Returning from London to Paris, we learned that the annual auto show was on, and the only hotel room we could find was a *very* modest one at an inflated price. The stall shower that was included looked and sounded like a tall tin can sneaked into a corner to substitute for a more appropriate piece of furniture.

One of my missions in Paris was to collect some household goods stored in a basement room of Yordan's home on Boulevard Suchet. Merlyn was now living there, and when I called she was delighted to hear from me. I retrieved my car from the garage and drove to Yordan's where, in the late afternoon, Merlyn was hanging out in a dressing gown. She was still a late riser. She was eager to talk to me. She wanted my opinion about Yordan's settlement with her. Was it fair? Though I might have been tempted to be evasive rather than cross Yordan in such a matter, I was glad to tell her in all honesty that I thought it was.

Only then did she let me go about the chore of lugging odd pieces of furniture, lamps, and bric-a-brac, loading them into the car for the drive back to Madrid. In spite of the season, I had worked up a good sweat over this and, when I was through, I remembered the tin stall shower at the hotel with its pathetic trickle of lukewarm water. I considered asking permission to use the splendid green-tiled tub with the gold faucets of the Suchet bathroom for a clean-up, but I decided one close call with an ex-wife of Yordan in Paris was enough.

For the next months Julian and I alternated between Madrid and Rome, working out the story and a central character conflict between Lettow-Vorbeck and a British officer inspired by Denys Finch Hatton, the hero of the real-life love story of the Baroness von Blixen (later Isak Dinesen), the Danish author of *Out of Africa*. We moved on to the screenplay and eventually decided to call it *The Afrikan General*, with the German or Afrikaaner "K." We liked the title, we liked the script, we felt we had a real winner, something that would sell in Hollywood as well as *The Beach Boys*.

Other events were unfolding in Madrid. Yordan was in town to get *Bulge* underway with his co-producer, Milton Sperling. They had made a deal with Warner Bros. and, for studio offices, had rented some dingy apartments in a building across the street from Madrid's major *fútbol* (soccer) stadium. Yordan arrived back with a new wife, whom I met outside their hotel. Faith, an extremely pretty young woman in her twenties, was carrying in her arms an infant from a previous marriage. All I learned about her was that she had been an airline hostess, that she had come from a large and affectionate working-class family in San Diego.

Yordan had met Faith in a parking garage in Hollywood when his car failed to start and he was due at an important meeting. Hearing him frantically trying to arrange any kind of transportation, she simply offered him a ride. They became acquainted, he made a date to take her to dinner, one thing quickly led to another, and here he was back in Madrid with a ready-made family.

Young as she was, and totally at sea in a strange country with people she had never met, Faith became close to and dependent on Jean—a life-long friendship, even as the marriage became a lifelong marriage. With Yordan and Faith, Sperling and his wife, and the dozen or more members and families of Yordan's regular crew working on *Bulge*, social life in Madrid became lively—especially at our place, where we seemed to host a dinner every night. This was a happy circumstance for Jean, who was not as isolated in Madrid during the many weeks I spent in Rome, alternating with Julian on *The Afrikan General*. In early January we tried our story on Yordan. He said he was interested, and, when he next flew to Paris, he discussed it with the Cinerama people he had been working on for years. We got a big "maybe." Meanwhile, in Madrid, actual production on *Bulge* went forward.

Milton Sperling had considerable experience as a studio producer at Warners; he kept a tight rein on the production. Unlike Yordan, who was flitting around on his promotional chores with Cinerama, Sperling saw to it that the budget money was actually spent on the film and was visible on screen. This paid off in a film that was physically superior to any of the films Yordan had made, and I could only wish that *Triffids* and *Thin Red Line* had had the benefit of such production care.

B y early June 1965, Julian and I felt we had finished the screenplay of *The Afrikan General*. Of course, as Hemingway is alleged to have said, "You never finish a book, you only surrender it." So we surrendered, taking it off to London for a first-class mimeo job. We made last-minute script changes and got in touch with people in London who might be interested in acquiring it or helping us to place it. Our old friend Mary Baker was living in London; in Hollywood, she had sold *The Beach Boys* for us. Sam Jaffe, who had been head of the agency Mary Baker worked for, was now a producer in England. Tony Mann had just completed *The Heroes of Tele-mark* with Richard Harris and Kirk Douglas. Carl Foreman, blacklisted in Hollywood, had producer and writer credits on *The Guns of Navarone* and many other films and was now a power in the English motion picture industry. He welcomed us to his fine offices on Jermyn Street, promised to read our script promptly and get back to us. A couple of days later we took him to lunch at the Ecu de France, one of the really smart restaurants for the film crowd. He was encouraging about the script but was not in a position to use it himself, as his own production schedule was full.

Though we got the usual and predictable noncommittal reactions from some people, we were encouraged by Mary Baker's enthusiasm and by the fact that, thanks to Yordan, we had gotten the script to Irving "Swifty" Lazar in Hollywood, perhaps the most prestigious literary agent in the film community. He had read the script and agreed to handle it. This seemed to auger well for a sure sale. But we weren't waiting.

At the lovely Hampstead Heath home of Sam Wanamaker, another blacklisted actor who had made it big in England, we attended a great, crowded party with much eating and drinking and, it seemed, every black-listed person we knew in Europe. Among them was Bob Roberts, who had produced some of the best—the few—progressive films in the preblack-list days: *Body and Soul, Force of Evil, He Ran All the Way*. Bob greeted us as old friends. We told him we had a new script, and he immediately in-sisted on seeing it, but we weren't ready to give the script out for general circulation. He promised us that no one else would see it without our per-mission and told us that he had excellent connections with Richard Har-ris, who had just finished *Heroes of Telemark* and was eager to find a new project. Would our script have a role for him? Would it! We couldn't think of a better actor to play our Englishman. Bob read the script under the agreed-upon strictures and was enthusiastic. It was perfect for Harris. It would make an ideal vehicle for both Harris and Kirk Douglas, who had just worked together on *Telemark* and who were on the best of terms. He was convinced that we could get these two stars and with them write our own ticket for the script and see a production mounted. He begged us to let him take it to Harris. We agreed. The very next day, Bob called to say that Harris had read the script, loved it, and was agreeable to play either role, the Englishman or the German. We were expected at Harris's home next morning for breakfast.

Julian and I met Roberts at the Harris home, where we were welcomed by the actor and his very pretty wife. We sat with them at a breakfast table laden with eggs, bacon, ham, rolls, cheese, butter, and jam. Best of all, we listened to the actor's enthusiastic talk about our script. How could we proceed? Would we give him a free option? No, we were not prepared to do that. The talk finally got down to the notion that Kirk Douglas should be brought into the mix. If he liked the script as much as Harris did, all were confident that a deal could be cooked up in no time. After all, we un-derstood that stars were the key to raising funds for film production.

So then and there Harris got on the phone and called Kirk Douglas in

Tel Aviv, where he was making a film about an Israeli general. Douglas listened to Harris and agreed to read the script. Just send it on. I objected. I was not going to throw this precious jewel of ours out onto the waters to see if it would sink or float. However, I agreed that if Douglas would read the script, I would immediately hand-carry it to him in Tel Aviv. I was convinced that this kind of personal touch was necessary. I had seen too many scripts mailed here and there and treated like scrap paper. This was more than acceptable to Harris, who told Kirk Douglas to expect me and the script within a few days.

We left the Harris place and found that Roberts was insisting that he would not agree to let Julian or me see Kirk Douglas without him. We finally worked out that Roberts and I would fly to Tel Aviv to see Kirk Douglas. Julian and I would pick up the costs (Roberts was flat broke), and Julian would remain behind in London and wait for word.

In Tel Aviv we stayed at the hotel on the beach where Douglas was staying, but all my efforts to get him on the telephone were fruitless. He was ducking us. Bob, however, made himself comfortable with a bottle of Scotch whisky, which he nipped at continually. I realized that I had an alcoholic on my hands. After a couple of maddening days, I decided, as an old private investigator, that I had to use another approach. It was easy enough to find the number of Douglas's suite; I called, but instead of asking for Kirk Douglas and leaving my name, I simply asked for the room number. Douglas picked up the phone. I was inclined to call him a son-of-a-bitch but couldn't afford that luxury. Instead, I told him who I was and that Richard Harris had talked to him and arranged for us to come to Tel Aviv to see him and offer him our script.

"Oh," he murmured, "I thought it was someone else with a similar name trying to get in touch with me."

Since this was a Saturday, a Sabbath in Israel, there was no shooting on the film, so Douglas finally agreed to see us about five. We went to his suite, script in hand, and tried to make polite small talk for a time. Douglas took the script, looked at the title page, then looked at me, and asked with real irritation, "Aren't you the guys who wrote *The Beach Boys?*" Ignoring his tone, I eagerly nodded, recalling that he had liked that script enough to make an offer to buy it for $35,000. A good move? No. Instantly, he went on the attack. "I tried to buy that script," he complained, "and you guys sold it out from under me to someone else."

I couldn't believe this attitude but tried to stay reasonable. "We sold it to Columbia," I explained. "They paid us more than twice what you offered."

He was not appeased. Alien as it was to me, I suppressed my anger. "Actually," I said, "I'm sorry we didn't sell it to you. Then it would have been made. After Harry Cohn's death, it wasn't."

He shrugged this off irritably and began leafing through the script. Finding something else to quarrel about, he demanded, "How do I know you control this script? You come here and try to suck me in, and I have no idea where else you've been and whether you really own this."

I assured him that we'd only finished writing the script in the past week, that he was one of the very first to see it, and that Julian and I certainly did own it. At this point, my tipsy partner, Bob Roberts, opened his mouth for the first time and shouted at me, "What do you mean you own it? What about me? I get to produce it." All I needed now before the hostile Douglas was a quarrel with Roberts. I assured Roberts that no one was trying to ace him out of the deal. Douglas finally said, "Okay, I'll read it as soon as I can and get back to you."

I wanted him to understand that we were hanging around in Israel to await his word. I didn't want to wait for a few weeks. "Well, we're here only to get the script to you and get your answer," I said. "I hope you can get to it soon." He said he would and dismissed us.

This was my first trip to Israel. The next morning, with no word from Douglas, I decided to see something of the country while waiting for my favorite movie star to get back to us. I made a deal with a taxi driver to give me a one-day tour. Mordecai, an immigrant from North Africa, gave me the tour of a lifetime. He spoke every language one could hear in this polyglot land; he shouted flirtatious remarks at every woman we passed, and, since it was obviously harmless, they seemed to like it. He was driving a big old DeSoto sedan, an outdated model one saw everywhere. Some philanthropist must have bought up a job lot of old DeSotos and donated them to his favorite charity. But it went. We sailed along the hundred kilometers from Tel Aviv to Jerusalem with Mordecai pointing out every feature of interest, especially the burnt-out tanks that littered some sections and had been left in place as monuments to the last war.

In Jerusalem, he quickly steered me to the Holocaust Museum, then to the university, where, in the midst of the splendid Billy Rose sculpture garden, there was a special building displaying the Dead Sea Scrolls. We toured the original wall of the city and the Wailing Wall of the ancient temple, still the holiest site in Jerusalem or, I suppose, anywhere for religious Jews. We stopped long enough for me to take him to the King

David Hotel for lunch. Afterwards it was to the Mandelbaum Gate, which then marked the border between Arab East Jerusalem and Jewish West. While we were there an Arab goat crossed the border and, amidst much hilarity, was captured by the Jewish border guards, who dubbed it a Jewish goat and led it away.

Mordecai wanted to take me to the splendid hospital with the stained glass murals by Chagall. I okayed that, but when he then wanted me to attend a circumcision ceremony in the hospital room reserved for such occasions, I protested that I hadn't come all the way to the Holy Land to see a circumcision, but Mordecai was not to be dissuaded. So we attended the *bris* and watched the parents almost faint at the sight of blood from their new son. Then it became clear what Mordecai had in mind. The buffet table was opened, with all kinds of honey cakes and goodies and plenty of wine and brandy. As guests, invited or not, we were welcome to enjoy the feast in honor of the new boy brought into the Jewish fold.

Later we saw the Church of the Assumption, where Jesus was supposed to be buried (but didn't he rise to Heaven?) and the Via Dolorosa. Under Mordecai's energetic and informed guidance, I didn't miss anything in Jerusalem.

Back at the hotel in Tel Aviv, I paid Mordecai for a wonderful trip and promised him that I would use no other driver whenever I might return to Israel. He proudly gave me his card, which I still have among my souvenirs.

Later that evening came word from Douglas that he had read the script. It was okay, but he was now shooting a film in which he was playing a general, an Israeli general, and he didn't care to go into another film with a similar role. That was that. We returned to London next morning on the El Al flight, which served us kosher food that tasted to me like crow. I suppose it will be clear that after this encounter with Kirk Douglas I am not an admirer of his. I may even be biased. Having admitted that much, I think it is fair to report that I have long been irritated by his insistent trumpeting that he is the one who had the courage to smash the blacklist in Hollywood by giving screen credit to Dalton Trumbo for writing *Spartacus*.

Of course it's true that Trumbo received the credit, and that this could not have occurred without Douglas' consent, but in a recent conversation with Trumbo's widow, Cleo, one of the world's most gracious and honorable people, she offered a different version of the story—her information came from Trumbo himself at the time of the events. Trumbo was working on both *Spartacus* and *Exodus* at the same time. Douglas's company, Bryna Productions, was producing *Spartacus*; Universal Pictures was financing it. When Trumbo pressed Douglas for a commitment to award him screen credit, Douglas stalled and hedged, explaining that he would have to deal with Universal on that question and could not promise anything. Only after Otto Preminger, producer and director of *Exodus,* announced publicly that Trumbo would receive screen credit for *Exodus* did Douglas come forward and announce that Trumbo would be credited as the writer of *Spartacus.* Both films came out at virtually the same time, so the question of "first" is moot, but knowing that Preminger was a courageous and very independent producer, I think it unfair to forget him in this matter. And after my own experience with Kirk Douglas, I prefer to believe Dalton Trumbo's version of what happened.

In any event, after Trumbo's success in busting the blacklist—and my own experience—one wondered if the blacklist and its effects were over. For most of us, almost all of us, it wasn't. For ten years we had been forced to work, if we worked at all, using fronts or pseudonyms. We had been out of the circuit so far as filmmaking in Hollywood went. In my case, the best scripts, like *Triffids,* did not bear my name. A big credit for *Peking* bore Yordan's name above my own. What would I be able to offer potential employers in Hollywood? What did any of this mean after so many years of being totally out of touch? Contacts meant everything. Writers were hired because producers knew them, had worked with them, and trusted them to deliver. My only "live" contact now was Yordan, and it wasn't that clear to me how "live" he actually was. In effect, the blacklist was never over—not for me nor for any of the others.

In London Julian and I packed up our bundles of freshly printed scripts and returned home—he to Rome, I to Madrid. We had had enough positive reactions to the script to believe that we would, one place or another, make a good sale, and that matter would be left in the competent hands of Irving Lazar, who assured us from Hollywood that he was working on it. Hope springs.

20

After returning to Madrid from my ill-fated meeting with Kirk Douglas in Tel Aviv, I found that Yordan was around and hustling harder than ever. With Bronston now gone, Yordan's years of flirtation with Cinerama might be paying off.

But to go back to the beginning: When I had first started working in Paris with Yordan, my offices were in the building occupied by Gray Films, Louis Dollivet's film distribution company. Dollivet was tall, strongly built, about fifty; he had thick, dark hair, a prominent Frankenstein brow, piercing eyes, and a bearing that could easily be viewed as alarming, but around me he was the soul of warmth and friendliness. He had come initially from some Balkan country and looked as though he should be sporting a great moustache and carrying a Kalashnikov rifle over his shoulder. Dollivet was a man of mystery. He had been a Stalinist commissar in Spain during the civil war, but when that enterprise ended in disaster, he had managed an astonishing shift of gears and made it to America, where he married the heiress to the Whitney fortune. Like the Spanish Civil War, this marriage also ended tragically, when one of their daughters drowned in a swimming pool. Dollivet regrouped in France, seeing his future in the film industry.

He attached himself to a promoter named Reizini, who was the chief stockholder and CEO of the Cinerama company. Cinerama had come on the scene with great fanfare as a completely new film experience. A film was shot with three separate but synchronized cameras, then projected in a specially equipped theater with three synchronized projectors so that the audience would feel almost completely surrounded by the motion picture image. Though it was a clumsy system, that didn't concern the promoters, who saw it as a way to entice large audiences, at advanced prices, into theaters to be built in capital cities around the world. In fact, several films for this style Cinerama had been produced and had been exhibited with considerable success.

By all accounts, Reizini's greatest talent was his keen perception of his own interests. He had persuaded MGM, already in the process of disorderly transition, to advance $15 million for a Cinerama version of *How the West Was Won.* The film had been exhibited by Cinerama successfully, but Reizini never bothered to turn over any of the receipts to MGM, which was still on the hook for the $15 million. Dollivet saw an opportunity. Since there were others who lusted to own and control Cinerama, Dollivet would bring the right people together, pay off Reizini, and wind up controlling Cinerama himself. The instrument for this scheme was William Forman, the owner of almost all the drive-in theaters in the western United States. Forman wanted Cinerama. Despite his great wealth in real estate from the drive-ins, he didn't have the cash to become a player. Moreover, Forman couldn't borrow on his collateral because he had served time for a felony rap some years before, and the banks wouldn't deal with him. Enter Dollivet and Yordan.

Yordan had a clean company, so far as the banks were concerned, and a clean personal reputation. Yordan's company, Security Pictures, Inc., had been used as a vehicle to produce various films like the United Artists pictures *Studs Lonigan, God's Little Acre,* and *The Big Combo.* Money for these had been borrowed from banks against the distributor's "pick-up," and they had always been promptly and properly repaid. In other words, Yordan had credit. He also had a Hollywood record that looked good to the bank. But he didn't have nearly enough credit to borrow the $28 million Forman needed to take over Cinerama. When Forman agreed to back the loan with his real estate as collateral, everything became possible—especially since Dollivet had a tight relationship with the principal loan officer at the Bank of Boston, Serge Semenenko. The bank's money and Yordan's were both guaranteed.

Semenenko was highly esteemed at the bank for never making a bad loan. According to Yordan, the reason for this was that when a loan in his portfolio turned sour, Semenenko cured it when he worked on his next loan. He would simply tell the next hungry borrower that if he wanted a loan for, say, $10 million, he would have to agree to receive only $8 million of the $10 million, because the other $2 million had to be applied to repaying the default of $2 million on Semenenko's earlier loan. This sounds like a Ponzi scheme, but I'm told it worked. Semenenko loved to live high. His hotel rooms were always first-class and always stocked with the best liquor and wine. He was not above accepting substantial gifts, and, when Yordan became deeply involved in the deal, one of his obligations was to arrange a gift to Semenenko of a chalet in Acapulco, which, as he now recalls, only cost about $35,000 in those days.

At the time all I knew was that Yordan was "in meetings," which sometimes lasted all night, in hotel rooms heavy with Cuban cigar smoke (Semenenko, Dollivet, and Yordan), and pipe smoke (Forman). He was frequently away from Paris, inhaling cigar smoke in hotel rooms in Cannes, New York, and Hollywood. He went along with these plans because he wasn't risking any of his own money, and he saw himself becoming a real insider with Cinerama, a stockholder and the man in charge of all production. For example, I had suggested a film I called *Men of Courage*, worked on the script, and supervised other writers doing this. It seemed right for Cinerama. I expect Yordan used it as a bargaining chip when dealing with the Cinerama people, who cared little about annoyances like scripts but who realized at some level that films would eventually have to be made to fill the Cinerama screens that they envisioned in dozens of cities around the world.

All of this illustrates the kind of complicated ambitions that moved Yordan, even when he was trying to fulfill his obligations to Bronston. His telephone rang incessantly with calls from New York, Los Angeles, Madrid, London, and Rome. Some of the calls were about Bronston matters; some were from Nick Ray; some had to do with *Triffids*. Most, however, were about the endless complications of the Cinerama scheme. I had an inkling of this one day when I was sitting with Yordan in the foyer of his apartment—a chamber he used as his office. The phone rang. He answered, then turned to me and asked if I would please leave the room until he was finished. When he called me back, he explained. "It isn't that I have any secrets from you. It's just easier for me to lie when you aren't sitting there, staring at me."

I asked him if he could sleep nights with all these pressures on him.

"I sleep fine when I'm having trouble," he said. "I can't sleep when everything is going great. Then I lie awake figuring out how to make the most of it."

Back in Madrid in July 1965, after all the years with Bronston and my own efforts with *The Afrikan General* and after my encounter with Kirk Douglas, Yordan was waiting for me in Madrid. On my first day back he came to our apartment and talked about a new deal that would pay me a $100,000 per script, plus fifteen percent ownership. I listened to his blandishments without comment, inserting questions from time to time about how much money I would receive up front for the work. About this, Yordan avoided a commitment.

Yordan's new project involved Forman, now in control of Cinerama, who had decided he wanted his first film for that company to be about Krakatoa, the most violent known volcanic eruption in history, which had occurred in 1883. Forman was waiting for a story outline or treatment; only when he had that would he okay a budget and provide funds for the start of production. He was insisting on a film ready for exhibition by July 4, 1966. Yordan and Sidney Harmon had been trying to put together a story line, but they needed help.

Initially, my reaction was negative. "How do you build a story around a volcanic explosion? There's no warning or build-up to the climactic event, so how can there be any personal story or drama about something that happens unexpectedly and instantly?"

Yordan didn't want to listen. He shook his head impatiently, but I continued. "It's something beyond human control, and can't be anticipated. Unexpected destruction and disaster. Who wants to see a film about that?"

Yordan was not interested in my clinical story considerations. "Bernie, I can get $4 million to make a picture. I'll come up with $25,000 for you if you write a short treatment that Forman will approve."

This got my attention.

"But I need it right away. Like tomorrow. Just do it."

With this incentive, I read up on the disaster from the meager material Yordan and Harmon had collected about the historic event. I was surprised to learn that the giant tidal wave after the eruption had caused most of the destruction and loss of life. I began thinking about building a story around a shipload of characters, from the captain down to the lowest steerage passengers, who would survive the violence of the tsunami. We could people the ship with good guys, bad guys, bandits, smugglers, scientists, deep-sea divers—anyone! I went to work.

Pressured by Yordan, I turned out thirty pages of crude story in less than a week. Greedily, Yordan read it as always—with the pages an inch or two from his eyes, and a grin on his face that I'd learned meant only that he was concentrating. Before he even looked away, he nodded happily. "Great. Just what I need." Then he paid me a dubious compliment. "Bernie, you're the best one I know at faking this kind of crap." Treatment in hand, he headed for California and Bill Forman.

While I waited to find out how real this picture might be, I called Julian in Rome to tell him that Swifty Lazar had no news yet about *Afrikan General.* Julian reported that a man in London connected with

Peter O'Toole had given the script to O'Toole, who had read it and was interested.

Thus began the thirty-year saga with *Afrikan General.* O'Toole took an option for $10,000, and a few years later we sold another option for the same figure, and these led to serious interest and a chain of *almost* deals. But the script was never actually sold. Ridiculous as it seems, there is interest in the project to this day, but for some reason I am beginning to lose faith. *Afrikan General* is only one of a number of scripts I consider among the best I have ever written—the only really good ones, in fact—all scripts that have never seen the flickering light of a film screen. Most of my screenwriter friends tell the same melancholy story. If we are right that these unmade scripts represent our best work, a lesson lies buried here. The truth about the nature of filmmaking was something I would learn much about in the next years.

Battle of the Bulge had finished shooting. In the middle of August, Yordan asked me to sit in at the rough-cut screening, where I offered some suggestions for changes. The cut was screened for Warners a few days later, and Yordan called me from Hollywood to tell me that Warners was "thrilled" with it, that they were now discussing a multi-picture deal for a series of projects like *Camelot, Krakatoa, Paris 1900,* and others. I felt I might be busy making films for the rest of my life.

I was too absorbed in *Krakatoa* to think that far ahead. I still hadn't been paid, as promised, for the treatment, and I was still not on salary, but I decided to go along with Yordan and work on the script. He kept flying back and forth to Paris (to see Dollivet), and New York (to see Forman), to Hollywood with Sperling (to see Warner Bros.), carrying whatever new script pages I had ground out. Each time he got back, he would assure me that *Krakatoa* was going forward. But there was still no money to pay me.

Of course, when working on a project that was totally alien to me, one that had no existing story material, characters, or plot (*Peking* or *Circus*), I struggled to write a script. This one was even more difficult because I had to design material suitable for Cinerama and to consider reality problems like cost. Despite my misgivings, I had nothing but encouragement and support from Yordan, who only wanted to see pages turned out and who probably was convinced that neither Dollivet nor Forman could read scripts. Maybe he hoped they wouldn't bother to read, just heft the bundle of pages, look at the number on the last page, and say go.

By the end of September, with about half of a screenplay written, I felt worn out and ready to quit. Working up major special effects concepts, then tacking on personal stories seemed like more trouble than it was worth. With impeccable timing, Yordan came through with the $25,000 and put me back on salary. Cinerama had delivered on the money. The cash infusion reinvigorated my creative faculties, but before I had anything like a finished first draft, a dramatic shift of interest took place. With his fine sense of the possible, Yordan realized that a viable script would not be ready in time, so to keep the project alive, he decided to use my rough-draft script pages to go ahead and shoot exciting special effects anyway. This footage of ships in the maelstrom during the eruption, without any characters whatever, could then be cut together for a presentation reel, shown to various production or distribution companies to induce them to invest in the film. It was perfectly clear to Yordan, if not to me, that they would be buying effects, not story.

Work on this loony idea actually began. Les Sansom and Eugene Lourie, the art director, were sent to Cinecitta in Rome, where they used an existing tank and that entire facility for a paltry $85 a day. Working with a couple of fine miniature ships built in Spain, also for peanuts, they put my flagship, the *Batavia Queen*, into the fray and produced thirty minutes of a really splendid series of violent storms and volcanic effects for only $300,000.

The mandarins now decided to go for outside financing, realizing that special effects would be costly *and* time-consuming. Since it was now understood that *Krakatoa* could not conceivably be completed by the time Forman had to have a finished film in his theaters, he decided that the film he wanted to make, one that could be finished in time, was about our famed (or notorious) General George Armstrong Custer.

We were walking along Madrid's broad main drag when Yordan broke the news to me. "We're going to have to put *Krakatoa* on the back burner and do a script about Custer."

My most negative characteristics erupted. "Custer? My God. All I know about him is that he was an Indian killer, and the Indians finally killed *him* at Little Big Horn!"

Yordan shrugged.

"Who in this day and age would want to make a film hero out of someone who did his best to butcher Indians?"

"I don't give a damn about Custer, or the Indians. All I know is that Forman is paying us to do a film about Custer."

We walked in silence as I tried to digest all this. "Fine," I finally countered. "Let's do a film about Custer, a really modern film that tells the truth about him and the whole American policy at the time."

Yordan was annoyed. He turned on me. "It's people like you with your antihero ideas who are ruining Hollywood! We'll just figure a way to turn Custer into a hero!"

As far as Yordan was concerned, I still didn't get it. I still had the naive notion that I was in the business of trying to make good films. I didn't understand what Yordan understood so well—we were in the business of business, and the business of business was to make money. The first thing a businessman had to do was find the capital to stay in business. "Good" films were films for which you could raise production money. "Good" films were films that made money. Films that didn't make money were bad films. Despite what I had gone through, and what I'd continue to go through for quite a while, it took years for me to learn that bankers, lawyers, accountants, theater owners (meaning real estate owners), and Wall Street investors were the people who really decided what films and what kind of films were made. Even when I finally understood this, I found it problematic that this was particularly true of Hollywood; France, Italy, England, Germany, even tiny Denmark and troubled Poland occasionally made what I considered a "good" film. Why not Hollywood? Regardless of my thinking and feeling, I too was interested in the money aspects of all this. As much as Yordan, I wanted the money to keep rolling in. I settled down to struggle with another killer script about George Armstrong Custer.

In February of 1966, with what I believed was a half-finished script of *Krakatoa* and a treatment of *Custer*, my energy and drive were about gone. Again, with good timing, Yordan announced he was taking me on a trip to the States. I never did understand why Yordan wanted to drag me along on this trip. Forman and Cinerama were paying for it, so there were various possibilities: 1) he just wanted company (possible); 2) he knew I was worn out and ready to quit so a break in the routine would help (maybe); 3) he wanted a living, breathing specimen to display to Forman to prove he was actually paying a writer (not unlikely); 4) he wanted to keep me hacking away at numerous ideas he could present as possible projects (not unlike him); 5) with me around, he would never have to spend a day or even an "unproductive" hour alone (sounds right); 6) he hoped I would impress Forman with my talent and dedication so that Forman would keep shelling out production money (least likely). Forman was tight with a buck and whatever might help was worth a try.

America seemed impressive from the moment I arrived at Kennedy

Airport, where we took a helicopter into the city and landed atop the PanAm building above Grand Central Station. My first ride in a helicopter. We put up at the two-bedroom suite Forman maintained at the Navarro Hotel on 59th Street, overlooking Central Park. I felt, even more than in Madrid, that I had lived up to my Hollywood hopes, when, all those years ago, I had paid $16 for a share-the-ride to California.

Yordan and I had one moment of disagreement. As we were riding up in the hotel elevator one day, he mentioned that he was taller than I was. "You're not taller," I grumbled. "You just think you're bigger than anyone else." He *insisted* he was taller. We decided to settle the matter and stood back-to-back as close together as possible so we could measure any difference in height with a hand at the top of our heads. We were standing like this, totally absorbed in this momentous question, when the elevator doors opened. An astonished woman, another guest at the hotel, stared at us. Feeling foolish, we grinned weakly and separated. We never decided who was taller.

Though I tapped out a few story ideas on a typewriter we found in the suite, I did little work there. I met with relatives and friends, and even hopped down to Philadelphia to see my father and his wife. After a week of this, Forman showed up and moved into his suite; I moved to another room on another floor. Yordan and Forman put their heads together, concocting their promotional schemes. After a few days we all flew to Los Angeles. Yordan arranged for me to be seated beside Forman in the first-class section. I tried to talk constructively about what I was planning on the Custer script, but Forman was preoccupied with another problem. He complained bitterly about a passenger in first class who had brought his small dog along. The dog wasn't bothering anyone, but Forman insisted that dogs did not belong in the passenger cabin.

After an absence of almost five years, my return to Los Angeles was something like a triumph. Yordan and I stayed at a good hotel on Wilshire Boulevard in Beverly Hills. I visited friends I hadn't seen in all this time and was welcomed in my status as a successful expatriate writer. I managed to forget for a few days that I had to face insoluble problems on *Custer* and *Krakatoa*.

On the return flight Yordan gave me good news.

"I'm going to bring Julian back to Madrid to work with you on the two scripts."

This was more than a relief for me. It was like a breath of new life. As he went on, I realized there was good financial reason for this. He had money to spend. "ABC," he said, referring to the American Broadcasting Company, "is going into film production and they've signed to put $2.5 million into *Krakatoa* and $2.5 million into *Custer*." This was what Yordan and Forman had been busy putting together on this trip. We were on a roll.

Back in Madrid, Julian and I bore down on the *Custer* story problems, but, even together and even with Yordan's input, we made little progress. Despite this, Yordan invited us for dinner at one of Madrid's best seafood restaurants to meet Robert Siodmak. He had been brought over from his home in Switzerland to be considered for the job of directing *Custer*. Yordan wanted us to talk over the project with Siodmak and offer some judgment on Siodmak's suitability for the job. Over the fine fish and seafood we met Siodmak, who looked every bit of his seventy years. Short and rotund, perhaps the remnant of a strongly built figure, he was bald, and what hair remained on the fringe was white. Siodmak had a long and distinguished directing career, beginning with UFA in 1929, where he had directed Emil Jannings; in Europe he had worked with stars like Charles Boyer and Danielle Darrieux. He had directed many films in Hollywood, including *The Spiral Staircase*, *Dark Mirror*, and dozens of others. He had been out of the circuit for years, living in involuntary retirement in Switzerland. He was eager to do another film.

After a dinner of small talk, we went to Siodmak's hotel room. For reasons known only to himself, Yordan quietly urged me to carry the ball and question Siodmak about his ideas for the film. Julian and I had only managed to produce a thirty-page treatment for *Custer*. We weren't satisfied with it, and we were looking for ideas to help develop a three-act story structure. Since he had read the material, had time to think about it, and had agreed to do the job, I assumed the director would have opinions and suggestions. I've seldom met a director who didn't think he could tell the writer how to write.

Yordan didn't jump into the discussion. I was left with the job of prodding Siodmak.

"We were wondering what ideas you have for the script."

Siodmak just shrugged.

"You know it isn't easy to make a hero out of Custer. He didn't do much except kill a lot of Indians and wind up getting killed himself."

Siodmak nodded. He glanced over at Yordan and was clearly aware that Yordan was not joining in the quiz.

I tried to go on. "We need a dramatic structure, a beginning, middle, and end. We know how it has to end with him and his whole troupe massacred by the Indians. But that's not the same as having a good ending for a film, some kind of payoff for the character."

"I agree," was all I got out of Siodmak.

"We were hoping you might come up with something."

Siodmak was an experienced and wily old boy. He probably understood what was going on better than I. He turned the discussion into an attack on me. "You're asking me for answers? You've been working on this for how many weeks? And what have you got to show?" He waved the pages of the treatment at me. "After two days, you want me to come up with answers!"

Before I could respond to the attack and tell him that if he wanted to direct the damned picture, he should have some notion of the story he wanted to tell, Yordan broke it up. He had heard enough.

"Okay, Robert," he said, standing up. "Get yourself a night's sleep. We'll talk again in the morning."

He ushered Julian and me out. In the elevator on the way down, I expressed my annoyance. "The man is useless. He hasn't an idea in his head. You want my opinion? Don't even consider him."

"I'm hiring him."

I was really astonished. "Why?"

Yordan gave me my next lesson in the *Realpolitik* of filmmaking. "We need a star or we have no deal. We have no script to show to a star, so what do I do? I go to Robert Shaw and ask him to do the picture. He wants to be helpful. But without a script, how can he agree? I tell him I'll get him a good director. He agrees that he'll sign on if I get an experienced director. How do I get a respectable director to take the job? I still have no script. I find out Siodmak is hungry. He has an impressive track record, but he's out of work in Switzerland. The phone isn't ringing. He's dying to do another picture and pick up another fee. So I get Siodmak and I've got Shaw—and I get the four million bucks to make a picture."

I swallowed hard and didn't bother to ask Yordan why we had gone through the whole charade. These were answers I had to figure out for myself. Even if I am a slow learner.

The final twist on all this Yordan didn't bother to mention until years later. Siodmak came cheap. He was paid only $100,000, probably a third of what any established director would have been paid for a four-million-dollar epic.

Siodmak showed up for work even though we only had half a script for him to start shooting. So did Robert Shaw and his wife, the actress Mary Ure, who was to play Custer's wife in the film. Julian and I slaved away on the script, trying to keep one scene ahead of the shooting. Siodmak and I never became friends. I never liked anything he shot; he never liked anything I wrote. He even persuaded Yordan to bring an old colleague of his, a writer, down from Paris, but weeks of effort from that writer did not produce a single scene.

Yordan was busy thinking of important things like how to shift another $100,000 from the film budget to his construction operation: Yordan liked to function out of his home, or as close to it as possible; therefore, his dream project at this time was building a studio headquarters on an entire floor downstairs from his own top-floor apartment in a new high-rise building. I presumed he had already managed to use production money to purchase and decorate his own quarters.

Because of unresolved script problems, the *Custer* shoot was an unending agony all through that hot Madrid summer of 1966. Ellen graduated from the American School of Madrid and was accepted as a student at the Davis campus of the University of California. She thought she wanted to be a veterinarian because of her interest in horses and animals in general. We were pleased the school had accepted her, but Ellen was unhappy about leaving for America and living so far from us and the places she had come to know as home. She also had to sell Ayuco, the white Arab horse she loved so much—a real trauma. Fortunately, Faith Yordan, who was already pregnant, decided, like an earlier Yordan wife, that if we could have a horse, then so could she; she admired Ayuco and decided that Yordan should buy him for her. Inexplicably, Jean thought Ellen would be consoled if we acquired another animal to replace the horse. She and Ellen went shopping and I learned we now had an Irish Setter puppy that would live with us in Madrid, not with Ellen in Davis, California. But the act was done.

The puppy had to be given a name. After the usual struggle to come up with exactly the right one, I suggested that we call her Chica, since she was such a pretty little female—*chica* means "girl" in Spanish. Jean and Ellen agreed. Chica she was, and she seemed happy enough with her name, but after a while we realized that the maid, housekeeper, and chauffeur were all calling her something unintelligible that sounded like "Chuspi." I finally asked our wonderful housekeeper, Maruja, what "Chuspi" meant. She looked at me, astonished, and said, in Spanish, "That's an English word." English? I was stumped. Maruja finally managed to convey that I used that word when I would come into the kitchen and say, "Excuse me, but could you make us a pot of tea . . . or coffee?" So "excuse me" was "chuspi" to them, the one English word they had learned. They preferred that to Chica, because I had insensitively named the dog by a term used for women of almost any age who work in the household, just as the word "girl" is or was used in our country to refer to such workers. Chica became Chuspi until we returned to America with her.

Jean took Ellen for a final tour of Europe on their way back to the States, where Ellen would be installed at school. It was high summer by now, and I was left at home to work, run the household, and train the puppy.

Another personal drama was playing out at the studio. Alfred Brown was an American in his forties who years before had emigrated to Europe and settled in Spain with an Italian wife. They had two young sons and struggled to survive under difficult circumstances. Yordan used him as a gofer and found him useful because Alfred had a better command of Spanish than any of us, and Alfred had attached himself to Yordan even more insistently than the Irish Setter attached itself to me.

Alfred suffered from bleeding ulcers that were a threat to his life. The midsummer heat that year in Madrid was stifling. One night as we were all working in the close quarters of the apartment, our "studio," the film editor complained to Yordan that it was unbearable to work under these conditions without an air conditioner. Without a moment's hesitation Yordan said, "There's an air conditioner in Alfred's room. Take it." I couldn't believe my ears.

"That air conditioner is the only thing keeping Alfred alive," I objected.

The British film editor was a decent sort; Alfred's air conditioner was saved for the moment.

His brother, according to Alfred, was a distinguished physician in Boston.

"Why don't you take off for Boston and have your brother take care of you?" I asked him one day.

"I couldn't afford that," he replied.

I spoke to Julian, Les Sansom, and Gene Lourie, all of us earning good money, and suggested that we each put up $1,000 and give the $4,000 to Alfred for a trip to Boston. They agreed with no hesitation. With the money in hand I went to Alfred and told him to take it and leave for Boston.

He shook his head. "I can't do that."

"Why not?"

"I can't leave Phil now in the middle of a production." Evidently Alfred could not accept the reality of his insignificant position.

"But you have bleeding ulcers. They can kill you."

"I wouldn't leave Phil now," he insisted. He wouldn't budge. I returned the money I had collected.

A week later Alfred Brown dropped dead on the street. The funeral was scheduled for the next day.

"Do we go to the funeral?" Julian asked me, wondering what to expect.

"Of course." I was sure all of us who had worked with him would be there.

Julian and I and all our fellow workers showed up at work in respectful suits, jackets, white shirts, and ties. Yordan showed up in especially grungy wash trousers and a shirt suitable only for the torrid weather. It was painfully clear that Yordan was not going to the funeral. Julian tossed a worried look at Yordan. "What do you think?" he asked me. He was concerned about taking off from work.

"I don't care what he does," I answered. Later I confronted Yordan. "Aren't you going to the funeral?"

Decisively, even angrily, he replied, "The only funeral I'm going to is my own."

Afterwards, at the offices, the buzz was about Yordan. How could he fail to pay final respects to Alfred, who had been so attached to him? I thought I understood. "Yordan is first and last a deal maker," I supplied my own explanation. "He's convinced he can make a deal to handle any trouble he gets into. Maybe he realizes there's one final deal he won't be able to make. Even he can't swing that one, and he hates to look that in the face."

The coda came a few weeks later. Julian, Les Sansom, Gene Lourie, and I were in Yordan's office discussing script problems when Yordan suddenly asked Les about the installation of air conditioners in the new offices that were being prepared in the high-rise up the street. Les shrugged and said he didn't know anything about that—Alfred had dealt with the workmen in Spanish.

Yordan squinted, puzzled. "Alfred? Alfred who?"

We got out of that meeting as quickly as possible and collapsed into chairs in Les's office. Julian looked around, squinting, then stared at me, and, mimicking Yordan's voice and manner, said, "Bernie? Bernie who?" We laughed immoderately; the joke was on all of us, the faithful retainers. Julian had summed it up perfectly.

Production stumbled along on *Custer* as Julian and I tried to give the Indians a fair shake. Robert Shaw was helpful. A bright man and a fine writer, he approved of our point of view that the Indians were victims right to the end. He even wrote one speech for Custer, his character, that made this point sharply. Yordan didn't care about any of this one way or another.

His focus was getting the picture shot and finished with as little cost as possible. He constantly bled money from the budget to invest in the new studio offices. In one scene Custer addresses the Congress of the United States, a historically accurate event and one the film needed for story progression. It was inconceivable that we should build a replica of the real chamber and people it with the dozens of representatives and senators in period dress. Yordan solved the problem economically by having Shaw, as Custer, pose in front of a painting of the crowded congressional chamber. I thought it looked fake but few other people noticed or cared.

On another occasion we needed Custer traveling west on a period paddle-wheel riverboat down the Ohio River to the Mississippi and St. Louis, then getting off the boat at a wharf. Another expensive nuisance. Yordan understood that a few scenes like this were necessary for the overall look of the production. Instead of trying to eliminate them, he turned to the special-effects crew and had them build a miniature paddle-wheel steamer that traveled in a tank. Shots of this were intercut with live shots of Custer disembarking from the "deck" of a limited but full-size set. Despite the stringent economy of building and using a hand-sized miniature, I felt we got away with this one and admired the trickery.

With principal photography completed, we all gathered one sweltering evening to look at the film cut together, viewing reel after reel on the moviola in the editing room. The moviola was an outdated and old-fashioned machine even then. We had to look at the image on a lens fixed over a spot where the film frames appeared. Yordan sat hunched over the machine, peering closely at the image in the lens. The rest of us made do as well as we could looking over his shoulders. The hot, exhausting night went on and on as each reel ran. When the last reel finished, the tail end of film leader slapped noisily until it came to a stop, and the lights came on. We waited for Yordan's judgment on our four-million-dollar epic.

He looked up. "Yeah," he announced wearily, "it sure looks like a million."

We didn't know whether to laugh or cry.

Reading some of the press notices in the scrapbook lovingly assembled by Jean, I can only conclude I was dead wrong about the production, about the direction, and even about our feeble scripting attempts to deal fairly with the Native Americans, as we now know them.

Custer of the West was so poorly received by the public that it was hard to find it in an American theater. But you would never guess that from the favorable reviews. Even a respected critic like Kevin Thomas of the *Los Angeles Times* managed to say some nice things:

Custer of the West . . . expresses today's compassionate attitude towards Indians . . . Writers Bernard Gordon's and Julian Halevy's Custer is a man of
considerable complexity, alternately a realist, idealist and egotist, allowing
for our historic attitude and treatment of the Indians to illuminate our
hypocrisy and greed . . .

The *Jewish Chronicle* . . . The *Jewish Chronicle?* Where did Jean find
this one? She probably included it because it says that Robert Shaw gives
an Oscar-nominee performance.

Although the legendary general is left as an all-time hero after the famous
"Last Stand," he is never whitewashed. Indeed, he is shown as a ruthless
man willing to carry out actions motivated entirely by political considerations. This rousing picture has a little bit of everything . . . Another
Cinerama smash hit.

The *Motion Picture Herald* reported that,

First of all, the protagonist is not a heroic hero . . . Secondly, this is a giant
spectacle of a film in the Cinerama process . . . And finally, there is an intelligent screenplay with realistic conflicts and human frustration.

I particularly love this bit from the London *Showguide:*

The script of the film—based on several years of research—has been splendidly written by Bernard Gordon and Julian Halevy, who delved into a private library of more than 1000 books, folios and letters to find their facts.

I can't believe Forman paid off all these reviewers, but I can see that, despite Yordan, we may have managed to get a bit of antihero into the picture
as well as some historical truth. Today I find it particularly annoying when
a film like *Dances with Wolves* appears, the same or equivalent reviewers,
however mistakenly, salute it as the first film to treat Native Americans
fairly. What about *Cheyenne Autumn, Little Big Man, A Man Called Horse?*
But so far as I was concerned, some thirty years earlier, a couple of blacklisted writers did succeed in smuggling a bit of red propaganda into a Hollywood film . . . well, redskin propaganda anyway.

Even after completion of principal photography and the departure of
the cast, as Julian and I were writing *Krakatoa*, I was occasionally pulled off
to work on *Custer*'s post-production problems. I was put in charge of a

scouting crew sent to Almeria Province to look for an appropriate "Western" location. Siodmak and I were as usual at swords' points even before the train left the station. In Almeria, good professional Spanish help made it possible to find what I considered suitable sites almost immediately, but Siodmak refused to be satisfied. We argued. I had written the damned scenes and I thought I had a good notion of what was needed. I gave it one more day. When nothing better showed up, I called off the search, convinced we were wasting time and money.

Much later Yordan told me that Siodmak had been suffering from cancer and was urinating blood during the shooting of the film. This altered my feelings toward the man, and, in retrospect, I think of him as functioning gallantly in the face of a fatal condition.

Back on the barricades, Julian and I kept churning out different scenes, different openings, different character constellations for *Krakatoa*. On one occasion Julian turned in a scene Yordan actually liked. "Good," he muttered sourly. "Now I know you aren't here just because you're a friend of Bernie's."

Unlike me, Julian is not combative or contentious; he finds it hard to express anger. He is universally liked by the people he works with and the people he knows. He laughed off Yordan's crack, and refused to take offense. He does have a few weaknesses, however. One of them is that he is a good cook and proud of it. In Madrid he began preparing lunches for a group of us who would cross the boulevard to his apartment. Most of the actual work was done by his carefully instructed housekeeper, while we struggled through the mornings at the office. Julian frequently came to work later than the rest of us because he had to survey the local food stores for the best fresh fish, meat, or produce. Then he had to instruct his housekeeper about the preparation. This delayed the start of his working day. At last Yordan took notice. "Julian," he barked. "I can afford you as a writer but not as a cook."

Once the lunch routine at Julian's became a regular practice, Yordan wanted to be included. "Why don't I get invited to these wonderful lunches?" he asked.

Julian took the hint. When Yordan joined us for lunch, he considered it his privilege as boss, I suppose, to be critical. We were eating a fine meal of braised veal ribs. Typically, the ribs or riblets had a good deal of fat and connective tissue, not the kind of food to Yordan's taste.

"My God, Julian," he complained, "did you get the cheapest meat in the place?" Julian took this uncomplainingly, but I was outraged. Even though I knew Yordan's taste in food had been indelibly fixed by his domineering mother way back in Chicago, he didn't have the right to complain to the host.

After another one of these episodes, I said, "Julian, why don't you just tell Phil that if he doesn't like your cooking, he doesn't have to come here?" Julian never liked confrontations. He just kept serving the food, feeling perhaps that my angry words were enough. None of this was at all serious, of course, but it probably reflected the increasing tension we all felt about the problem of getting *Krakatoa* on the road.

In the food department Yordan had one more trick up his sleeve. He had come to like a simple dish consisting of canned tuna fish mixed with Campbell's cream of mushroom soup and a few minor additives, topped with crumbled potato chips, and browned in the oven. No gourmet treat but not bad if eaten once in a while for a quick, light lunch. Yordan developed a taste for it though, and when he liked something, he wanted to eat it until he tired of it. Then he would never eat it again.

Yordan was in the tuna lunch mode. He figured he could cut down Julian's focus on cooking by inviting us to his place for lunch. Naturally, we accepted his invitation, and we ate the creamed tuna. No complaint. The next day, Yordan asked us for lunch. Creamed tuna again!

Julian said nothing until he got me alone. "What the hell goes on? Does he eat that garbage every day?"

"Sure," I responded cheerfully, "until he gets tired of it."

"Well, I'm not going to eat that again."

I thought the whole matter a joke, unlikely to be repeated.

On the third day, Yordan asked us for lunch again. This time, Julian inquired about the menu. "Creamed tuna," Yordan said blithely.

I really don't think he was playing a game. He was just providing a decent lunch that was not time-consuming, one he liked and assumed we would like. Politely, Julian turned down the invitation. He was not going to eat creamed tuna a third time. He had had it. And Yordan had finally managed to push Julian's button.

In addition to the endless stress of the work on *Custer* and *Krakatoa*— and it wasn't all about creamed tuna—our personal lives were crammed with all the usual and unusual concerns. From the very first, Ellen was not happy in school at Davis, and she never accommodated to life there, although we didn't understand that until much later.

For years Jean and I had agonized over the right course to take with a beloved daughter, an only child. Other friends took their young children to demonstrations and picket lines, involved them in their political lives. Jean and I felt that a very young child couldn't possibly understand our political struggles and had to be shielded from them. What effect did this have? Did it create a sense of secrecy, of ominous and incomprehensible threat, of insecurity in the household that reached into the psyche even of a four-year-old who was told not to answer the door to the "magazine salesman?"

What was the effect of uprooting a bright and winning little girl of ten from her school at home and dropping her into a Swiss boarding school she hated? Of uprooting her again, a couple of years later, to go to the English School of Paris, then to the American School of Paris, and, finally, to the American School of Madrid? We knew that her attitude toward school suffered, but we didn't know what to do about it. Did buying her a beautiful horse in Madrid balance the books?

I don't know at what age Ellen became aware of the blacklist, either as a word or as a fact of life. Probably not until too late. I don't know how much responsibility we, her parents, bear for whatever difficulties Ellen has known. I do know that, despite HUAC and McCarthy, Ellen has surmounted some years of personal turmoil and grown into a fine woman who is bright, warm, and loving. She now looks back on her years in Europe—where she learned a couple of languages, made some enduring friendships, and knew a rich and very special life—with pleasure and appreciation.

Nineteen sixty-six marked the end of six years of living and working in France and Spain, not just for Ellen, but also for Jean and me.

Despite our tenacious efforts with *Krakatoa*, Julian and I were unable to write a script that satisfied Yordan, Forman, and whoever else lurked behind the Cinerama scenes. I was not in on any of the financing complexities of Forman's grab for control of Cinerama, but I know that the Wall Street sharks took him for $30 million. They first drove up the price of the stock dollar by dollar to $30 per share as Forman bought it all in; then they let it drop to less than $1 per share, which is certainly all that it was worth. But before the stock collapsed, Forman acquired substantial confidence in his own expertise as a filmmaker. He wasn't the first film exhibitor who assumed he knew more about filmmaking than the people in Hollywood. A number of such men, after acquiring chains of theaters, became major players in film production. Forman was on his way.

He had met Bernard Kowalski, a director of a successful television series, who, so far as I knew, had no meaningful feature credits. Kowalski persuaded Forman he could deliver Kirk Douglas as the star for *Krakatoa* and he would guarantee to make a star of Barbara Werle, Forman's steady lady friend. Based on those promises, Forman brought Kowalski over to take charge of *Krakatoa*. Although Julian and I were working a few doors from him in the new high-rise where Yordan had his own apartment, I don't recall ever meeting Kowalski. A climate of uneasiness and confusion settled over the place. Kowalski brought in his own writer, Clifford Newton Gould, whose other credits escape me, and who lists no credits in the Writers Guild Directory as late as 1995. Again, no contact was made. We never met Gould.

In a matter of days everything was made clear. Yordan called us in. Julian and I were terminated. Later I learned that Yordan was also, in a sense, terminated. Forman told him that he would continue on the payroll but asked him to take a "vacation" while Kowalski took charge. Kowalski then led an entire troupe down to the coastal town of Cartagena, where, having rented an old tub of a ship, he proceeded to shoot and shoot and shoot (with no Kirk Douglas). Our Spanish old-timers who continued in the production crew sent back stories of horrendous episodes as Kowalski, inexperienced in this type of production and ignoring all practical considerations, called off production each afternoon with the sun still at the right angle, which forced him to wait out most of the next day for the light to be right again. As money kept going down the drain, I could only recall Yordan refusing to let my soldiers in *The Thin Red Line* walk into a mud hole because of the laundry costs. The production costs on *Krakatoa* mounted astronomically, but Forman, who went down personally to the location to watch the filming (his first), seemed to enjoy it.

More than a year later, when I was back in Hollywood, the Screen Writers Guild was deciding the matter of writing credits. I ignored the notice, assuming that I had long since been written out of the *Krakatoa* script. Millard Kaufman, an old friend, called me. He was a distinguished writer with two Academy Award nominations. He told me Yordan had brought him to Madrid in a desperate attempt to rescue the film from Gould's and Kowalski's devastation. Kaufman had worked for several weeks until he learned that Kowalski was tossing out whatever he wrote because Gould's contract specified that if Gould received a sole screenplay credit, he would be paid a bonus of $5,000!

Bitterly critical of this unprofessional behavior, Kaufman pleaded with me to ask the guild for credit arbitration and to submit my own original versions of the script. He assured me that a great deal remained from my first drafts, and that I would at least be awarded a story credit. He was determined to see that Gould not receive sole credit because he wasn't entitled to it and because Kaufman was so offended by the wasteful disregard of writing propriety. I acceded. When the results were announced, I was surprised to learn I had been awarded, not merely story credit, but the much more significant co-screenplay credit. This deprived Gould of his bonus and saved Forman $5,000.

But before that, back in Madrid, Jean and I had packed for home. By that time we had lived more years in Madrid than anywhere else in our married life. We felt comfortable there, at home. Moreover, this had been the site of truly fruitful years, times of financial rewards, of life with the high-rollers, and of professional success. It was indeed wrenching to have to wrap it all up and return to the United States and a future that appeared very uncertain. We drove with our Irish Setter and our personal belongings to Barcelona, where we boarded the new Italian liner, the *Leonardo da Vinci*, and sailed away. Our twenty trunks and pieces of luggage with six years of accumulated possessions were stored in the ship's hold. I didn't know if or when we might return to Europe, if or when I would next find work, but we decided to do it in style and enjoy a first-class voyage across the Atlantic.

It was a fine crossing with bright, sunny weather most of the way. Only when we approached the North American coast were we hit by a violent storm that battered the great ship and scattered the dishes on the dining room tables. On our last night aboard, our stateroom rocked as though we were afloat in a rowboat. We were passing Nantucket, where the Italian liner *Andrea Doria* had gone down with tragic results some years before. I lay awake imagining the scene: all passengers were ordered into lifeboats, and, after helping Jean into one, I would insist on taking our beloved setter in with me. An argument ensues, with the Italian officers refusing to let me rescue my dog. Room in the lifeboats was reserved for people! What would I do?

Our ship didn't go down, and I didn't have to face the prospect of abandoning Chica or staying behind and sinking with her into the briny depths. The next morning, as we entered the lower bay of New York Harbor, the sky was brilliantly clear, though a gale wind was still blowing. The ship was safe; I could see the Manhattan skyline in the distance. I went up to the top deck to retrieve Chica from her kennel, to assure her that we would all land safely. There she was, her red feathers blowing and flapping splendidly, when the captain appeared. He was a short, roly-poly man who didn't seem nearly substantial enough to command such an impressive vessel. He began to skip lightly up the companionway to the bridge with the graceful steps of so many heavy-set men. I wondered if he had gotten any sleep through the stormy night. Halfway up, he stopped, glanced down at us, at Chica, and exclaimed in true Italian style, "*Que bella ragazza!*" Even at that distance, he could tell Chica was a girl, a beautiful girl.

The drive across the States was a pleasure. We took a northerly route so that we would hit California near Davis, where we could stop and see Ellen and the school. This meant driving through towns and places that had only been dots on a map: Columbus, Ohio; Indianapolis, where we watched the trial runs for the Memorial Day 500 race; Rapid City, South Dakota, from which we took off to visit Mount Rushmore, and where I finally got to see the Little Bighorn of Custer's Last Stand.

America was a big, exciting, and wonderful land. After years abroad, coupled with our quick tour "from sea to shining sea," we both felt a renewed sense of wonder, of pride and affection for home. It was more than geography. It was the awesome infrastructure of highways and communications; it was the complete convenience and availability of everything, including sour cream in Iowa, and it was the casual friendliness of people who really did make their own apple pie in a coffee shop on some forgotten road in the Dakotas. For this special time, the negatives were forgotten. There were so many positives. America was also "the land of the free," a golden place. Jean and I felt lucky to be home.

When *Krakatoa* was released, the distribution people titled it *Krakatoa, East of Java*—evidently "east" sells better than "west." To this day I am teased by friends who attribute the title to me and insist that I don't know that Krakatoa is west of Java. I would like readers to know that I do know where Krakatoa is.

21

In 1967 we rented a small, comfortable house on the flats of Beverly Hills for the summer as we hunted for a home to buy and I worked on restarting a career in Hollywood. The blacklist was over but the effects lingered. The agents I had known were all gone. The credits I had garnered in Europe were not impressive enough to open doors for me, especially since my name didn't appear on many of the films, and Yordan's name dominated others. Twenty years had passed since the first HUAC hearings of the Hollywood people in Washington, and almost as long since the start of the blacklist. Since the blacklist had never been an acknowledged fact, there was never any official end to it, but by 1967 it was effectively over—except that for hundreds of writers, directors, and actors, it could never truly end. After almost twenty years of not working in the industry (or working under pseudonyms or fronts), after almost a working lifetime as salespeople, bartenders, or whatever, after such a long time of being in the closet and out of the circuit, most of the affected people never did get back to work.

There were exceptions, of course. Dalton Trumbo, who was charming, witty, talented, admired, and loved by many in the industry, had never been altogether without work. After credits on *Spartacus* and *Exodus*, not to mention his hilarious dealing as Robert Rich on *The Brave One*, for which he had won an Oscar, he was able to continue working. Even the hard-nosed Academy (AMPAS), which had stubbornly refused to recognize blacklisted writers, was in the process of change. It had accepted the nomination of Carl Foreman as producer and writer of *The Guns of Navarone* and was shortly to award blacklisted writers Ring Lardner Jr. and Waldo Salt writing Oscars for *M*A*S*H* and *Midnight Cowboy*, respectively.

Other profound changes had occurred in these twenty years. The studios no longer functioned as integrated film factories with writers, directors, actors, and producers under contract. The offices and suites that had once been assigned to these workers were now available rent-free to producers who were trying to arrange packages of scripts, stars, and directors (and sometimes financing), the package to be turned over to the studio for distribution and either partial or complete financing. Under these circumstances, writers had to work on spec, creating not only stories (which in the past had been turned over to agents for submission to studio story departments) but completed screenplays, which would then be taken under arm by the producer—promoter? hustler?—whose function was to exploit his contacts to create the "package." The writer received nothing up front for his work and lived in hope.

This was a completely new hand for me . . . and for all of us. Even highly esteemed writers like Michael Wilson were now hung out to dry. What were the chances of getting back into the swim?

It is true, of course, that the old studio system had created many fine films and a great worldwide industry in its so-called Golden Age. This had all changed. We who were trying to recover from the blacklist found ourselves in a very different game. Despite the difficulties this presented, it was still clear that the results of breaking away from the old studio monopoly were certainly not all bad. Many refreshingly different films appeared that had the stamp of independent writers, directors, and producers. Films like *Easy Rider, Bonnie and Clyde,* and *They Shoot Horses, Don't They?* came out of the new Hollywood. England had a splendid flowering, with filmmakers like Tony Richardson, Carol Reisz, Lindsay Anderson, Carol Reed, and many others turning out such films as *Tom Jones, A Taste of Honey, Look Back in Anger, Saturday Night and Sunday Morning, Georgy Girl, Our Man in Havana, The Man in the White Suit, The Lavender Hill Mob, The Captain's Paradise, The Horse's Mouth.* In France, the New Wave developed young directors Louis Malle, Truffaut, Godard, Bertrand Tavernier, and many more, who were making films like *Breathless, Jules and Jim, The Four Hundred Blows, The Lovers, Murmurs of the Heart, Zazie in the Subway, Clean Slate, Coup de Torchon, Sunday in the Country.*

Italy offered directors like Fellini, Antonioni, and De Sica, who contributed such films as *The Bicycle Thief, Garden of the Finizi Continis, Umberto D, La Dolce Vita, La Strada, 8½, Divorce Italian Style,* and so many more. And there was Rossellini, who with his *Open City* virtually initiated an entirely new way of making feature films, shooting in the streets and in real apartments rather than in studio sets. Nor may we forget the spaghetti Westerns of Sergio Leone, which were among the first foreign films to achieve profitable distribution in the States. The German and Japanese renaissance came a bit later, of course, but come it did.

To what can we ascribe this great creative outburst, which, for me at least, produced many of the films I treasure most? As with any significant historic development, there are probably more causes than can be counted. But I can count quite a few: First was the energy that arose from the recovery from such a destructive war, World War II. In England it meant evolving from the empire on which the sun never set into a very different kind of society that had reason to look inward and examine itself in interesting terms. For Italy, of course, it meant ridding itself of the shackles of fascism. France had to recover from the destruction and defeat of the war and from a long period that, under Vichy, certainly resembled fascism.

Closer to the actual business of filmmaking, Hollywood and its major studios no longer dominated and smothered the international film world as it had for so long. There was now room for local product as never before. Out of this also came the export of American talent (blacklisted and other), which contributed to the creative juices, even in countries like Italy and France, but especially in England. Equally important, Hollywood money now became available for production abroad, and Hollywood know-how made a significant contribution even as the New Wave transcended the limits of the old Hollywood product. Further, the countries of Europe made an effort to encourage local production with tax programs and subsidies that made funds available for filmmaking. In most instances, these funds were relatively small, not enough to entice the major directors and producers, so new people entered the field, people who were prepared to work on small budgets and produce the kind of searching, personal stories that so often characterized these new films. This was all fine. It was stimulating. It reminded us of why we had wanted to become filmmakers from the start. Unfortunately, with the exception of very few blacklisted people like Jules Dassin (*Never on Sunday, Topkapi*) most of us had to enjoy these films as audience, not as creators.

Television had taken over. As a newcomer to this land of television, the medium was foreign to me. What I saw troubled me. Children were glued to the set hour after hour watching as one commercial proved that Colgate was the best dentifrice only to be followed moments later by another brilliant and irrefutable commercial that proved that Crest was the best. Or that this battery or that battery lasted longer, and so on and on. These messages came out of the air, out of the sky; they might be coming from God. Who could refute them? And how could you believe them? What kind of confusion did all this produce in children's minds? Our very language was deliberately warped when the godlike voice said: "No deodorant (or laxative or whatever) has been proved to be more effective than Brand X," which is meant to be heard as "Brand X has been proved to be the best." *Caveat emptor!* The vendors had discovered the glory of the indefinite comparative. I was forcibly struck by all this, and especially by the impact of the commercials. What would happen to a generation of children who grew up trusting nothing? I wondered about the future. Now that the future is here, I still wonder how much of the trouble we lament can be traced to something as simple and basic as this.

Was all of this strictly an American phenomenon or was it much broader? How much of the same was true in Europe? I didn't have a definitive answer, since I had lived in Europe without a television set, but I had seen enough to know that American brands and American advertising had penetrated to a considerable extent, and it seemed to me that the insistent pressure of consumerism would eventually arrive and dominate, and, in this sense at least, represent the triumph of the "American Century." I suppose that all of this proves only that my leftish bias remains exactly that.

Even if I could turn off the television set at home in Hollywood, the problem remained: how to find work and earn a living. Arnaud d'Usseau and I had both been involved closely with Yordan for a long time in Europe. We had become very good friends. Despite the odds, we decided to try working together on an original story as a way of breaking back into film work. My focus on the impact of television on our culture determined our subject. We wrote a treatment for a story of how a nincompoop with no political background and nothing to recommend him is elevated to national status by an advertising genius who understands the power of the TV medium and sets out to run the idiot as a candidate for president of the United States. Of course, he wins. We called the story *How to Become President of the United States, Dad.*

While working with Arnaud, Jean and I found a wonderful house on a terrace above the Sunset Strip. All the years in Europe that might have been a miracle, a gift of God, a ball for some women, had been a time of anxiety for Jean. How long would our miraculous prosperity last? What would come after? How could we make a home in rented, furnished apartments in foreign countries (no matter how luxurious), knowing that one way or another all this would have to end? She wanted to build a home for us. Perched above the Sunset Strip, for the first time in her life, she had the money to do just that.

One episode cast a flickering shadow over our complacency. As the house was just about settled in the handsome order we had arranged, a couple of men in suits and snap-brim hats made their way up the steep driveway onto our porch and rang the doorbell. When I opened the door,

I saw they were unmistakably FBI men. Many of our friends had been approached by Mr. Hoover's minions. We never had, but times had changed and I felt reasonably relaxed and secure. As they glanced through the door and around at the outside of the house, one of them murmured, "Very nice place." It was on the tip of my tongue to say, "Moscow gold." They politely asked if they might come in and ask me a few questions. I had been warned never to permit this or to get into any kind of discussion with these people without the presence of an attorney, but I couldn't resist. I wanted to know what they knew or thought they knew about me and just how closely they had followed me around Europe.

I let them in. We sat around an occasional table in the living room and they proceeded to inquire about the people I had known or associated with in Europe. They named quite a few friends of ours in Europe and even some people I didn't know. I was interested to learn who was on their laundry list of suspects and undesirables, so I let them go on. Soon enough they wanted me to talk. I told them that I had nothing to conceal from the government and didn't mind talking about myself but would answer no questions about anyone else. Their tone altered slightly from very amiable to threatening. I can't recall exactly how, but the word "treason" was dropped. My hackles went up and so did my guard. I backed off and said, "If you're talking about anything as serious as treason, I think you had better leave. You'll have to talk to me in the presence of my attorney." They remonstrated that they had not meant to accuse me of anything that serious, but the fat was in the fire and I insisted that they leave. They shrugged and took off.

I won't pretend I wasn't shaken by this. Even though McCarthy had gone, Hoover's men were still busily pursuing "subversives," adding to their files, waiting for their time to come again. What means did they use to track people so carefully in distant places, people who couldn't possibly be a threat to the security of the country?

When I reported this to my friend and attorney Ben Margolis, he berated me soundly for getting into a discussion with the FBI without the presence and advice of an attorney. Nothing more came of this visit except, I presume, more pages in my file at the Bureau.

Arnaud and I kept writing, changing, and rewriting *President* before we finally decided to send it out. An old friend, George Willner, who had been blacklisted as an agent, was working again. He liked our story and agreed to handle it. We were in his office at the agency when luckily we ran into one of its clients, Walter Matthau, already an important star. He had started his career as an actor on Broadway in a play, *Ladies of the Corridor*, written by Arnaud and Dorothy Parker. Matthau greeted Arnaud warmly, asked about our story, expressed interest in it, and turned the matter over to the producer he was working with, Howard Koch. We entered into intense negotiations and held out for our price of $150,000, which would include rights to the story plus our services to write the screenplay. Because of Matthau's interest, and with Paramout financing, Koch finally agreed.

Through the summer of that year and into the fall, Arnaud and I worked on the screenplay of *President* in offices at the ABC headquarters on Vine Street in Hollywood. We felt we had an imaginative and hilarious farce in the works; our agent encouraged us; so did Howard Koch, once or twice, though he was content to let us work away on our own at ABC while he was busy with other projects at his Paramount Studios office. We completed our screenplay at the end of September, turned it in, and waited for a reaction. It was slow in coming and not promising when it came. Matthau was not convinced it was right and seemed to be backing out. Koch called to assure us that he loved the script and would guarantee that the film would be made. This was important for a number of reasons, one of them being that the second half of the payment to us, $75,000, seemed to hinge on the acceptance of the screenplay. We were never clear about this, and it appeared that the attorney at the agency had done a poor job of drawing up our contract, leaving a loophole that permitted ABC to refuse to pay us the remainder of the deal. Normally we would expect to receive that money after delivering the script, without consideration of whether it was approved. Ultimately, it all fell through. We didn't get the rest of the money. Battling with ABC achieved nothing. Even when we submitted the script elsewhere and found interest, we were unable to clear our rights to the material without paying ABC all they had advanced us plus additional fees and overhead, so no other deal was ever made. The world would have to wait until 1979 for the film *Being There*, based on Jerzy Kosinski's book, to deal with this very theme.

By April of 1968 Jean and I had been back in the States for almost a year. Occasionally I had heard from Yordan, who, no longer involved with Cinerama, had embarked on a project of his own. Uncharacteristically, he was for the first time risking his own money on a production without other financing and without a release deal. He had purchased the film rights to Peter Shaffer's splendid play, *Royal Hunt of the Sun*, which I had seen during its premiere run in London. It was the story of the Spanish conquest of

Peru, of the fascinating relationship between Pizarro and the Inca prince
Atahualpa. But having embarked on what would have been an expensive
historical production, Yordan approached it in a most cost-conscious manner. He wrote the new scenes the film needed himself (no cost); he hired
Irving Lerner to direct the film for a measly $25,000 instead of employ-
ing an established major director who would have cost several hundred
thousand; he hired a friend of Irving's, Roger Barlow, as first cameraman
for a minimal salary. Roger had been a documentary film cameraman without major feature-film experience. Yordan never stopped bitching about
Roger's work and blamed Irving for the blunder. He scrounged Madrid
for whatever existing sets and flats he could find and dressed the native Pe-
ruvians in green cheesecloth and sandals patched together from cut-up
rubber tires.

Irving's appeal to Yordan was not merely a matter of salary. Yordan was
constantly aware that he must have a director he could control, one who
would not run up production costs by demanding good sets and locations,
by insisting on retakes, by catering to the whims of actors, or in any other
way battling the producer for quality results. Irving was also an asset because he had a close relationship with Robert Shaw, who had agreed to accept Irving as director. It's doubtful that any other star would. Shaw's affection for him meant that at last Irving would get a crack at directing a
major film. With that locked in, other members of the cast went along.
The fine actor Christopher Plummer played Atahualpa to Shaw's Pizarro.
I understand that Yordan brought the entire film in for $2 million, a pro-
duction that would have cost Bronston at least $10 million. Somehow,
along the way, Yordan managed to get ABC to give him a pickup of $2 mil-
lion for the theatrical rights. This guaranteed Yordan against loss for *Royal
Hunt of the Sun*. When the film was completed and out for release more
than a year later, its reception was a disaster. ABC took a full-page ad in
the *New York Times*, opened the film in one theater in New York, and closed
it down for good in less than a week. I don't believe it has ever been released elsewhere again.

In February of the following year, 1969, Yordan finally returned, *en
famille*, to reclaim his splendid home in Beverly Hills. As usual, he managed to stir up a great deal of activity, with people coming and going from
early to late, people with all kinds of business proposals, whether for films,
real estate investments, or stock promotions. I saw a good deal of him, and
he and Faith were regulars at our dinner table.

Meanwhile, Arnaud and I had embarked on another major spec writing project, a screenplay about the Vietnam War, one which would tell

the truth about that venture. When we finished, proud of our work, we showed it to Yordan. He read it, then looked at us as though we were crazy. Saying little, he dropped the script as though it might burn him. In 1969 we were about ten years premature in presenting the brutality and insanity of that venture. He was right—we got nowhere with the script we had titled *Firebase Domino*. Another one of my better efforts for the trunk.

In May Yordan made certain that I received two tickets to the grand premiere of *Krakatoa, East of Java*, which was held at the flagship Cinerama Dome theater in Hollywood. Personally, I felt it was the least Bill Forman could do, since I had saved him the five-thousand-dollar bonus he would otherwise have been forced to pay to the other writer, Clifford Gould, but I refrained from pointing this out to Forman at the premiere. Well, it was a big, noisy film. My greatest satisfaction was seeing my name up on that very wide screen. My own reservations about the film were more severe than the critics' reception of it. To my amazement, Kevin Thomas of the *Los Angeles Times* enthused, safely enough, that it is "one of the best movies ever made in Cinerama" and went on to say, "Excellent in all aspects, it is an artistic as well as a technical triumph." The *Hollywood Reporter* was less generous and managed to squeeze in, "Several Mack David songs are intrusively planted, and at one point when Miss Werle breaks into song, it appears as if the course of the film has shifted to a musical." Apparently, Kowalski's efforts to make a star of Forman's friend Barbara Werle would not succeed.

As I continued to work on my own projects, Yordan often asked me over to his beehive of activity on Benedict Canyon. Increasingly, he seemed to want me involved in everything, and I spent a good deal of time with him in the office he worked from at the very entrance of his mansion. Typical of the way he operated, everyone, including the man delivering groceries, had to pass by his desk.

At this time, apart from his many projects, Yordan's most urgent problem was his eyesight, since a cataract operation done in Paris had long since deteriorated. His vision was even worse than before. Learning, naturally, about the "best ophthalmologist in the world," who worked in San Francisco, Yordan flew up there for a corneal transplant. Yordan pressed me into service to accompany him to San Francisco for the surgery, then to return him home from the hospital, and to accompany him again for checkups. Regrettably, the new cornea eventually clouded over and was useless. Finally, a proper and up-to-date cataract operation restored excellent vision in one eye, and he has done well with that ever since.

After I had left Madrid, while Yordan was still in Europe working on *Royal Hunt of the Sun*, he had also been developing new contacts and financing sources in England. His new associates were Ben Fisz (pronounced "Fish"), a shamelessly extravagant promoter with overweening filmmaking ambitions, and Bobby Marmor, a pleasant, low-key man who had made a fortune in London real estate. Fisz interested Marmor in the romance of filmmaking; Yordan plugged into this combo because Marmor had money and excellent financial connections with the London merchant banks. Yordan could provide the Hollywood contacts and expertise plus invaluable Madrid contacts and know-how. With the money he had earned from Bronston, he was also in a position to contribute his share to the creation of a small studio in or around Madrid, the site of their new empire.

To my surprise, this dream seemed to be evolving credibly. With money supplied by Marmor and Yordan, and with Yordan using his film and legal connections in Madrid, they acquired a property just outside Madrid. Working on and off with my own projects, I was startled to learn that they had developed the lot with a few buildings for offices and dressing rooms. A warehouse was to serve as a sound stage, and they had constructed a modest Western street on top of the hill dominating the property. Yordan, commuting back and forth to London and Madrid, showed me the script of the first film they planned to shoot. Under Ben Fisz's supervision, a writer in London had scripted *A Town Called Bastard*. Yordan was supposed to rewrite and cure its problems. He gave me the script to read. I wasn't asked to participate, so I refrained from any criticism of the work, but since this looked like a "go" project, I felt left out. I speculated on the meaning of this. Did Yordan feel he could handle the rewrite on his own without my help? Or had he not asked me because Bronston wasn't around to foot the bill for my work? Or did Yordan need to prove to his new partners that he, personally, was the man who could be trusted to deal with all the script problems?

I kept my mouth shut until Yordan finally asked me, "What do you think of the script?"

"It's interesting," I said, "though I think it has some problems."

Never insensitive, Yordan let it go at that. If I wasn't interested in volunteering comments, he wouldn't ask for them. Actually, the *Bastard* script was a bloody, violent, and confusing exercise that, presumably, catered to the booming desire for more and more sensational films. After much travail that did involve me, it was eventually made into a film, but Halliwell dismisses it as a "sadistic Western with an opening massacre followed by twenty-two killings (count 'em). Pretty dull otherwise."

Yordan got my attention when he announced, "They started shooting *Bastard* in Madrid."

"Who's the director?"

"Bob Parrish." Parrish was an American director with many substantial credits who was at the time working principally out of England.

"Who's the producer?"

"Ben Fisz is in charge until I get over there."

So it was real.

"You want to go back there with me?"

"Doing what?"

"You'll be a producer."

I was ready. "When do we go?"

"September." He was unequivocal.

I had heard this kind of talk from him before. As usual, Yordan didn't give a vague date in the future. I recalled our first encounter outside a projection room when he had promised to get me to Madrid in "six weeks," and I hadn't heard from him until Irving Lerner reached me in Paris much later in a very different context. But this seemed real because they were actually shooting a film at a studio he had helped to pay for.

"How do I get paid?"

"You won't. Same as me. You'll have a big expense account and own a piece of the pictures along with me. You'll make a lot more than salary that way." I had my doubts, but the way things were going for me in Hollywood, I couldn't say no. He went on. "I have to get another script ready to shoot in September." It was early summer.

"I'm going to work with Milton [Sperling]. He owns a book." He was referring to a paperback Western, *Captain Apache*, which in fact Yordan did work on full-time with Sperling. "Meanwhile, I'd like you to start working on some scripts. We'll need a whole program."

He set me up with a desk, a Selectric typewriter, and plenty of paper in a fine apartment he had fixed up above the very spacious garage at one edge of his Beverly Hills property. For source material, he dumped on me a stack of scripts he had acquired at bargain rates. These scripts had all been written by an American, Marc Behm, who lived in Paris. Behm was a compulsive writer who could and did turn out screenplays in a matter of days, and, according to Yordan, had a closet bulging with such scripts. Yordan bought them wholesale for about $1,000 apiece. Then he pawed through them to see, from time to time, if there was anything there he could use. Actually, Behm was a talented writer who had a few respectable credits, such as co-writer on the Beatles' second feature, *Help*. But none of the Behm scripts Yordan bought ever made it to the screen.

I went to work reading these scripts to try to find at least an idea or basis for a practical production. As once before on *Krakatoa*, I had to work on spec, but the genuine prospect of returning to Madrid and of becoming a producer made me willing to gamble.

I finally settled on a Western of Behm's that turned me on. It was about a beautiful Indian girl who, having been raped by a gang of scruffy outlaws, for revenge sets out to kill them all. *By herself.* The script had some of Marc's originality, weirdness, and whimsy, but it was woefully weak in character motivation, story development, theme, and the kind of ideas necessary to give it unity and direction. I pounded away at the typewriter, pleased with the way the script was going. When I finished and gave it to Yordan, he read it swiftly and, for the only time in my experience with him, compared my writing to his own.

"It's just what I would have written," he said. "Only better."

He put Sidney Harmon to work on casting. It looked as though this would be the next picture on the schedule after *Captain Apache*. I called my version of the script *They All Came to Kill.*

B y September 1970, our move back to Madrid was becoming a reality. Jean was not at all happy to leave the lovely home we'd just finished creating, especially since it was agreed that with the new prospect of my producing pictures and taking over a studio in Madrid, we would be there for a very extended period, and it would be advisable to sell the house. We put it on the market. Only in retrospect and with considerable regret do I understand how much of a blow this was to Jean.

Y ordan was looking for a director for *Captain Apache*. This involved me with a close connection. Alex Singer was married to Judy, Julian's young sister. Alex had started out in the Bronx as a hopeful filmmaker and a close friend of Stanley Kubrick. Kubrick was already on his way with a number of major accomplishments, but, after a promising start with a single low-budget feature, Alex had stalled. As it turned out, he spent much of the rest of his life trying to compete with and catch up to the Kubrick who had been his young buddy in the Bronx. In 1970 this still lay in the future. Alex wanted any crack at directing a feature film. He asked me to get him together with Yordan.

Though Alex's feature-film credits were not impressive, he had a number of television shows under his belt. Yordan decided he was a competent professional. What's more, Alex was willing to do the job for a minimal fee of $25,000, something that inevitably appealed to Yordan, who also calculated that Alex would be amenable and manageable. He was right on all scores. Judy, Alex, and their twelve-year-old son, Jethro, packed up and prepared to move to Madrid as I was making my own arrangements, which involved leaving Jean behind on her own for a month to settle up with the buyers of our house, get our possessions into storage, resettle Ellen in an apartment now that she had transferred to UCLA, and clean up a thousand odds and ends.

With the help of a most cooperative personnel agent at TWA who appreciated all the first-class tickets the company was now purchasing for our flight to Madrid, I arranged for Jean to depart later with our mountain of excess baggage, plus Chica, who would be returning to her native land. I took off for Spain with the Singers. In those days first-class flying was truly first class. The brand new 747 gave us every amenity, including an exclusive upstairs barroom with the best drinks and the fanciest hors d'oeuvres in the sky. All at once, I felt like a true producer . . . more than that, I felt like a man who would be running a studio. It was amazingly easy to become accustomed to this kind of service.

22

At the Madrid airport, I was pleased to see the familiar face of Herminio, the police lieutenant who had for years been moonlighting—night and day!—for the Bronston studio and now was continuing with the new setup. He quickly hustled the Singers and me through customs and immigration, then into a car to the new Eurobuilding Hotel. The hotel bustled with Yordan, Milton Sperling, and any number of minions who seemed to be occupying an entire floor. I looked appreciatively at the modern amenities of this hostelry with its grand marble bathrooms, dressing rooms, bedroom and living room suites. Unfortunately, all the suites were occupied except one. Looking at the exhausted three Singers, I decided that it would be a kindness to let them dump their baggage and rest up after the overnight flight. It was no problem for me to ride over to my old home away from home—the Hilton—where I was greeted warmly by the familiar staff.

Curiously, my feelings were mixed about my return, but I attributed that to the fatigue of the flight. I took a hot shower and tried to nap. I was delighted to be back and to be involved in a more important way in the process of filmmaking, but I realized I would be surrounded by other producers and money men like Yordan, Sperling, and Ben Fisz; I couldn't help wondering exactly what my role would be. I unpacked and managed a couple of hours of rest before I dressed and taxied over to the Eurobuilding where, with Yordan and Sperling, I rode out to the new studio.

Shooting on *A Town Called Bastard* was completed and the editing was under way. The "studio" was not much—offices, dressing rooms, a warehouse, and a standing Western street with a substantial wall, a tower, and a well-built church, finished inside and out. The street was minimal, not much more than a *cantina*, which was all that the Mexican pueblo of *Bastard* had called for. But the wall, tower, and church were impressive enough, and we could see how, with the erection of a few storefronts and a hotel, the requirements for *Captain Apache* would be met. There was no soundstage, and interiors would have to be shot inside the church, in the warehouse, or in the interior of the hotel, still to be built. Since shooting on *Apache* was due to start shortly, the construction had to start immediately.

The next few months, until the end of 1970, were a time of madness. Nothing went right, but everything finally worked out—if the quality of the picture-making is ignored. I was involved in every aspect of production: construction, casting, wardrobe, locations, sets, publicity, even makeup, yet I had no real authority. Most of all, there were endless hassles over the script. The *Apache* script was a dreary mess. Sperling knew it and wanted rewrites. I found that working with Sperling was impossible. For weeks I held conferences, listened to his comments, reached agreement on changes, went back to my hotel (now a nice suite at the Commodore) and wrote late into the night. The next day Sperling liked nothing, had changed his mind, demanded a rewrite of the rewrite. Yordan was too involved with more important matters about financing and co-production to concern himself with script. I suspect, also, that he may have resented the notion that we were rewriting his work. Eventually I tossed the pages back to Sperling, told him I was not being paid as a writer, and if he knew better than anyone what was needed, he could make the script changes himself.

Impatiently, Yordan cut through all this. "Forget about making changes. You're wasting time. You're not making it any better. We're going to shoot the script the way it is."

A Town Called Bastard still had to be attended to. When we viewed the first cut of *Bastard*, we all agreed it didn't make sense and that production would have to be reopened. Again, I realized this was a commonplace with Yordan. Finish a film inadequately, then worry about making changes when it was, in effect, too late. Strangle a production with too little money, then spend a great deal more than was saved on fixing up. Like *Triffids*.

I was asked to write an "envelope" for *Bastard*, something to help to make sense of the plot's mishmash. Yordan got Robert Shaw, one of the principals in the original film, to come back for the new scenes. I wrote a half-dozen envelopes. Some were rejected by Yordan, some by Ben Fisz. I don't know how we ever agreed about anything. Meanwhile, *Captain Apache* had to start shooting. Lee Van Cleef had been signed as the lead. He was an ex-stuntman who had become a leading man in spaghetti Westerns. In appearance he was well cast to play the Indian-who-became-a-lawman-for-the-whites called for by our script. He was tall, well-built, with a strong, aquiline face. He had been signed for two back-to-back features at $150,000 each, but he seemed to resent everything about work. I found him a clod and wondered why he appeared sullen. I decided it wasn't the script—I doubted he'd bothered to read through it. Still, we had to be concerned about getting another script ready for him after *Apache*.

Carroll Baker had been signed for the female lead. She was a delight. True, she got in a flap over getting exactly the right brand of bleach for her very blonde hair. I picked up the phone and reached Jean just before she left Los Angeles and asked her to get a stock of the special bleach; I had to make arrangements for a hairdresser at the Hilton beauty salon to report each morning at five a.m. to get Baker ready for the day's work. Carroll was serious about her work, though, was always on time, always knew her lines, and laughed readily at all the right moments. My sessions with her in her suite at the Hilton were entertaining. She traveled with a very small dog, a Yorkie that couldn't have weighed more than five pounds. She carried it with her on airplanes in a little overnight bag that had been fitted with a plastic window and air holes. The Yorkie was so small that whatever mess it made was easily picked up, and Baker was relaxed about this, as she seemed to be about everything. Always considerate about sex, she also carried with her a small stuffed dog about the same size as her terrier. The real dog had a fine time humping the stuffed dog, much to Baker's satisfaction. "The little fellow simply has to have an outlet," she explained to me. And why not?

We were well along in the production when she had to play a fairly explicit sex scene with Van Cleef, both of them lightly clad under the covers and presumably naked. Baker went along without demur and disrobed above the waist. Van Cleef, also undressed, had to appear to be making love with her.

He was alarmed. "What will I do if I get an erection?" he demanded. I was not on the set at the time and the problem did not have to be resolved by me. After a hurried consultation with Alex, the matter was turned over to Milton Sperling, who came up with a quick answer.

"Fuck her," Sperling replied gleefully.

These were the good times that kept Yordan awake nights. Money was coming in. Films being made. The sky was the limit. He concentrated on the trickery of co-production deals with France and Italy, but this wasn't enough. He made a serious foray into purchasing foreign-made films, mostly Italian Westerns that could be dubbed into English and then marketed to the burgeoning American television market. To move into the vast Italian marketplace, which was producing Westerns by the dozen that could be picked up for almost nothing in American dollars, Yordan asked Julian to help. Back home in Rome, Julian was to look at the films offered for sale, then report back to Yordan on those he thought useful for the American market. Julian would be paid for his time, and, sometime in the by-and-by, take a cut of profits.

I too was working for pie-in-the-sky—no salary, just a peseta expense account, but this amounted to $500 a week in local currency—a princely sum, considering the cost of living in Spain at the time. Yordan freely, as always, wrote up fine documents guaranteeing me percentages of the profits of all the films I worked on. I knew enough by now to demand such contracts but to pay little heed to them. This was, after all, a great learning experience, and I was having a ball.

The co-production problems were trying. We received funds in the currency of each participating country, then used that currency for payment for goods and services in that country. For instance, we had to be certain to hire enough Italian actors or production personnel—or French or Spanish—or use the post-production facilities of a given country to prove the money contributed by each country was actually spent for film industry functions in that country. This led to many problems and compromises, corner-cutting or bending the rules, sometimes breaking the laws. The end result was significant because, in addition to finding funds to help finance the films, a co-production meant a favorable and highly desirable "nationality" for the film. If a film had nationality, that film had great tax advantages as well as favored distribution and exhibition in each country. The film would then be considered a local product, not subject to import quotas. It was not possible to get investors from a given country unless the film had nationality for that country. I was learning.

With all of this going on, Yordan was too preoccupied to concern himself with scripts. I believe he devoutly wished I would take all script problems off his hands and simply deliver the necessary changes without troubling him. Even so, he couldn't keep his hands off the scripts, and, as the Academy Award–winner and author of so many distinguished films, he was expected to be in charge of that function.

I was not the only faithful old sidekick and retainer Yordan had brought over to Madrid. Irving Lerner was there, too, not as the distinguished director of *Royal Hunt of the Sun* but in his other general capacity as a supervising film editor, music consultant, expert on every phase of filmmaking . . . and gofer. Yordan treated Irving shabbily—he wasn't even offered a company-paid hotel room, and he wound up on a spare bed in my suite at the Commodore. Still, when things got going and a director was needed for shooting the new sequences of *Bastard*, Irving was pressed into service. It became my responsibility to work with him.

I also had to work with Ben Fisz, who was the pipeline to the British money. Fisz had been entirely in charge in Madrid during the building of the studio and then during the shooting of *Bastard*, before the rest of us landed. He was despised by the Spaniards who had been in charge of the land acquisition and the construction. They had also been the principals of all the below-the-line work, from production manager to *telefonista*. Most of them were holdovers from the Bronston days. To a man, they complained to me that Fisz had been irresponsible, that he seldom appeared at the studio during the shoot and spent most of his time back in Madrid in card games with friends. He would come out to the studio mainly to complain about such things as the sewer stink around the newly constructed dressing-room building.

When Jean arrived, I went to the airport to meet her. This time Chica had been forced to cross the Atlantic in a huge kennel box in the baggage hold of the plane. She was calm enough about her arrival, but the Spanish were puzzled about the problem of admitting her. Evidently there were no clear regulations about dogs flying into Spain. I explained that Chica was born and bred in Spain and therefore had full citizenship and was merely returning to the land she loved. The Spaniards liked this and waved her in. I immediately took her outside to let her relieve herself after the long flight. Instead, she lay down and rolled on the ground. Maybe she was only relieved to be out of confinement, but it certainly looked as though she rejoiced at returning home. The watching immigration officers were delighted. They recognized a good Spaniard, even if she looked Irish.

Alex Singer struggled with *Captain Apache*. I thought that some of the scenes he directed were good—and some weren't. But Alex never bit the bullet and complained about the script pages he was handed to shoot. Van Cleef liked him, which may or may not have yielded him Brownie points in my book, but Alex did have a way of getting along with actors. He didn't get along with Sperling, who complained about him and to him endlessly. Once, after Sperling and his wife Margit had dinner at our home, Sperling got Alex on the phone and proceeded to chew him out mercilessly. I was very angry about this. I landed on Sperling and told him I never wanted to hear him talking to the director like that again. I told Yordan I thought Sperling was demoralizing Alex and I wouldn't take any more responsibility unless Sperling was barred from the set. Yordan did warn Sperling to stay away, but the carping never ended.

Sometimes it was Yordan who found fault, usually with Irving. Back on *Bastard*, one scene involved Robert Shaw on a horse leading a captive prisoner on another horse across a small stream. It seemed simple enough to me, but this time Yordan complained about the scene no matter how many times we shot it. I was lunching with Yordan and Robert Shaw when Yordan vented his vexation at Irving for not knowing how to direct the scene. "You'd think by now he'd know how to shoot two men on a horse so that it looks like something is happening."

This kind of buck passing annoyed me. "Did it ever occur to you that the director needs something to work with?" I asked. "If he had a scene with anything written, anything but two men on horses crossing a stream, he might be able to put a little drama into it."

Shaw, who knew Yordan was responsible for the script and had a fine sense of it all, was delighted to hear Yordan taken to task. He chortled happily.

Irving did make some real contributions. As we were shooting a lively scene of dancing in the *cantina*, he wanted the cameraman to move around loosely, catching shots of the dancers from different angles. He knew, as a film editor, how he could use such snippets of action, but the cameraman insisted he had to light the scene for one angle, then stop and relight it for another. It would have taken a week to do the scene that way, and it still wouldn't have been right. Irving told the cameraman to put the camera on his shoulder, sit in a wheelchair, and have it pushed around among the dancers. Hand-held? No tripod? No light changes? The cameraman froze. With my authority, Irving handed the camera to the assistant, sat him in the wheelchair, turned on the music, started the dancers, then pushed the wheelchair with the assistant and the camera all through the moving crowd. It worked beautifully.

During the shooting of that *cantina* scene, Jean and I were sitting in the trailer with Shaw and another fine English actor, Michael Craig. We were cozy in there with the butane heater to fight off the freezing winter night. We reminisced, killed a couple of bottles of good Spanish brandy, got pretty high, and had a fine time. When this was all over about two A.M., we returned to town in Shaw's Mercedes 600. Still not ready for bed, Shaw came up to our apartment and sat around another couple of hours while we killed another bottle. Jean fell into bed long before this was over. I couldn't keep up with drinkers like Shaw, but in the interest of a career, I tried. To my admiration, as I watched helplessly from a chair, Shaw was able to get up finally and walk steadily out of the apartment.

For foreigners, eating and drinking seemed even more important in Spain than anywhere else. After work, what else could we do, given that country's crazy, historically mandated hours for working, resting, and eating? On that score, even Franco's attempts to bring Spain into the twentieth century failed. The day began with a light breakfast of coffee and a bun, followed in midmorning by the "elevenses," a snack of coffee, toast or sweet roll, and, usually, for the Spanish, a generous dollop of brandy. That carried a worker through the long morning session until about two o'clock, when everything shut down for the midday siesta; ordinary people went home for a heavy meal and a nap, consuming about three hours before work started up again at five or six and lasted until eight or nine in the evening. No respectable Spaniard ate his dinner at home or in a restaurant before ten at night. In a decent restaurant, the meal lasted until midnight—time to go home and sleep.

I asked a Spanish acquaintance about this schedule: "At night, you go home, eat a meal, spend some time with the children, go to bed, make love to your wife, and go to sleep. Right?" He nodded agreeably. "But what do you do in the three or four hours of the afternoon siesta?"

He grinned and said, "Exactly the same things."

Foreigners had few of the normal outlets. By law, almost all films were exhibited in Spanish regardless of origin. Plays were also in Spanish. What else could you do but eat, drink, sleep . . . and hope you had a willing spouse? These hours seriously hampered film production—it was impossible to break for a siesta in midday, especially when the studio was out of town, adding transportation and travel time back and forth. We tried to operate on western work hours of nine to five, or eight to five, with an hour's break for lunch, but the film workers were unhappy about missing their accustomed siesta. As a matter of habit and right, they managed to put away quite a bit of wine or brandy during the lunch break, so that starting work after lunch was an uphill battle. Later, when I fully took charge of the studio, I tried to tackle some of these matters constructively, but I battled in vain against millennia of culture and habit.

In the early days, my producer chores included quite a bit about meals and eating. At first I tried to socialize with Lee Van Cleef and his wife. I invited them to dinner at one of Madrid's premier seafood restaurants. At the Bajamar, I urged them to order the *angulas*, which were the choicest item on the menu and one of my favorites. These were tiny eels that came out of the kitchen looking like a dish of three- or four-inch strands of white spaghetti. They were prepared in a steaming sauce of olive oil, garlic, and red pepper, served in a hot earthenware bowl. You couldn't tell that they were anything but spaghetti unless you looked closely and found the two tiny black spots at one end that were due to grow into eyes. This sounds disgustingly carnivorous, but I'm sure the baby eels, not more than a day or two old when plucked from the sea, didn't suffer as much as a carp or a trout. The Van Cleefs looked at this dish and shoved it away in disgust. I had blown it with them again.

Other meals I arranged were more successful. I organized a real American turkey dinner for Thanksgiving at the Hilton. We had a couple of tables with celebrants who included most of the stars and the American personnel. On another occasion, I arranged for an evening at the splendid Puerta de Moros restaurant. Over the years, Luigi, the owner, had become a good personal friend. Luigi outdid himself. He prepared a great, round table that seated a dozen of us. The centerpiece looked like an acre of fresh flowers. Luigi went around personally offering my guests all the best Spanish wines and liqueurs. He was pleased to have such a gathering of important movie names, but he made an extra effort to please me, and I was grateful. Even Sperling, who was accustomed to the best that the world's capitals had to offer, complimented me on that one. Christmas Eve dinner was held at our home and a we had unique evening for New Year's Eve at the Jockey. Producers, it seemed, had responsibilities outside the sound stage.

Increasingly I was working with the Spaniards, who were important to this enterprise. With them we solved the sewer stink in the dressing-room building, a case of poor ventilation of sewage in the septic tank. It was not very difficult or expensive to arrange for a tall vent pipe which carried the odors safely away. I took some satisfaction in this accomplishment as a producer, even though none of this ever appeared on the screen. At least I was the only American there who tackled the problem, which was, I suppose, one of the reasons Yordan liked having me around.

The principal Spaniard I worked with was Gregorio Sacristan. He was probably the most important film person in Madrid, because, first of all, he ran the Mole Richardson facility, a branch of the worldwide company that rented film production equipment of every conceivable variety, from gelatin filters for lamps to great 5,000-watt "brutes" to light up sets, to cameras, cranes, even mobile generators and the trucks to go with them. Because of this position, he was close to every production in Spain, familiar with every aspect of filmmaking, knew everyone who worked in the field, from film stars to electricians. He also had excellent connections with the banks. Yordan happily acquired his services as our production manager, which he was clearly able to carry out in addition to his responsibilities at Mole Richardson. He was a lean, swarthy man, almost six feet tall, with penetrating dark eyes and a thatch of black hair. I thought of him as a gypsy, though neither his name nor his family suggested such a background. He radiated authority and growled out orders to subordinates, who always responded with alacrity. He had an excellent sense of political reality and exhibited proper deference, though certainly not humility, to the foreigners who were bringing in all the money for this work. With me he was not certain. He was not sure how much power I represented, so he treated me with friendly respect, almost as an equal. I liked him. I learned from him as he took charge of all the endless details of running a production office.

The other key Spaniard was Paco (Francisco) Lizarza, our attorney. Paco was a chunky man of about fifty who dressed in the impeccably formal style of the Spanish businessman: buttoned up jacket, dress shirt, tie, polished handmade boots. He knew his way in and out of Spanish law and in and out of some Spanish banks. These two men were Yordan's main allies in Spain and probably accounted for much of his clout with other foreigners who wanted to work there but didn't know their way around. Paco and Gregorio were loyal to Yordan because he had—before, with Cinerama, and now with the new company—brought real money into Spain for production. Whether Yordan liked these two men, I never knew. He couldn't be bothered with such personal considerations. That was a waste of time.

I was a neophyte. I liked Sacristan and disliked Lizarza—his name did not mean "lizard" in Spanish, but I always thought of him that way. He was a coldly calculating man, and I figured I could depend on him only so long as he could also work his own angle. His thick, white hair constantly shed dandruff on his otherwise impeccable shoulders. His fine offices discreetly displayed a signed photo of Franco, and I was given to understand that there was a basis of regard between Franco and Paco's family. He had access to high-level ministers in the regime and was able to work local municipal authorities like a Tammany politico. All this was certainly useful when, for example, we ran into zoning problems with the municipality where the studio was located. I respected the man's usefulness but I couldn't bring myself to like or trust him.

During these last months of 1970, as I was getting my feet wet in production, I also wanted to schedule my script of *They All Came to Kill*, but we proceeded instead with another old potboiler of Yordan's, *Bad Man's River*. This was something he or someone had written years ago in Hollywood, one of the many scripts in Yordan's backlog. When I protested that *Kill* was a good script and ready to go, Yordan agreed that others liked it too, but he told me that Ben Fisz had nixed it because he didn't believe that a Western should be made with a woman lead. End of story—except that not much later another major American film was shot in Spain, a

Western with Raquel Welch in the lead. *Hannie Caulder* bore a startling resemblance to *They All Came to Kill:* a woman raped by an evil gang deals with a bounty hunter, personally exacts revenge on her violators. I was bitter about this and wondered whether it was possible that Yordan felt it necessary to reinforce his position by supplying a script with his own name attached.

The year was ending and so was the shooting of *Captain Apache.* As usual, Yordan kept trying to patch up the holes with new and irrelevant scenes that only further confused the story. It kept Alex Singer working, if not happy. Alex was devastated when, despite all his hard work and strenuous efforts to please, the next film was slated to be made without him. The decision to use another director had nothing to do with Alex. It was a necessity born of circumstance: Lizarza had managed to torture the rules of Spanish nationality, and the next film would be "Spanish." This was a great coup and a significant advantage, but it meant even more emphasis on hiring Spanish film workers. Specifically, we would need a Spanish director.

By New Year's Eve most of our Americans had left for the holidays. The Sperlings had let us know that they were going to Italy to enjoy a weekend on the yacht of the Agnellis, the Fiat family. Ben Fisz had long since happily given up on Spain and was putting together a fine set of company offices in the heart of London. Since Yordan and Faith were still with us, I asked him if he wanted to make plans for New Year's Eve. He said no. The Lerners also had no plans. Jean and I decided we would settle for a quiet evening at home.

That evening, a few hours before dinner, Yordan called. "Can you find a place to go out for dinner?"

"You said you didn't want to go out."

"Faith wants to go out," Yordan said irritably.

"Where?"

"Anywhere. But no paper hats and noisemakers."

"New Years Eve! I doubt it."

"Someplace with decent food. Try."

To my surprise, my modest connection with the Jockey Club, which I considered the best restaurant in Madrid, worked. They were conscious of the importance of film names among their clientele.

I still recall fondly the poetic name of the street where the fine restaurant was located: *Amador de los Rios,* Lover of the Rivers. We were welcomed by the well-trained staff, who always acted as though they knew us personally. The menus were printed for the occasion, with specialties and regular favorites. There were no prices listed. I wondered if it was a *prix fixe* dinner but doubted that when the waiters started coming around with impressive and expensive goodies to eat and drink. We were presented with a large, freshly opened can of Beluga caviar, which Jean and Yordan, to my surprise, greedily accepted as the waiter spooned heap after heap into their plates and then came around again and added more as the two recently born gourmands nodded. Of course, we ordered a bottle of French champagne. Faith discovered she really liked the bubbly, and we were soon into a second and a third bottle. The rest of the meal consisted of local sensations like partridge in grape sauce. I was too busy wondering how much all this would cost to wonder where the fresh grapes came from at this season.

It was a grand meal. When the bill was presented, it came to 18,000 pesetas, approximately $300. This was a modest charge for such a meal for six. I believe that today, even in Spain, such a meal would cost at least five times that much. I only had about 10,000 pesetas in my wallet and I knew that the Jockey had not yet gotten around to accepting credit cards. I asked Yordan and Irving to produce their wallets. Yordan just shook his head indicating that he had no cash on him. Irving produced a meager 2,000 pesetas. We were a $100 short. "Well," I shrugged, "it looks as though we're going to wind up in the kitchen washing dishes." Yordan was unmoved. It occurred to me that he was dispassionately considering the possibility that he would sacrifice Irving to the kitchen detail if necessary . . . and even me. But I wouldn't buy that.

"Come on, Phil, I don't believe you came out without any cash on you."

He persisted for a while with the charade but finally, reluctantly, produced his wallet and was forced to reveal that it contained a secret pocket from which he produced a $100 bill. "This enough?"

I nodded. "They'll be happy to take American money."

"Make sure Ramón [the studio accountant] reimburses me." So the meal ended happily. And so did 1970.

23

1971 began on an unpromising note. Yordan had purchased a very large apartment on the northern outskirts of the city, and he had locked himself up there for ten days with instructions that he not be called or disturbed. He was writing a new version, suitable for filming in Spain on our Western street, of the old turkey, *Bad Man's River*, that he had been unable to unload in Hollywood. At the end of his self-imposed exile, he emerged cheerfully and handed me the new script.

"I wrote this in ten days," he boasted, "and Faith read it and says it's the best script she's ever read."

I was surprised to hear that Faith had ever read a script before. What could I say? I just swallowed hard and replied, "I'll read it right away. Get back to you."

"Oh," he said, "I've also given a copy to Irving to read."

When I finished reading it and found it as bad as I'd feared, I wondered whether I should tell the proud chief how I really felt, whether I should hedge or just go hide. For advice and comfort, I called Irving. "Have you read Phil's script?" I began neutrally.

"Yes."

"What do you think?"

"Not bad," he replied.

I was astonished. "You mean you liked it?" I was still trying to restrain my anger at what appeared to me a cowardly sell-out.

"Well," he said, starting to hedge, "I thought there were some pretty good things."

"Have you talked to him about it?"

"Yes."

"What did you tell him?"

"I told him I liked it."

"Look, Irving, how could you? It's a total mish-mash with characters dropping in and out, no continuity, no credibility, nobody to root for. It isn't comedy. It isn't melodrama. It isn't anything . . ." I couldn't go on.

"Well," Irving tried, backing off, "it isn't as bad as you think. I . . ."

Valuable as he was, I understood that Irving had no status or security around there and had to be careful not to offend Yordan. Unlike Irving, I was supposed to function as a producer on this next film—my first real production experience. I had responsibility. I would have to deal with a director, with actors, and, ultimately, with the people who were investing over $1 million in this venture. I knew I didn't have the Teflon veneer to slide away and pass the buck. I was no Yordan. He was never responsible for any disaster. There were always a dozen other people and circumstances to explain failure. He knew how never to admit any association with failure. This was a valuable talent I didn't have. I saw myself drowning on job number one. Since I was absolutely unable to echo Faith's enthusiasm about the script, I dictated three pages of notes about the problems I saw. I figured that at least, being specific might shield me from voicing an overall judgment.

"I can see a few problems," I said when we finally got together, and I handed him my lengthy notes.

"Sure," said Yordan. "I'll read them. Thanks. There's always some little fixing you can do." If he was impressed with my acuity or industry, he concealed it well. He went on, "You know, we've got to move ahead right away. Lee Van Cleef gets here in ten days. We have to do more casting so we can start shooting. We have to get moving with a production and a budget so we can pay the bills at the studio. The budget's gonna be done from this script the way it is." This was a lecture. I was being given a lesson in the realities of filmmaking.

The story was about four notorious bank robbers in the Old West who are hired to slip into Mexico and blow up a Mexican ammunition dump. Normally, it might have been difficult to get a director to go with this script, though recalling Yordan's ploy with Siodmak and *Custer*, I had no doubt that he would find a way to cross that ditch, and it was even easier this time, because, to get Spanish nationality for the film, we had to have a Spanish director. Sacristan came through with a recommendation, a local director who had even made a couple of films in England, a man with excellent English. We ran the films he had made in England and found them quite professional by our own standards. A man of about forty, Eugenio Martín was slender, sensitive, and pleasant-looking. He had grown up in Granada, the site of some of Franco's worst brutalities, including the murder of the poet Federico García Lorca, but Eugenio had been a boy at that time and grew up to become a teacher and professor of English. I always assumed that Eugenio was civilized enough to deplore Franco, but this was still Franco's time in Spain and people did not express any negative opinions about their generalissimo. Eugenio was thrilled to be hired for an American feature, to be paid well by Spanish standards, and to be working with the distinguished Academy Award–winning Philip Yordan.

The principal casting was, as usual, done out of London by Ben Fisz. He assembled a fairly impressive cast. In addition to Lee Van Cleef, we now had Gina Lollobrigida as our female lead and James Mason as the heavy. Julian, our man in Rome, had to work with Lollobrigida to order her wardrobe. She had expensive tastes and carefully reserved her approval for gowns she intended to take with her after finishing the film. Julian called, troubled about how to handle this, but nothing could be done, as he discovered, without enraging her.

When our star reported for work in Madrid, I picked her up at the airport. She was sullen and instantly let me know where things stood. "You know I don't usually work for this kind of money," she sniffed, "$50,000."

Since I knew nothing about the deal she had made and didn't want to let her know that was the kind of producer I was, I hesitated to get into this but was saved because she went right on.

"My agent made this deal for me to be paid at the back end and get a participation. It's a tax deal," she concluded airily.

My problems with Lollobrigida were just beginning. Absolutely nothing pleased her. She even refused to submit to the routine doctor's examination required for our insurance. "I know these doctors," she snapped. "They're all the same. They just want to look up under my skirt!"

"You know, Gina, it's the same on every film. We have no choice. We have to have the insurance for the Errors and Omissions policy."

She ungraciously agreed to see the doctor at his office, but, having conceded this, she figured she had me at a disadvantage and used the moment to ask me for a favor. "My good friend is here. He's a marvelous photographer, and he's going to stay here with me. I'd like you to give him a job as still cameraman on the film." Working on the kind of stringent budget limits we had, I regretfully turned her down and found her even more resentful and uncooperative after that. I was learning that no matter how much they earned, some stars never stop trying to milk more money out of a production.

Her complaints continued until the very last day of her schedule. On an evening when our friends David and Betty Lewin had arrived in Madrid and were having dinner with us, Lollobrigida called me. David was a very successful journalist who specialized in writing about film personalities for the London press. He personally knew almost every screen star on either side of the Atlantic.

"I've never been paid!" Lollobrigida was screaming into the phone. "It's the last day of filming and the money was never deposited in Rome!"

I knew nothing about this. "I'll look into it right away," I promised.

"Right away! Right away! That's not soon enough. I'm supposed to finish work here tomorrow!"

"I'll call Rome now. I'm sure I can straighten it out."

She didn't believe me. "If the money isn't paid tonight, I don't come to work tomorrow. I leave."

If she really did leave, we would miss her important final scene. "That won't be necessary, Gina. I'll get it worked out tonight." But I had no idea how I would do that. She hung up.

I found Yordan and Fisz at a hotel in Rome, explained the matter to Yordan, who turned me over to Fisz, who started to give me a lot of double-talk. "Don't worry. She'll be paid. It's complicated because they want a tax deal. Tell her to relax."

It was my turn to scream. "Never mind all that crap, Benny. You get in touch with her or her agent and get this settled. Tonight. I need her on the set tomorrow."

"Tonight? You want me to open the banks tonight? There's nothing I can do tonight. You shouldn't be so excitable. And you shouldn't talk to me that way. You just go ahead and talk to her." The ball was in my court. I was left on my own.

My loud shouting on the telephone, even from my office in the apartment, had easily been heard in the living room. I explained the impasse to David Lewin. He was amused. "I know her very well," he said. "Let me talk to her." I didn't think that was a good idea, not at the moment.

I called her back. "I just talked to Mr. Fisz in Rome. He's the executive producer who made the deal with your agent. He said he'll get it all settled tomorrow. There's nothing he can do tonight."

She wasn't satisfied. "You can forget about me for tomorrow."

"In that case, Gina, what can I do? I'll have to rewrite the scene, write you out of it. That's a pity. It's one of my favorite scenes in the film and one of your best. You know it's the pay-off for your funny double-crossing character." This hit the actress where she lived, but she still wouldn't budge.

As a last desperate ploy, I said, "Listen, Gina, I have a friend of yours here, David Lewin. He knows we're working together and wants to say hello."

"David Lewin?" Her voice rose in pitch. "Don't tell me he knows what's going on?"

"He doesn't know anything. I'm back in my office. He just wants to say hello."

I hurriedly briefed David. He was to know nothing about our problem. He understood and got on the phone. They talked about nothing consequential, just that he was a good friend of mine and had heard good things about the film and was looking forward to seeing it. When he was through, she asked to talk to me again. "I'm glad you were able to work things out in Rome," she now told me. "I'll see you on the set tomorrow."

I believed that Lollobrigida was right to worry that the deferred salary would be slow in coming—if it ever came. There are many escape routes for contracts made across national borders and Fisz knew them all. But that was not my department.

My initial contact with James Mason was even more trying. I admired him greatly as an actor and considered it a coup to get him to work for us. I wondered how he had fallen on such hard times as to agree to work on *Bad Man's River*, but I was looking forward to meeting him. Two days before he was due to start working, I still hadn't heard from him. Frantically, I began trying to find him. At last, I got the right number in Switzerland. "Where are you?" I demanded testily.

"Who wants to know?"

"I'm Bernie Gordon, producer of the film."

"I never heard of you," he dismissed me.

"That's neither here nor there. It's just two days before you're due to start work here, and I've never heard from you."

"I don't like your tone, Mr. Gordon."

"Well, now that I've tracked you down, I have to know whether or not you intend to be in Madrid no later than tomorrow." I knew he had been provided with a couple of first-class tickets. "If you will get to Barajas (the Madrid airport) on a flight from Geneva, I will have time to get you to wardrobe so that you can start work the following day."

He barely managed to say all right and hung up. I wasn't certain whether he would appear. At the airport the next day, I was nervously trying to spot the actor in the crowds getting off a plane. I knew James Mason's looks well from dozens of films. I searched the line of arrivals but no one even remotely resembled Mason. At last a man approached me. He had long, unkempt hair, wore a casual shirt and trousers that looked as if he had slept in them not once but for a month. "You look like a CIA man. If you're looking for me, I'm James Mason."

I never asked him but had to assume he was in his hippie mode. This was, after all, 1971. He was not the clean-shaven, bowler-hatted English gentleman in impeccable Bond Street attire I had expected. He was accompanied by a handsome woman, Clarissa, who was also casually dressed but was more presentable than he. Clarissa, I later learned, was a bright and attractive Australian circus performer. I believe they were married.

I succeeded in getting them settled at the Commodore hotel, then hurried him downtown to Cornejo, the one and only wardrobe company in Madrid. I sat with him as he tried on various costumes appropriate to the time and place of the script and also to his character as a con man. We agreed about everything and by the time we rode out to the studio in the car, we were getting along famously. Mason turned out to be one of my happier encounters with film stars.

There were other star problems. Lee Van Cleef was furious with me for failing to use Alex Singer again on this second film. He liked Alex. Alex had a great gift as a director: he knew how to kiss the right end of his stars, a talent I might well have studied. I tried to explain to Van Cleef.

"It has nothing to do with Alex," I said. "He's a great friend of mine, but this is a Spanish production, so we have to use a Spanish director."

Van Cleef was not appeased. He didn't like me and was only too glad to manufacture an excuse to attack me. "I'm not interested in your problems. And I'm not interested in working with someone who is learning how to be a producer. You can practice on someone else. Not me."

Van Cleef made other problems that challenged my inexperience. He didn't want to ride a horse. He hated horses. As a stuntman, he'd had too many bones broken while riding or falling off the damned animals. On occasion, the director had to call on me to persuade the actor to do a scene. Van Cleef balked again when we were shooting night scenes in the bitter cold of the Madrid winter. It was too cold, he said. He wanted to go back to his comfortable hotel room, but it was expensive shooting at night, and the actor was holding up the works. I compromised with Van Cleef, promising him that we would make the scene in one take so he could then leave.

The real problems, though, were script problems. Yordan had a talent for writing amusing and original personal scenes that pleased the actors and dressed up the dreary story. But he had no sense at all for story structure. When the continuity made no sense, he would rip off another cute scene and tell the director to shoot it. Most of my Sundays were spent either with Yordan and Sperling thrashing out script problems, or with Yordan and Martín. Little as I liked Sperling, he was more serious and critical of the script; the two would get into loud and nasty exchanges, Sperling insisting on significant rewrites, Yordan snarling that Sperling was no writer and couldn't tell him, Yordan, what to do. Once I thought the battle would become physical. I stood up and announced that my presence wasn't needed and walked out.

On another Sunday, Martín, the director, begged for help with a transition that made no sense. Yordan made a typical and tiresome suggestion.

"Every time we get into trouble on this script," I said impatiently, "you come up with another cute scene. One more comic scene, and the picture is out the window. No audience will take any of the action or suspense seriously."

Instead of addressing the problem, Yordan looked pained. "Look, Bernie, let me handle this. I know what I'm doing."

Furious at this put-down, I got up to go. "Since I can't be any help here, there's no point in my staying."

Yordan was as irritated as I. "Since this is your first job as a producer, why don't you just stay around and learn?"

Cravenly, I subsided. Could he be right? I still wasn't certain how much he really did know. Eugenio Martín was altogether under his spell, and, despite all the trouble he was having with the script, he believed.

On our next film, Yordan was far away in London. Martín depended entirely on me as producer and, when required, as writer. It was a real satisfaction when he said to me with heartfelt sincerity, "I thought Yordan had the answers, but you're the one who's serious about helping. When I have a problem and come to you, you work it out for me. You're the best producer I've ever worked with." As you can imagine, Eugenio and I have remained friends ever since.

Even as we struggled with *Bad Man's River*, we re-opened production on *Captain Apache*, with demands on me for rewrites and demands on poor Alex Singer, long since off the payroll, to reshoot.

As in that apocryphal Hemingway remark, neither *Bad Man's River* nor *Captain Apache* were ever finished. They were terminated (surrendered) and flung into the cold world to sink or swim. For those, and for *A Town Called Bastard*, I found the British trade press very kind. I suspected that they were inclined to favor any film with a British label. *Bastard* was reviewed in the *Kinematograph Weekly* as "A brooding violent story, this has considerable force of the kind that is popular just now. Very strong X attraction." *Captain Apache* was hailed in *Today's Cinema* as "A smashing Western just sufficiently tongue-in-cheek to delight the more sophisticated but not enough of a send-up to spoil the enjoyment of those addicts who prefer their Westerns to be deadly serious."

Bad Man's River is, perhaps, best characterized by a quote from James Mason, who allegedly said, "When shooting a Western in Spain, one should not say to oneself, 'Never mind, no one is going to see it,' because that will be just the film the Rank Organization will choose to release in England." After *Bad Man's River* and *Captain Apache*, we had to get another script ready for the next film. My old friend Bob Williams, who had helped me on *The Law Vs. Billy the Kid*, sent me a few pages, an idea of a story about Pancho Villa, who had actually invaded the United States at a border town in New Mexico, the one and only foreign invasion of the United States. This historical curiosity has been ignored, at least by Americans, but it seemed a promising idea. Williams was starving in Hollywood, never having recovered from the blacklist days. I persuaded Yordan to send him $1,000 for the idea. There was no story.

Van Cleef finished work on *Bad Man's River* in the middle of March, but we had to go back and clean up *Captain Apache*. Yordan kept writing new scenes to be shot, first a prologue, then a prologue to the prologue, then a third prologue. At the beginning of April, I lugged cans of film to Rome so I could direct Van Cleef and Carroll Baker in dialogue looping at a sound studio. That was a learning experience and I enjoyed it.

I stayed with Julian and tried to talk him into coming back to Madrid to work on *Pancho Villa*. Money was tight; Yordan would only come up with $1,000 per month and his usual promises of future rewards. But Julian, unemployed, with few prospects, accepted; he followed me back to Madrid and moved into our spare bedroom. Julian worked full-time on the script, meeting frequently with Yordan and me. In a few weeks we were casting: Telly Savalas as Villa; Clint Walker as his American buddy; Chuck Connors as Villa's nemesis, General Pershing; and Anne Francis as Walker's ex-wife, with whom he has a fighting romance.

All this was done, as usual, before we had a finished script. We were having difficulty figuring out a solid action climax. We decided on Villa and Pershing pursuing one another by train, but how to wind up with a wallop? While we were all kicking around ideas, I came up with something. "Maybe we could have the two of them, Villa and Pershing, in two trains roaring toward each other. Neither of the idiots will give in, stop his train, and reverse to avoid a fatal collision. It's a double game of chicken."

"Then what?" asked Yordan.

I couldn't come up with an answer. I shook my head. "Nah, it's crazy. I can't see any way out."

Yordan didn't want to drop it. As always, he had a good sense of theater, or cinema. "It's exciting. Let's try to make it work."

"It's like having your hero jump off the Empire State Building, then telling me to figure out a way to save him while he's on the way down." Eventually we came up with an answer that worked very well. We shot the horrendous collision, then cut immediately to a hospital room where Pershing is in bed, covered head-to-toe in a plaster cast and able to communicate only by whistling through a hole cut open for his mouth. We inserted some gag with the pretty nurse. There was nothing gruesome or gory. Pershing recovers, of course. We saw no injured, maimed, or dead at the crash scene. The audience buys it as a joke, but buys it because there is at least one symbolic victim.

We prepared the production and ordered a beautiful set of miniature trains from a specialty firm in London. The miniatures were quite large, each rail car and locomotive about six feet long, motorized, controlled by radio. The locomotives were equipped with a device that emitted smoke from the stack. Any child's dream. In fact, each car was big enough for a child to lie down in. We built a railroad track at the studio that was long enough for two trains to be photographed racing toward each other in a single shot that, also, would not include any background of modern buildings or incompatible power lines. The ground was carefully leveled so that the speeding trains would not jump the track. None of this was routine. The Spanish set constructors had to overcome real problems, but they worked everything out quite well in spite of my worried interference.

When Telly Savalas showed up to begin shooting, he was already an old hand in Madrid. Because I hadn't been around during the shooting of *A Town Called Bastard*, I had never met Telly. I found him easy, friendly, cooperative. He was having a tough time making ends meet and was working in bottom-of-the-barrel Italian features—before *Kojak*. Had he read the script? I didn't know. His attitude was that the film and its fate were my problem. Just so long as he got paid.

"You know," I said, "we have a problem because a lot of people know Villa had thick black hair."

Telly shrugged. "I'll wear a hairpiece."

I was surprised at this since I assumed he prized his trademark bald-as-an-egg hairstyle. Believing he would have a problem about this, I had worked out a solution in advance. "I had an idea, Telly. What do you think of this? We'll start the film with you as a captive of the Mexican general who's your nemesis. He's got you in a railroad car heading for Mexico City, where he plans to have you hanged. Meantime, to humiliate you, he has you strapped in a chair and is having your head shaved. Then, you're rescued and play the rest of the film without any hair."

"Fine." He smiled. "Good idea."

I was pleased because I felt that Telly was an asset playing his recognizable self. "I'll send a car for you in the morning, get you to the studio, work on your wardrobe, and we'll be ready to shoot."

"No problem." Telly was ready to go. I found Telly to be smart, educated, and tough without being mean. He gambled compulsively, drank, and was usually deeply in debt.

By early July, Yordan decided to leave the Spanish operation entirely to me and settle in London "where the real action is." As part of the deal Jean and I were able to move into the huge, if barren, apartment Yordan had bought on the Burgos road leading north from Madrid. We got the place painted and somewhat refurnished and moved in to what seemed like acres of space.

Shooting on *Villa* progressed. Telly was fun to work with and gave me a taste of the kind of Hollywood I hadn't known. He had a gofer, a man who hopped around on a peg leg and performed whatever task Telly wanted him to handle. Mostly he would go into a bar, look for some attractive women, and invite them over to Telly's place for drinks and the evening. Surprisingly, often they agreed, and one thing usually led to another. Telly eventually settled down with a couple of attractive English girls he brought out to the set while he was shooting. At lunchtime we all ate the hearty food prepared for the entire cast and crew by some miracle-workers who operated from a trailer equipped with butane stoves. The studio paid for all this, being charged each day for the number of meals served. Because Telly's two lady friends ate in his trailer with him, one of the production assistants finally came to me and complained that we were paying for people who weren't on the payroll. What to do? I told him to get lost. I didn't need trouble with the star over the cost of a couple of lunches, and though I was curious what this threesome did during the lunch break, I didn't think it was the right time to inquire.

Further along in the production, we had to make a major move to a location near Granada, where a small town, Guadix, had a railroad spur line from a mine.

I was beginning to have problems with Sacristan. He had loaded the crew with relatives and friends who weren't needed on the production. Sacristan was what might have been called in Spanish, a *cacique*, a kind of chieftain who doled out jobs and favors and expected loyalty in return. This was fine with me except that the salaries were coming out of the budget and I was fighting to complete the picture on budget. I could not afford to confront Sacristan, but I raised a question about some of these hirelings to let him know someone was looking into costs. He had also insisted on bringing along the sound crew, a tremendous waste of money because I knew the awful rattling of the period train we had shipped down would never permit recording synch sound. He strongly disagreed, but I was right. We weren't able to record a single line of dialogue and sent the crew back.

Other problems were typical, but some were not. For example, Telly was bored riding back and forth all day on the rattle-trap period train. He liked to climb up and ride on top. Eugenio Martín was terrified that a sudden stop would topple him off the train, and he was right, but he couldn't cope with the American star. I was called to climb up top and insist that Telly desist. Telly also made problems with his co-star, Clint Walker. Walker had recently survived a horrifying skiing accident, when a ski pole virtually penetrated his heart. As a result of this intimation of mortality, Walker informed me on arrival that he was through with any ego trips; he only wanted a peaceful existence and friendly relations with everyone. He had gotten religion. Only too happy to take advantage of this, Telly upstaged Walker whenever he could. Walker kept to his word and swallowed Telly's tricks until the last day of shooting.

In the final scene, the two of them are riding the tail end of a railroad car they have detached from General Pershing's train. The picture comes to an end as they disappear into the distance. Telly wasn't happy with this setup. He talked the director into a change that would result in his being featured solo instead of in a two-shot. This time Walker abandoned religion. He exploded and refused to do the scene. The director sent for me.

"Look, Bernie," Telly said, reasonably, "the picture is about Pancho Villa, not some fake invented American friend [Walker's role]. Villa just had a great scene with General Pershing. Now we're ready for the fade out. Should it be on Villa, who everyone knows got away from Pershing? Or should it be played with the fake American friend you invented for the film?"

"You're absolutely right, Telly," I agreed. "But you've been getting your way every time. Clint knows it. Everyone knows it. And Clint's been very nice about it. Right?"

Telly had the grace to grin and shrug.

"This time he's had a bellyful, and he won't do the scene any other way but how it's written." I pointed at the afternoon light. "It's getting late. We're losing the light. We're returning to Madrid tomorrow. If we don't get the shot right now, we're dead. So do the damned scene."

Telly shrugged. "Sure, Bernie. Whatever you say."

He acted like a good gambler (which he was), who makes a bad bet, loses, takes his lumps, and goes on.

Because of scheduling, our other star on the film, Chuck Connors, didn't have to report until we were halfway through the shoot. Connors was delighted with his role in the film. A comic role was a rare opportunity for him and he hammed it up with gusto, playing the insanely spit-and-polish general who was being driven mad by the slippery, unpredictable Mexican.

After returning from Granada we had some heavy post-production work to do, principally the stupendous final crash of the two trains. We were all unwilling to actually permit the two beautiful and expensive locomotives to collide, blow up, and be destroyed. The Spanish special effects people came up with a splendid solution. We ran the two trains together as close as possible and stopped them just before contact. Then we substituted two imitation locomotives, hollow shells made of sheet lead that looked just like the real thing. For the final few feet before contact, the two fake locomotives were pushed together with poles by men out of camera range. As the sheet lead collapsed convincingly, fireworks inside the locomotives were set off to create a tremendous explosion. The scene was rehearsed as realistically as possible after long discussions with the cameraman about how many frames per second to use, how many cameras to use, and so on. The actual shoot worked beautifully in a single take.

Since we hadn't needed the cast for this work, they had all dispersed. We found, though, that an important scene shot in Guadix of Telly riding in an open flatcar had missed the crucial close-up shots of Telly. I called him in Rome and explained that we needed him back for one day. He wanted to be paid. I told him I had no money but agreed to provide him with a week at a hotel plus a chauffeur and car during his stay.

"Okay. Send me three first-class round-trip tickets Rome–Madrid."

"Three tickets?" I howled. "We only need you. Just you here for one day."

"Three tickets," he insisted.

"Why only three? Why not four or five or six while you're at it?"

He considered this and offered to compromise. "Send me one first-class round-trip ticket for Los Angeles–Madrid."

We settled for two-first class tickets Rome–Madrid. I was beginning to feel like a producer. After he arrived and while he was playing the scene, Telly never let me forget that he was doing me a favor, but it was all good-natured.

When *Pancho Villa* was finally released, the British trade press treated it kindly, though this time, since it was much more my own baby and the comments seemed right on, I was more inclined to accept the kindness. Marjorie Bilbow of *Cinema TV Today*, had this critical comment:

Like all the best jokes, this film does not start off with its punch lines and gives a deceptive impression of being just another ropey old Western — although there are a few sly in-jokes providing clues for those of us whose bottoms are sore with riding the Italian-Spanish-German range . . . I suppose you could say it's deplorable to make fun of national heroes — but that is an old English custom and Pancho Villa is in some pretty good company.

Thank you, Marjorie Bilbow. At least one person really understood what we were trying to do.

With Ben Fisz long departed and Yordan also gone to live and work in London, I was, finally, truly in charge in Madrid, not only of film production but of running and managing a studio. When the cold winter descended on us, I ordered good heaters for the sets where we worked; when I questioned the need to rent expensive generator trucks to provide electricity for production, I arranged to have a new heavy-duty electrical line run to the property. I was warned that this was risky because we might suffer an interruption of current while shooting. I decided to take that risk and never regretted it. I had a restaurant built at the studio and contracted with a company to provide meals at an agreed-upon price schedule. There were similar problems to solve about parking and the paving of a road up to the hilltop permanent sets. None of this was accomplished without sometimes rancorous disputes, but it all got done.

Pancho Villa, the first production I might call my own, is not a film I would nominate for any kind of award, but, despite script problems, it was finished on time and on budget, was completed, for once, without the endless reshooting of every other Yordan production, and it even received some favorable notices. I was beginning to feel confident in my new role and hoped to go on to bigger and better films.

24

In London, now that he had a source of funds, Yordan was working with Ben Fisz to promote a vertical operation with its own distribution company and a program of cheap horror films. He hired Julian and Arnaud d'Usseau at his standard $1,000 a month to come to London to write scripts. Occasionally Yordan popped over to Madrid to check on the production progress, look at some dailies, and deal with the financing.

In Madrid a great deal of the production money came from a revolving credit line at the Banco de Bilbao, one of the leading Spanish banks, where Lizarza and Sacristan had good connections. Yordan became a player. A number of times he took me to meetings with the bank's principal officers at their downtown headquarters so that they could become familiar with me, know that I was now in charge of the local operation, and deal directly with me when necessary.

On one visit to Madrid, Yordan showed up while I was deeply involved in shooting *Villa*. "We're going to have to come up with another picture to keep the studio going."

I was much too busy to want to consider this, but keeping the studio going was very much a concern of mine.

"No more Westerns," Yordan went on. "You can't give them away in the States anymore. And without the American market, there's no way to recoup costs."

"So what do we do?"

"I think we should do a horror film. You can always find a market for them—anywhere. You have any ideas?"

The weather was rainy and dark as I drove us back to town from the studio on a back road. I became so involved in thinking about what film we might do next that I took a wrong turn. Though we were close to the city, I found myself lost in a remarkably remote rural byway and had trouble finding a way to get back on track.

"How the hell did this happen?" I muttered, trying to read the road signs through the gloomy rain.

"You took a wrong turn," Yordan said helpfully. He was not a man who liked being lost. "Get us back on the right road."

I was trying to do that. "Since we've got that beautiful miniature railroad," I said, "and the track, why don't we do a horror story on a train?" I suppose I was thinking of something like *Murder on the Orient Express.*

This kind of economy was right up Yordan's alley. He agreed at once. "What can we title it?"

A title already? I was scarcely back on the road to Madrid. I threw out the most obvious suggestion. "*Horror Express.* What else?"

As far as he was concerned, that was it. He had already leaped ahead, seeing ways to finance and promote such a film. To my regret, the title stuck. I've always felt it sounded cheap and lessened the value of what was otherwise a good effort. The Spaniards had better taste. When it came to translating the film title for Spanish release, they called it *Pánico en el Transsiberiano* (Panic on the Trans-Siberian Express).

An insignificant footnote to all this has irritated me for years. Somewhere, somehow, it was reported that our lovely miniature trains were obtained from the production of David Lean's film *Dr. Zhivago*, which was also shot, in part, in Madrid. For the record, that is not true. We had our own trains that, I believe, were as good as the ones for Lean's fifteen-million-dollar film. Aside from this, I think *Zhivago* was a fine film and a great production.

I borrowed Arnaud from his hated London chores of writing horror film scripts under Yordan's supervision. He was pleased to return to Spain and go to work with me writing a script he felt had more promise. The *Pancho Villa* production absorbed me and I had little time to work with Arnaud. I liked his idea of placing a troupe of circus performers on the period train and playing out a suspense story with them. He wrote a script draft, and though it had its charms, it didn't have the action, suspense, and horror elements that I was expected to deliver. After a couple of more passes, I decided Arnaud was stuck with his initial concept, and, difficult as it was for me to switch from one friend to another, I got Julian to come in and work on a quite different story. I was functioning now as a producer in a way I didn't particularly enjoy, as I had spent much of my working life assailing stupid producers who only knew how to switch writers, but I was under pressure from London to get a script and a production going pronto.

Julian and I worked out a more traditional story outline. He wrote his version of the script, a first draft. An archeologist unearths a creature from outer space that has been trapped in an icy Siberian wasteland since a prehistoric period, before even hominids existed. The creature is crated for shipment back to Europe on the Trans-Siberian Express. It revives. Having witnessed the development of the Earth and of mankind, the creature intends to survive and return to his own galaxy. You can take it from there. Eugenio, our Spanish director, consulted with us, but, like any director actively shooting a film, he scarcely had the time or energy to breathe.

By September, with *Villa* in the can, we all wound up in London for consultation. Eugenio and Julian were there. Eugenio and I were not satisfied yet with the script, but he was more emphatic—he wouldn't direct the film in its present form. Julian and I met with Yordan in the new offices on Audley Street. I told Yordan we were not ready to go. "The script needs more work."

Yordan wouldn't hear of it. We had to get a picture started right away. "You can rewrite until the cows come home," he insisted in his intimidating mode, "and it won't make a dime more at the box office."

"Eugenio won't direct it as it is," I replied.

"I'll handle Eugenio," Yordan came back.

"Dammit, Phil, I've heard this kind of talk from you too many times. Maybe you can muscle Eugenio. I've seen what happens with those films where you say the script is good enough. If you want me to do this film, Julian comes back to Madrid with me and we rewrite the script."

Shouting matches did not startle Yordan. He took this calmly, but Julian turned white (saying later that in all our years together he had never seen me so enraged).

Yordan backed off. "Okay. But remember it's now September. We'll have a thirty-day schedule, so we have to go in November and finish before the end of the year." The holidays were always expensive in lost time and money.

"I'll do my best." That's all I could promise.

For our return to Madrid, Jean and I detoured through France. Having finally cleared away their divorces from former spouses, Arnaud and Marie Christine, the French woman he had been living with for years, were to be married in Marie Christine's home town in Burgundy. We flew to Paris and took a train to Chalon-sur-Saône. Arnaud met us and drove us to the tiny town of Buxy. He had arranged a room for us in the only hotel. Modest as it was, we were surprised that there was any hotel in a settlement boasting no other buildings.

Marie Christine's mother lived in a fine old country home that sat in the middle of beautiful and extensive gardens. It was the remains and last gasp of a once-important provincial family. A few minutes outside Buxy, the estate was the scene of great festivity: other American friends had come down from Paris, the champagne flowed, neighbors hosted parties around the countryside, and the guests were feted in local restaurants, all run by friends of the family. We were treated to the best food and wine of Burgundy and lived in a happy, sated haze for a weekend. Even the wedding ceremony in the local *mairie* was anything but routine as Marie Christine's two lovely children (whom we had known well from Hollywood) snapped photos and embraced Arnaud as their beloved new father. This weekend remains one of the happiest and most delightful memories of all of our European years. It was especially gratifying that Arnaud, who had suffered more than most from the blacklist, plunging from successful and esteemed Broadway playwright to bottom-fishing for handout assignments from Yordan, had finally found real happiness in a marriage that lasted the rest of his life.

In Madrid Julian was working disconsolately on the *Horror Express* rewrite. He had been away from home and wife in Rome too long and was impatient to finish. I worked with him as much as possible, but I was overwhelmed by the problems of getting the production organized. This was to be an entirely new experience because I had bitten the bullet, fired Sacristan, and undertaken full responsibility for the production. Even forgetting the multi-million dollar Bronston budgets, Sacristan had grown accustomed to working with us as foreigners who had money to burn. None of the previous three films at Daganzo had been brought in for less than a million dollars. I was now determined to work in the local mode and produce films for much less. With the help of a truly Spanish crew, including my new production manager, I budgeted *Horror Express* at $300,000, apart from any British or American cast. My production manager, cameraman, special-effects person, art director, makeup artist, and all the crew spoke no English. For me it was another learning experience.

I was now a one-man operator, entirely in charge and entirely responsible. My only real help, aside from Eugenio, who was having the usual director's jitters at the prospect of starting a film, was my new production secretary, Lisa Doty, an American woman who spoke serviceable Spanish. She had worked extensively in Canada on documentary and television films so she was not without production experience. Lisa and I became good and lasting friends.

At work on *Horror Express*, I made every effort to respect Sacristan's special status and macho image. I let him keep his office and saw to it that the new production manager trod carefully in dealing with the *cacique*, but word must have spread through the small Madrid film community that Sacristan was out at the only foreign-run studio. Out was out and my effort to remain on good terms with him were doomed, as I later learned.

Another complication arose, one I didn't anticipate. The studio real estate had been purchased and paid for by Bobby Marmor and Yordan. Everything—all the construction of the sets and buildings—had also been paid for by them, but Spanish law did not permit foreign ownership of any media, including film studios, so the nominal ownership had been vested in some Spaniards (one being Sacristan) and our studio accountant. The attorney, Paco Lizarza, may also have had a piece, though he was careful to keep his skirts clean, since what had been done contravened the law. The studio's muddled ownership would come back to haunt us.

Creating a truly Spanish production company to produce *Horror Express* and subsequent Spanish nationality films was even more complicated. The same nominees who "owned" the studio became officers and shareholders, plus Eugenio Martín and me. Amused, I gave my consent to become one of the minor corporate officers, with a share or two of meaningless stock. There were no assets and the stock had no value. Since I was strictly a minority shareholder, there was no conflict with Spanish law. When the film was almost completed, Lizarza informed me that Spanish fiscal inspectors were snooping around, suspicious that our financing was not really Spanish and that the whole operation was fraudulent.

"You have to understand, Bernie," he said, so earnestly that I could see sweat on his brow as well as the dandruff on his shoulders, "the fiscal inspectors here are the most highly educated and trained officials in the whole country. Something like the people they send to the *École Normale Supérieure* in France." I was familiar with that setup. "You have to understand," he emphasized again, "in Spain maybe you can get away with murder if you have the right connections. But you don't get away with violating the currency laws. You'd be surprised at the people they send to prison for that." He paused to let that sink in. "It doesn't matter who you are or who you know."

I could only assume that he was referring to the fact that I was a foreigner. "So what do we do now?"

He hunched his shoulders. "We're not in trouble yet. I'll try to handle it."

I had never considered the legal violations involved as truly significant because we were in fact bringing money into the country, honestly financing the films and creating employment for Spaniards. Where was the harm? But the government took a dim view of all this because, under the cover of Spanish nationality and its benefits, we would ultimately be exporting films to lucrative markets all over the world and never repatriating the proceeds to Spain. When Eugenio, not the most courageous man in the world, heard what was going on, he almost fell apart. I didn't feel very snappy either and made myself scarce when the inspectors came around to the studio. I never heard the end of this saga but assumed that Lizarza and Sacristan had somehow satisfied the expert snoopers.

Back in Madrid, after a full month of rewrites, Julian insisted on taking off for Rome. He was fed up with the script. With misgivings, I let him go but immediately regretted it. Eugenio was uncharacteristically stubborn about needing changes, and I had to agree that further work would help. I was back on the phone to Rome. "I hate to do this, Julian, but I need you back here."

"Not a chance," he replied.

"The script needs work, and I'm too busy to do it myself."

"I'm sorry." He meant it. "I have a life here and a wife who's been neglected for too long. I just can't leave again so soon."

"I'm sorry, too. And I understand. But I wish you wouldn't force my hand."

"What does that mean?"

"It means you're putting me in a lousy position. It means that if you're not back here in a couple of days, I'll have to get someone else to work on the script."

Julian snorted. "Fat chance. Who will you find in Madrid?"

Actually, I had anticipated this impasse and had checked around. I knew that John Melson (from the *Battle of the Bulge* script) was still around and eager for work. "Johnny Melson is here and he wants to work. You remember him."

Long pause. Julian was considering. "How long will it take?"

"A week. Maybe two. Not more."

Julian came back, worked quickly and well, and in another ten days we had the script in satisfactory shape. Eugenio kept dragging his feet. I began to wonder why. He had a script that was much better than either one he had worked on before. Why was he so negative? Yordan was gone. Didn't he feel secure working on an English-American production where I was in charge? I was learning that most directors had to be dragged kicking and screaming to the set for the first day's shooting. Was that the problem? Or was it something else? I was not fated to get a good answer to this because, fewer than three days before our start date, I had an emergency call from him.

"I'm sorry, Bernie, but I have to go into the hospital for an operation. I won't be able to do the picture."

Get another director? *Now?* And a Spanish director at that, because of the damned Spanish nationality problem? Alarmed as I was, I had the decency to ask Eugenio about his condition. "What's the problem? What kind of operation are you having?"

"It's for hemorrhoids," he explained. "I've put it off as long as I could. I can't wait any longer."

This struck me as less than a life-and-death matter. "How long will you be in the hospital?"

"Three or four days."

"I'll postpone production for a week. We'll just have to start a week later." He was stuck. He would have to go on. We didn't get started until the second week of December 1972, which meant we ran through the Christmas and New Year's holidays. Despite problems, I felt I was really making a film—no Ben Fisz, no Milton Sperling, no Yordan. Not even Sacristan. I have never enjoyed anything so much in my life.

In London, Ben Fisz had cast two highly regarded stars of the Hammer horror films, Christopher Lee and Peter Cushing. He had also made a deal for Telly Savalas to return to Madrid briefly for a truncated role. It was creative casting, and so was the deal made with Telly, who was, predictably, broke again. They had agreed to purchase a seven-year lease on a West End apartment, which would be his gift to the lovely lady with whom he was living. The added inducement—the gift was tax-free. I understood the cost was $22,000, which was a bargain for his services.

Christopher Lee was the first star scheduled to work. He showed up on time and conducted himself professionally. Tall, well-built, with strong, handsome features, he looked more like a leading man than a creature from the bog, but this suited his role in our film splendidly. He was pleased with his role and with the script. We worked out his wardrobe, he reported to the set promptly and knew his lines. He was cordial with me, with Eugenio, with everyone. When he wasn't working on the set, he roamed the hall of our dressing-room building where my office was located and sang arias from *Boris Godunov* at the top of his excellent baritone.

After the first week of shooting, Peter Cushing was due to start. I went to the airport to welcome the actor, whom I had never met, never even seen on screen, since I was not a fan of horror films. I had no trouble spotting Cushing: a refined looking English gentleman in a perfect British tweed suit, handmade London boots, proper necktie. He was slender, not tall, very fair, with delicate features—not what I had expected from one of the world's leading actors of horror films. No Frankenstein monster he.

My admiration for him faltered from the moment we got into the car for the drive to the studio. In quiet but insistent tones he made a startling announcement. "You know Mr. Gordon, I don't intend to work in your film." He was not a man who was making a rude joke.

I tried to digest this. "Then why are you here?"

"Mr. Fisz in London explained that I had to report and explain matters to you. I agreed to do the film on the basis of having read the first draft of the script, but when I read the final one, the one you're shooting, I told Mr. Fisz that I didn't care to work in the film."

"You could have called and told me that from London. I would have arranged for another actor. You're supposed to start working tomorrow."

Cushing was genuinely contrite. "I entirely agree. That's what I told Mr. Fisz, but he insisted that I come here and report directly to you."

Since the studio property virtually adjoined the airport, we had arrived by the time we had concluded our brief conversation. I settled Cushing somewhere while I grabbed a telephone and called London.

"What in the hell is going on?" I demanded of Fisz and reported my conversation with Cushing. "I'm supposed to start shooting with this man tomorrow."

Fisz's attitude was that he had provided the actor and the problem was now mine. "You're the producer," he virtually sneered. "So produce."

My shouting accomplished nothing except to entertain the considerable gathering that had assembled outside my office door to listen to my very loud and angry epithets. Completely at a loss, I sought out Christopher Lee, who was an old colleague of Cushing's.

Lee smiled. "That doesn't mean a thing. Peter is always like this at the start of every film."

"What am I supposed to do about it?"

"We'll meet with him at the hotel after work," Lee said, "and everything will be fine."

We met outside Cushing's room at the Eurobuilding in a small public area, where the three of us sat in easy chairs away from any other guests. I had no notion what to say or how to begin, but my efforts were not needed. Voluble under any circumstances, Christopher started to talk, a virtual filibuster of anecdotes and irrelevant remarks. Neither Cushing nor I could get a word in. No mention was made of Cushing's refusal to come to work, and if Cushing had any notion of voicing his intentions, he never had a chance. The whole performance was cleverly designed to keep Cushing from opening his mouth.

After about forty minutes of nonstop monologue, Christopher stood up. "All right, Peter, see you at work tomorrow."

If Cushing was surprised, he didn't betray it. I was dumbfounded, but Cushing reported to work the next day.

After a week, Peter, who was a truly gentle and decent man, serious about his work, dropped into my office. "I want to tell you, Mr. Gordon, how sorry I am for the way I behaved the day I arrived. I want you to know that I've studied the script again, and I really like it. I like the way the work is going, too."

I learned that Peter's wife, with whom he had been very close for almost fifty years, had died not long before, that this was his first venture outside of Britain since her death, that he was feeling devastated and alone in a foreign clime. Apart from his usual resistance to starting a film, Christopher believed that Cushing's intense sense of loss may have contributed to his initial feelings.

One of the first sequences I had planned for filming with both of them was at the abandoned Delicias railroad station in central Madrid. Aging and decrepit, the station was no longer in active use by the Spanish rail system except to store obsolete locomotives and carriages, but it was a magnificent structure of wrought-iron arches and columns supporting a glass roof, originally designed and built by Alexandre-Gustave Eiffel, the genius with wrought iron who built the Eiffel Tower in Paris. It was perfect for our period film set in the year 1906. More than that, we had the use of full-size period trains and locomotives, so we could see our characters climbing in and out of real trains, then see a real locomotive billowing great clouds of steam as it chugged from the station with our characters aboard. Since almost the entire action of our film was on the train, we needed many exterior shots of our miniature traversing the snowy wasteland of Siberia. I decided we should establish an authentic, full-size train at the very beginning to convince the audience that all subsequent train shots were just as real. The initial sequence in the station worked out beautifully and gave the film a very handsome and substantial start. The strategy worked—no one complained that our miniatures looked fake.

We were deep into the film when it was time for Telly Savalas to report. Having already worked together, Telly and I were good friends. I had met the beautiful lady for whom he had acquired the London apartment. Sally was one of the loveliest women I have ever seen. She was Anglo-Indian, with burnished coppery hair and a glowing, golden complexion. She was a show-stopper in any country, but in any language she was also the most languid person I had ever met. She seemed to drift along in a dreamworld of her own, never really responding to anyone or any situation.

Shortly after their arrival in Madrid, I called Telly at his hotel. Sally answered.

"How are you, Sally?" I asked in my heartiest tone, genuinely pleased to talk with her.

"I don't know," she murmured.

"Are you glad to be back here?" I asked, trying to make friendly conversation.

"I don't know," she replied.

"Don't you ever say 'yes'?" I coaxed her. "To anything?"

A pause. "Try me," she replied.

Her tone didn't suggest she really meant that, but her tone never betrayed anything. I confess she was so attractive that for a fleeting moment, a stray thought rippled through my mind. After all, what did I know about what went on behind closed doors with these two? But if opportunity it was, I let it pass.

Because our budget was stringent, we had to resort to many tricks and shortcuts in filming. I found my Spanish crew resourceful and willing. We had no proper full-size train interiors. Instead, we had acquired a set of flats that could be erected to represent the interior of a railway carriage. One was reserved for the interior of the freight car that carried the crate where the creature was stored and where much action occurred; the other was constantly redressed to represent the interior of either the dining car (sumptuous), a sleeping compartment (convincingly period), or the fine private car of the wealthy and important Russian count who was aboard with his young and delicious wife. We mounted the two sets on springs so they could be rocked during shooting to simulate the motion of a train.

That was only the beginning of our effects. We had to see the passing countryside through a car window when we occasionally played the action during daylight. The Spanish art director, ingenious and effective, prepared a large roll of heavy paper on which he had painted his version of the Siberian countryside. Set up outside the car window, this arrangement was slowly unrolled, suggesting the passage of the train across the tundra. It looked quite Mickey Mouse to me, but I was surprised to see how well it filmed. Much of this was new to me, and I was amazed by (and I appreciated) the cunning.

Other effects problems were more trying. Our premise required the creature, whether in his original form or in his subsequent forms (after he had inhabited the bodies of many of our characters), to turn burning red eyes toward the character he had chosen to take over. With the lights dimmed, these frightful red eyes had the power to drain the contents of the victim's brain and add it to the accumulated knowledge in the creature's brain. When this happened, the victim's eyes turned a blank white, signifying that the victim had suffered a brain-drain that left him good and dead. In the story, our leads, Cushing and Lee, playing the anthropologists, verified this when they began to catch on to the process and performed autopsies in our all-purpose freight car. They found the exposed brains to be smooth as bowling balls, having lost their normal wrinkles!

It was relatively simple to have the eyes go white. Carefully supervised by an accredited ophthalmologist, we arranged with a local optometrist (in exchange for a screen credit) to insert blank white plastic covers under the eyelids. The actor could see nothing through these, but he (or she) didn't have to do much except lie down dead. Turning the eyes into red headlights as the audience watched was more difficult. I urged the cameraman to try working with the red reflective material used in roadside warning signs, the material that appears to light up brilliantly when the headlights of a car hit it at the right angle. My notion was to seal a bit of this material over the actor's closed eyelid. The cameraman was dubious, but he arranged a trial. That never worked. I felt I was running into resistance, that the film crew didn't like my idea and didn't make a strong effort to get the angle of the lighting right so that the red reflection would be caught by the camera.

I was willing to consider anything that would work. The special-effects people came up with a dandy solution. It sounds tricky, but it worked easily. A tiny package was concocted of a very small flashlight bulb behind a red glass lens. A hidden wire led from this to a switch held in the actor's hand and connected to a battery pack. The eye package with the bulb and red lens was sealed over each of the actor's closed eyes. When the tiny bulb inside the package was switched on, the light shone through the red glass lens and produced the appearance of a "normal" eye that glowed red. It wasn't possible to see that the entire package, including the red lens, was actually placed over the actor's closed eye. This was certainly a case where the Spanish effects people and cameramen knew a lot more than I.

Irving Lerner helped me in every department. As associate producer, he worked with the cameraman and the film editor, a youthful Englishman, Bob Dearberg, who benefited enormously from Irving's expertise. Irving knew a great deal about laboratory work, film editing, and cameras, but his greatest expertise was music. He had started life as a musician. Irving and Telly Savalas persuaded me to hire John Cacavas to do the score of the film, even though we had to throw in a Spanish composer for nationality reasons. Cacavas was of Greek extraction, automatically making him a close friend of Telly, but Cacavas was very much an American who had been raised in the Midwest, perhaps in one of the Dakotas. He was a talented and experienced conductor and composer but had never done a film score. He was willing to work for practically nothing to get started in the business. For *Horror Express*, John Cacavas really took over, writing and conducting the entire score. Working with Irving, he developed a series of special themes or motifs that represented different characters or movements of our story. We came away with a superior score that has been commented on by people who know. Cacavas went on with Telly to make a distinguished career at Universal doing the *Kojak* series and many more.

My problems during this filming were not all technical or creative. Because of a variety of obstacles in London, including the disappointing performance of the earlier Westerns, it was increasingly difficult to carve out funds for my production. At the end of each week I had to have money to pay salaries; excuses were not accepted. The fascist Franco government did not permit unions or any kind of worker organization; but it did have a "corporate" structure that was supposed to protect workers' rights. In practice, this kept wages low, but an absolutely rigid rule was that wages due must be paid on the dot. If I let a payday pass without payout, I would be shut down the next day. *¡Ojala!*, as they say in Spanish. (Working with an all-Spanish crew greatly improved my command of the language.)

Saturday was payday. Each Friday the accountant assured me there were no funds for the payroll. I would get on the phone to Yordan in London, explaining that I desperately needed money. This was Spain. No excuses would be accepted. All stalling tactics were out. These discussions would wind up with him telling me to write a check on my Los Angeles bank for $30,000 or $40,000 (money I did not have on deposit) and to send it down to the Banco de Bilbao, which would honor my check immediately and provide the necessary pesetas. He would also assure me that he would see that my check in Los Angeles would be covered because a bad check of that size would land me quickly in a Spanish hoosegow. Bad checks were a criminal offense in Spain and other continental countries.

Could I trust Yordan to cover my bum checks? I really didn't know. He seemed more relaxed about such transgressions than I, and I didn't feel this was the occasion to test the flexibility of the Spanish financial system. What choice did I have? We went through this routine repeatedly. Friday was shouting-on-the-telephone day.

Although my checks were covered, there were times when, in the days before electronic transfers, it took an unreasonably long time for checks to clear, and I heard complaints, short of threats, from my friends at the Banco de Bilbao. Sometimes the delays worked to my advantage, but more often, they resulted in protests. I became convinced that the bank, like most banks, enjoyed working on a float, enjoying the use of my money for a number of days before making payouts.

As usual, Telly Savalas had to make his own creative contribution to the scenes, especially if that meant stealing the scene from everyone else. One day I had a frantic call to come to the set because Telly, playing the brutal Cossack colonel, was under a blanket making love to a girl in the telegraph station we had situated in the middle of Siberia.

Hurrying to the set and wondering how I could stop Telly from having such a good time, I arrived to find that, in the midst of this freezing Siberian scene, Telly had decided it would be wise to warm himself under a fur robe with the local girl. He wasn't making love to her, scarcely cuddling—a friendly encounter for mutual warmth. I liked it and told the director to shoot it just that way.

Telly came to me one day. "Bernie, you're the luckiest man I've ever met in the film business." This puzzled me. "Not because you're rich," he went on. He assumed that since I was in sole command of this studio operation I was at least being well paid. I didn't dare tell him that I was still on a meager "expense only" account—it would have lowered me in his estimation. "You're the only one I've met in this business who sends a few pages, a new scene, up to the set, tells us to shoot it, and then gets to see it in the projection room next day. Most writers have to wait months, even years, if they ever get to see their work on the screen, and then it has usually been fucked up. But you get to see it exactly as you've written it immediately."

For all of his screwing around and his shticks, Telly was an exceptionally bright and perceptive man, and he had hit the nail on the head: I had been feeling fortunate for precisely the reason he indicated. I was able to see a scene in the dailies within a day of writing it. I learned which scenes worked and which lay on the screen like dead fish. I learned to distrust reliance on dialogue instead of image.

Mark Miller's book, *Christopher Lee and Peter Cushing and Horror Cinema*, a filmography of their twenty-two films together, describes *Horror Express* as "the ultimate Lee/Cushing film," praising their performances extravagantly. He also notes, "Savalas plays his small role of an unpredictable, arrogant bulldog for every ruble it's worth and practically steals the film from his two co-stars."

Christmas of 1972 arrived before we were able to finish principal photography. Jean and I decided to have a big Christmas party in the cavernous apartment we had inherited from Yordan. We invited all the cast and principal crew personnel. We served traditional roast turkeys on the buffet table and, another rare treat, a real Smithfield ham we had sneaked out of the American PX. We also had all the other dishes and sweetmeats, both American and Spanish, that we could assemble. The party was a glittering affair. Telly and Sally; Christopher Lee and his handsome Danish wife, Gitte, with their nine-year-old daughter, Christina; Peter Cushing, polite and cordial, but painfully missing his wife; Eugenio, the director, with the pretty woman he was seeing, a Danish girl he had met when shooting *Bad Man's River*; and all the Americans, British, and Spanish connected with the production.

Feeling alone in this festive gathering and needing to be occupied, Cushing asked permission to carve the ham. He was wearing the white cotton gloves he used to preserve the appearance of his fingers from smoking stains. He did a fine job on what I still remember as the best ham I've ever eaten. The surprise of the party was nine-year-old Christina. We were playing recorded dance music, and in order to start things off, Jean took the girl by the hand and started to dance with her. Christina moved into this enthusiastically and never quit dancing and prancing around the middle of the floor for the rest of the evening. I expected her parents to pull her off and tell her to quit, but both Lee and his wife kept watching the child with keen pleasure. I was puzzled, until someone explained to me that Christina had been born with both feet turned completely backward and had undergone numerous operations in Switzerland to correct the condition. This was her coming-out party. Nothing could have thrilled her parents more than to see her performing on her feet with such ease and to see her, after so much torment, carry on in public like any other happy, spoiled little girl.

Although production was not quite completed, this Christmas party became something like a traditional Hollywood wrap party. Most of the cast and crew were here, feeling good about the film. Work had gone smoothly; there had been no unpleasantness; I felt that the people here liked and respected me and were not merely being deferential because I was the boss. I drifted around as a host offering food and drink, dancing with Christopher's handsome Danish wife and thinking all the while about the years that had passed, the years of selling plastic, of coaxing statements from accident witnesses, of sweating out the worst assignments with Sam Katzman. I had a keen sense of how fortunate I had been, compared to almost any of the other blacklistees, who had never had an opportunity to achieve any kind of success or gratification. This was a kind of culmination, a tribute more to extraordinary luck than any special virtue. How else could I explain winding up so happily giving such a Christmas party in Madrid, Spain?

We had one more major sequence to film. To finish off our monster, we would send our train hurtling off a cliff to burning and exploding destruction. In principle, and as written, the train was to be deliberately shunted off onto a spur line that ended at the face of a cliff rising 300 feet above the plain. For some reason that I have never understood, the director and our skilled cameraman insisted it was necessary to scout the area for an appropriate 300-foot cliff in the mountains near Madrid or elsewhere in Spain. I protested that since our model trains were built on a six- or seven-to-one ratio to real trains, a drop of forty feet or less would achieve the effect of a full-size train rolling off a 300-foot cliff. I couldn't convince them. It cost nothing to let them go look. I sat back, knowing that even if they found such a cliff, it would look ridiculous to send our miniatures off it. I also knew I didn't have the money to mount a location shoot for the crash.

In the end, the excellent art director painted a matte of the side of a mountain, then placed that between the camera and the 40-foot tower of our standing set. The model trains were to be pushed off a ramp at the top of the tower; it would look exactly as if they were careening off a very high cliff. After the camera test, and after everyone finally agreed this would work, we still had a problem: we didn't want to wreck our finely made and expensive model trains. Again, the Spaniards came to the rescue, tacking together simple wooden duplicates that cost almost nothing. We would shove these duplicate trains off the cliff.

One more battle remained to be fought. I asked the cameraman what camera speed he intended to use. He looked at me, surprised. "Normal. Twenty-four frames."

I shook my head. "If you do that, the whole shot will only last a second or two—the time it takes the cars to fall 40 feet to the ground." He shrugged. (Maybe that's why he had been looking for a 300-foot drop.) "We'll have to roll the cameras as fast as possible," I insisted.

He shook his head. "Then the whole thing will look false. It'll be in slow motion." By this time, the director had joined us and nodded in agreement with the cameraman. Any fool knew this!

"I don't care if it looks that way. We can't have the whole sequence over in a fraction of a second." I was emphatic. I felt odd. Where did I come off to argue with these professionals? I was not an expert cameraman. "How fast can our cameras turn?"

"Two times normal. Not more."

"Can we find a camera in Madrid that will go ninety-six frames per second?"

"I know where there is one," the cameraman admitted reluctantly.

"Let's rent it."

Irving agreed with me in this dispute. He knew enough about camerawork and about editing to understand exactly what should be done. Translating into Spanish, I explained Irving's plan to intercut angles from the different cameras so we could eliminate the slow-motion effect and also prolong the time of the drop without giving the appearance of trickery.

The big day came. Madrid gave us a wintry January sky that was exactly right for our Siberian express. With four cameras rolling and up to speed, action was called. The *mozos* on top of the tower pushed the cars off the ramp. They fell as required and when they hit the ground, they exploded and burst into flame just as we planned. When cut together under Irving's supervision, the effect was perfect. No complaints were voiced then or later.

The rest of the work was done at the excellent sound studio just outside Madrid on the highway from the airport. First we dubbed into English all the dialogue that had been spoken by the Spanish cast members, who had merely tried to mouth the English words they were speaking during the shoot, though they didn't understand what they were saying. This looping process was painstaking and wearing, but it was relatively new to me and I found it interesting. After we had a final cut, the post-production meant extensive dubbing. Now we put together the picture, dialogue, sound effects, and music. I learned that each craft looked out for itself. During shooting, the cameraman worried about how his colleagues would judge his photography; the makeup man his makeup; the wardrobe man his costumes; and so on, for special effects, sound recording, and everything else down the line. Even the director, I felt, was more concerned with how his special contribution would be received than with the final effect of the film. Of course, the actors worried about their performances quite apart from how it might contribute to the overall effect. In the dubbing sessions, the sound-effects man wanted his work to be heard —loud. The composer/conductor wanted his music to be heard—loud. Everyone was so tired of listening to the dialogue over and over again that they knew it by heart and couldn't care less whether it was comprehensible to an audience that had never heard the dialogue before.

As a neophyte producer, I was in an unenviable position. "I don't know what's right, but I know what I like," I said, like any ignoramus. By now I had enough confidence in my picture sense to insist and to prevail, saying to myself and to others, if it turns out wrong, it will be on my head. Despite this, the final phase of filmmaking was the most rewarding. We had all the pieces in place and were putting them together to create a whole.

The end result was gratifying. I had plenty of good helpers to whom I owed much. I also felt that I had controlled the process enough to take pride in my accomplishment.

Miller quotes reviews of *Horror Express* from the British press in his book about Christopher Lee and Peter Cushing. In the *Evening Standard* review, Alexander Walker noted, "It was made in Spain, had far more style and much, much more speed than the home-grown horrors but catches the national characteristics nicely." In the *Evening News*, Felix Barker proclaimed, "It is a rather splendid compound of old-fashioned melodrama." Reviewing the film for the *Monthly Film Bulletin*, Tom Milne praised the script: "[It] unwinds itself with sufficient cunning to keep interest alive, always one step ahead of the audience with a new revelation to come . . . "

Joe Dante, the esteemed American filmmaker and a director of excellent horror films, called *Horror Express* one of his five all-time favorite horror films: "Cossacks, countesses, and mad monks abound, the plotting achieves astonishing complexity for a film of this type, and the level of humor is surprisingly sophisticated. Cushing and Lee are especially amusing . . . In short, it is a real treat."

Years later, in California, I was dragged out to speak about my science-fiction films, and found myself next to Joe Dante on the platform. He turned to me and said how pleased he was to meet the producer of *Horror Express*.

What happened to the film in the U.S. and why didn't I become the king of horror filmmakers?

Bobby Marmor's real estate operations in London suffered sudden and serious financial reversals. He could not come up with the money to repay loans from the Banco de Bilbao. All I knew at the time was that Ben Fisz kept hammering at me to get hold of the negative and send it to London so that release prints could be made. Sacristan kept dodging with one excuse after another, but we had a debt of $150,000 to the Banco de Bilbao, money for which Spaniards had signed. The Spaniards were Sacristan and our accountant, Ramón, who were both acting for their British and American backers. Nevertheless, when the money to repay the bank was not forthcoming from London, these Spaniards properly exercised their rights to grab the negative, which was, of course, in the laboratory in Madrid. They had the legal right to do this since the negative was collateral for the loan. I was told nothing about this at the time. Typically, Sacristan would not tell me the truth, dodging with one excuse after another. Our already strained relationship became aggravated.

Because of the financial stress in London, Fisz made a wretched deal to sell the picture to an American company for release in the States for something like $100,000. The company acquiring the film was getting it virtually free—thanks to a tax deal that was in effect at the time. Fisz took the beat-up, faded, miserable, work print, which was all he had in London, made an inter-negative from that, and proceeded to run off release prints! Friends of mine who went to the theater to see the film in Hollywood reported back to me that it was almost impossible to see anything on the screen—everything was dark and unintelligible. I was completely bewildered, because I knew from many hours of fighting for film quality at the Madrid laboratory that we had an excellent negative, one that had been photographed with care and skill. At that time, Yordan had not seen fit to fill me in on these complications. The film he later said could have been a real hit and a moneymaker was trashed.

In 1972, at an international festival of horror films held in Spain, *Horror Express* was up for the grand prize. It lost to an American production, *The Other*, directed by Robert Mulligan, but *Horror Express* won the consolation prize for best story. This accolade went to Eugenio Martín, who had been listed, for nationality reasons, as the writer of the story—much to Julian's lasting irritation.

What might have been the start of a career I would really have enjoyed was, instead, finished. I may have had what it took to be an effective line producer, but I didn't have what it took to be a promoter. My own effort to promote an independent film in Spain was a dismal failure; I had lived comfortably under Yordan's umbrella too long, doing my share of writing and producing while he did his job of hustling, packaging, finding connections, financing, and distribution. The film operation in Spain folded. The studio was abandoned.

Jean and I wrapped up everything and we returned to Hollywood from Spain in early 1973.

Yordan had by now purchased an apartment in St. John's Wood, a pleasant suburb of London. He was working with Fisz and Marmor to develop a vertical film operation with its own distribution company, but none of the films from Spain or the ones they produced in London succeeded sufficiently. Yordan eventually abandoned the effort and returned to Beverly Hills.

Back in Hollywood all of Yordan's connections had soured: he had used up his goodwill in the film community. He had seen the demise of Bronston and of the London operation, which had gone broke. Installed again in his splendid home in Benedict Canyon, he wanted me to work with him, but he had nothing to offer. He became involved in a number of get-rich-quick schemes that had nothing to do with films. They drained him of the money he had managed to accumulate, but, rising from the ashes once again, he made another financing connection and actually started a studio in a deconsecrated church in Salt Lake City. He made friends with the Mormons and produced a film about Brigham Young. The project, another of his filmed messes, was in and out of work for years. Regardless, the Mormons were thrilled to have this important Hollywood writer, producer, and Academy Award-winner among them, working to tell their story and proselytize their cause. He had large plans, half-a-dozen projects based on old properties, and financing from people in the Midwest who were convinced he had put them on the Hollywood map in a big way. He even ferried me up to Salt Lake City and offered me an apartment. I found the place cheerless in winter and was uncomfortable working in a church, even a deconsecrated one. I tried to come up with some ideas to rescue his project, but he had no money for me, and it all seemed hopelessly tacky.

Eventually, everything petered out for Yordan. He sold his fine home in Beverly Hills at the very bottom of the real estate market and moved to San Diego, where he and Faith could be near her family. The two of them remain very devoted to each other. It's a fine marriage, his best by far. Yordan still dreams of making a killing in the stock market by floating an initial public offering based on his old properties. I have heard so much about this over the years that I've become something of an expert. At least I can look intelligent when I hear the plans for a stock prospectus.

His other obsession is to make a blockbuster film entirely from stock footage. It's so logical. There are millions, perhaps billions, of feet of film which have been shot on every conceivable situation. Why go to the bother and expense of shooting a new film with new footage, costing millions of dollars, when the stock can be picked up for a dollar a foot, assembled for about ten thousand bucks (for ten reels, plus a bit more for editing and lab work . . .), and presto! It's like saying that all the possible words are in the dictionary, so why bother to hire a hard-nosed, expensive writer (like Shakespeare) when you can get some bum to go through the dictionary and assemble the same words for practically nothing. Bring on the monkeys!

Yordan has been generous about filling me in with some of the stories I've related in these pages, spending hours on the telephone with me. I may not have portrayed him as an unsullied hero, but I hope he comes through as the fascinating, unflappable, if flawed, human being he is. We did, indeed, have a long and symbiotic relationship. (Symbiosis is defined in Webster's Dictionary as "the intimate living together of two dissimilar organisms in a mutually beneficial relationship," and this seems to describe us.) Yordan has become something of a Hollywood legend and enigma, and, because of my relationship with him, I am constantly asked for the "bottom line": Was he a phony, a fraud, someone without talent for anything but self-promotion? Could he write? How did he amass so many respectable writing credits?

Granted that I would not, under any circumstances, wish to trash him, it is fortunate that I do not feel the need to do that. I knew him as a man who genuinely considered himself a writer, a man who could and did sit down and write scripts—as when he wrote the script for *Bad Man's River*, and as, in the same suite with me, he tried to turn out scenes for *Battle of the Bulge*. The same was true when we were struggling to come up with scenes and ideas for *Krakatoa*. In more recent years I have known him to turn out many scripts that he has tried to promote. None of these writing efforts appealed to me as good professional work, but that is just my opinion. In any case, this does not make him a fraud, who, unable to write himself, exploited others to do his work for him. I certainly knew him as a man who could and did contribute creatively with good ideas and concepts for improving scripts, making them work, as for example in *Peking, Triffids,* and other instances not recounted in these pages. Perhaps it would have been better if he had settled in as a producer who would work productively with writers, but, in any event, I have always known him as a man who took himself seriously as a writer, took pride in that, and did not deliberately wish to hide behind the work of others. I respect that.

25

Back in the Hollywood Hills, Jean and I found another home we liked almost as much as the one we had so lovingly furnished and decorated before we left for Spain in 1970. Situated in our favorite area above the Sunset Strip, we were on a quiet, tree-lined street that wound into the hills toward Mulholland Drive.

In 1973 I was fifty-five years old and had neither the inclination nor resources to retire, but I was virtually a stranger in Hollywood—again. My credits in Spain were of no use, especially since the distribution of the films had been badly mangled. Besides, you don't become a film producer because of talent or ability. Unlike writing, where there is a long-shot chance you may sell a spec script or bring yourself to the attention of someone, producers have no way to offer a spec project. More than ever, it's not what you know and can do, but who.

I was unsuccessful seeking work. Fortunately, my good friend, Lisa Doty, who had been my production secretary in Madrid, had friends and connections in Canada, and when she learned they were looking for a screenwriter, she recommended me. I spent many months on and off in Toronto working on a script of Margaret Atwood's novel *Surfacing*. Beryl Fox was a first-time producer, very determined, very gutsy. The film was finally shot with Claude Jutra as director. Although Beryl and I became fast friends, it was unfortunate that with Beryl's stubborn insistence on the feminist angle and Jutra's utter indifference to that, the film was disappointing. All other efforts to film Margaret Atwood's excellent novels have been notably unsuccessful.

At home, the motion picture industry was experiencing probably its worst ever decline. Attendance in the States had dropped from a peak of 80 million people a week in 1946 to 17 million in the early 1970s. According to Jack Valenti, the president of the Motion Picture Association of America, "we had to practically subpoena people to get them to go to the theaters." (I appreciate his sensitive use of the term "subpoena," but that

goes with the territory.) Further, as we have noted, for reasons of economy, a great deal of production had shifted abroad, causing consternation
in the local community.

The major studios were in the hands of financial conglomerates or were
clearly headed that way. MGM, grand old dame, had become nothing but
an old whore to be used and passed around from hand to hand. She finally
had her garments auctioned off to people who evidently got an erotic
thrill from handling Judy Garland's old slippers from *The Wizard of Oz* at
$4,000 a pair. All of this at the hands of Kirk Kerkorian, a ruthless manip-
ulator of stock prices, real estate, and Las Vegas casinos.

Much of 20th-Century's real estate was sold for the development of
Century City. Zanuck was long gone. A real estate mogul, Marvin Davis,
bought the studio. He played the Hollywood game by opening a delicatessen on Beverly Drive. When that "production" flopped, he eventually sold the whole studio at a profit to Rupert Murdoch, the Australian
magnate who had already gutted the London *Times* and has now gobbled
up another sacred icon, the Los Angeles Dodgers baseball team.

Columbia and Universal were already in the hands of agents or conglomerates and would eventually be put on the block for other corporations
very far removed from Hollywood. Paramount had long been controlled
by Charles Bludhorn, whose corporate assets, via stock manipulation, extended worldwide and for whom a movie studio seemed a plaything. In
the hands of agents, bankers, and lawyers, blockbuster films like *Jaws* and
Star Wars would become the norm.

In spite of all this, talent would out and did occasionally pop up. *The
Godfather* was a good, big film and a financial success. And even if I am a
grumpy old man, I confess I liked *Rocky*, the first one, as well as many other
smaller productions of (roughly) the period: *Five Easy Pieces*, *M*A*S*H*,
A Clockwork Orange, *The Last Picture Show*, *Cabaret*, *Deliverance*, *American
Graffiti*, *Dog Day Afternoon*, and *Taxi Driver*, plus one very big flop, *Apoc-
alypse Now*, which I consider a film in the grand old style going all the way
back to Griffith's *Intolerance*. So perhaps all is not lost.

Though I look back on the years with Yordan and Bronston, the years
in Spain and France, as good years, when, despite the blacklist, I was able
to function meaningfully as a screenwriter and producer, my own good
experience in no way lessens the bitter meaning of the blacklist for all the
hundreds who never got to work again. Do I regret things? Of course. I
would like to believe that under normal circumstances, I might have had

a bigger and more rewarding career in Hollywood, might have been able to write or produce films that would have won the respect of the film community and the world, films that might have done something to change the world a bit for the better. Why not an Oscar? I think that some of my better scripts deserve such consideration. Is there a scribe with soul so dead who never to himself hath said . . . Where is *my* Oscar?

The years are passing, and so are dear friends. Irving Lerner died in 1980, Arnaud in 1990. My heaviest blow was the loss of Jean in 1995. Even though we did not marry until 1946, we had really been together since 1940—fifty-five years. It's difficult to convey how loyal and supportive she was and how necessary for me she became. In working on this memoir, I've studied the old agendas she kept so faithfully, reliving via her scrupulous hand the days that passed, page after page, volume after volume. It's a too-familiar story of years that go by unnoticed, the most important things not valued and never recovered. It's painful, but it also reminds me of the many truly wonderful times we shared. Covering this ground again reminds me that there was more good than bad, that we were luckier than most.

Julian lives in Rome with Anna Maria. I visit there occasionally. They come here almost every year. Ellen had her rough years trying to adjust again to America and to American schools but she finally earned her BSN degree, started work as a nurse at the Cedars-Sinai Medical Center, and worked up to a good administrative job.

Over the years in Hollywood there were occasional rumblings about proper credits for the blacklisted writers. By 1980, spurred and driven by the energy and determination of Paul Jarrico, the Writers Guild set up a committee to restore the credits to blacklisted writers who had worked under assumed names or with fronts. This had to be done very carefully in order to assure accuracy and avoid contention from persons whose names did appear on the screen. It was tedious, seemingly endless. But at last, in 1997, the committee and the guild were ready to announce the names of some of us for whom proper credit had been restored. Rather to my surprise, it turned out that I had more credits as a blacklisted writer than anyone else—nine. And this does not include several more to which I feel entitled, as explained in these pages. This has been picked up by the press and the media. I have appeared on television on the Canadian Broadcasting Company and CNN as well as local stations; I have been written up repeatedly in the press, ranging from major articles in the *Hollywood Reporter* to more than one piece in the *New York Times, USA Today, Le Monde* of Paris, the *Guardian* of London, the Italian press, and any number of other periodicals and newspapers who picked up the story from the AP. So I have had my "fifteen minutes of fame" (*pace* Andy Warhol). Is this important? I think it is worthwhile to call attention, especially to a new generation, that events such as blacklisting—and worse—can and do occur in a society that, more than most, prides itself on democracy, justice, and freedom for all.

As a culmination to the "celebration" of the 50th anniversary of the 1947 HUAC hearings in Washington, a major event was scheduled by four Hollywood unions, the Writers Guild, Screen Actors Guild, Directors Guild, and AFTRA (American Federation of Television and Radio Artists). I was very much involved in the preparations for and participation in this event, which was set for the beautiful Academy theater, but I was concerned that the event would simply be a *mea culpa* affair, with the union presidents predictably expressing regret for the events of fifty years ago and, of course, taking no responsibility for matters that occurred before many of them were born, like Germans expressing regret for the Holocaust. Then what? What about now?

In the course of a glittering evening at the Academy, Paul Jarrico was impressively honored with an award for his efforts to correct the credits of blacklisted writers. His outstanding and eloquent appearance before HUAC was acted out by Kevin Spacey, from the transcript record. In a meaningful way, the evening was a special tribute to Jarrico for his unwavering devotion to principle as well as his unstinting efforts to correct the injustices of the blacklist. So it came as an unbelievable shock to all of us when we learned that, only twenty-four hours following this affair, Paul apparently had been overcome with exhaustion from several days of preparation and participation in the tribute. He fell asleep at the wheel while driving home and died crashing into a tree, but this grievous event only occurred the following evening.

At the Academy's program eleven of us, the remaining handful of blacklistees, were present and honored. My own participation was a recounting of the bitter event at the Screen Writers Guild meeting in 1953, when my friend Eddie Huebsch was subpoenaed with the enthusiastic consent of members of the guild. This story was potent enough to elicit an audible gasp from the contemporary audience of eleven hundred.

Considerable drama was provided by a reenactment taken from the actual transcripts of the testimony and cross-examination of several other witnesses before the House Un-American Activities Committee. Billy Crystal offered a moving portrayal of the painful and reluctant testimony of Larry Parks. John Lithgow was brilliantly effective in the role of Sterling Hayden, who crawled before the committee and lived to express his everlasting regret for cooperating with them. Other fine actors played the roles of HUAC inquisitors. Alfre Woodard was hostess for the evening and lit up the auditorium with her enchanting presence.

A most impressive and important contribution was made in the speeches of the four union presidents who actually told it the way it was . . . and is.

Daniel Petrie Jr. of the Writers Guild said:

We look back in sadness and in shame that our guild at that time supported, in effect, the Waldorf declaration, which committed the industry to the blacklist. At one time, the board authorized the guild president to turn over all union records to HUAC, which meant, among other things, pen names . . .

Now, I am humbled by the privilege of offering, directly to those seated in the theater who suffered as a result of those actions taken so long ago, and to your families: a pledge, on behalf of the Writers Guild of America, that we will be *out in front* of all efforts today and in the future to prevent any governmental move to restrict expression and conform thought. It must not happen again. It will not happen again.

Richard Masur, president of Screen Actors Guild, spoke at length and with shame and horror about the fact that the Actors Guild had made a loyalty oath a condition of membership. It was not until 1974 that the loyalty oath was finally removed from the Screen Actors Guild bylaws. He went on to say:

Screen Actors Guild would like to express how deeply we regret that the poison of fear so paralyzed our organization when courage and conviction were needed to oppose the blacklist. Only our sister union, Actors' Equity Association, had the courage to stand behind its members and help them to continue their creative lives in the theater. For that we honor them tonight.

Jack Shea, president of the Directors Guild, related how hard and successfully Herbert Biberman had worked as one of the founders of the guild. But in 1947, when Biberman became one of the Hollywood Ten and was later sentenced to prison for contempt of Congress, he became the first member expelled from the guild he had helped to create. His name was removed from the list of founders. "Tonight," Shea said, "we restore Herbert Biberman's membership in the Directors Guild of America and officially return him to the list of giants who founded the Screen Directors Guild." This action, regretfully, was posthumous.

I found the very best words were spoken by Susan Boyd, president of the AFTRA local.

Usually when so many members of the creative community get together, it's to commemorate a happy event. Clearly this gathering is exceptional in so many ways.

Tonight we acknowledge a bitter episode in the history of television, radio, and motion pictures. I did not personally live through the blacklist. I didn't experience the suffering as many of you did. But I have felt its effects. I still do. So does my union, AFTRA.

I know people whose careers were destroyed. I know performers who spoke out in defense of colleagues who were smeared—and although their numbers were not so great as one might hope—their refusal to "go along," to "get along," was all the more heroic because they stood fast against the national tide of fear; they did not hide from *Red Channels*, the *Counterattacks*, the Madison Avenue slander, even the government itself. These heroes are here in this room; I salute you. And so does my union, AFTRA.

Is the age of blacklist finally over? Or is each generation doomed to repeat the sad mistakes of its predecessors? We've seen in just the last two decades the damage done to so many in our community from whispers circulated about HIV and AIDS. That's what makes this more than a commemoration of those terrifying days which poisoned our profession fifty years ago. It is a lesson in vigilance for those among us who may believe we are safe from lists and files, dossiers, and subpoenas. The words we say here tonight must live on to teach our children that compassion without action is hollow; that words are weapons and labels are equal opportunity destroyers of lives.

And the most important lesson: though the blacklist of the fifties is over, there are others waiting in the wings.

Well, that's the point, isn't it? What about today? I hate to think that such meanness can ever return. But it can. In many ways it has. Three strikes and you're out. Kick the immigrant kids out of school and the immigrant sick out of the hospitals. Blame all violence on gangs but do nothing to change conditions in the ghettos. Fill the prisons with more Blacks.

Build more prisons to house them because we don't know what else to do and there are no jobs for them.

Do I still believe we can build a better world? Was I wrong to think we could? I am no longer certain how to go about it. Maybe this old world has to be treated like an old house. It's a "fixer-upper." You can't turn it into a grand new mansion, but maybe you can make it habitable by fixing the leaky roof and plumbing, and improving the heating, and making it a place with living space for all, regardless of race, color, creed. But keep hammering away.

America is a grand old place, but it has some bad old ways and some bad new ones. I still believe it needs a lot of fixing.

Flesh and Fury (1952) Universal
    Tony Curtis, Jan Sterling, Mona Freeman, Wallace Ford
    Directed by Joseph Pevney
    Written by William Alland (story), Bernard Gordon (screenplay)
    Produced by Leonard Goldstein

The Lawless Breed (1953) Universal
    Rock Hudson, Julie Adams
    Directed by Raoul Walsh
    Written by William Alland (story), Bernard Gordon (screenplay)
    Produced by William Alland

The Law Versus Billy the Kid (1954) Columbia Pictures
    Scott Brady, Alan Hale Jr., Betta St. John
    Directed by William Castle
    Written by Janet and Philip Stevenson (play), Bernard Gordon (screenplay)
    Produced by Sam Katzman

Crime Wave (1954) Warner Bros.
    Sterling Hayden, Gene Nelson, Phyllis Kirk
    Directed by André de Toth
    Written by John and Ward Hawkins (story), Bernard Gordon, Crane
    Wilbur, Richard Wormser (screenplay)
    Produced by Bryan Foy

Earth Vs. the Flying Saucers (1956) Columbia Pictures
    Hugh Marlowe, Joan Taylor, Donald Curtis
    Directed by Fred F. Sears
    Written by Donald B. Keyhoe (book), Curt Siodmak (story),
    George Worthing Yates, Bernard Gordon (screenplay)
    Produced by Sam Katzman

Zombies of Mora Tau (1957) Columbia
    Gregg Palmer, Allison Hayes, Autumn Russell, Joel Ashley
    Directed by Edward L. Cahn
    Written by George H. Plympton (story), Bernard Gordon (screenplay)
    Produced by Sam Katzman

Chicago Confidential (1957) United Artists
    Brian Keith, Beverly Garland, Dick Foran, Elisha Cook Jr.
    Written by Jack Lait and Lee Mortimer (book), Hugh King (story),
    Bernard Gordon (screenplay)
    Produced by Robert B. Kent

The Man Who Turned to Stone (1957) Columbia
    Victor Jory, Charlotte Austin, Barbara Wilson
    Directed by Leslie Kardos
    Written by Bernard Gordon
    Produced by Sam Katzman

Escape from San Quentin (1957) Columbia
    Johnny Desmond, Merry Anders
    Directed by Fred F. Sears
    Written by Bernard Gordon
    Produced by Sam Katzman

Hellcats of the Navy (1957) Columbia
    Ronald Reagan, Nancy Davis (Reagan), Arthur Franz
    Directed by Nathan Juran
    Written by Charles A. Lockwood, Hans Christian Adamson (book),
    David Lang, Bernard Gordon (screenplay)
    Produced by Charles Schneer

The Case against Brooklyn (1958) Columbia
    Darren McGavin, Maggie Hayes, Peggy McCay
    Directed by Paul Wendkos
    Written by Ed Reid (book), Daniel B. Uliman (story), Bernard Gordon,
    Julian Zimet (screenplay)
    Produced by Charles Schneer

The Day of the Triffids (1962) Allied Artists, Rank
    Howard Keel, Nicole Maurey, Janet Scott, Kieron Moore
    Directed by Steve Sekely
    Written by John Wyndham (book) Bernard Gordon (screenplay)
    Produced by Philip Yordan (Security Pictures)

55 Days at Peking (1963)
    Ava Gardner, Charlton Heston, David Niven
    Directed by Nicholas Ray
    Written by Bernard Gordon
    Produced by Samuel Bronston

Cry of Battle (1963) Allied Artists
    Van Heflin, Rita Moreno, James MacArthur
    Directed by Irving Lerner
    Written by Benjamin Appel (book), Bernard Gordon (screenplay)
    Produced by Joe Steinberg

The Thin Red Line (1964) Warner Bros.
    Keir Dullea, Jason Fithian, Ben Tatar, Jack Warden
    Directed by Andrew Marton
    Written by James Jones (novel), Bernard Gordon (screenplay)

Circus World (1964) Paramount
    John Wayne, Claudia Cardinale, Rita Hayworth, Lloyd Nolan,
        Richard Conte
    Directed by Henry Hathaway
    Written by Bernard Gordon (story uncredited), Ben Hecht, Julian Zimet,
        James B. Grant (screenplay)
    Produced by Samuel Bronston

Battle of the Bulge (1965) Warner Bros.
    Henry Fonda, Robert Shaw, Robert Ryan, Dana Andrews, Pier Angeli,
        Charles Bronson, Telly Savalas
    Directed by Ken Annakin
    Written by John Melson, Bernard Gordon (uncredited)
    Produced by Philip Yordan

Custer of the West (1968) Cinerama Releasing
    Robert Shaw, Mary Ure, Jeffrey Hunter, Robert Ryan
    Directed by Robert Siodmak
    Written by Bernard Gordon and Julian Zimet
    Produced by Irving Lerner, Philip Yordan

Krakatoa, East of Java (1969) American Broadcasting Co.
    Rossano Brazzi, Brian Keith, Maximilian Schell
    Directed by Bernard L. Kowalski
    Written by Bernard Gordon, Clifford Newton Gould
    Produced by William R. Forman, Philip Yordan

Bad Man's River (1972) Zurbano Film S~A.
    James Mason, Gina Lollobrigida, Lee Van Cleef
    Directed by Eugenio Martín
    Written by Philip Yordan
    Produced by Irving Lerner, Bernard Gordon

Horror Express (1972) Benmar/Granada
    Christopher Lee, Peter Cushing, Telly Savalas
    Directed by Eugenio Martín
    Written by Arnaud d'Usseau, Julian Zimet
    Produced by Bernard Gordon

Pancho Villa (1972) Scotia International/Granada
    Telly Savalas, Clint Walker, Chuck Connors, Anne Francis
    Directed by Eugenio Martín
    Written by Julian Zimet
    Produced by Bernard Gordon

Surfacing (1981) Famous Players (Canada)
    Joseph Bottoms, Kathleen Beller
    Directed by Claude Jutra
    Written by Margaret Atwood (novel), Bernard Gordon (screenplay)